Lynne D. Geller

INSTRUCT
MA

THE DOLPHIN READER

Third Edition

DOUGLAS HUNT
University of Missouri

MELODY RICHARDSON DAILY
University of Missouri

CAROLYN PERRY
Westminster College

HOUGHTON MIFFLIN COMPANY BOSTON TORONTO
DALLAS GENEVA, ILL PALO ALTO PRINCETON, NJ

Senior Sponsoring Editor: Dean Johnson
Special Projects Editor: Lynn Walterick
Production and Design Coordinator: Caroline Ryan
Electronic Publishing Specialist: Linnea Meyer
Senior Manufacturing Coordinator: Holly Schuster
Marketing Manager: George Kane

Printed in the U.S.A.

ISBN: 0–395–61959–9

123456789-B-96 95 94 93 92

CONTENTS

Note: An asterisk (*) denotes fiction or drama.

INTRODUCTION

As with the earlier editions of the *Instructor's Resource Manual to The Dolphin Reader*, we have worked to build an instructor's guide that will be of practical help, remembering that an hour of footwork here might save scores of hours of preparation for our far-flung users.

If you used either of the first two editions, you know the *Manual*'s general layout. In the second edition we added an index to help instructors locate examples of particular rhetorical strategies and find links among selections. In this edition we are adding sixty-one style lessons, about which we will have more to say in a moment.

Our "**work-up**" of each selection includes a sketch of the general nature of the piece, comments on types of student writing that might develop from it, and 3–5 discussion/writing questions. The questions are "answered" with some notes from us to you about what may arise in class discussion and some suggestions about how you might direct the discussion. Discussion is something we take seriously, assuming that talk, good and plenty, inside class and out, is the best invention strategy. Accordingly, we have posed the questions we thought would lead to the most productive talk. In some cases, you will want to narrow these questions to turn them into writing assignments, but students who tackle a large question as part of a lively discussion often find their own ways to sharpen the focus. An interested student is never as vague as a bored one.

The **style lessons**, most of which were prepared by Carolyn Perry, are based on short passages—often a single sentence—from the essays. Typical tasks set in these lessons include sentence imitation, sentence combining, and the reordering of a scrambled paragraph. The physical layout of the lesson depends on the task: in an imitation lesson, for example, the sentence is visually broken up into phrases so that it can be more easily imitated phrase by phrase; in a sentence-combining exercise the author's fairly long sentence might be broken into a dozen "kernel" sentences containing (roughly) one idea each.

Some of the lessons—such as the sentence-combining exercises—are clearly best used in the classroom and are a good way to open a class period. Since we have built the lessons, whenever possible, on key passages, working with them can serve as a prelude to discussing the essay as a whole. Other lessons—especially some of the sentence imitation exercises—could be used as homework assignments to be completed either before or after an essay is discussed.

At the end of the *Manual* you will find **appendixes** intended to help you build your syllabus: a rhetorical table of contents, two tables of estimated reading difficulty, and a table of estimated reading times.

Writing this *Manual* turns us into undergraduates once more. Answering the discussion questions sharpens our minds and forces us to grapple with some intriguing ideas. We hope this book works as well for your students as it does for us.

Doug Hunt
Melody Daily
Carolyn Perry

CHILDHOOD

OVERVIEW OF UNIT

The *Childhood* unit, new in this edition, has the great practical advantage of accessibility. Students sometimes complain that they are required to write about topics about which they have neither interest nor knowledge, but *everyone* has had a childhood and everyone is interested in the development of his or her own personality.

At the same time, childhood is not a matter of merely personal concern. Once your ear becomes attuned to it, you hear on the airwaves and in the streets a great deal of concerned talk about how our children are being raised and what the consequences are for the society. In national politics, this discussion shows as posturing about "family values"; in the lives of working women (and, increasingly, working men), it appears a nagging worry about the long-term effects of day care; in the courts, it emerges in custody and desegregation cases. If childhood is a subject on which all of us have done a good deal of first-hand research, it is also one that has inexhaustible ramifications.

Two of the selections in this unit, the excerpts from Marie Winn and John Holt, raise the broad question of whether children need primarily to be sheltered from the adult world until they are ready to face it, or need instead to be exposed to the adult world as quickly as they develop a curiosity about it: childhood as a walled garden versus childhood as an apprenticeship. The other selections are arranged in a roughly developmental sequence. Essays by Dillard and Angelou recollect memories of fairly early childhood; essays by Anderson, Rivera, Mitford, and Twain deal with the "tween" years of late childhood; stories by Hamilton and Cameron deal with adolescents coming of age. The essays and stories touch on issues that resonate in the adult world, particularly race (Angelou and Rivera), class (Rivera and Mitford), ethics (Twain and Hamilton).

ANNIE DILLARD

Skin

Like much of Annie Dillard's best work, this chapter from *An American Childhood* is remarkable chiefly for what it allows us to see. There is an Edenic quality to some of her descriptions, as if she could strip away our daily expectations and preconceptions and look on the most common objects freshly. In this case, she sets herself almost precisely that task, taking herself back in memory (or imagination) to early childhood and looking at the bodies of adults as if she had just discovered that they were different from her own. The result is a tour-de-force that makes us aware again of the peculiarities of our own bodies: the skin's tautness or looseness, the peculiar shape of our shinbones, the flatness of the bottoms of our feet.

In a sense, the chapter falls into the "martian" genre of descriptive writing; that is, Dillard describes everyday phenomena from the perspective of an alien to planet earth. But this particular alien is psychologically recognizable; we may not be able to recall our childhood perceptions as vividly as Dillard seems to, but her descriptions have (to me, at least) a familiar feeling. I can't remember when I first noticed the bumps on shinbones or the way that the cheek takes an impression from the surface we lay it on, but I remember noticing and being fascinated.

Setting students the task of writing an essay that, like Dillard's, describes things as a young child would see them engages three types of thinking. It encourages them to search through remembered objects toward a recollection of their pasts (Patricia Hampl discusses this search very well in "Memory and Imagination"). When recollection fails, it encourages them to imagine what a child's perception of the world must be like, an exercise that can be educational in itself. And, like all "martian" writing, it encourages them to look harder at the world around them and to find fresh language to describe what they see.

QUESTIONS

1. [Close your books.] List the everyday sights that Dillard's essay made you think about more clearly than you had thought about them before.

This is a straightforward recall question to help students bring the essay back to mind and start talking about it. I'd suggest having students close their books before asking it so that you won't get a mechanical listing, but a more freewheeling discussion of the images students were most struck by. You might want to list the images on the board and then ask students to rank them from most striking on down. Here are five that are likely to appear, in the order most striking to me.

- The impression of the cushion's upholstery on Dillard's mother's cheek (paragraphs 14–16). What strikes me most strongly here is the way that we learn to *ignore* these marks, just as her mother does. At the risk of sounding like Yogi Berra, if they weren't so familiar, we'd notice them all the time.
- The shinbones, both their description of their general shape ("like the slats of a Venetian blind") and the enumerating of their irregularities (paragraph 20). I used to wonder whether my own shinbones were diseased because of the "nicks, bumps, small hard balls, shallow ridges, and soft spots," but I hadn't thought of this for about thirty years until I read Dillard's book.
- The "joined trapezoids" of the skin (paragraph 9). Dillard's associating these with the dust specks with which God made Adam adds charm, of course, but the sheer closeness of the observation shows us how much we miss by not looking at the things nearest us.
- The flattened bottoms of the toes (paragraph 21).

- The "skeletal rays" of the thin bones in the feet (paragraph 21). I think Dillard's accomplishment here is to make us remember how "terrible" this sight is.

2. Where do Dillard's observations sound like those of a child? Where do they sound like those of an adult?

Some students may take the position that Dillard never sounds like a child, assuming that children chirp in monosyllables and have no striking thoughts. But surely everyone would concede that some passages here evoke childhood more clearly than others. Most children must be struck at some point by the "knuckly" hands of adults (paragraph 2) and the way that the skin on them can be pinched into ridges (paragraph 4). Most children must have episodes when they pester their parents with the sort of pulling and poking Dillard remembers and provoke a somewhat irritated response "That's getting boring," or "Ouch! Enough of that." Surely it occurs to every child that the amusements of adults are not very amusing compared to Kick the Can or some other uproarious children's game (paragraph 26).

But Dillard doesn't choose to express the child's insights entirely in the child's language. No eight-year-old would talk about the "absolute figural splendor" of adults and contrast the beauty of children which "was, in the long run, merely elfin." Paragraph 3 is packed with such expressions, but they appear throughout the essay.

Paragraph 2 gives a pretty good picture of how childlike observation and adult language mix in the essay. Let's consider it sentence-by-sentence. *We children had, for instance, proper hands; our fluid, pliant fingers joined their skin.* No child, of course, would use words like "fluid" and "pliant" to describe fingers, and the idea of opposing "proper" hands to the odd hands of adults may be outside the conceptual range of a child. I don't find much in this sentence that belongs authentically to childhood. *Adults had misshapen, knuckly hands loose in their skin like bones in bags; it was a wonder they could open jars.* The knuckliness of the hands is something that would strike a child, and the observation about "bones in bags" and opening jars, though ingenious and precise, are within the range of some bright ten-year-olds I have known. In fact, the image of an adult's loose skin clinging to a jar lid while the bones slide around it has the grotesqueness of childhood's imagination. *They were loose in their skins all over, except at the wrists and ankles, like rabbits.* The comparison to rabbits is the only thing that might sound too adult here, but only to those who assume that children haven't handled rabbits. To the child that has, the looseness of the skin is, as we used to say, "weird" and so memorable.

The sense that things are weird is, in fact, what I find most convincingly childlike in this chapter. Dillard seems to have remembered her way back to a time when things were far more wonderful and awful than they are to any adult.

—D.H.—

Style Lesson 1: Dillard's Diction

Annie Dillard's care in the choice of words is by now proverbial. To see it more clearly, close your book and examine the following passage from paragraphs 11–13 of "Skin." Try to determine which word in each set of brackets is Dillard's original choice. Be prepared to explain the merits of your choice in class discussion.

The skin of my mother's face was smooth, fair, and tender; it took [marks/impressions] readily. She [slept/napped] on her side on the couch. Her face skin [pooled/gathered] on the low side; it [bunched/piled] up in the low corners of her deep-set eyes and [drew/hauled] down her lips and cheeks. How [plastic/flexible] was it? I pushed at a [puddle/wad] of it by her nose.

She [stirred/moved] and opened her eyes. I [stood/jumped] back.

She reminded me not to touch her face while she was sleeping. Anybody's face.

When she sat up, her cheek and brow bone [bore/sported] a red deep [gash/mark], the mark of the cushion's [reinforced seam/welting]. It was [stamped/textured] inside precisely with the upholstery's weave and [pattern/brocade].

MAYA ANGELOU

Momma

"Momma" deals with one of the central themes of childhood, the mysteriousness of adults and the world they inhabit. In this case, the mystery about the world involves relations between the races in Stamps, Arkansas, in the 1930s. Young Maya Angelou can't understand why the "powhitetrash" children are able to insult her grandmother as they do. The mystery about adults is not just why she puts up with these insults, but why she does it in the manner that she does, standing motionless in the doorway, humming a hymn under her breath, scrupulously polite, until the children are out of sight. As a child, Angelou couldn't see the encounter as a victory for her grandmother, another occasion where she has preserved her dignity and kept control of an explosive situation. As Angelou says, "Something had happened out there, which I couldn't completely understand, but I could see that she was happy."

Most students, if they think hard about their childhood, will recall instances—dramatic or comic—where they found themselves as confused as Angelou was by the way adults deal with their lives. The recollection of such confusion could be the germ of an essay.

QUESTIONS

1. To what extent does Angelou's memoir sound like a recreation of the experiences and thoughts of a child, and to what extent does it sound like the reflections of a mature woman? What does she gain by her mixture of the child's perspective and the adult's?

This question should prevent your students' overlooking the dual perspective Angelou creates in this passage. To be sure, the child's perspective is dominant. With a keen eye to detail, she captures a child's view of life: from the nuisance of bathing, to the fear of the dark and of snakes, to her angle of vision when she hides behind the screen door or looks up to see Momma hovering over her. Small details as well reveal a black child's confusion over differences among people; Angelou can't resist pinching a white child to see if it is real, and she mentally resists Momma's acknowledging the white girls as "Miz."

But what makes the memoir complete is the voice of the adult Angelou looking back on the experience. When she pauses to assert that her "lifelong paranoia was born in those cold, molasses-slow minutes" (paragraph 18) or to realize that she was "as clearly imprisoned behind the scene as the actors outside were confined to their roles" (paragraph 22) we know that Angelou the adult is making sense of what had happened. She recognizes the event as an introduction to the injustice of racial conflict, but also to the complexity of it: In spite of her intense anger, she knows that the white girls are simply acting out learned behavior. The Angelou who makes these comments is clearly not the same one who wants to throw black pepper in the faces of the girls and call them "dirty, scummy peckerwoods."

These hints of an adult consciousness behind the essay are crucial to its success. Without them, we would have difficulty putting the incident into perspective, seeing what was hidden from the child.

2. Divide the essay into four sections by putting a check mark after paragraphs 5, 14, and 32. What does Angelou accomplish in each of these sections?

The aim here is partly to get students to see that even when an essay is organized as a narrative, it will have subparts with somewhat different functions and purposes. In a general way, the essay stresses two sets of contrasts: the one between Momma's personality and the narrator's and the one between Momma's code of behavior and that of the "powhitetrash."

Paragraphs 1–5 set forth the "customary laws" that both reveal Momma's character and establish a means of comparing "correct" behavior with that of the powhitetrash who will soon appear.

Paragraphs 6–14 then complete the contrast by describing the girls who tormented Angelou by their behavior in Momma's store. Angelou suggests their inferiority by subtly comparing them to animals (they are a smelly "gaggle" that "crawl" over everything in the store). By presenting Momma's and Uncle Willie's response to them, Angelou emphasizes the irony of the social scene: though the white people rented land from Momma and were clearly her inferiors in cleanliness and behavior, they still had the power to treat her as an inferior. By briefly mentioning her own reaction (pinching the girls and feeling a "crying shame" when Uncle Willie followed their orders) she shows that she has not come to terms with the injustice.

Paragraphs 15–32 take the scene in the yard through its climax (the handstand) and ending (the goodbyes). Here Angelou is using the pattern of conflict and rising action characteristic of storytelling in our culture. The girls break into a scene of order and harmony (the raked yard); they first mimic Annie, then make faces at her, then do the puppet dance and the obscene handstand. The climax past, the girls leave and Momma bids them a calm farewell, restoring a kind of order. As she develops this narrative, Angelou provides us with contrasting views of Momma's calm and her rage.

Paragraphs 33–37 serve as a coda, connecting Momma's restrained dignity in the encounter with the values of cleanliness and respect she taught her granddaughter in the opening paragraphs. Like the grandmother who faces the indignities of life in a white apron "so stiff by virtue of starch that it could have stood on its own," the granddaughter knows that the best way to deal with this unpleasantness to do something "just for nice," as Iowans put it. She rakes the yard again ("The smudged footprints were easy to erase") and creates a design her grandmother can praise as "right pretty."

3. What exactly did Momma win?

Angelou's memoir draws its strength largely from what it does not tell us directly. It is as if Angelou knows that we will understand Momma's victory better emotionally than we would intellectually, so she focuses her attention on helping us to *feel* what was going on. Notice what details Angelou has selected to keep our attention focused on the "battle" and Momma's fight. Angelou points out that Momma could have avoided the confrontation by coming into the house, and in the middle of the incident, we may find ourselves wishing she had. As the girls grow more and more insulting, Momma continues to hum softly and steadily to herself; only the occasional trembling of her apron strings indicated her struggle to maintain control. The battle culminates, of course, in Momma's determination to give the girls respect by calling each by "Miz" despite their despicable behavior. We *know* at this point, without being told, that Momma has proven that personal dignity can be maintained in the face of racial injustice. Her goal was not to prove anything to the white girls, who may or may not have understood the impact of the incident, but to teach Angelou what her response should be—and given the resulting memoir, we know she succeeded.

—D.H.—

Style Lesson 2:
Imitating a Descriptive Sentence

The structure of Angelou's sentences often creates opportunities to add layers of detail. The two sentences below are from her description of the "powhitetrash" children as they enter the store. Have your students write sentences that parallel hers phrase-by-phrase, detail-by-detail, but that present a different subject (perhaps ants invading a cabinet or leaves blowing into the sheltered corner of a building).

Sometimes a gaggle of them came into the store
    filling the whole room
    chasing out the air and even
    changing the well-known scents.
The children crawled
    over the shelves and
    into the potato and onion bins,
        twanging all the time in their sharp voices
        like cigar-box guitars.

SHERWOOD ANDERSON

Discovery of a Father

This very short essay, a classic of its kind, follows the simplest of organizational patterns. The narrator describes his old feelings on a subject, describes an event that changed those feelings, and describes his new feelings. Since emotion is the heart of such an essay, students won't find much logical development here. They will find strong development at the social and visceral levels: Anderson implies a contrast between the juvenile values that made his father repugnant to him and the more mature values that made him attractive, and the scene where he and his father swim in the pond during a thunderstorm perfectly illustrates Scott Russell Sanders's point that "the body has its reasons that reason knows nothing of."

QUESTIONS

1. What is it that made the swim with Anderson's father such a powerful experience?

When students write papers about events that change their lives, the narration of the event often falls flat either because it is underdeveloped or because it is developed by the laying on of adjectives—as though it were possible to prove that an event were "extraordinary" or "moving" or "amazing" simply by saying so. Or they turn to pyrotechnic displays of thesaurus language.

Some of the effectiveness of this passage comes from the understatedness of the style. The episode begins with paragraph 30. You might have students begin there and look for the first word of three or more syllables they can find. The first I see is *intended* in paragraph 34. You might have them look for the first sentence longer than 16 words. It is the 25-worder in the middle of paragraph 33, but even this sentence is so gaunt that its ribs show: "We went along a dirt road that led down into a valley, about a mile out of town, where there was a pond" not "We paced along a deserted, unpaved, country road that descended into an isolated valley fully a mile from the town, where there was a pond with no one in sight." While I wouldn't want to claim that the plain style is the only effective one (Annie Dillard's is far from plain), it does avoid the danger of distracting the reader from the action and situation. Anderson gives us few words, a very few elaborate ones.

The plain words make some broad contrasts clear, and these contrasts do a good deal of the work at the visceral and social level:

- When the episode begins Anderson's mother is at church and Anderson is reading at the kitchen table. Their behavior makes them representatives of everything that is conventional and sedate. Anderson's father bursts into the kitchen after a two- or three-week absence, soaked from the rain. In defiance of rules of ordinary courtesy, he says nothing, then gives a brief command, "Come on with me." His behavior makes him a representative of everything that is outlandish and unpredictable.

- Throughout the essay, the son has been preoccupied with the social world, with what people thought of his father, how they interacted with him, how ashamed he was of his father's behavior. In this episode, the father leads him away from the house into the solitude of the night. He tells him to take off his clothes (almost inevitably symbolic of civilization) and exposes him to the natural elements—water, lightning, thunder—that have nothing to do with society.
- The son is small and a poor swimmer. The father is "a man with big shoulders, a powerful swimmer." Paragraphs 39, 41, and 42 repeatedly draw attention to the contrast between the weakness of the "clinging boy" and the father's large hands, strong shoulders, and general muscularity.

In general, Anderson gives us the impression that the "world of the schoolboy" (paragraph 41) has been overwhelmed by something much larger and less predictable, something that comes not from books and self-consciousness, but from the body and from nature.

2. Are experiences like the one Anderson had with his father typically male? That is, do sons typically have such experiences with their fathers, but daughters typically not have them with either father or mother?

It's hard to miss the element of male romanticism in Anderson's essay, particularly if you have read Robert Bly's *Iron John* or come into contact with those who have. Anderson is getting in contact with his "wild man" by having this primal experience with his father. Muscles, silence, male bonding.

Whether students say that girls have similar experiences must depend partly on how they define Anderson's experience. If they see his reconciliation with his father as an embracing of a masculine rejection of mere (feminized) respectability, then they will perhaps say that this sort of thing doesn't happen to girls. They may also say that it doesn't happen very often to boys.

But they may recognize a broader pattern: the child sees in the parent the self he or she may become and doesn't want to, he or she exaggerates the parent's defects, then (perhaps as a result of a particular encounter) gets over this "stage" and views the parent with admiration (or at least understanding). This kind of experience is surely more common among both sexes. Students can read about a girl's parallel experience in Alice Munro's "Boys and Girls."

3. In a sentence, write a *positive* summary of the character of Anderson's father.

If we look back on the information Anderson gives about his father and remove the boy's shame and anger, we can see his father as one of the most popular men in town—the man whose company everyone (even the soberest of citizens) found delightful and the man chosen to be grand marshal of the parades. We also understand why he was popular. He was a marvelous storyteller, he had a sense of humor about himself, and he was so generous that he let his business fail rather than collect debts from his poor neighbors. Even his absences from home during lean times might *possibly* be seen in a positive light; when there was too little food to go around, he foraged for himself, returning with food in hand.

Your students, working from recall and writing a single sentence can't be expected to note all this, but to understand the essay, the reader needs to recognize the ambiguity of the evidence young Anderson used to condemn his father. Failing to see that most of his supposed faults could be virtues amounts to missing the boat.

—D.H.—

Style Lesson 3: Simplifying a Style

The following passage, while it follows the wording of Anderson's paragraphs 2 and 3 fairly closely, destroys the effectiveness of his simple, direct style. Close your book and take about five minutes to try to recreate the style of the original.

I know that as a small boy I wanted my father to be a certain thing that he was not—a proud, silent, dignified father who, when he passed along the street, made me feel a glow of pride—"There he is, my father."

But he wasn't such a one, and couldn't be, because, as it seemed to me then, he was always showing off, as (for example) when someone in our town had got up a show, which they were always doing: the druggist would be in it, the shoe-store clerk, the horse doctor, and a lot of women and girls, and my father would manage to get the comedy part, which in the case of, let's say, a Civil War play was a comic Irish soldier, and he had to do the most absurd things, and although they thought he was funny, I didn't.

EDWARD RIVERA

First Communion

In this section of *Family Installments: Memories of Growing Up Hispanic,* Rivera presents childhood from the vantage point of a third grader who does not belong to the dominant Anglo culture. Santo, the narrator, tells the story of his teacher, Sister Felicia, an Irish-American nun "both cold-hearted and generous" (paragraph 1), who ridicules her students' families and their cultural heritage, but uses her meager funds to purchase new clothes for the children to wear for their first communion.

Like all of the pieces in this unit, "First Communion" considers the ways in which children develop a sense of their own identities. In addition, this story, like Maya Angelou's "Momma," presents the unique problems of children struggling to see themselves in a mirror distorted by the majority culture's delusions of grandeur.

This selection may prompt many of your students to recall growing up with a sense of cultural inferiority unrelated to differences of race or language. I was reminded that, as a girl who grew up in Missouri, I always suspected that New Yorkers would consider me a hillbilly, even when I did wear shoes.

QUESTIONS

1. How do the nuns feel about their students? How do the students feel about the nuns?

Although we are never privy to the nuns' thoughts or private conversations, their actions certainly offer clues about their attitudes toward their Hispanic students. The story involving Marta Cuevas is particularly telling. When Sister Mary Felicia sees Marta picking her nose, the nun publicly humiliates the child by "hinting that in Marta's home personal habits were still primitive," much like those of her cannibalistic ancestors, the Carib Indians (paragraph 29). Clearly the nuns, who are Irish-American, consider themselves culturally superior to their students. Although Sister Felicia cares about the children, or at least about their religious training, she has nothing but contempt for their cultural heritage.

At the beginning of the story Santo characterizes the nuns as both "cold-hearted and generous." This mix thoroughly puzzles the children, who can't comprehend that a nun's religious convictions might lead her to dedicate her life to educating children even though she feels no personal affection for them. Santo expresses his confusion in these lines: "For one thing they were Irish, all of them, so why should they give a damn for people like me? But they did sometimes" (paragraph 27). The students respond to these mixed signals with respect and gratitude but with none of the love third-graders often feel for their teachers.

2. To what extent are the children aware of the limits to the nuns' authority?

The children understand that the nuns are all powerful within Saint Miseria's. They accept the nuns' right to punish them for some sin they have "committed unawares" (paragraph 28). After all, the nuns knew "what sin was and wasn't; they had technical training in those things and they didn't miss a thing" (paragraph 28). And the students recognize the nuns' absolute power to expel a child who would then be exiled to public school, which was "as close as you could come to perdition before actually dying with your sins unconfessed" (paragraph 40).

But the students also suspect that neither the nuns nor their beliefs command the same respect outside the school. Mami jokingly tells Santo, "Making your First Communion is almost as important as making your first *caca* all by yourself" (paragraph 24). And one of the ushers remarks that "after the Pope said you had to use English in church," it "gave the whole game away" (paragraph 35). When Sister Felicia takes the children shopping, Santo realizes that the merchant is teasing her when he refers to the tie clasps as "crucifixion claps" and then winks at the boys (paragraph 67–69). All these incidents lead Santo to understand that nuns rule the school but not the earth.

3. How does the author make this story humorous as well as heartrending?

A bare-bones summary of this story is anything but funny: a nun humiliates a little girl in front of her classmates; that same nun later buys new first-communion outfits for her students on ADC. But Rivera manages to keep us chuckling throughout the narrative. He sets the tone immediately by naming the school Saint Miseria, and he follows through with other ironic names: Sister Felicia, Sister Mary Monitor, and Jorge Mercado (the merchant). Most important, the author permits us to smile by allowing us to *hope,* at least, that the students aren't permanently damaged by the incidents we witness. Marta's knuckles hurt for a while, but she probably won't need years of psychoanalysis to get over the nun's insults. Santo even suggests that "in a way Marta got herself off the hook" because the nun didn't call on her the rest of that day, and Santo suspects that Marta hadn't "studied too much the night before" (paragraph 34). We also have reason to hope that Santo's psyche won't be irreparably scarred because he was forced to accept the nuns' charity. After all, he is confident Papi would have "found a way to scrounge up the funds" for his new clothes (paragraph 23).

In addition, the narrator's droll asides remind us that, at least in retrospect, he can see the humor of his adventures as a third grader. For example, we have his description of the shoes purchased for First Communion: "Thom McAn shoes (blisters guaranteed) that expanded like John's Bargain Store sponges as soon as it rained" (paragraph 23)—hardly the remark of a child overcome by the munificence of his benefactor. He watches Marta staring up at Sister Felicia and—undaunted by the revelation of her primitive progenitors—notes that he "got a good look at the attractive cannibal profile" (paragraph 32). He tells us that after the nuns bought them new clothes, the children realized they had "a lot to be grateful for as well," but he then remarks "Not that we had much choice, but still . . ." (paragraph 36).

In one of the funniest passages, the humor builds level by level. Rivera begins by describing a mildly amusing sight: a pig's head sporting a sailor's cap and the message "Eat me, Im' Delishious." He then adds another level of humor with Santo's remark, "Moses would have passed out" (paragraph 38), a joke based on the juxtaposition of ancient Jewish law and tasteless modern advertising. He adds the third level by reporting Sister Felicia's observation: "That man can't spell" (paragraphs 38 and 39). Because the nun's pedantic condemnation of the sign exposes her own humorlessness, it becomes, without her knowing it, a joke on her.

4. Do the nuns succeed in persuading the students to think of their Hispanic culture as inferior?

It is clear that the *adult* narrator understands that the nuns were selling cultural imperialism, and he isn't buying it. His account of Marta's punishment shows us that it is the nun, not the child, who behaves like a savage. Sister Felicia booms "Stand up, Marta Cuevas!" in a voice that "could have scared the loincloth off Huracán himself" (paragraph 33), then brutally strikes the child's knuckles with her ruler (paragraph 34). Marta, with the courage and dignity of a Christian martyr, takes her punishment without screaming.

But it is not so evident that the *students*—when they were third graders—were able to recognize the deficiencies of the nuns' world view and escape from the third grade with their self-esteem intact. The narrator admits that after Sister Felicia condemned the vendor's spelling, he sided with her:

> Here was a grown man, probably the father of half a dozen or more, and he didn't know where to put his apostrophe. This was the kind of father who passed down his ignorance to his children . . . (paragraph 39).

The child Santo is willing to label a successful merchant ignorant merely because he doesn't follow the orthographic conventions of English, but neither Santo nor the other children seem to expect the nuns to speak or write Spanish. The students' acceptance of this double standard suggests that they have learned one of the lessons of cultural chauvinism.

—M.R.D.—

Style Lesson 4: Imitating a Sentence with a Simile

The sentence that ends "First Communion" divides into three parts: a firm statement, a modification, and a striking simile.

1. Nobody started trouble with our nuns,
2. at least not before the drug pushers and their customers entered our neighborhood
3. like the great Medieval plague she had told us about during our history period.

Imitate this pattern, writing on a subject of your choice. If you have difficulty getting started, try one of these substitutions for "our nuns"—George Bush, Madonna, Hammer.

JESSICA MITFORD

Thirteen

Jessica Mitford is best known for her exposès of American institutions such as the funeral industry (*The American Way of Death*) and the prison system (*Unusual Punishment: The Prison Business*). In this excerpt from the first volume of her autobiography, *Daughters and Rebels*, Mitford scrutinizes her own adolescence with the same uncompromising honesty.

In "Thirteen" Mitford recalls struggling to establish her personal identity and discovering that she is different from her family yet indelibly marked by them. As an upper-class English child, young Jessica lives on a country estate run by a staff of servants and supervised by a loving mother who plans "amusements" for her six children, including excursions to Switzerland and Sweden. In spite of this privileged existence, or perhaps because of it, Mitford "at the discontent age of thirteen" suddenly begins to find "the unvarying sameness of life . . . unbearable" (paragraph 2). Nanny encourages Jessica to join an organization called Sunbeams, which matches rich children and poor children as correspondents, and eventually Jessica persuades her mother to enable her pen pal, Rose, to escape her wretched existence in London by inviting her to live at Swinbrook as "Between Maid, or Tweeny" (paragraph 14). What is supposed to be a "fairy tale come true" (paragraph 15) turns into a disaster. Face to face, Jessica and Rose have nothing to say to each other, and Rose is miserably homesick. Rose returns to London leaving Jessica worried about her inability to solve the problems of society and puzzled about the class system she has inherited.

You might want to pair this selection with Liliana Heker's "The Stolen Party," another story that examines the complexities of the class system but from the perspective of a maid's daughter.

QUESTIONS

1. How is young Jessica's attitude toward class different from that of her mother? How has Jessica been shaped by her own status in the class system?

Muv is ambivalent toward the "delicate matter" of class. She shares her children's amusement over their grandmother's politically incorrect question: "Is she *one of us*, dear child?" (paragraph 24), but finds herself in the uncomfortable position of having to maintain a tradition she would prefer not to discuss. When Jessica wants to invite Rose for a visit, Muv responds, "I really don't think that would do, Little D. . . . Think of how dreadfully *uncomfortable* she'd feel" (paragraph 14). And later when Jessica wants to ask her school friends to tea, Muv—with logic from the other side of the looking glass—explains why that is impossible: "If you have them to tea they'll invite you to tea with them, and you wouldn't be able to go. You see, I don't know any of their mothers" (paragraph 23).

Jessica consciously rejects the class biases of her parents, who would never think of themselves as snobbish yet cling to a view of history where the various classes are "destined to travel forever harmoniously down the ages on parallel tracks which could never meet or cross" (paragraph 27). But Jessica is a product of her environment. Jessica's education makes her aware of "the extremely flowery style and strictly phonetic spelling" (paragraph 13) of Rose's letters. Jessica's ignorance of any life other than her own allows her to imagine that her letters, containing romanticized accounts of her pampered life, will "bring great rays of joy into [Rose's] otherwise drab existence" (paragraph 12). And Jessica's narrow range of experiences makes it impossible for her to imagine homesickness or to understand Rose's longing for her impoverished family. Regardless of what Jessica thinks about the class structure, her own place in it guarantees the failure of her friendship with Rose.

Jessica, like all adolescents, comes to the discomfiting realization that, long before she was old enough to examine and reject the pattern of her parents' lives, she had been cut to fit it quite nicely.

2. What are the "invisible boundaries that keep Jessica "boxed in from the real life of other people going on all around" (paragraph 3)? To what extent are those boundaries like those that surround all adolescents?

Jessica lists five of the boundaries that confine her (paragraph 3). The first three are similar to the restraints that chafe most adolescents who are ready to emerge from childhood: "there were rules against talking to strangers, seeing a film unless Muv had seen and approved it first, going anywhere without a grownup." Although the parental rules common today are less restrictive, most of your students can probably list at least five family rules that they considered too confining.

The fourth boundary—"the company of my own family exclusively" is unique to people of Jessica's social class (and to the minority of other children who are schooled at home). Although it's difficult for most of us to imagine that situation, you might ask your students to name ways in which such an experience would have changed them.

The fifth is the most interesting: "there was, above all, the crushing realization of my own limitations." Jessica's personal limitations include her failure to find a self that measures up to the standards set by the books she reads (paragraph 7), her inability to grasp the reality of other people (paragraph 8), and her powerlessness to discover an answer to the problems of poverty and class. Like most adolescents Jessica seems to believe that she will not be able to overcome these limitations until she can achieve the independence and self-knowledge found only on the other side of the garden wall, in the land of adulthood (paragraph 4).

3. How does the author feel about her younger self?

This question is intended to focus your students' attention on the distinction between the narrator and the narrator's younger self. This piece was written in 1960, thirty years after the events occurred and long after Mitford settled the question of class for herself by becoming an active supporter of the Communist party. Even without that biographical information, your students should be able to see how Mitford the narrator distances herself from Jessica the teenager by characterizing her in ways that would not have occurred to the child. For example, the narrator refers to the "discontent age of thirteen" (paragraph 2), and she comments that a "thirteen-year-old is a kaleidoscope of different personalities, if not in most ways a mere figment of her own imagination" (paragraph 6).

Once your students recognize that the narrator is not the teenager, they can move on to the more interesting question of Mitford's feelings about her adolescent self. Although Mitford is critical of Jessica's romanticized view of the world and her naive hope that she can solve the problems of poverty by sending letters and parcels to her Sunbeam or by inviting her to become a Tweeny, the narrator does not condemn the teenager. Instead, she charitably presents a young Jessica we can like and sympathize with—an adolescent well aware of her physical imperfections, concerned about the misfortunes of others, and able to laugh at her own suffering, which "you know is largely of your own making" (paragraph 9). Mitford seems to have forgiven herself for her youthful ignorance, a feat many of us never accomplish.

You may want to have your students examine the other first-person narratives in this unit and consider the attitudes of each narrator toward his or her earlier self. In Cameron's "Homework," for example, the narrator, Michael, is relating incidents that occurred only a few days earlier. Because there is little if any difference between the narrator and his younger self, the narrator has no distant vantage point from which he can comfortably look back to try to understand himself. Consequently, he offers no "mature" interpretation of his earlier actions and feelings.

In Anderson's "Discovery of a Father," the narrator deliberately and completely separates his old self from his new self in a way Mitford does not. He may recognize the kid he once was, but he wants to make it clear that the kid has been left behind. Mitford, on the other hand, makes a point of telling us that putting childish things behind isn't as easy as the Bible says it is (paragraph 4).

—M.R.D.—

Style Lesson 5: Imitating a Periodic Sentence

To get a sense of how a sentence builds to a climax, imitate the structure of Mitford's intricate one below (from paragraph 21). Instead of "glorying in every minute of school," you might describe an encounter with a drive-through car wash, a supreme pizza, a theatrical performance, or the weight room in the gym.

The clatter
    of hundreds of girls
        rushing through the corridors,
the unfamiliar business
    of competing in lessons,
the huge smelly meals
    in an enormous dining room
        with an endless choice
            of people to talk to,
the vast pleasure
    of "showing off" and
    baiting the mistresses
        in front of the other pupils—
even the irrational rules
    against whistling in the corridors
    or putting your feet up on your desk—
it all went to my head
    like wine.

MARK TWAIN

The Mesmerizer

Twain's memoir may serve as a springboard for memoirs by some of your students. It recalls an episode which he pretends, at least, to be ashamed of: ten days of dishonest glory when he pretended to be hypnotized by a traveling "mesmerizer." Twain was then "fourteen or fifteen years old, the age at which a boy is willing to endure all things, suffer all things short of death by fire, if thereby he may be conspicuous and show off before the public." But your sharper students may notice that in addition to being a portrait of the boy Twain was, the story serves as a hint of the man he would become. Ingenuity in acting and storytelling was the key to Twain's success as the mesmerizer's assistant, and the same ingenuity made Twain famous as a writer and public speaker. Thus the memoir, like many memoirs of adolescence, shows with humor and detachment the emergence of the adult personality.

Before your students read this memoir, you may want to make sure that they are aware of the time that has elapsed between the event and Twain's writing about it. "The Mesmerizer" is part of Twain's autobiography, which was compiled rather haphazardly over a number of years; this segment was written in 1903. Twain would have been 68 years old, looking back on an incident that happened more than fifty years earlier. Students may be confused by the shift in time in paragraphs 13–15, which recall an earlier incident in order to set up the rest of the memoir. You may want to warn your class that the memoir will contain a flashback to a still earlier time.

QUESTIONS

1. What does this memoir reveal about the personality of Sam Clemens (Mark Twain) as a teenager?

This may be a particularly important question to ask if you are going to have students write autobiographical essays. Some students feel that the unstated purpose of an autobiographical essay is to make a good impression, and so they tend to write about episodes in which they figure as heroes or as saints. Twain's memoir, like most successful ones (humorous or serious), avoids praising its subject too highly. It portrays Sam Clemens as a boy eager to "show off before the public," a boy capable of lying to everyone in town, including his own mother, and at the same time a boy capable (for a time, at least) of being fooled by a showman like the mesmerizer. On the other hand, young Sam Clemens shows intelligence and ingenuity in his lies (particularly in his manipulation of Dr. Peake) and he shows an almost astonishing will power when he allows the "dear good people" of the town to drive pins into his arm as part of the mesmerizer's act.

Independent of praise or blame, the memoir shows us that the teenager Sam Clemens understood what it meant to assume a role, and that he did so with great gusto. The boy foreshadows the man, who spent a long public life in the carefully constructed (and marketed) role of Mark Twain, folk humorist.

2. Does Twain tell this story from his teenage years from a teenager's perspective or from an adult's?

The joy of a well-written memoir is the sense of being in two places at once, caught up in the story of youth at the same time that we are joining the adult writer in observing and interpreting from a distance. In some memoirs (like Maya Angelou's "Momma"), the adult voice is muted so that we can experience with little apparent mediation what the narrator experienced at the time. In Twain's memoir, the adult perspective and the teenager's are about equally present.

You can clarify Twain's dual perspective by looking at extreme cases to begin with. Paragraphs 7–10 come closest to being narrated strictly from the boy's perspective: "I perceived by the tense and expectant faces of the people that Simmons was behind me," for example, seems to recreate the experience without comment. The introductory paragraph and the concluding paragraph are "spoken" by the 68-year-old Twain: "An exciting event in our village was the arrival of the mesmerizer. I think the year was 1850. As to that I am not sure but. . . ." After identifying the extreme cases students should be ready to see the effect of bringing the perspectives together in a passage like this one that bridges paragraphs 11 and 12:

> They would stick a pin in my arm and bear on it until they drove it a third of its length in, and then be lost in wonder that by a mere exercise of will power the professor could turn my arm to iron and make it insensible to pain. Whereas it was not insensible at all; I was suffering agonies of pain.
>
> After that fourth night, that proud night, that triumphant night, I was the only subject. Simmons invited no more candidates to the platform. I performed alone every night the rest of the fortnight. Up to that time a dozen wise old heads, the intellectual aristocracy of the town, had held out as implacable unbelievers. I was as hurt by this as if I were engaged in some honest occupation. There is nothing surprising about this. Human beings feel dishonor the most, sometimes, when they most deserve it.

We start, so to speak, "in the story" as told from the boy's perspective, but by the last three sentences, we are "out of the story," hearing an adult, detached, humorous comment not only on the action, but on human nature generally. The spice in many of Twain's autobiographical writing comes from this mixture of perspectives—the (relative) innocence of youth is brought into contact with the cynicism of age.

You may not want to encourage cynicism in your student writers, but you may want them to consider in their own memoirs taking advantage of the opportunity to contrast the naiveté of the person they were to the relative knowingness of the person they are.

3. How truthful do you think Twain's account of this episode is?

Built into this memoir are layers and layers of fabrication. Because Twain is recreating an event from the distant past, we can assume that he relies on his imagination as well as his memory. The text itself is full of warnings about credibility: It makes the point that people can be easily fooled into believing that a lie is the truth and lets us know up front that Twain is the best liar of all. And in recreating his performance as the mesmerizer's assistant, he demonstrates to us his duplicity, telling us specifically how he managed to make his vision of the Richmond fire believable by feeding his audience a little at a time, building momentum as he got them hooked, and then throwing "the valves wide open and [turning] on all the steam." Taken as a whole, the story compares a marginally good fake, the mesmerizer, to a more successful one, Twain himself. Without the ending, the description of a repentant man attempting to persuade his own mother of his falsehood and to make us see the horrible burden of being a great liar, we might think the entire episode was essentially a fiction. But perhaps the ending is Twain's "throwing the valves wide open"—duping the reader by adding a lie that creates verisimilitude.

Twain's mother's argument alone is wonderfully humorous and ironic; it may be fun to try to sort out her reasoning and look at its logic and illogic. But it may also be interesting to pull apart the complete memoir and have your class decide how much memory and how much imagination went into Twain's account of the mesmerizer coming to town.

—D.H.—

Style Lesson 6: Balanced Sentences

In paragraph 5, Twain contrasts his own personality to that of Hicks in a series of carefully balanced sentences. Imitate Twain's technique by contrasting yourself to a childhood rival.

Hicks was born honest,
    I without that incumbrance—so some people said.
Hicks saw what he saw and reported accordingly,
    I saw more than was visible and added to it such details as could help.
Hicks had no imagination;
    I had a double supply.
He was born calm,
    I was born excited.
No vision could start a rapture in him and he was constipated as to language, anyway;
    but if I saw a vision I emptied the dictionary onto it and lost the remnant of my mind into the bargain.

MARIE WINN

Children Without Childhood

Winn's "Children Without Childhood" and John Holt's "Escape From Childhood" could be assigned together to present contrasting metaphors of the child's world. Winn pictures childhood as a distinct stage of life, and she worries that its innocent inhabitants are no longer surrounded by the "protective membrane" (paragraph 6) that should shelter them from premature exposure to the adult world. Holt, however, envisions childhood as the first segment of the curve of human life, a single curve of "continual growth and change" (paragraph 8). He argues that the artificial "institution of childhood" constructs a "walled garden" (paragraph 13) that unwisely separates children from the society around them and prolongs their years of dependency and subservience. Both essays offer your students the opportunity to test the authors' visions of childhood by comparing those visions to their own experiences as children.

QUESTIONS

1. Winn lists a number of the social forces beating down childhood's door. What are others?

This question could open class discussion or lead to personal experience essays. Winn blames the present situation on the "social upheavals" of the 1960s and 1970s (paragraph 10), and she points specifically to "the rise in two-career families," "the mounting divorce rate," and the "fascinating presence of television" (paragraph 11). Your students can undoubtedly list many other pressures, ranging from child abuse to AIDS, that shove children into the adult world.

They may also note that the outline Winn sketches looks somewhat middle class. To flesh out that outline, your students might list some of the additional problems faced by children who are growing up in impoverished urban or rural areas.

2. Do you agree with Winn's argument that the pressures to become an adult are stronger today than ever before?

Winn asserts that children have been perceived as "special creatures with special needs" ever since the end of the Middle Ages (paragraph 9), and that the social changes occurring since the 1960s have radically changed that time-honored perception.

To evaluate the strength of Winn's argument, your students will need to consider two underlying assumptions. First, we have Winn's characterization of children a generation ago: the girls "guileless and innocent creatures with their shiny Mary Janes and pigtails, their scraped knees and trusting ways" (paragraph 2) and the boys "climbing around a construction site," "having a crabapple war," or "mowing the lawn" (paragraph 3). Although most of your students will be too young to challenge this "Leave It To Beaver" version of childhood by recalling their own experiences in the 1950s or 1960s, they can certainly weigh Winn's evidence, which amounts to little more than her unsupported assertion that schoolchildren today are more akin to Lolita than to the children a generation earlier (paragraph 2) and her reliance on *National Lampoon's* satirical comparison of the boys of today and yesteryear (paragraph 3). Although these vivid illustrations tug at our hearts, they fail to convince our minds.

Your students should also note that if such idyllic childhoods ever existed, they belonged to white, middle-class, or upper-class families. Other selections in this unit address the problems of less favored children. In "Momma" Maya Angelou captures the pain of an African-American child taunted by racists. In "First Communion" Edward Rivera reflects on the complex relationship between Hispanic school children and their teachers—Irish-American nuns who disparage their students' families and ancestry, but who also buy the children new clothes for first communion. In "Thirteen" Jessica Mitford contrasts the lives of lower-class and upper-class English children.

Winn's second unstated assumption is that the sheltered state of suburban children of the 1950s is typical of the position of children ever since the end of the Middle Ages. Your students who have read novels such as Dickens's *Oliver Twist* or *Hard Times* will realize that the working class children of 19th century England were neither cherished nor protected from the harsh realities of the Industrial Revolution. And those who know about U.S. laws regulating child labor and requiring school attendance will understand that such laws were necessary because children in this country were being exploited. After conducting a little historical research or interviewing grandparents who grew up on farms, your students may conclude that the concept of childhood as "The Age of Protection" is the exception, not the rule.

3. Can you recall instances when the adults in your life attempted to protect you from "the harsh realities of life"? Do you think children should be sheltered from such knowledge?

You might begin this discussion by giving your students ten minutes to write brief answers to a few questions about their own experiences. You will probably want to assure them at the outset that their responses are confidential, and that they will not have to read them aloud or allow anyone else to see what they have written. Then ask the following:

> Do you remember a specific incident when you noticed that adults were protecting you or another child? If so, describe it.
>
> If you did notice active protection, describe what you felt at that time. Relief? Resentment? Fear?

> Now that you are an adult, do you think the adult did the right thing? Under similar circumstances, would you try to provide the same protection for a child? Why or why not?

Because some students may not recall personally observing protectionism of this sort, you can also offer the option of writing about any experiences they believe children should or should not be protected from.

Your students' answers will be as varied as their childhoods, but most will probably recall at least a few times when their parents tried to shield them from disturbing or unhappy experiences. You might prompt your class by asking them to recall the births of younger siblings or the illnesses or deaths of relatives. Unlike the children of earlier eras, children today seldom observe childbirth or death, partly because those events usually occur in hospitals where small children are not admitted, partly because adults no longer consider it appropriate for children to view such things. For similar reasons, some parents choose not to take their children to funerals.

Parents today may wrap their children in fewer layers of protective padding, but they still try to cushion a few of the bumps of life.

—M.R.D.—

Style Lesson 7: "Oratorical" Antitheses

In paragraph 7 of "Children Without Childhood," Winn uses an orator's technique of rhetorical questions based on antitheses. (In this case the antithesis of the adult world and the child's world.) As an exercise in invention and sentence patterning, choose another pair of contrasts—men versus women, perhaps, or television versus real life, or play versus work—and then develop rhetorical questions that parallel Winn's in structure.

There is nothing wrong with sex, the modern adult has come to understand well,
but what about sex at age twelve?

Lassitude, indifference, cynicism, are understandable defenses against the hardships of modern adult life,
but aren't these states antithetical to childhood?

Shouldn't these kids be out at the old fishing hole or playing with their dolls or stamp albums
instead of reading *Screw* or *Hustler*, or flicking the TV dial to see what's playing, just like weary adults after a hard day's work?

JOHN HOLT

Escape from Childhood

Holt's essay and Marie Winn's "Children Without Childhood" are good ones to assign in tandem because Winn believes that childhood *should* be a walled garden protecting the young from the outside world, but that the wall now has too many holes in it, while Holt believes that wall should either come down or be fitted with many well-marked exits. At the heart of their disagreement are two different visions of children: Winn views them as vulnerable creatures who should not be prematurely exposed to "sorrowful knowledge of the adult world," while Holt sees them as resilient and resourceful creatures eager to deal with the adult world. Holt's book *Escape from Childhood* is essentially a proposal to allow children to declare themselves adults when they wish to, and to face both the opportunities and responsibilities of that declaration.

QUESTIONS

1. Would you have been better off in a society that treats childhood as Holt recommends? Would you want your children raised in such a society?

The first question of this pair invites students to think autobiographically, with all the particular details that their own particular lives provide. The second forces them to think prudentially, as parents must. Thinking autobiographically myself, I don't think I would have been better or worse off under Holt's plan, since I enjoyed my childhood and actually found it freer than I am finding my adult life. Then, on a summer day, I might have chosen among going fishing or playing football with kids in the neighborhood or reading whatever book I liked. Now, I *know* that I will take care of the baby, do the dishes, go to a department meeting, and write this comment. Some of these things are pleasant enough and all are the result of free will exercised on another day, but I may never again have the day-by-day freedom I enjoyed when I was twelve.

I have known people whose experience was very different, of course, and who really wanted, as Holt suspects most older children do, to get *out*—out of an unpleasant or abusive home life, out into the workplace, out into sexual freedom, out into that never-never land that consumer culture seems to offer, where adults can buy whatever they want just because they want it. Some students, looking back on their own childhood, may have reason to argue that they would have been better off getting out. Others may say that if they had been allowed to get out, they would have married that creep or stopped playing the piano or got a dead-end job at a pizza place, or otherwise messed up.

When your students imagine themselves as parents, they will probably see some problems with Holt's scheme, or at least some need for clarification. Is the eight-year-old going to have a legal right to leave the house in a tizzy and try to hitch a ride to Los Angeles to work as a child porn star, while the parent is forbidden to stop her? Does the suddenly depressed twelve-year-old's right to privacy mean that he can take his parents to court if, while they are putting clean underwear in his dresser drawer, they check to see whether the bottle they find there contains quaaludes? If discussion on such questions waxes hot, you may want to suggest that reading the whole of Holt's book (it is not long or difficult) and evaluating his success in dealing with them might be a good paper topic.

3. Holt says that in human life "growth and change are continuous. There are no breaks or gaps in it. We do not, like some insects, suddenly turn from one sort of creature into another that is very different" (paragraph 8). How accurately does this statement describe your experience of growing up?

Holt is a mathematician by training, and I can't resist suggesting at this point that his metaphorical description of each human life as "a single curve, a wholeness" reflects a mathematician's eagerness to find behind all phenomena a set of smooth curves, without "breaks and gaps" that are inexplicable by formula.

Everyone who has taken literature classes has encountered the *bildungsroman* or "initiation story" often enough to suspect that some transitions from childhood to adulthood *must* be dramatic. In this unit we have an autobiographical initiation story by Sherwood Anderson and a fictional one by Jane Hamilton. Here there are apparent "breaks and gaps" and the adult does pop quickly from the chrysalis of childhood.

My own life offered nothing so dramatic (which has sometimes made me think that by comparison to the characters of literature, I had no life), but it seems an exaggeration to me to say that growth and change are so entirely continuous. Boys do have first shaves, girls first periods. We do fall in and out of love for the first time, and we do have a first bitter experience with our ability to decide wrongly in a matter that affects us and others. Getting your students to think about the breaks and gaps that Holt so briskly dismisses may also point the way to a good essay topic.

4. Is it true, as Holt says, that "we *act* as if the differences between any sixteen-year-old and any twenty-two-year-old were far greater and more important than the differences between someone aged two and someone aged sixteen, or between someone aged twenty-two and someone aged seventy" (paragraph 20).

Here I think Holt has let his enthusiasm for his position lead him to a kind of blindness. The important thing (from Holt's perspective) that the two-year-old and the sixteen-year-old have in common is that they are minors, unable to enter into legally enforceable contracts—including marriage, enlistment in the military, and so forth. But law is not custom in this society, and custom is ordinarily the stronger of the two. We don't let two-year-olds leave the house alone; we don't let them own or handle sharp objects; we don't expect them to fend for themselves at lunch time. We don't (most of us) decide what clothes sixteen-year-olds will put on every morning; we don't routinely carry them to the car and strap them in despite their loud protests; we don't even (many of us) have the nerve to suggest what movies they will go to or what books they will read during their leisure time. Holt knows this, of course, but chooses to ignore it in order, I assume, not to dilute his argument.

This instance of exaggeration is trivial in terms of the logic of Holt's whole argument, but some readers will not think it rhetorically trivial. Here's a chance to remind your students that in argumentative prose especially, the writer needs to avoid making statements that damage his credibility.

—D.H.—

Style Lesson 8:
Narrative Sequence

To study Holt's technique as a narrator, close your book and work with classmates to fill the blanks in this excerpt from paragraph 23 of "Escape from Childhood:"

I asked three questions, for a show-of-hands response. The ________ was "If you could legally vote in political elections, how many of you think that at least some of the time you would vote?" About two-thirds of the students raised their hands, many of them ________ and ________. The ________ was, "If you could legally work for money, how many of you think at least some of the time you would work? One boy in the front row, who had not spoken during the discussion, said, "Hey, ________

____

________________, what's the big hurry to start?" People ________, but the hands________ ________. ________, almost as an ________, not expecting any particular response, I asked the ________: "If you could legally live away from home, how many of you think that at least some of the time you would do so?" Every ________ ________ into the air, so ________ and ________ that I half expected ________ to ________ out of ________.

*Hint: Holt uses simple transitions (*first, second*) and creates a climax by starting with the least dramatic question-and-answer and building to the most dramatic.*

PETER CAMERON

Homework

Michael, the narrator of this short story, is an eighteen-year-old high school student who is saddened by the prospect of entering the adult world where lives seem trivial and drearily alike. For Michael that world is symbolized by the Photo-Matica:

> There's a machine in the booth that looks like a printing press, only snapshots ride down a conveyor belt and fall into a bin and then disappear. The machine gives the illusion that your photographs are being developed on the sport. It's a fake. The same fifty photographs roll through over and over, and my sister says no one notices, because everyone in town is taking the same pictures (paragraph 69).

Unfortunately, Michael is not a rarity. The teen suicide rate, the alarming number of teens who suffer from depression, and the popularity of teen-problem movies ranging from *Pretty In Pink* to *Heathers* to *Pump Up the Volume* attest to the despair of many young people. "Homework" will allow your students to discuss and write about a peculiarly adolescent type of sorrow that most of us have experienced.

QUESTIONS

1. Why is Michael sad?

This is the puzzler. Although the adults in the story assume that Michael is sad because his dog Keds died, Michael tells us that he was unhappy even before Keds' death (paragraph 80). Michael's unhappiness cannot be attributed to any obvious cause: he isn't poor, he doesn't have a drug problem, and his parents aren't divorced. Instead, Michael has had the good fortune to grow up in a loving, protective, two-parent, two-child, one-dog family—precisely the kind of environment Marie Winn ("Children Without Childhood") would wish for every child. So what is his problem?

Perhaps, as John Holt ("Escape From Childhood") might suggest, Michael feels trapped in the limbo of a childhood that has extended too long. He is eighteen years old, still living at home, and still attending high school. Cameron highlights the awkwardness of this boy-man status with the excuse-to-the-teacher incident. Although the school recognizes that Michael is old enough to write his own excuse, the guidance counselor rejects the honest excuse Michael offers—that he was unhappy. Michael is patronized by an adult institution that refuses to recognize the legitimacy of his grief. Perhaps Michael is sad because he is a grownup who is not yet allowed to live his own life. Like a contemporary Holden Caulfield, Michael seems to be too old for the stage of life he's stuck in.

On the other hand, it may be that Michael's sadness stems from his reluctance to enter adulthood, which is—to Michael's way of thinking—an imperfect world with little to recommend it. Michael has outgrown the comforting childhood conviction that mommy and daddy can make everything all right. He suffers from the knowledge that adults are neither omniscient nor omnipotent, and that no one can understand him or help him.

In fact, Michael is acutely conscious of the inadequacies of the adults in his life. He recognizes that his father "is very good at bringing things up and letting them drop" and that a "lot gets dropped" (paragraph 15). He notes that his mother "is afraid to acknowledge [his preparations for going to school] for fear it won't be true" (paragraph 35). He remarks that his guidance counselor "used to be a history teacher, but she couldn't take it anymore, so she was moved into guidance" (paragraph 42). Perhaps Michael fears that he too will soon be forced to don an ill-fitting costume for his role in the tragicomedy of adulthood.

2. What is the significance of the story's title?

Near the beginning of the story, Michael confesses that since he started cutting school, the one thing he misses is homework. Consequently, he sets himself difficult algebraic problems that he attempts to solve (paragraph 3). Michael refers to these problems again in paragraphs 8 and 34 and in the final paragraph. On one level, homework is an escape from the real world. While Michael ponders the boat sailing down the river and the jeep driving along the bank, he doesn't have to think about Keds or the other causes of his sadness.

On another level, the algebraic problems are a metaphor for the real world: "Find the value for *n* such that *n* plus everything else in your life makes you feel all right. What would *n* equal?" (paragraph 82). If *n* represents whatever it is that gives meaning to life, Michael has not yet solved the equation, and he doesn't think anyone else has either. He suspects that Julie's attempt to answer to the problem lies in her relentless quest for beauty (paragraph 2); that his father's attempt involves securing the hearth and home, a goal that explains his father's need to repair the garage door and his conviction that bicycles shouldn't be locked up at his own house (paragraphs 10, 11, and 15); that his mother's attempt is revealed by the love she showers on her plants (paragraph 6) and children; and that his guidance counselor's failure even to venture an answer is suggested by her "calendar blotter with 'LUNCH' written across the middle of every box, including Saturday and Sunday" (paragraph 42).

Maybe Cameron wants us to realize that the algebra problem is a bad metaphor for life, but one that we use constantly, all of us looking for *n*, all of us disappointed because *n* "is never a whole number. It is always a fraction" (paragraph 3).

3. Is Michael a believable teenager or does he seem to be a fictional character dreamed up by an adult author? Which of his qualities, thoughts, and actions make him either believable or unrealistic?

I would predict that your students will judge Michael atypical (because he seems to have no friends and no social life) but generally convincing.

Few people recall their teenage years as so happy that they would want to repeat them, so your students will probably find Michael's inexplicable sadness credible.

Some readers may doubt that a teenager could have Michael's uncanny ability to predict and manipulate adults. However, as the mother of three teenagers, I'm convinced that this talent arrives on the thirteenth birthday. In any event, Michael knows exactly which buttons to push when he is dealing with his father, his mother, and his guidance counselor. When Michael comes home, he locks his bike, knowing that his act "infuriates [his] father, who doesn't believe in locking things up in his own house" (paragraph 11). When his mother watches him write his excuse but doesn't ask to see it, he leaves it on the table while he goes to the bathroom. Then he comes back to get the note, certain she has read it (paragraph 37). When he realizes that his guidance counselor is "embarrassed to be talking about a dead dog," he escapes from the conference by repeating, "I don't want to talk about it" (paragraphs 62 and 63).

A second look at these incidents reveals another of the characteristics that make Michael believable as a teenager—his absolute certainty that he is right. He is confident that locking the bike "infuriates his father" even though his father "pretends not to notice" (paragraph 11). Maybe his father really didn't notice that Michael had locked his bike; maybe his mother didn't read his excuse; maybe his counselor wasn't embarrassed to discuss a pet's death. Michael never suspects that other people might be as enigmatic as he is.

The one false note in the story may be Michael's deliberate use of the algebra problem as a metaphor for life: "Find the value for *n* such that *n* plus everything else in your life makes you feel all right" (paragraph 82). Your students may find it improbable that Michael, in the midst of his suffering, could so perfectly conceptualize and express the cause of his pain.

—M.R.D.—

JANE HAMILTON

Rehearsing "The Firebird"

When your students are ready for comic relief, assign "Rehearsing 'The Firebird,'" which could have been subtitled "Portrait of the Writer As A Young Girl." This is the story of twelve-year-old GeorgeAnne Mealy, an aspiring author who decides to entertain herself and her friend Tiffany by concocting an unlikely romance between two of her teachers: Mr. Smedley, the hapless musician who conducts the sixth-grade All Village Orchestra, and Mrs. Vogel, the French teacher whose husband was murdered on the el train. GeorgeAnne and Tiffany compose a series of love letters (which the girls exchange only with each other) featuring lines wretched enough to have been lifted from a romance novel:

> Dear Patricia,
>
> When I see you I am reminded of the grove of poplars near my uncle's farm. It was a refuge for me when I was a boy, a place of shimmering wetness (paragraph 21).

The letters continue, along with sketches of the outfits the two lovers are to wear on their various dates, until Mrs. Vogel intercepts a note and then "with her infallible teacher radar" searches out the "plain blue spiral notebook" that contains the entire correspondence (paragraph 41).

Before you assign this reading, you might want to tell your students the story of the Firebird, which comes from a Russian fairy tale. In the ballet, Prince Ivan is hunting in the forest and captures the Firebird. She persuades him to release her by giving him a magic feather that he can use to call her whenever he needs her assistance. Ivan then meets a group of young princesses who have been enchanted by the wicked Kotschei. Ivan falls in love with one of the princesses, but before he can leave the forest with her, the Kotschei and his followers return. Ivan despairs of vanquishing the Kotschei, who is immortal, until he summons the Firebird. She directs him to the egg that holds the Kotschei's life, Ivan destroys the egg, the Kotschei dies, and the enchantment ends. In the final scene, Ivan is crowned, he and his beloved are married, and all the other princesses are reunited with their true loves.

QUESTIONS

1. What makes this story humorous?

The fun of this story is not in its plot but in its plotter—sixth grader GeorgeAnne Mealy, a little girl made of no sugar but plenty of spice. GeorgeAnne's observations about people are brutally honest, wonderfully imaginative, and wickedly funny. For example, she describes her friend Mr. Smedley in this way:

> He looked as if he had been put on a medieval stretching rack and stretched beyond what his poor sunken frame could support. His skin was red and sore and pockmarked. His one suit was always wrinkled and too short in the sleeves. There his hands were hanging limp like dead chickens at his side; even when he brought them up, his baton between his chapped thumb and first finger, those hands were lifeless, something to throw in a pot with an onion and cook, and endure for Monday-night supper (paragraph 2).

GeorgeAnne is equally honest in assessing herself: "I had no talent. I had never practiced except under duress. I would never go anywhere in the musical world beyond lip-syncing "Climb Ev'ry Mountain" (paragraph 3).

GeorgeAnne also amuses us with her outlandish metaphors. You might ask your students to list their favorites. Here are a few possibilities.

> We played the tremolo parts and sounded as we looked, like spastic electric toothbrushes (paragraph 8).

> The violins made the sort of noise that must surely fill your ears when you are being suffocated in the dark by a strange man (paragraph 9).
>
> I waited for the blast of horn to come down to the swamp waters of the strings (paragraph 17).
>
> Mr. Smedley might just as well have been teaching a pack of hyenas to sing the *Messiah* (paragraph 17).
>
> Sitting at supper I would feel a letter come up my throat and sit on my tongue (paragraph 24).
>
> Mrs. Vogel . . . was like a little dog yapping at an imaginary postman (paragraph 46).
>
> When I went back to school I was welcomed with the measured warmth a leper receives at the village square (paragraph 56).

If your students have read Cameron's "Homework," you might ask them how this story would change if it were told by Michael, the narrator of "Homework." They are likely to conclude that the same incidents that delight GeorgeAnne (at least the GeorgeAnne who exists at the beginning of the story) would depress Michael.

2. What is the basis of GeorgeAnne's special relationship with Mr. Smedley?

This unusual friendship seems to be grounded on their love of art and their respect for each other, a respect based in part on their shared sense of the inadequacy and sorrow of life. Both of them recognize and appreciate artistic talent. GeorgeAnne knows that Mary Clare's horn solo sings above and beyond the other instruments, "the notes floating out into the auditorium, away from the mire" (paragraph 9), and Mr. Smedley closes his eyes while he conducts that solo (paragraph 18). Mr. Smedley also recognizes GeorgeAnne's talent as a writer. After reading the love notes, he shocks the other adults by remarking, "If these girls were as good at their music as they are at writing there'd be some hope for the concert halls of America" (paragraph 46). Perhaps what he responds to in her story is her potential to someday transform sorrow into art.

GeorgeAnne seems to respect Mr. Smedley's dedication to music, and she pities him because he is trying to conduct a sixth-grade orchestra when he would rather play violin at Carnegie Hall (paragraph 8). Mr. Smedley's respect for GeorgeAnne is demonstrated by his recognition of her writing talent. When she asks him what the horn solo means, he doesn't give her the typical smug adult answer: "Don't worry. You'll understand when you're older." Instead, he first tries to explain:

> "Uh"—he took a pass over his thin wet hair with his hand —"I think it's about resolution, and"—he looked out into the dark theater—"it's something you feel here." He pounded with his fist on

> his sunken chest. I guess I can't say it in words; I'm not very good at that sort of thing." He looked at me in a way that made me think a sparkler had been lit at my throat and then sizzled all the way down to my toes (paragraph 61).

Then he pays her the supreme compliment: "I leave it to you to describe it some day, GeorgeAnne" (paragraph 61).

3. Why is it that GeorgeAnne never regrets writing the notes, even though they obviously upset Mrs. Vogel?

When GeorgeAnne is ready to pass her last note, and Mrs. Vogel commands, "GeorgeAnne, FREEZE," GeorgeAnne thinks, "In retrospect it all seemed so inevitable; we should have . . . (paragraph 29). At that point the reader might expect GeorgeAnne to complete her sentence by wishing that they had never written the notes or that they had been more discreet. But no. She continues: "we should have had a getaway car or some plan for spontaneous combustion." GeorgeAnne continues to treat the incident humorously, even though her mother and father are quite upset that she caused Mrs. Vogel to suffer, "to SUFFER, DID I UNDERSTAND?" (paragraph 53).

There are at least two possible explanations for GeorgeAnne's seemingly callous behavior. One is that she never regrets writing the notes because, by doing so, she seals her friendship with Mr. Smedley and thus wins admission to the adult world. However, this interpretation requires us to believe that GeorgeAnne consciously decides that her gain outweighs Mrs. Vogel's pain, and I see nothing to suggest that she is so calculating.

Another possible explanation is that GeorgeAnne is a child. She is fascinated by adults, but—as her love notes prove—she doesn't understand them at all. For GeorgeAnne, the murder of Mrs. Vogel's husband is no more real than the romantic escapades she invents. Both are excuses for word play. Imaginative though she is, GeorgeAnne cannot imagine the grief Mrs. Vogel must feel when she reads the playful description of a "sniper flattening" her "husband on the corrugated doormat of the el train" (paragraph 28). Although the narrator of the story is GeorgeAnne as an adult, she chooses not to reflect on her later understanding. Instead, she gives us an unretouched photo of a child too innocent to repent.

4. How is GeorgeAnne like the firebird described in the opening paragraph?

After first viewing the ballet, GeorgeAnne knows she loves the girl-bird: "she had the power too, the power of the storyteller. She was the one who made the story take its course; it was she who arranged for true love to prevail" (paragraph 1). As this story progresses, GeorgeAnne begins to recognize her own potential: "It occurred to me sometime during the first weeks of orchestra that if a bird has the power of love—the power to enchant, the power to destroy—what magic ought a young girl like myself, GeorgeAnne Mealy, have within her beating heart?" (paragraph 10).

GeorgeAnne has no musical talent, but she can write, and she begins to pen notes that construct an imaginary romance between Mr. Smedley and Mrs. Vogel. Like the firebird, GeorgeAnne tries to arrange for true love to prevail. Even when it is obvious that her efforts have failed miserably, and the culprits are sitting in the principal's office while he reads the confiscated letters, GeorgeAnne finds herself imagining yet another note to Mrs. Vogel, "telling her to calm down, to acknowledge to herself that she was behaving like a lunatic" (paragraph 41). GeorgeAnne is hooked on writing, and near the end of the story, she recognizes the qualities that compel her to write:

> For GeorgeAnne Mealy there were two things: There was the lurking power of words, words to tell any dream in the world; but most of all there was the feeling in the back of my throat, at the roots of my hair, in the goose bumps on my knees, the knot in my stomach, of pity. I had finally found its name. Pity ran so deep in my blood I had to kneel on the wood floor and cry into my wastebasket (paragraph 64).

GeorgeAnne's eventual success as a storyteller is demonstrated by "Rehearsing 'The Firebird,'" an adult version of the notes she and Tiffany passed back and forth. Although the story can't bring Mr. Smedley and Mrs. Vogel together, it can—like Mary Clare's horn solo and the firebird's dance—offer us the beauty, order, and consolation of art.

—M.R.D.—

FEMININITY AND MASCULINITY

OVERVIEW OF UNIT

One of the difficulties of teaching a composition class is finding topics that all the students in the classroom are interested in and that also have enough depth and ambiguity about them to require the exercise of rhetorical skills. The ways that society shapes our sexual identities may be an ideal topic, engaging the students' personal experience and opening some possibilities for research inside the library or out.

Users of earlier editions of *The Dolphin Reader* will notice some change of approach in this unit. Rather than trying to systematically demonstrate the change of sex roles over several decades, this edition concentrates on the various ways that roles are defined in a multi-cultural society. The historical note is still present: since most of the writers are now in middle age, students will be reading about how sex roles were defined "back then" and are in a position to write about how much (or how little) things have changed.

We particularly recommend Lois Gould's "X", a playful essay that nonetheless raises all the key questions about how our sexual identities are shaped. We also want to point out several essays from other units that touch on the theme of *Femininity and Masculinity:*

Sherwood Anderson, "Discovery of a Father"
Toni Cade Bambara, "Hammer Man"
Edna O'Brien, "Sister Imelda"
Doris Lessing, "A Sunrise on the Veld"
Jomo Kenyatta, "Gikuyu Industries"
Katha Politt, "The Smurfette Principle"
Gloria Steinem, "Sex, Lies, and Advertising"
Adrienne Rich, "Claiming an Education"
Susan Glaspell, "Trifles"

Clearly, this is a theme that could unite an entire semester.

LOIS GOULD

X

When my children were little tykes, "X" was their favorite read-to-me story. They no longer want me to read to them, but they still love "X," a modern fairy tale that asks us to imagine what it would be like to grow up free of the pressures to behave "like a girl" or "like a boy." The story begins: "Once upon a time, a Baby named X was born. It was named X so that no one could tell whether it was a boy or a girl." We then learn that—although X's parents know what X is—they have sworn not to tell anyone because they are participating in a "Secret Scientific Xperiment, known officially as Project Baby X."

Your students will be curious to find out how X fares in a world where everything from games to bathrooms to clothing is labeled either "boys" or "girls." And they should be intrigued by the revolutionary idea that it might not be necessary to identify young children by gender because "by the time it matters which sex [a child] is, it won't be a secret anymore."

The other selections in this unit force us to notice how we are conditioned to conform to our society's stereotypes of masculinity and femininity and to consider whether such conditioning is desirable, but only this piece invites us to visualize childhood as an X.

QUESTIONS

1. Would our society be better off if we all grew up as Xes? Would you be better off if you had been brought up as an X? Would you bring your child up as an X?

For class discussion, I would pose these questions in this order to demonstrate that ideas are often like roses—beautiful from a distance but thorny up close.

Gould's answer to the first question is clearly "yes." Not only does her story demonstrate X's excellence, it also shows us that the other children recognize X's superiority and strive to be just like X. Some of your students will accept Gould's basic proposition that it's all right for both boys and girls to excel in spelling bees, relay races, and cake baking, and those students may agree that—in theory—we would indeed be better off as Xes. If you are lucky, you will also have some students who will be courageous enough to speak out in support of traditional gender differentiation, or at least argue that we can offer our children all the opportunities X is given without robbing them of their sexual identities.

The second question is tougher because it requires your students to apply a general theory to the particular facts of their own lives and—with the 20/20 vision of hindsight—consider how a different upbringing might have affected them. I doubt that many will opt to revise their personal histories. When they begin to consider their own childhoods, they will realize how many problems an X has to face. An X would never get to spend the night with a friend. An X couldn't belong to Boy Scouts or Girl Scouts. An X couldn't use public bathrooms. An X might feel rejected by its grandparents, aunts, uncles, and cousins. An X might not like being called an "it." Worst of all, an X would always be an outsider because it would be neither one of the boys nor one of the girls. It's one thing to grow up in a world full of Xes; it's quite another to be the only X in the neighborhood.

The third question will get the fewest affirmative responses. Although "X" is a delightful story, it leaves potential parents with many unanswered questions: What if little X sets its heart on becoming a professional football player or a nanny and then discovers that it is the wrong gender for that occupation? What if X reaches adolescence and becomes confused and frightened when other people begin to respond to it as a female or a male? What if the adult X finds that he or she has so little in common with either males or females that she or he doesn't have any friends? What if the adult X overcompensates by adopting exaggerated feminine or masculine characteristics? Students who want to explore these possibilities may want to write another chapter in the life of X.

2. Would X be as popular with the other children if X did not excel in every school activity?

This question will insure that your students notice how Gould stacks the deck. The children at school hate X until X wins the spelling bee, wins the relay race, and almost wins the baking contest (paragraphs 79 and 80). Apparently, it is not X's Xness, but its superiority that impresses the other children. A child who is clearly exceptional will usually be allowed one idiosyncracy. Gould wants us to believe that X is excellent primarily because it has been taught to do both boys' stuff and girls' stuff, but such training merely gives X a wider range of abilities. It doesn't guarantee excellence. You might ask your students to consider whether X would have been as popular if X had been an average student, or a student with a learning disability, or a student who was physically disabled.

3. Would you find it difficult to be friends with an X or with a former X? Why or why not?

Surely everyone will have to answer "yes" to this one. We might well decide to befriend an X in spite of the difficulties, but it's hard to imagine that they wouldn't exist. For most of us, gender is so essential to identity that it's the first thing we notice about other people. I'm not an observant person, and I seldom recall a person's eye color, height, or clothing, but I do remember whether that person was male or female. In fact, we don't quite know how to respond to a person so androgynous in appearance that we can't label him or her appropriately. That's the theme of the *Saturday Night Live* skits involving Pat, a person whose gender is not obvious to his or her co-workers. The other employees are obsessed with learning what Pat is, and each episode features a new scheme (such as strip poker) for discovering this essential information.

The interesting question is why such information is essential. Unless we are looking for dates or mates, gender shouldn't matter. But of course it does. Because males and females in our society are not raised as Xes, we have different backgrounds and experiences, and we assume—perhaps incorrectly—that people who are of the same gender have certain things in common. I know I would never walk into a room filled with women and strike up a conversation by asking, "What did you think of that Cardinals game last night?"

4. Do you think this story would appeal to children? Why or why not? Is there anything about the tone or style that might affect adult readers negatively?

These questions will allow you to discuss the problems of writing for a particular audience. "X" was first published in *MS.* as a "Story for Free Children," and its appeal for young readers is obvious. The story begins with a traditional fairy tale opening, focuses on the adventures of a child hero, and ends happily with proof that the children—who all want to be like X—are wiser than their benighted parents. The sentence structure is simple, the tone is light, and the novel spelling of "Xperts," "Xperiment," and other words that usually begin with "ex-" reinforces the theme that we don't always have to follow established rules.

Your adult readers should also enjoy "X," probably because they will be fascinated by the idea of a genderless childhood, but they may find the eccentric spelling distracting rather than amusing, especially if they read the story more than once. Gould is right. We grown-ups feel more comfortable when everyone plays by our rules.

—M.R.D.—

Style Lesson 9:
Gender-Marked Language

Gould's interest in what she sees as obsessive sexual differentiation shows in her playfulness with the gender markings in language itself. Sharpen your sense of how frequently language indirectly comments on sexuality by attempting to find the ten words omitted below.

X liked being (1). But X cried a lot that night. So (2) (3) held (3) tight, and cried a little, too. X's (4) cheered (5) up with an Xciting story about an enchanted (6) called Sleeping (7), who woke up when (8) (9) kissed (10).

The key below will tell you what sort of word you are looking for:

1. *reflexive pronoun*
2. *possessive noun or pronoun*
3. *noun or pronoun*
4. *noun*
5. *noun or pronoun*
6. *noun*
7. *name*
8. *highborn title*
9. *name*
10. *pronoun*

ALICE WALKER

Brothers and Sisters

Alice Walker is sometimes taken to task by reviewers who find her portrayal of men venomous (think of *The Color Purple*). "Brothers and Sisters" goes a way toward explaining the bitterness Walker feels toward many men and also shows that it is not indiscriminate. Walker seems to suspect that *most* men raised in her father's generation or earlier were and are sexists in theory and practice. I gather from her footnote about her brothers' having taken responsibility for children conceived during their Saturday night forays that she sees the possibility of individual men improving as the attitudes of society improve. And her response to her oldest brother shows us that she can delight in the company of *some* men who were raised in what she would surely regard as the bad old days.

Walker's essay is based entirely on personal experience and could be an excellent springboard for an essay in which students discuss the ways they learned about sex and sex roles in their own families. The fact that Walker first published the essay under a pseudonym, however, reminds us that even a bold professional writer may be somewhat reticent about discussing intimate things. If you are going to make such an assignment, you may want to assure your students that their experience will provide them with material they will be comfortable with: Susan Brownmiller, for example, writes about learning sex roles while setting a table, and Noel Perrin talks about what he learned from a masculinity/femininity quiz in a magazine. You may also want to guarantee students that you will not read their essays aloud or distribute them without getting permission in advance and disguising the identity of the author.

QUESTIONS

1. Clearly Walker's essay shows her father and most of her brothers to be sexists. Is her mother also a sexist? Is Walker herself?

This question should help your class see how much misunderstanding can be created by a loosely defined term and the clarification of an issue that can come when we attempt to find a more precise definition. Most students, I suspect, will have a mental image of a sexist as a male bigot much like Walker's father. This picture fits fairly well with the first definition of *sexism* given in *The American Heritage Dictionary*: "Prejudice against the female sex." It fits less well with the second definition: "Any arbitrary stereotyping of males and females on the basis of gender."

Make "arbitrary stereotyping" of both sexes your criterion, and you look at the essay with somewhat different eyes. Yes, Walker's father is a sexist, but his sexism shows more in what he has to say about men than what he has to say about women. "'Like bulls,' he said, "a man *needs* to get a little something on his stick'" (paragraph 7). I think we can assume that this stereotyping is arbitrary; he must have known some men (like his oldest son) who didn't feel a need for indiscriminate and irresponsible sex every Saturday night. We actually don't see much evidence that Walker's father has stereotyped women at all. His daughters are restricted so severely because his stereotype of men has created a world in which they are not safe.

Was Walker's mother a sexist? Yes, I think so. Her "saying girls did not need to know about such things" and that those who asked were being "womanish" (paragraph 2) seems arbitrarily to divide women into perpetual innocents and lascivious tarts, a myth she might have exploded by a frank examination of her own life and the lives of other women around her. But how can we tell what is arbitrary when we don't know the workings of a person's mind? Perhaps both of Walker's parents were expressing opinions wrung from a close, impartial examination of their experience. Walker does not think so. In paragraph 25 she says she now understands that her father's "sexist behavior was not something uniquely his own, but, rather, an imitation of the behavior of the society around us." "Arbitrary stereotyping" is contagious.

Now, is Walker herself a sexist? That she harbors some bitter feelings toward her father and younger brothers is evident, and her other writings confirm that she feels their attitudes to be widespread among men. But is this "arbitrary stereotyping"? Some have said so, but it seems to me to be far from arbitrary. She has thought a good deal about the causes of men's attitudes, she has noted that they are capable of change, and she has shown that not all men are alike. There is too much reason and flexibility here to deserve the label "arbitrary."

Let's consider again the implications of the "arbitrary stereotyping" definition. It allows us to distinguish between a sexist, a bigot, and a simple villain. Imagine a man who lives in our time and believes that women are incapable of doing executive-level work, but who is supportive and helpful whenever he talks with a female executive. Is he a sexist? Yes, most of us would say so. Is he a bigot? No. Imagine a man who believes that women are absolutely as capable as men, but who undercuts them with behind-the-back innuendoes at every turn. Is he a sexist? No. A bigot? No, simply a villain.

2. What price do Walker and her siblings pay for the attitudes of their parents?

Most obvious and most disturbing is the effect on Walker's sister (paragraphs 4–18). This is the intellectual and emotional heart of the essay. Because her parents are so close-mouthed about menstruation, she grew up feeling ashamed and foolish during her period. Clearly, Walker believes that her severe cramps, nausea, and headaches are more psychosomatic than physiological. The mysterious silence with which her parents veiled sexuality and the strict denial of access to men created in her a craving that Walker clearly feels was pathological: "She fell for the first man who loved her enough to beat her for looking at someone else, and . . . married him" (paragraph 17). In some ways, the story of Walker's sister is a very familiar one: you can hear it over and over again if you listen either to the blues or to country and western music. What Walker has done is trace the outcome to the source.

The younger brothers suffer, too, though we don't know the nature of their suffering as well. The footnote at the essay's end tells us that they eventually felt a need to acknowledge all their children, illegitimate as well as legitimate. Perhaps they found little satisfaction in an irresponsible life of sowing and abandoning wild oats. One wonders, too, how satisfying their relationships with women could have been if they thought of them only as "a little something on their stick."

The oldest brother enters the essay like an angel, unscathed, but Walker does not present herself as entirely unscathed. There is a dark side to her vow "early in my life" that she would not suffer as her sister had (paragraph 4). It separated Walker emotionally from her sister and made her view her with some contempt: "I hated her for giggling, and it was at those times I would think of her as dim-witted," she says in paragraph 6, and her summary of her sister's courtship and marriage is not very sympathetic. One suspects that there must be scars from this separation, just as one suspects that the scars left by her father's words and actions have darkened her view of men.

3. Where in this essay does Walker freely admit having feelings that many of us would be inclined to hide? What is the effect of these revelations?

Perhaps my reaction is idiosyncratic, but I was surprised by the frankness with which Walker talks about her dislike of members of her family. Her father, of course, gets roundly condemned throughout the essay, and she says rather proudly that at his funeral "my oldest brother and I did not shed a tear between us" (paragraph 22). The mother of whom she speaks so fondly in "In Search of Our Mothers' Gardens" is presented in unflattering terms here. The sister is treated with what must be called contempt: "Oh, that Alfred!" she would moon over some mediocre, square-headed boy, "he's so *sweet!* And she would take his ugly picture out of her bosom and kiss it" (paragraph 16). The brothers are portrayed as "not bright enough" to grasp the fact that sex leads to pregnancy (paragraph 3) and not responsible enough to care for the children they have fathered (paragraph 24). At their father's funeral, all the siblings except the oldest brother are portrayed (I think) as hypocrites (paragraph 22).

None of this is in the Norman Rockwell or Hallmark tradition, and Walker must be perfectly well aware that she is not portraying herself as an ideal daughter and sister. But to tell the truth that she knows, she has to be willing to reveal some uncomfortable things about herself and her past. The essay is a good illustration of the price an autobiographical writer pays for honesty and the reward he or she may reap.

—D.H.—

Style Lesson 10:
Use of a Rhetorical Question and Parallel Answers

In paragraph 5 of "Brothers and Sisters," Walker uses the sentences below to discuss the plight of her sister. Practice her question-and-answer technique by writing a set of parallel sentences on a subject of your choice.

On the farm it is impossible
    not to be conscious of sex,
        to wonder about it,
        to dream . . .
but to whom was she to speak her feelings?
Not to my father,
    who thought all young women perverse.
Not to my mother,
    who pretended all her children grew out of stumps
        she magically found in the forest.
Not to me,
    who never found anything wrong with this lie.

MAXINE HONG KINGSTON

Daughter

In "Daughter," which is an excerpt from *The Woman Warrior*, Kingston describes the conflict experienced by a Chinese-American girl who is presented with two contrasting models of womanhood. The Chinese emigrants of her neighborhood consider girls worthless. They sympathize with the narrator's parents because their first two children are girls, and when the narrator throws tantrums, they comment, "I would hit her if she were mine. But then there's no use wasting all that discipline on a girl" (paragraph 14). She learns that there is "a Chinese word for the female *I*—which is 'slave'" (paragraph 26). On the other hand the narrator listens to her mother talking-story and discovers that women can become heroines, swordswomen who courageously lead armies into battle and slay the enemies who would harm their families. The narrator remarks, "[My mother] said I would grow up a wife and a slave, but she taught me the song of the warrior woman, Fa Mu Lan" (paragraph 3).

This selection will allow your students to consider how the traditions of a particular society might lead to the devaluing of females. It should also force them to recognize that the denigration of women is not as foreign as we might like to believe.

QUESTIONS

1. How does the remark "Feeding girls is feeding cowbirds" (paragraph 11) explain why females were not valued by traditional Chinese culture?

Some of your students will probably know that cowbirds are blackbirds that lay their eggs in the nests of other birds. The female cowbird lays one egg in the nest of a smaller bird and then abandons it. Apparently, the foster parent birds usually don't realize that they are hatching and feeding an outsider. However, because the cowbird chick is bigger than the other chicks in the nest, it sometimes grabs all the food, and the other baby birds starve.

In traditional, patriarchal Chinese culture, once a female married, she belonged to her husband's family. In another part of *The Woman Warrior* Kingston tells us that "a synonym for marriage in Chinese is 'taking a daughter-in-law.'" The daughter-in-law lived with her husband's family, she assisted her mother-in-law with her work, she bore sons who would someday marry and bring more daughters-in-law into the family, she cared for her husband's parents when they were old or ill, and she offered food and prayers to her husband's dead ancestors. But a married woman could do none of these things for her own parents.

In an agrarian society where families need as many workers as possible and where there are no retirement benefits or Medicare programs for old people, the tradition of giving females to their husbands' families does make feeding a daughter like feeding a cowbird, who will eat her parents out of house and home and then abandon them.

Although the emigrant villagers' remarks about girls horrify the narrator and us, the villagers are not trying to be cruel. When they say, "There's no profit in raising girls. Better to raise geese than girls" (paragraph 13), they are stating a hard economic truth.

2. When you were growing up, what—if anything—caused you to believe that it was better to be a boy or better to be a girl?

This question will encourage your students to compare their experiences to Kingston's and will lead to a more general discussion of the social forces that shape males' and females' perceptions of their own value. I hope your students will not have been subjected to comments as disparaging to females as those Kingston recounts, but I think most people can recall incidents suggesting that females are not as capable or as important as men. Perhaps your students dealt with a high school guidance counselor who encouraged girls but not boys to take typing and shorthand. Perhaps they heard people say to the parents of a baby daughter, "Well, you'll have to try again for a boy." Perhaps they attend a college where most high level administrators and tenured professors are men. Even if they have had none of those experiences, they live in a country where positions of power are occupied primarily by men, where the work customarily assigned to women—child care and housework—is unpaid or underpaid, and where one woman out of every four is the victim of domestic violence. It's easy for us to condemn the Chinese emigrants' anti-female attitudes, but we cannot pretend that we have already achieved the ideal of gender equality.

3. What does Kingston mean when she says, "Even now China wraps double binds around my feet" (paragraph 32)?

With this metaphor Kingston reminds us of what she has escaped and what she cannot escape. At one time high-born Chinese girls had their feet bound when they were five or six years old. The procedure involved forcing the toes down and toward the heel and then binding them in that contorted position. Eventually the bones in the arch broke, and the foot was reshaped as a hideously deformed but tiny hook. The excruciating pain lasted for years, and a woman with bound feet was crippled for life, but she could wear beautiful embroidered slippers no larger than baby shoes. No mother wanted to inflict such suffering on her daughter, and some women hired professional foot binders to distance themselves from the binding. But if a girl's feet were not bound, she would be a failure in life because no aristocratic man would marry her. For a Chinese woman the choice was between two painful alternatives.

Kingston is not compelled to have her feet bound, but she too faces impossible choices. If she chooses to conform to the traditional feminine ideal by cooking and washing dishes, she cripples herself, but she will find a husband. If she rejects the traditional role, she can walk on her own two healthy feet, but no man will love and support her.

—M.R.D.—

ALICE MUNRO

Boys and Girls

Munro's story, set in rural Ontario in the 1940s, captures the feelings of a girl growing up and learning what her role in life will be. Because of the first-person narration, your students may be inclined to think that it is at least partly autobiographical, and I'm not sure I would discourage this supposition, which seems valid for many of Munro's early stories. The details of the story are surely a mix of memories and imaginations, but we shouldn't forget that we are reading a woman's account of growing up in a time and place where she actually *did* grow up.

That said, we should also note that the story is meticulously plotted to conform to the familiar pattern of

- introduction establishing a conflict (the narrator's desire to grow up like her father versus society's desire that she should follow her mother's pattern of femininity)
- rising action (feed salesman dismisses narrator as girl, narrator hears parents planning the end of her masculine choring, grandmother comes and insists on feminine behavior, narrator sets out to prove her "manhood" by viewing the killing of a horse)
- climax (the narrator betrays her father by rescuing a second horse)
- falling action (the narrator deliberately takes on feminine ways)
- dénouement (disgraced by having the rescue of the horse revealed, the narrator accepts her father's judgment that she is "only a girl.")

The resolution of the conflict may sit uncomfortably for some of your students, who will bridle at the narrator's not protesting her father's judgment "even in my heart." We could deal with this discomfort by saying that Munro was writing in 1968 and that her ending would have been more acceptable then than now. This is an intelligent enough observation, but I think it misreads and diminishes the story, which surely *invites* discomfort.

QUESTIONS

1. Why does the narrator open the gate for the second horse?

There are many possible answers here, and getting them on the table may productively consume all the discussion time you will have for this story. I would try to deal with three, at least.

The first is simply that the killing of the first horse, Mack, had been so disgusting to her that she instinctively wants to free the second, Flora. The narrator herself says that in thinking about the killing she did not have "any great feeling of horror and opposition, such as a city child might have had" but that she was "a little ashamed" (paragraph 43). Nonetheless, her legs had been "a little shaky" when she witnessed the scene (paragraph 37).

More important in terms of the theme of the story is the narrator's movement away from identifying with the masculine and toward identifying with the feminine (as these terms are defined in the story). Earlier, she had viewed the skinning of the foxes placidly enough and had even found the smell of the pelting operation "reassuringly seasonal, like the smell of oranges and pine needles" (paragraph 2). But seeing Henry Bailey (who is throughout the story a caricature of masculinity) laugh at Mack's dying contortions and seeing "the easy, practiced way" her father did the shooting creates (or crystallizes) some uneasiness about the masculine world, and she experiences "a new wariness, a sense of holding off, in my attitude to my father and his work" (paragraph 43). Refusing to participate in the killing of Flora is a turning toward the feminine, an echo the mother's disliking the pelting operation and refusing to talk about the slaughter of horses.

This second reason, neatly suiting the story's theme, is complicated by a third. The better readers in your class may notice that Mack and Flora are curiously similar to the humans of the same sex. Mack, in broken health like Henry Bailey, is an old "workhorse, sooty and indifferent" and so rather like the taciturn father and the matter-of-fact brother. (Laird, despite the narrator's fears for him is not frightened by the shooting of Mack; he is "remote and concentrating." In the final scene, he reports "matter-of-factly" that his sister is crying.) Flora, a "driver" (carriage horse) is skittish, but the family loves "her speed and high-stepping, her general air of gallantry and abandon" (paragraph 20). In these respects, she matches the high-spirited narrator well, but also suggests the girl the hard-working mother had been, the girl that shows in her chatter about "the name of a dog she had had when she was a little girl, the names of boys she had gone out with later on when she was grown up, and what certain dresses of hers had looked like" (paragraph 10). As the mother is locked up in the house most of the day, and as the narrator will someday be, so Flora is kept in the barn all winter. When she is let out in the barnyard in the spring, she "rear[s] at the fences, clattering her hooves against the rail" in a way that reminds us of the narrator's rebellion against her confining feminine role. So I suppose that we might give identification as a third reason for the narrator's releasing Flora: she is "on Flora's side" (paragraph 50).

Being on Flora's side implies not just turning away from the masculine world (as though femininity were no more than the absence of masculinity), but turning to something positive that can be set in opposition to it—the feminine world, where squeamishness about killing may be a positive virtue and where some notions of beauty and joy can be kept alive (in talk at least), even in a life of constant choring. When she releases Flora, she seems symbolically to be both embracing the feminine role and breaking the shackles that come with it.

2. Does this story suggest that masculine and feminine roles are assigned by nature or by social conditioning?

Like life itself, the story yields ambiguous answers if we pose the nature-nurture question. I certainly see no signs that Munro wants to answer it directly: she is interested in what it felt like to be growing up female in a particular time and place, not in what could theoretically have been different if society had been different. Nonetheless, the story (like life itself) offers some toeholds for those who want to see anatomy as destiny and for those who want to see sex roles as artificial.

Those who are inclined to read this as a story about a girl's ceasing to struggle against her inherent feminine nature can point out that the changes in her attitude toward the masculine and feminine worlds is connected with maturation. As she approaches adolescence, even her dreams begin to change; they may start out with situations of spectacular danger, but she appears in them as a victim rather than as a rescuer, and she spends a disproportionate amount of dream-time working out the details of her appearance (paragraph 52). It is arguable that she is "feminizing" from the inside out, discovering an identity that grows out of her body. Some might argue that she is simply working out the Electra complex that makes many young girls into tomboys eager to mimic their fathers. At the very end of the story, when her father announces that she's "only a girl," she acknowledges that it may be true, which sounds like a capitulation to the anatomy-as-destiny school.

On the other hand, it is possible to read this as a story about a girl fitted for a "manly" role in life—a role like that of the "plumed adventurers" she sees on the Hudson Bay Company and Montreal Fur Company calendars that hang in the kitchen. It is she, not Laird, who initiates adventures in the story, she whose early dreams are filled with "courage, boldness, and self-sacrifice," she who loves the foxes for the "pure hostility" of their faces. It's true that at the story's climax, she finds her father's casual killing of the horse repugnant, but by then, she has been pretty heavily propagandized about the difference between the masculine and feminine worlds and so is prepared to turn away from the masculine with the slightest provocation. And how heavily stacked the deck is! In the miniature society of the story, to embrace masculinity seems to mean not only embracing an active life outdoors (which the narrator would gladly do) but embracing a crudeness that includes spitting in the kitchen fire and laughing at the death spasms of animals. If masculine and feminine roles weren't defined in such an exaggerated way, our narrator might have found a way to include more of the supposedly masculine life in her own. In some ways, Laird and the narrator are like the foxes who "inhabited a little world [her] father made for them" (paragraph 7). Inside the little world of this household, adolescence marks an absolute fork in the road. The narrator might take a few steps up the masculine route, but with so little support that she will be easily turned back. And Laird, who is capable in childhood of naming a fox Mexico, will soon learn to restrict himself, as his father does, to "names like Prince, Bob, Wally, and Betty." Only an individual of extraordinary strength can *identify* his or her nature when "nurture" makes its demands so clear.

—D.H.—

SUSAN BROWNMILLER

Femininity

Brownmiller rose to the forefront of the feminist movement in 1975 with the publication of *Against Our Will: Men, Women, and Rape.* In that book, which is based on extensive research, she examines the history of rape as a political rather than a sexual crime and concludes that rape is "nothing more or less than a conscious process of intimidation by which *all men* keep *all women* in a state of fear." The controversial best seller has been praised as one of the most politically important works of our time and has been criticized as biased and one-sided.

Needless to say, many feminists were shocked when Brownmiller published her next book, *Femininity* in 1983. *Femininity,* another work of scholarship, describes the various ways in which women throughout the ages have pursued the elusive and ever-changing ideal of femininity. In cataloging the hair styles, body shapes, and fashions that have been in vogue, Brownmiller describes feminine wiles without condemning them. But the introduction to *Femininity,* which is the selection included in *The Dolphin Reader,* provides a framework that makes the book more than a history of fashion. In this essay, Brownmiller defines femininity as "a romantic sentiment, a nostalgic tradition of imposed limitations." She argues that our society prevents women from succeeding by persuading them to cultivate the qualities associated with femininity. In Brownmiller's view, it is not accidental that those qualities "lie outside the established route to success."

In *Femininity* the personal and the political are inextricably intertwined as Brownmiller uses a personal experience to illustrate a significant cultural issue. The thesis of this essay is guaranteed to provoke a spirited classroom discussion, and its organization demonstrates one way that the personal experience essay can become more than anecdotal.

QUESTIONS

1. How does Brownmiller define femininity?

Brownmiller defines femininity in political terms. She says, "Femininity, in essence, is a romantic sentiment, a nostalgic tradition of imposed limitations" (paragraph 5). She goes on to explain that femininity is more than biological femaleness; it is an active effort to emphasize, or to create, a difference between male and female. Later she compares the masculine and the feminine principles (paragraph 8). According to Brownmiller, traits that are likely to "inspire straightforward, confident success" are defined as masculine. In contrast, femininity is characterized by "vulnerability, the need for protection, the formalities of compliance and the avoidance of conflict." She argues that "whimsy, unpredictability and patterns of thinking and behavior that are dominated by emotion . . . are thought to be feminine precisely because they lie outside the established route to success" (paragraph 9).

Brownmiller's statements are likely to stir a few emotions among both male and female students. If I were going to teach this essay, I would want to get some information from my students before they read the essay and take sides. A few days before assigning this essay, you can ask the class to compile a list of traits that are likely to help a person become a success. On another day (possibly when discussing Sayers, Woolf, or Brophy), ask them to list the qualities they associate with femininity. You then have a relatively objective base line that you can use to assess the validity of Brownmiller's position.

2. How does Brownmiller explain the renewed interest in femininity in the 1980s?

She suggests a number of possible causes. One is that femininity can offer esthetic pleasure. After all, it is sometimes great fun to try a new hair style, to wear silky lingerie, or to take bubble baths. Given the opportunity, men might enjoy such activities as much as women do, but Brownmiller suggests that most men would not dare to so indulge themselves.

Brownmiller believes the chief attraction of femininity is the advantage it seems to promise in the fierce "female competition for two scarce resources—men and jobs " (paragraph 10). The irony, of course, is that the competitive edge gained through femininity is illusory, "for one works at femininity by accepting restrictions, by limiting one's sights, by choosing an indirect route, by scattering concentration and not giving one's all as a man would to his own, certifiably masculine, interests" (paragraph 7).

Brownmiller seems to be saying that "indulgence in the art of feminine illusion" (paragraph 12) may enable a woman who happens to be good at it to win a few skirmishes, but only at the cost of losing the final victory. For example, when a woman interviews with a male *or* female supervisor for a job, it may well be true that if she is attractive and feminine as well as qualified, she is more likely to be hired than an unfeminine applicant. But by playing the role men expect her to play, she is in effect accepting their right to judge women on a basis other than their ability to do the job. And since femininity, according to Brownmiller, is something each woman has less of as she becomes older, she has unknowingly acquiesced to play the game by rules that must ultimately defeat her.

3. Are girls today as pressured to become feminine as Brownmiller was?

Brownmiller opens the essay by recounting one of her childhood lessons in gender identification, a game called "setting the table." She then details the "white organdy pinafores," "the miniature tea sets," "the fairy tales," "the brightly colored advertisements," and the "radio soap operas" that taught her the "art of being feminine." The specifics have changed, but your female students should have no trouble recalling how they learned what is still essentially the same lesson. And, of course, boys receive equally clear messages about appropriate male behavior.

Today there are more parents who conscientiously attempt to avoid relaying those messages, but societal pressures are difficult to counteract. When our daughter Shannon, who is now seventeen, was small, we did our best to keep her toys gender neutral, or at least balanced. For every doll she owned, we bought a truck. But the commercials on television and the pictures on the packages showed girls playing with dolls and boys playing with trucks. Her trucks, cars, and tractors still look new. Complaints by irate consumer-parents have brought some progress in this area, but the messages conveyed though advertisements aimed at children are still far from gender free.

The problem obviously goes far beyond advertising. Children are at least as sensitive to cultural norms as adults are. By the time Shannon was three, she had decided that she could not play in her wading pool unless she wore the totally unnecessary top of her two-piece bathing suit.

4. Can the cost of femininity be balanced against its affirming advantage?

Brownmiller does not answer this question, at least not directly. She does insist that femininity is costly. She argues that true acceptance of the "feminine ideal" results in the economic and emotional dependency of women. And she suggests that even a woman who resists the trap of "believing" in femininity but who chooses to indulge occasionally for the sake of "fun, or art, or attention" must weigh the "time and cost factors," the "deflection of energy," and the risk of "absorption in fakery" (paragraph 12).

On the positive side, femininity offers an exquisite esthetic. In addition, it "operates as a value system of niceness, a code of thoughtfulness and sensitivity that in modern society is sadly in short supply" (paragraph 11). Obviously, Brownmiller is not claiming that the world would be better if we eliminated thoughtfulness and sensitivity altogether, but she is stating that unless those qualities are encouraged in men as well as in women, women may have to abandon them to achieve political equality.

—M.R.D.—

Style Lesson 11: Sentence Combining

The following list breaks two of Brownmiller's sentences into thirteen one-idea kernel sentences. Close your book and combine the kernels to form sentences like the originals, cutting, adding, or rearranging as necessary.

1. The world smiles favorably on the feminine woman.
2. It extends courtesies and privileges.
3. The courtesies are little.
4. The privileges are minor.

5. This situation creates a competitive edge.
6. Yet the nature of this edge is ironic at best.
7. One works at femininity by accepting restrictions.
8. One's sights are limited.
9. The route one chooses is indirect.
10. One scatters one's concentration.
11. One does not give one's all to one's own interests.
12. A man would give his all to them.
13. His interests would be certifiably masculine.

Keys to Brownmiller's style in the more difficult second sentence are a subordinator (<u>for</u>) at 7, parallel construction in 8–13, and subordination at 12.

VIRGINIA WOOLF

Professions for Women

In this address to the Women's Service League, given in 1931, Virginia Woolf, the famous English novelist, essayist, and critic, discusses women at the beginning of the era in which they would, for the first time in history, be practicing in professions formerly reserved for men. As Woolf so aptly puts it, women had finally won rooms of their own in the house hitherto owned exclusively by men.

Most of the essay details the two major battles Woolf (and all other women writers of her time) fought to win her room. In the first, she struggled with the Angel in the House, the phantom who epitomized the Victorian ideal of womanhood. Because the Angel whispered to Woolf that a woman writer should be sympathetic, should charm, should conciliate, and should never let anyone guess that she had a mind of her own, Woolf could not write until she had killed the Angel. In the second battle, which Woolf says she had not yet won, she fought the conventional notion that it is unfitting for a woman to write about her experiences as a body, to speak the truth about her passions.

As the earliest of the writers included in this section, Woolf initiates the dialogue that continues in the other essays. At the end of her address, she notes that the rooms women have won are still bare. And she poses three crucial questions: "How are you going to furnish [your room], how are you going to decorate it? With whom are you going to share it, and upon what terms?" We are still struggling with the answers.

QUESTIONS

1. How dead is the Angel of the House?

Woolf claims that she finally killed the Angel, but she admits that she may be flattering herself (paragraph 3). She expresses the hope that the women in her audience who are of a "younger and happier generation" may not have heard of the Angel. I think she was too optimistic. Certainly the ideal of womanhood has changed since Woolf's time, but the notion that certain forms of behavior are inappropriate for women persists. (See Susan Brownmiller's essay, "Femininity.") Woolf was more accurate in her later prediction: "Indeed it will be a long time still, I think, before a woman can sit down to write a book without finding a phantom to be slain, a rock to be dashed against" (paragraph 6). Unfortunately, even when the Angel is ultimately defeated, she extracts a heavy price. Woolf regrets the time she spent struggling with the Angel, time that would have been better spent "learning Greek grammar" or "roaming the world in search of adventures" (paragraph 3). Every woman who has spent hours, days, or years pondering some question labeled "For Women Only" will recognize the cost of battling the Angel.

During the seventeen years that I have been a mother, I have always been a student, a teacher, or an attorney as well. Not a day has passed without a reminder from the Angel that a "good" mother would be willing to postpone her career for a few years so that she could be home with her children while they need her. My husband is as good a father as I can imagine, and I recently asked him if he ever felt guilty about going to work instead of staying home with our children. His answer: "No, I never thought about it that way." Like Woolf, I sometimes regret that I have wasted so much emotional energy in a battle that should not have been necessary.

2. Does "the extreme conventionality of the other sex" (paragraph 5) still prevent women from telling the truth about their bodies?

Any generalization about all women is obviously inaccurate, but with that caveat, I will blunder ahead. That women are freer to express themselves now than they were in Woolf's day is a truism. At the very least, we have given up certain euphemisms. Even in the politest society, it is quite proper to order breast of chicken rather than white meat.

But the evidence indicates that our society, as a whole, remains basically ambivalent in its attitude toward women's bodies. Writers such as Erica Jong seem quite comfortable in telling the truth about their physical experiences. At the same time, however, we have an explosion of popular romances in which the writer can allude to romantic encounters in carefully prescribed formulas but can never describe sexual experiences directly. Women characters in soap operas engage in one sexual adventure after another, but apparently they never menstruate. Television movies show nude women in a variety of provocative poses, but a televised health program that demonstrates breast cancer detection techniques must use drawings or plastic models. A woman wearing the skimpiest of bikinis on the beach is unlikely to receive the scowls of disapproval that will be directed at a mother who nurses her baby in public.

Teachers of Women's Studies classes frequently find that their female students are initially reluctant to discuss their bodies, and their reluctance is even greater if there are male students in the class. The idea that it is not quite proper for women to have bodies (except when those bodies are used to entertain men) is still with us.

3. How seriously does Woolf seem to take herself in the essay?

Woolf must have realized that she was between Scylla and Charybdis when she agreed to give this address. Her audience was composed of women who were themselves exemplars, and undoubtedly a number of them had made substantial economic sacrifices to achieve their goals. Woolf's dilemma arose because she was born into a wealthy family and inherited a comfortable yearly income. If she claimed that it was as difficult for her to choose to write as it was for any other woman, her audience would have resented her. On the other hand, if she minimized the challenges every woman writer—wealthy or poor—must face, she would have been dishonest.

She handles the problem with her tone. Although she is completely serious about her topic, she uses a gently humorous tone when describing herself. In the first paragraph she openly admits there were few material obstacles to prevent her writing. As she charmingly describes the situation: "Writing was a reputable and harmless occupation. The family peace was not broken by the scratching of a pen. No demand was made upon the family purse."

With the same disarming charm she explains how simple it was for her to become a journalist: "You have only got to figure to yourselves a girl in a bedroom with a pen in her hand. She had only to move that pen from left to right—from ten o'clock to one. Then it occurred to her to do what is simple and cheap enough after all—to slip a few of those pages into an envelope, fix a penny stamp in the corner, and drop the envelope into the red box at the corner" (paragraph 2).

She further endears herself to the audience by conceding that she does not deserve to be called a professional woman because she does not know the struggles and difficulties of such lives. She confides that the first check she received for writing was spent not for "bread and butter, rent, shoes and stockings, or butcher bills," but for a beautiful Persian cat (paragraph 2).

Woolf never apologizes for her money, but she cheerfully confesses that it made her way easier: "I now record the one act for which I take some credit to myself, though the credit rightly belongs to some excellent ancestors of mine who left me a certain sum of money—shall we say five hundred pounds a year?—so that it was not necessary for me to depend solely on charm for my living" (paragraph 3).

In another of her essays, "The Patriarchy" Woolf gives a somewhat bleaker view of her attempts to make a living before she received her inheritance, chronicling the "chief occupations" (odd jobs) that were open to women before 1918. That account demonstrates how, in this essay, Woolf deliberately glossed over her personal difficulties to avoid alienating her audience.

—M.R.D.—

Style Lesson 12: Examination of an Extended Metaphor

In paragraph 5 of "Professions for Women," Woolf uses the metaphor of a fisherman who hooks something unimaginably large to explain the situation of the female novelist whose imagination (likened to the minnow used as bait) runs up against "something about the body, about the passions." The metaphor is complex and worth thinking about. Try to recover the words for which capitalized words are substituted below. You may wish to work with your classmates.

The image that comes to my mind when I think of this girl is the image of a WRITER lying sunk in dreams on the verge of a deep SUBJECT with a PEN held out over the PAPER. She was letting her imagination sweep unchecked round every NOOK and cranny of the world that lies REPRESSED in the depths of our unconscious being. Now came the experience, the experience that I believe to be far commoner with women writers than with men. The AGITATION raced through the girl's CONSCIOUSNESS. Her imagination had rushed away. It had sought the SOURCES, the depths, the dark places where the STRONGEST EXPERIENCES slumber. And then there was a smash. There was an explosion. There was TURMOIL and confusion. The imagination had dashed itself against something hard.

JAN MORRIS

To Everest

Morris's essay will be baffling to students who don't read the headnote. In her autobiography *Conundrum*, from which this chapter is taken, she says that at the age of three or four she realized that she "had been born into the wrong body, and should really be a girl." Boy, however, she was. For the first thirty-eight years of her life, she was James Morris, male, and externally very successful in the role, rising to the rank of lieutenant in the British army in World War II, becoming well-known as a travel writer, marrying, and having children. Nonetheless, the feeling of being a female trapped in a male body continued, and in 1964 he began taking hormone pills to initiate his transformation into the female Jan Morris. The process was completed surgically in 1972.

The testimony of someone who has crossed the boundary between the sexes would always be interesting, but Morris's case is doubly so because of the clarity of her writing and thinking. In a sense, *Conundrum* is yet another travel book, and Morris manages to guide us wisely and intelligently through an unfamiliar interior landscape. What makes "To Everest" particularly pertinent to the Femininity and Masculinity section is the importance she attaches to the psychological or (as she once put it) spiritual differences between masculine and feminine temperaments. Here, obviously, is someone who saw the gulf between the sexes as so great that she found it intolerable to be stranded on the wrong side. In a letter, however, she told me that if she had been living in the more androgynous 1980s, she is not sure she would have felt compelled to go through with the surgery.

QUESTIONS

1. How does Morris characterize the difference between the masculine and feminine temperaments?

The focus here is on maleness, which Morris describes in terms most Victorians would have accepted. Men, first of all, are "constant," capable of "influctuating control" of both mind and body (paragraphs 8 and 9). The popular Victorian metaphor would, I think, be that men are sturdy oaks and women are clinging vines. The feeling that the body and mind are running reliably at a constant high speed leads to the subjective feeling of being "brilliant," leads to "conceit," leads to "swagger" (paragraph 10). Men, more than women, are inclined to pursue an abstract, even senseless goal at great cost out of sheer "masochistic relish of challenge" (paragraphs 13 and 14). Finally, men conform more readily than women to the "team spirit"; they can work together like a mechanism (paragraph 16).

This list of male attributes should be profoundly irritating to some of your students. Such characteristics are, after all, part of the stereotype of masculine competence and feminine incompetence that the women's movement has been trying to erase for the last sixty years. When the discussion heats up, it is probably worth pointing out that Morris admires the male attributes, but not enough to want to be male herself. She no longer wants to be solid, mechanical, arrogant, and masochistic.

2. Do you believe that Morris's description of the difference between maleness and femaleness is accurate?

The $64,000 question, which you will want your students to discuss energetically. Morris says some things that may bring light to the discussion. On the one hand, she tells us (paragraph 9) that the feeling of influctuating control comes "specifically from the body." To a degree, she seems to think that it is unrelated to cultural conditioning. On the other hand, she concedes (paragraph 18) that "the barrier between the genders is flimsier now" than in 1953, which presumably means that her description is somewhat dated. A fair question, one that surprisingly seems not to occur to Morris, is how much of the difference between her feelings as James in 1953 and Jan in 1974 comes from age rather than gender. Perhaps 27-year-old women in peak condition feel the same sense of brilliance that 27-year-old men do.

3. What is the effect of the last four paragraphs?

I would love to ask Morris why she added these paragraphs to the chapter. Perhaps it was simply that they record a memory too vivid to suppress. Some people might argue that they are extraneous. I think, though, that they add a new dimension to the chapter, opening it into something larger than it might otherwise be. Suddenly the whole vexing mystery of gender is swallowed up in the larger mysteries of nature and religion. Notice that even the visual detail adds scope. The holy man appears at such a distance that he is at first "a small black swaying speck" (paragraph 21), and he recedes to become a speck again. Morris's personal concerns seemed dwarfed by the scale. Morris is terribly good at altering the scale of things to bring them to us freshly. Note, for instance, the bowl simile in paragraphs 6 and 7, which reduces the slope of Everest "to miniscule proportions" and allows us for a moment to see the whole enterprise as if through God's eyes.

—D.H.—

Style Lesson 13: Building Densely Packed Sentences

Jan Morris's style features many sentences honeycombed with modifying phrases and clauses, including absolute constructions. Into the cells this style creates are crammed the details that make her story interesting. The kernel sentences below are extracted from the third sentence of paragraph 10 of "To Everest." Rearrange, cut, and add as necessary to construct from them a single sentence in Morris's style.

1. I had already sent a message.
2. I had done this by a combination of cunning and ingenuity.
3. The message was coded.
4. I had sent it through an Indian Army radio transmitter.
5. The transmitter was located at Namche Bazar.
6. Namche Bazar is located twenty miles south of Everest.
7. The radio operators were unaware of the message's meaning.
8. I did not know if it had reached London safely.
9. I was myself hastening to the cable office.
10. I was carrying my own final dispatch.
11. The cable office was back in Katmandu.

NOEL PERRIN

The Androgynous Man

In preparing this section I was surprised by how little good introspective writing there is on masculinity compared to the amount available on femininity. I suppose that the explanation must be partly historical: women were writing well about their condition for about a century before men began to think they might have a condition to write about. Today there are some interesting *studies* of masculinity available, either by social scientists or by writers like Morris or Wolfe who stand outside the subject because of gender or journalistic detachment. And there is, of course, a great deal of fiction (one thinks of Hemingway) in which masculinity is explored. But good first-person writing on the subject is rare.

The New York Times Magazine has opened an avenue for such writing in its "About Men" column, from which both Perrin's and Norman's essays are drawn. Perrin's appeared February 5, 1984, and Norman's April 1, 1984. I suspect that Norman's is an answer to Perrin. At any rate, the two form a little debate and should provoke a good deal of discussion if taught together.

As examples of introspective or persuasive writing, both pale in comparison to the wonderful essays by Sayers, Woolf, and Brophy included in this section. As springboards to writing and thought, though, they should be at least as good. I am sympathetic with both writers, and my uneasiness with the way they articulate their positions has forced me to rethink my own.

QUESTIONS

1. Does Perrin see androgyny and "all-maleness" as two equally desirable alternatives?

In paragraph 10 Perrin says that men are indirectly indebted to the women's movement because it has "released a lot of men from the *single ideal* [my emphasis] of the dominant male." He goes on to say that not all men need this release, implying that the "dominant male"—the he-man—is as acceptable as the androgynous male. Apparently this is *not* his real position. His comments about he-men are often derogatory. Note that, in paragraph 7, he-men (though they have some good qualities) are said to be unfree: for them biology is destiny, right down to the inevitability of watching football on television. And, of course, the last paragraph insists that God is androgynous. To be fair to Perrin, his main point is that *imitation* he-men are a wretched lot, but he muddies the water by belittling (amid seeming compliments) the real he-man. The effect is to make him an advocate of yet another single ideal.

2. How does Perrin keep the reader from seeing him as a wimp?

This is to me the most interesting element of the essay. Perrin seems to assume, perhaps rightly, that the androgynous male may be dismissed as a mere wimp unless he establishes some of the typical manly credentials. To establish these, he fills the essay with so many references to his he-man pursuits that he sounds like a composite put together from John Wayne films. He is a former wrangler and combat leader who had "a very good time" in battle. Although he loves his daughter's cat, it is a very doggy, outdoorsy type of cat, "the adventurous kind of cat that likes to climb hills with you" (paragraph 12). And although he cries at plays, he assures us that "true he-men" do the same, that it is only the imitators who work hard to suppress their emotions. Even while he is advocating a sprint toward androgyny, he is keeping one foot safely on the base of old-fashioned masculinity.

3. Beyond Perrin's comment in paragraph 7, what is a "completely masculine man"?

Perrin reduces the old ideal of masculinity to an interest in physical power, dominance, and televised football. The business about being unconsciously at ease is a vague and rather left-handed compliment, since in the context it almost implies mindlessness. Surely this is too narrow a definition. What else there may be to masculinity is a very open question. The most articulate of my male sexist friends often says that manliness implies not only courage but forbearance. The real man, he argues, knowing that he has advantages over others because of body size and social custom, has faced down the temptation to use these advantages unfairly. The forbearance from taking unfair advantage is tied up with the old-fashioned codes of male courtesy: the opening of doors, the surrender of umbrellas on rainy days, the reluctance to climb into the lifeboat until everyone else is out of the water.

—D.H.—

STEPHEN HARRIGAN

Answering the Howl

Harrigan opens this short, funny essay with a Theophrastan character sketch of the kind of man he most admires, "a solitary wanderer, impatient with civilization, indifferent to comfort, lulled by the sounds of howling beasts" (paragraph 4). He then contrasts that vision with a picture of himself, a suburbanite who dreams of lighting out for the wilderness but actually sets "aside 'Walden' to read a newspaper article about Ted Danson's hairpiece" (paragraph 5).

During the class period before you assign this essay, you might want to give your students 10 or 15 minutes to write their own definitions of "a real man" or of a "he-man." Then collect the writings to see how many people share Harrigan's idea of a man: "a lone wolf, austere and independent, a secular saint of the wilderness" (paragraph 4).

QUESTIONS

1. Why does Harrigan regret that he is not a lone wolf?

Usually our regrets are reserved for things we want to do but can't. For example, college basketball players who aren't drafted to play professionally may go on to become successful attorneys, sportscasters, or business people, but they continue to harbor a tiny regret that they can't spend their lives playing the game they love. Harrigan's regret is different because he laments his failure to become something he knows he would hate. It's like hearing someone who detests classical music wish she could play oboe for the New York Philharmonic.

Harrigan makes it clear that he is not a born outdoorsman so tied down by his job in the city that he never has time to mush across the frozen Arctic or hack through steaming jungles. No, the barrier separating Harrigan from the wilderness is internal. As his comical description of his adventures in the Big Thicket shows, Harrigan is bored by the Great Outdoors. "I just sat there in my tent crestfallen, counting the hours till it might be respectable for me to return home" (paragraph 8).

So if Harrigan hates doing the kind of things lone wolves do, why would he want to be one? There are at least two possible answers. One is that he admires the lone wolf's ability to live outside the silliness and pampering of the consumer economy. In "Advertising: The Standard-Gauge Railway" (an essay in *Media*), Jerry Mander argues that a capitalist economy cannot thrive unless it persuades people (through advertising) to reject natural nonconsumer experiences and to seek instead "vaginal sprays, chemical and artificial milk, drugs to smooth out emotional ups and downs, and commodities to substitute for experience." In contrast, Harrigan's lone wolf takes his experiences straight, "sucking air against the exposed nerve [in his chipped tooth] just to feel the pain" (paragraph 2). The lone wolf doesn't play Peter Pan Golf, and his famous dog Denali doesn't munch Pup-Peroni snacks.

On the other hand, Harrigan's admiration of the lone wolf may signal the triumph rather than the failure of Madison Avenue. Now that we are totally estranged from nature, our advertisers are eager to sell it back to us. Television commercials promise us that all it takes to be a "mountain man" is buying the right brand of beer. As soon as we begin to see ourselves for what we are—consumers whose identities are circumscribed by what we own—advertisers hold up a more attractive image, that of the wilderness adventurer. And all we have to do to reestablish our bond with nature is to purchase the necessary accoutrements: a back pack, hiking boots, freeze-dried food, a canteen, some cooking utensils, a light-weight tent, and maybe a canoe and a. . . .

2. After reading this essay, which do you admire more—the lone wolf or Harrigan? Which would you choose for a friend?

You might begin by asking your students to list admirable traits for the lone wolf and for Harrigan while you write them on the board. Those for the lone wolf will be fairly obvious: physical strength, courage, self-reliance, the ability to survive in the wild, and an indifference to pain that borders on catatonia—in short, all the qualities we love in Indiana Jones, Crocodile Dundee, and other icons of popular culture. Harrigan's strong points are less evident. They include his self-deprecating humor, his willingness to catalog his own shortcomings, and his quixotic devotion to an unattainable ideal. Any decision to choose one as more admirable than the other undoubtedly tells us more about the chooser than the chosen.

The second question probably has only one realistic answer because friendship requires reciprocation. I might invite the lone wolf to join my circle of friends, but he would decline the honor. By definition he is a loner. Like Muir he is "locked in a lifelong spiritual embrace that [makes] his human-to-human relationships a mere afterthought" (paragraph 9). He would be a fascinating acquaintance, but I can't imagine that he would volunteer to pick up my mail or mow my lawn while I went on vacation. I'll bet Harrigan would do those things for his friends.

3. Would this essay be more or less effective if Harrigan opened it with a description of himself and then described the lone wolf?

This question is meant to demonstrate the importance of organization. Your students should see that much of the comic effect would be lost if Harrigan began with his own description. Instead, he opens the essay with a rhapsodic characterization of his idol, a man as awe-inspiring as the mountains he scales. Then Harrigan juxtaposes that image with a caricature of himself, first as "a teenager, sporting glasses, braces, global acne, and Lee's 'Husky' jeans" (paragraph 4), and later as an adult "lining up a putt on the tricky Tyrannosaurus Rex hole at Peter Pan golf" (paragraph 5). Out of context, Harrigan's self-portrait might be mildly amusing; contrasted with our vision of the lone wolf, it's hilarious.

—M.R.D.—

Style Lesson 14:
Use of Humorous Details

A good deal of the humor in "Answering the Howl" comes from Stephen Harrigan's use of details—often drawn from popular culture—that illustrate the ridiculousness of his situation. The details in paragraphs 4 and 5 are particularly eloquent. See how many you can recall.

I've always wanted to be one of these guys: a lone wolf, austere and independent, a secular saint of the wilderness. As a teenager, sporting ___1___, ___2___, global ___3___ and ___4___ ___5___ jeans, I found it consoling to think of myself in years to come as a solitary wanderer, impatient with civilization, indifferent to comfort, lulled by the sound of ___6___ ___7___.

And yet, here you find me: lining up a putt on the tricky ___8___ ___9___ hole at ___10___ ___11___ Golf; sitting out in the backyard chucking ___12___ snacks to an overstimulated and mentally deficient dog; setting aside ___13___ to read a newspaper article about ___14___ ___15___ ___16___.

Hints: 1, 2, and 3 are things associated with the face; 4/5 forms a brand name; 8/9 and 10/11 are proper names; 12 is a brand name; 14/15 names a person; 16 names an item the person wears.

SCOTT RUSSELL SANDERS

Reasons of the Body

Sanders's essay, primarily narrative and descriptive, could belong equally to three units in *The Dolphin Reader:* Childhood, Nature, and (of course) Femininity and Masculinity. It involves the relation of father to son, focusing on the crucial stage when, as Sanders says, the adolescent son is "midway up the slope" of life and the middle-aged father is "over the crest and digging in [his] heels" on the way down. Among the most interesting ideas raised by the essay is reflected in the title: Our body, as Sanders, borrowing from Pascal, says, "has reasons reason knows nothing of." Schooling tends to make abstractionists of us all, and one of the virtues of this essay is that it reminds us how much of our lives (especially our emotional lives) inevitably comes from the body rather than from the mind.

One of the contributions of feminist thinkers in our time has been to challenge the lionization of abstract thought and the denigration of "reasons of the body." Sanders pursues the same point, but from a distinctly masculine point of view.

QUESTIONS

1. What justification does Sanders offer for men's interest in sports, and how convincing are these justifications?

A good technique for discussing this question is to ask students who are not particularly interested in sports to talk first. This will prevent them from feeling excluded from the discussion and may have the advantage of testing how much sense Sanders's justifications make to someone whose experiences are different from his own. After your non-sportspeople have had their say, let the athletes talk. It may be that the justifications make more sense to those who have participated very actively in sports than to those who haven't. This would, of course, be a sort of confirmation of the essay's thesis, showing that our understanding is shaped by our body's experiences.

Here are some of Sanders's justifications:

- That sports are one of the principal ways that fathers and sons forge a relationship. In paragraphs 12 and 13, for example, Sanders puts a game of catch into both the context of other dialogues (including call-and-response preaching) and the context of every son's imitation (or rejection) of his father's ways. In effect, the movements of sports dance out the relationship between father and son, a relationship notoriously difficult to talk out.
- That sports have replaced hunting, farming, war, and shamanism as masculine heritages to be passed from father to son (see paragraph 22). This almost amounts to saying that boys learn to be men by learning sports.

- That sports provide men (especially) with a common bond, something to talk about in the household or in the office (paragraph 19).
- That sports allow people to experience joy in their bodies, to "dwell in the flesh without rancor . . . for moments at a time" (paragraph 42). Sanders hints that this may be particularly important because of the loss of the physical dimension in modern life.
- That sports get us into contact with our own mortality and immortality (see paragraphs 43–46). This may sound like highfalutin language to apply to games, but Sanders means something simple and concrete: As one generation replaces another on the diamond or the court, we see enacted both the inevitable curve of the individual's aging and death and the continuity of life.

I believe that something like this list will fill the chalkboard after a good deal of class discussion. Along the way, you will have had some talk about how convincing or important the various justifications are. I think that some students will dismiss number two as bunk—the sort of easy-to-parody, male-as-wild-man mythology that has come into the mainstream with the publication of Robert Bly's *Iron John* and Sam Keene's *Fire in the Belly*. The others are less likely to draw criticism, but are not all equally weighty: number three does not seem as important in Sanders's essay as numbers four and five.

2. Is Sanders correct in identifying the bond through sports as characteristically masculine? Are there similar physical bonds forged between mothers and daughters? Do they involve something other than sports?

These really are two different questions, but one leads us to the other. It appears to me that by the standards of the nineties, Sanders's family seems more polarized about sports than most families are. This question will allow some of your female students to talk about their experiences with sports and the way that basketball or hockey (or whatever) linked them to the previous generation and may link them to the next. It will be interesting to hear how many women students felt that their sporting life linked them to their mother, how many to their father, how many to male coaches, how many to female.

Women who are less oriented to sports are likely to mention in the process of discussion that our society is relatively rich in *other* physical connections between mothers and daughters or among women generally. Daughters have traditionally lived in households where their mothers did the bulk of the physical work—the cooking, the cleaning, the decorating, the shopping, perhaps the gardening—and have traditionally spent many hours imitating, first as play, then in earnest, this physical work. Sons of my generation typically spent little time watching their fathers at work. (What work did they do anyhow, when they went off to the mysterious office? How could we know?) When my wife talks to her mother on the phone, they are likely to discuss a refinishing or quilting project. When I talk with my father, we are likely to talk politics. (Of course, this oversimplifies things somewhat: We all discuss health, weather, and children). It is possible that the importance of sports in forging bonds between men reflects the relatively *unphysical* nature of men's lives together and that women have richer daily opportunities to experience the "reasons of the body."

3. If you were Sanders and if you faced an editor who told you to cut the length of this essay by half, what would you delete?

This question is essentially a way to get students to decide between baby and bath water. Of course, students may legitimately differ from each other about what is central and what is peripheral in this essay, but discussion is likely to focus on paragraphs 22–39, where Sanders tells four family stories: the hole-in-one, Satchel Paige, the boxing coach, and the fight with Olaf Magnuson. Paragraphs 20 (the catalogue of sports paraphernalia) and 21 (the philology of sport) may also get some attention. Those who argue that some or all of these things should be omitted are holding Sanders's essay to standards of tight organization that have not traditionally been applied to an informal essay (which I seem to recall Dr. Johnson's defining as "an undisciplined ramble") and are assuming that the real business of the essay is an attempt to explain the role of sports in the lives of men generally. The Satchel Paige story has some explanatory power (the sports myth links the generations as stories are passed from father to son) but it isn't as essential to Sanders's explanation as, for example, the opening description of the game of catch is. It is there because Sanders feels that it is too good a story to omit and because it has the quirky resonances of personal experience.

Asking your students to reconfigure the essay as a less rambling, more focused piece should help them remember that not every style is suited to every occasion. The looseness of the informal essay allows Sanders to collect material attractive in its own right, though not governed very clearly by a thesis. It allows him to write with a great deal of visceral and social impact. But students need to be aware that it would not be an appropriate model for the organization of an academic essay or a news story.

—D.H.—

Style Lesson 15:
Using Parallel Gerund Phrases to Show Movement

In paragraph 12, Sanders describes the "dialogue carried on with muscle and bone" between people engaged in sport. The sentence below illustrates this point with a series of gerunds that evoke particular sports and particular movement. Fill in the blanks, then (if time permits) write a sentence patterned on Sanders's, perhaps one describing two people flirting or two political candidates skirmishing.

One body speaks by _____ a _____ [think of baseball or football],
or a _____ [boxing],
by _____ with a _____ [fencing],
_____ a _____ [tennis or racquetball],
_____ a _____ [golf],
_____ a _____ [bowling],
_____ a _____ toward the corner of the _____ [soccer];

the other replies by _____ [arm movement],
_____ [movement up],
_____ [movement down or over],
_____ [contact with opponent],
_____ [reaction to opponent],
_____ [movement of recovery].

DAVE BARRY

Lost in the Kitchen

Barry's essay is about as uncomplicated as they come, a good one to read on a day when the class needs some comic relief. Nonetheless, it can help you teach some valuable lessons about variations in tone and diction, which are the bases of Barry's humor.

Assigned with Perrin, Norman, and Riskin, "Lost in the Kitchen" could provide an interesting day of discussion about the changing roles of men. Because the four essays are so short, they could serve as models for short student essays on the same subject.

QUESTIONS

1. What generally accepted rules of good writing does Barry's essay violate?

If your students are like mine, there is no telling what they will come up with in response to this question. You may find that their notion of generally accepted rules is very different from your own, which could lead to a valuable discussion that has little to do with the essay.

My list of Barry's "lapses" is fairly long. The essay is ill organized (see question 2), is filled with overstatements, uses jargon, mixes very informal and very formal language recklessly, and contains a sentence fragment of a type that drives some composition teachers right up a wall. All of these supposed faults help to establish the essay's casual, humorous tone. Here's a good chance to remind your students that rules of writing are almost entirely rules of thumb, and that a writer who is *demonstrably in control* can take liberties with them.

Let's look at Barry's overstatements. Even those who think that the essay's first sentence is a plain statement of fact will not think that men are literally "as useful around the kitchen as ill-trained Labrador retrievers" (paragraph 2). The dog may be stupid, but her brain cannot have been "long ago eaten by fleas," nor are the children "running as fast as they can directly into things, trying to injure themselves" (paragraph 3). This vein of overstatement is worked throughout the essay, particularly well in the case of some similes of heroic proportions: "I would no more enter that kitchen than I would attempt to park an aircraft carrier" (paragraph 4) and "for which they expect to be praised as if they had developed, right there in the kitchen, a cure for heart disease" (paragraph 7).

The wildly mixed diction often has the effect of overstatement, too. "It is a scientific finding based on an exhaustive study of what happened last Thanksgiving when my family had dinner at the home of friends . . ." puffs up with the sort of inflated diction we hear when someone is emphasizing the importance of a supposedly scientific study and then returns to plain language. Better still is the "famous law of physics that goes: 'You cannot watch small children and the Detroit Lions at the same time, and let's face it, the Detroit Lions are more interesting'" (paragraph 6). Somehow I can't remember any other law of physics that contains the phrase "let's face it."

"Which we try to do" (paragraph 5) is a sentence fragment of a type one sees sometimes in advertisements and often in student papers. Used well, it has the clipped sound of a wisecrack. In this case, it is almost as if Barry had winked after it.

2. In what ways is Barry's essay badly organized?

The essay contains two absolutely off-the-wall digressions, one to "human sexual activity" (more inflated diction) in the opening paragraph, one to women's liberation and automobiles in the closing paragraph. Barry makes the situation worse by the transitions he uses to glue the digressions to the body of the essay: "But that, as far as I can tell, is not my point," "I asked my wife to read this and tell me what she thought," and "This seemed pretty accurate to me, so I thought I'd just tack it on the end here." These transitions remind me of many horrible freshman papers filled with phrases such as "Before beginning to discuss abortion, it is important to define the issues" or "In conclusion, let me say . . ." Part of the humor of Barry's essay comes from its skillful imitation of ineptness.

3. What is Barry's attitude toward himself and his behavior?

A friend of mine read this essay and was concerned that Barry's tone seemed to countenance the faults he pretends to find in his behavior. I suppose that there is some truth in this. Unlike Perrin and Norman, he is not out primarily to persuade or inform or shape our attitudes. People burning to reform their lives or the lives of others aren't notable for their senses of humor. Still, as Fielding observed, it may be possible to laugh people out of their vices. The essence of Barry's humor is a combination of pride and humility: he is scum and he knows it.

—D.H.—

Style Lesson 16:
Casual Style, Loose Sentences

The casual style of Dave Barry relies on frequent loose (cumulative) sentences that begin with a simple statement and then add on a series of modifying phrases and clauses that take the reader in unexpected directions. To appreciate how loose and casual the style is, close your book and combine the following short sentences (from paragraph 7) into one, trying to recapture the rambling effect of the original.

I think most males rarely prepare food for others. They sometimes do. Then they have one specialty dish. In my case it is spaghetti. They prepare it maybe twice a year. It is a very elaborate production. They expect to be praised for it. It is as if they had developed a cure for heart disease, right there in the kitchen.

COMMUNITIES

OVERVIEW OF UNIT

There are two ways to view the *Communities* unit. One, which I will characterize without bias as the low road, is to see it merely as an invitation to write about places and the people who inhabit them. I have had students react to a reading like Toni Cade Bambara's "The Hammer Man" or Edna O'Brien's "Sister Imelda" or Richard Rodriguez's "Going Home Again" viscerally because it struck a note sympathetic to the students' own experience, and these students have sometimes produced fine essays in response.

The cerebral "high road" puts in the foreground what these visceral and personal responses often keep in the back: the questions of what a community essentially *is* and why some communities function better than others do. The high road involves us in philosophical and political questions. Is a community essentially a family writ large? What is the connection between the quality of a community and the prosperity of the individuals who live in it? What makes it possible for someone to live geographically in the middle of a community without politically or socially having a place in it? How does the community put its stamp on the individual? H. D. F. Kitto's "The Polis" and Plato's "Crito," both of which present Greek community life as an ideal, help us get at such questions, as do James Baldwin's "Fifth Avenue, Uptown" and Charles Murray's "What's So Bad about Being Poor?"

I would encourage you to keep both the high road and the low road in your students' view as they read and discuss the selections in this unit. The stereoscopic effect of keeping one eye on each may sharpen their insight into what "community" means, both viscerally and abstractly.

JOAN DIDION

On Going Home

In "On Going Home," which is thematically linked with the Insiders and Outsiders unit, Didion focuses on one of the largest groups of outsiders in our society—the children who grow up, move away, marry, have children of their own, settle into different lifestyles, establish new allegiances, and are surprised to find that the people they become are outsiders in their parents' homes, outsiders who remember being insiders.

For Didion the word *home* has a special meaning. Five generations before Joan Didion's birth, her pioneer ancestors emigrated to the Central Valley of California and claimed huge areas of land. Those pioneers and their descendants became a local aristocracy who intermarried, multiplied, expanded their holdings, and prospered. In 1934 Didion was born into this stable and comfortable world of great-aunts and old family houses. She tells us that her earliest memory is of "running a boxer dog of my brother's over the same flat fields that our great-great-grandfather had found virgin and had planted. . . ." When Didion moved to the East in 1954 to take an editorial position at *Vogue,* she became the first member of her family to leave the Central Valley. In "On Going Home" Didion describes the bittersweet memories that assail her when she returns to her parents' home to celebrate her own daughter's first birthday.

QUESTIONS

1. Is Didion correct when she says that people born during the 1930s were "the last generation to carry the burden of 'home,' to find in family life the source of all tension and drama" (paragraph 2)?

Didion seems to be claiming that people her age were the last to feel a sense of connection to previous generations, that after the post "World War II fragmentation," there were no fixed traditions to abandon. Consequently, no one has to choose to abandon them. I would agree that few of us experience precisely the same kind of trauma Didion describes. Didion's experience of moving away from a ranch that had been owned by her family for five generations is undoubtedly different from that of a young woman who moves out of a condo her parents purchased while she was away at college. But even today some people have to decide whether to continue family traditions. I live in Glasgow, a tiny Missouri river town established in 1831. Downtown is Henderson's drugstore, which has been owned and operated by a single family for four generations. Behind the soda fountain is a picture of each of the family's pharmacists. David, son of the present proprietor, recently graduated from pharmaceutical school and returned to Glasgow to take his place behind the counter.

But even those of us who are less aware of our link to a number of generations can be securely tied to our parents, and I would guess that many people still find family life the source of most, if not all, tension and drama. Didion seems to believe that people who do not know their great-aunts and who have not lived in one house throughout childhood have no real understanding of "home" and never experience the emotional commitment and conflict she feels. Surely some of your students will disagree. In fact they may point out that the bonds between members of a small nuclear family become even stronger when that family is geographically separated from cousins, aunts, and grandparents. Your students may want to write essays comparing their own feelings about leaving home to Didion's.

2. Why does an essay about Didion's visit to her family's home have so many passages about her husband?

Didion seems to believe that the nuclear family is a closed community composed of individuals who share a set of experiences no one else will ever understand. Didion uses most of the first paragraph to show that her husband is not a member of her familial community and that her family's ways, "which are difficult, oblique, deliberately inarticulate," are not her husband's ways. He is critical of the dusty furniture, fails to appreciate the assay scales, and does not understand the code the family uses to talk about the things they like best.

Didion shares one community with her husband and another with her family, and she is torn between her conflicting allegiances. In that sense, marriage is indeed "the classic betrayal." No wonder Didion comes to dread her husband's evening call, a call that reminds her of her divided loyalties.

3. Does the evidence presented in the essay suggest that Didion still belongs to her family?

In many ways Didion is definitely a member of the family. She understands that discussions about sale-leasebacks are code for "the yellow fields and the cottonwoods and the rivers rising and falling and the mountain roads closing when the heavy snow comes in" (paragraph 1). She puts the mementos she intended to throw away back into her bedroom drawer. She visits the family graveyard.

But Didion learns that in more significant ways she "can't go home again." The graveyard has been vandalized since her last visit, the roundup she is invited to attend will take place after she returns to Los Angeles, and her great-aunts confuse her with other relatives. In the closing paragraph Didion adds up what she has lost, what her daughter will never have: "a sense of her cousins and of rivers and of her great-grandmother's teacups," "a picnic on a river with fried chicken and her hair uncombed," "home." Then, with her eyes open, she accepts the reality that "we live differently now, and I can promise her nothing like that."

The essay, however, ends on a note of optimism. In the final sentence Didion explains what she can give her daughter: "a xylophone and a sundress from Madeira" and a "promise to tell her a funny story." In other words, music, travel, literature, and, of course, love. The reason Didion doesn't find those beautiful gifts sufficient is suggested in an earlier line: "I would like to give her more." I think Didion means more *of* the childhood she herself experienced and also more *than* the childhood she experienced. Those of us who had happy childhoods always want to give our children exactly what we had—and more. We can't do both.

4. What passages in the essay suggest strong emotions Didion never quite articulates?

Didion keeps a journal filled with "flash-cuts," a film term that describes the technique of focusing the camera for just a few seconds on a scene that speaks for itself. Such flash-cuts frequently find their way into her essays as images that suggest far more than Didion actually says.

In paragraph 1, for example, she shows us that her husband neither understands nor appreciates her family. She then suggests the complexity of her feelings toward him by describing a particular moment: "We miss each other's points, have another drink and regard the fire." If you ask your students to explain how she feels about her husband, they should see how much she communicates with that image. Another poignant scene focuses on Didion trying to clean out a drawer. Again, ask your students how they think she feels when she looks at the teacups hand-painted by her grandmother. My favorite image is that of Didion having a cup of coffee with her mother. "We get along very well, veterans of a guerrilla war we never understood." The term "guerrilla war," with its implications that it is difficult to tell who is on which side, that the boundaries between enemy and friend are continually shifting, that the participants never know whether to expect peace or hostilities on a given day, is a perfect metaphor for the intrafamily tensions Didion cannot ignore.

Your students who like straightforward, clear, explanatory writing may be put off by Didion. In fact, she has been criticized for seducing her readers by indirection. But those who enjoy communication on an intuitive level should love this essay.

—M.R.D.—

Style Lesson 17: Details that Characterize a Community

The multi-layered sentence below is filled with details describing Didion's family. At each number, work with other students to try to recall the omitted words or phrases, then substitute details about another community, replacing the "him" (Didion's husband) with another outsider.

We live in [1] houses ([2])
filled with [3] quite without value to him
(what could the [4] mean to him?
how could he have known about the [5],
why should he care if he did know?),
and we appear to talk exclusively
about [6],
about [7]
and about [8],
particularly about [8, repeated],
[9], [10] and [11] and [12] and [13].

You might write about a sports-oriented family with a bookish visitor: "We live in sprawling houses (it takes a lot of elbow room to accommodate seven jocks) filled with sports memorabilia quite without value to him . . ." Or about a suburb as seen by a poor visitor from a third world country.

RICHARD RODRIGUEZ

Going Home Again: The New American Scholarship Boy

A student who merely skims Richard Rodriguez's essay will very likely see, correctly, that he is a man caught between two cultures. But such a student will probably think that the two cultures are Chicano and white. Not so. The two cultures are Chicano and academic, and the social pressures Rodriguez feels are not at all the same as those he would have felt if he had moved away from the barrio to live among illiterate Anglo factory workers, for instance. He comes to the academic world as an outsider and, by taking on academia's values, becomes an outsider to his native community. Many Anglo students with unscholarly parents have also had such experiences.

But the Spanish-speaking student and the academic world is part of the larger picture of minority-majority relations that has become critical in the last few decades in both the United States and Canada. In every sphere the white, English-speaking, and Protestant majority seems to occupy the center, while others are relegated to the periphery. In the discussion about how this situation is to be remedied, Rodriguez has become a very controversial figure, an opponent of affirmative action programs and bilingual education. As readers of this essay will see, Rodriguez is acutely aware of the psychological price minorities pay for assimilation. But he argues that members of minority groups can't simultaneously penetrate to the center of public society and retain the culture of their home communities.

QUESTIONS

1. Why does Rodriguez refuse to identify himself as a Chicano?

You may want to begin the discussion of this question by looking at one of the most dramatic points in the essay, in paragraph 23, where Rodriguez refuses to teach a course on the Chicano novel. This is the sort of refusal to take up the cause of the group that has made him so controversial. He has at least three reasons for not accepting the role of a Chicano intellectual:

- True Chicanos, as the word is used politically and culturally, are illiterate or semi-illiterate. They are certainly not Ph.D.'s in Renaissance literature. They are a deprived group; Rodriguez is not deprived. To claim a close identification would simply be to distort the truth.
- Worse yet, to claim to be a Chicano would be to exploit the suffering of actual Chicanos. In the present climate of affirmative action programs, someone who seems to represent a minority group—even though he suffers none of the cultural or educational disadvantages of the group—can become a "beneficiary" of that group's oppression (paragraph 14). No col-

lege is going to hire a genuine Chicano, a poor illiterate, as a professor, but they will pay very well for an imitation Chicano with degrees from Stanford, Columbia, and Berkeley.

- And so, to the extent that a promising *individual* identifies himself with a minority group, he raises in his own mind and others the question of how much of his success is due to his individual accomplishment: "The most dazzlingly talented minority students I know today refuse to believe that their success is wholly based on their own talent . . ." (paragraph 14).

Students who disagree with Rodriguez's views may imagine less charitable motives for his statements. It is worth noting that after this essay was published Rodriguez, swamped by job offers in the very crowded field of English literature, abandoned his academic career. The irony and the hypocrisy of being so courted as a member of a minority group to which he did not belong was overwhelming.

2. Is it only among members of racial and cultural minorities that education alienates the student from his or her home community?

Rodriguez points out in paragraph 4 that "one can grow up to enter the culture of the academy and find it a 'foreign' culture for a variety of reasons, ranging from economic status to religious heritage." On my own campus, perhaps a third of the students are outsiders of the sort Rodriguez has in mind. But many, many more of them are outsiders in another sense that Rodriguez only hints at: they see academic education as a tool for getting status and jobs, and so stand outside academia, appraising it with a foreign eye. They can't make themselves feel the value of the disinterested pursuit of truth and are nagged in their studies by the feeling that they are missing out on life itself, by which they don't mean running barefoot through the barrio, but watching movies, going out to eat pizza, playing softball, cruising the singles bars, vacationing in Italy, whatever their home culture (which is increasingly mass culture) has taught them are the *real* goals of life, toward which education is merely an end.

Except for the very few that come from families genuinely at home in the academy, most of us have some of the feelings of alienation that Rodriguez experienced as he sat in the reading room of the British Museum "depressed by the silence and what the silence implied—that my life as a scholar would require self-absorption" (paragraph 20). To the extent that we manage actually to become academics, we share some of his difficulties talking to the home folks about what we are doing. One of the penalties most students pay for a really good bit of research and writing is the uncomfortable feeling that their parents will appreciate the grade but not the paper itself. Somewhere in *Walden* Thoreau observes that every student reaches the point where he has more in common with Plato and Shakespeare than with the people he sees every day.

3. How does Rodriguez manage the difficult task of writing an essay about his personal feelings in a manner appropriate to an audience of educated strangers?

Your students should see from the headnote that the essay appeared in *The American Scholar*, a magazine slightly less frosty than its title, perhaps, but not an ideal vehicle for confession. Obviously, the situation creates difficulty in establishing the right tone.

At his best Rodriguez solves the problem of speaking publicly about private things by just the method that educated people have always employed in writing essays based on personal experience: he keeps his life in perspective by seeing that his experience is related to the experience of others. He doesn't write about his life at random, as diarists and letter writers may, but focuses on its publicly interesting aspects:

> The autobiographical facts pertinent to this essay are simply stated in two sentences, though they exist in somewhat awkward juxtaposition to each other. I am the son of Mexican-American parents, who speak a blend of Spanish and English, but who read neither language easily. I am about to receive a Ph.D. in English Renaissance literature (paragraph 2).

We know from the outset that though the essay is in the first person, it will not be a bit of self-indulgent wool-gathering. Too often students confuse the presence of first person with a failure to address public issues. I recently read an essay by Dean Rusk, former secretary of state, in which he questioned the reliability of high-tech weaponry by pointing to the most ordinary sort of personal experience: "Only once in sixty years have I had a clock in an automobile that would keep time. . . ."

Beyond the issue of personal content, though, there is the question of voice. Can one sound like a particular person while addressing an academic audience, or must one assume the protective armor of academic prose? I don't think Rodriguez had an answer to that question when he wrote this essay. We find passages that seem very personal and vivid: "Remembering my youth, a time when I was not restricted to a chair but ran barefoot under a summer sun that tightened my skin with its white heat, made the fact that it was only my mind that 'moved' each hour in the library painfully obvious" (paragraph 21). There are also passages of utterly impenetrable abstraction:

> The problem, however, with this sentimental solution is that it overlooks the way academic culture renders one capable of dealing with the transactions of mass society. Academic culture, with its habits of conceptualization and abstraction, allows those of us from other cultures to deal with each other in mass society. In this sense academic culture does have a profound political impact (paragraph 31).

It isn't surprising that a graduate student writing for *The American Scholar* should occasionally lapse into what he himself describes as the "tedious prose" too common in the academic world. In the years since "Going Home Again," Rodriguez has found another style that blends the personal and the public more completely. He recently told *Contemporary Authors* that his present model is George Orwell:

> Orwell is the great modern example. He embarrasses other journalists by being more. He never let the urgency of the moment overwhelm his concern for literary art. But, in like measure, he embarrasses other writers because he had the courage to attend to the voices outside the window, he was not afraid to look up from the paper.

If Orwell were editing "Going Home Again," he would find much to approve of, but his pencil might descend occasionally on the last two or three pages.

—D.H.—

Style Lesson 18: Suiting the Style to the Audience

To illustrate the way Rodriguez's style is suited to an academic audience, rewrite the following passage (from paragraph 31) for an audience of typical sixteen-year-olds. You will probably find that changes in diction aren't enough; Rodriguez's syntax is too convoluted for the audience proposed.

Awaiting the scholarship boy who finally acknowledges the fact that his perceptions of reality have changed is the dilemma of action. The sentimental reaction to this knowledge entails merely a refusal to renew contact with one's nonacademic culture lest one contaminate it. The problem, however, with this sentimental solution is that it overlooks the way academic culture renders one capable of dealing with the transactions of mass society. Academic culture, with its habits of conceptualization and abstraction, allows those of us from other cultures to deal with each other in a mass society. In this sense academic culture does have a profound political impact.

A rewrite might begin this way: "A problem faces the scholarship boy when he realizes that he sees the world differently than he once did."

JAMES BALDWIN

Fifth Avenue, Uptown: A Letter from Harlem

Like most Baldwin essays, "Fifth Avenue, Uptown" intertwines history with personal experience and observation. In this respect, it is closely akin to Scott Momaday's "The Way to Rainy Mountain." In both essays, the writer begins by establishing a clear sense of place: Momaday's landscape is barren and Baldwin's cityscape is bleak (paragraphs 1–4). As Momaday's grandmother seems to fit the landscape, so Baldwin's people seem to fit the cityscape, derelict as it is derelict: the environment shaping the people, the people shaping the environment.

All of this, naturally, Baldwin views with bitterness, but one of the things that makes him a great writer is that his bitterness doesn't taint his judgment or result in a protective callus. He sees that the suffering he and others have experienced in Harlem is only one aspect of racial oppression, and not even the worst aspect: racism in Birmingham, Alabama, may be worse, and if it is, "no doubt Johannesburg, South Africa, beats it by several miles, and Buchenwald was one of the worst things that ever happened in the entire history of the world" (paragraph 17). But he doesn't let his awareness that other places have been relatively worse blunt his condemnation of the racism that created Harlem's slums.

QUESTIONS

1. What changes does Baldwin notice when he returns to his old neighborhood?

The most obvious is the housing project that has supplanted his own house. We immediately discover that he does not find this an improvement. It becomes a symbol for the decline of the neighborhood. His view of what the neighborhood had been in his childhood is not altogether idyllic (note in the first paragraph that Baldwin's family never wore new shoes) but it *was* a neighborhood, a connected social fabric. We see this particularly in paragraph 3, where Baldwin remembers the interaction among the children on the block, and in paragraph 6, where Baldwin recalls the people engaged in civic or social activities: playing handball, going to church, going to school, going to war, getting married. Today he sees "immense human gaps" in the social fabric. Where have the productive, lively people gone? In paragraph 4, Baldwin counts them off, as if on his fingers: some have moved or are dead, but most have (1) turned into fanatical churchgoers, (2) turned to "moslems" or allied haters of "the white world and its works," (3) retreated into idleness, television, or drugs, or (4) turned to dope peddlers "on the way to prison or just coming out." All have had their energy tragically deflected. Some, he notes in paragraph 5, are still alive, still struggling to maintain their humanity and dignity, but against great odds.

Baldwin never quite says that social conditions were better during his childhood. Perhaps he can't know: as "Notes of a Native Son" shows us, he had other things to be concerned about then. But he does imply that things have gotten worse, that the attempts of white liberals (up to 1960, at least) have done more harm than good. Charles Murray ("What's So Bad about Being Poor?") would say that the same analysis could be made today.

2. What, according to Baldwin, is the root of Harlem's problem?

Baldwin, like Clarence Darrow and John Kenneth Galbraith, is inclined to put the blame at the doorstep of the wealthy and powerful and those who worship wealth and power:

> . . . the American equation of success with the big times reveals an awful disrespect for human life and human achievement. This equation has placed our cities among the most dangerous in the world and has placed our youth among the most empty and most bewildered. . . . [Our children] are imitating our immorality, our disrespect for the pain of others (paragraph 8).

Like Swift, Baldwin is particularly angry that large companies and local merchants exploit this misery by selling luxury goods at inflated prices to people desperate for a piece of the good life (paragraph 9). The general attitude of the white world toward blacks in another cause: "The people in Harlem know they are living there because white people do not think they are good enough to live anywhere else," and they resent being "corraled up" for economic exploitation (paragraphs 13 and 14). Baldwin says that the whole problem of what American blacks want has been made unnecessarily obtuse: they want "to be treated like men" (paragraph 16).

3. What is Baldwin's attitude toward whites?

Though he has the keenest sense of the wrongs whites have done, he clearly separates himself from those who hate "the white world and its works." He is willing to acknowledge the humanity of whites, and takes no pleasure in their suffering (paragraph 7). In paragraph 15 he goes so far as to give a sympathetic picture of the plight of the white policeman, who feels "like an occupying soldier in a bitterly hostile country." Students may appreciate the acuteness of this psychological portrait if they compare it with Orwell's description of his own feelings as a policeman in Burma in "Shooting an Elephant."

4. How does Baldwin distinguish between the attitudes of Northern and Southern whites?

The tidiest antitheses are seen in paragraph 19:

> He [the Northerner] never sees Negroes. Southerners see them all the time. Northerners never think about them whereas Southerners are never really thinking of anything else. Negroes are, therefore, ignored in the North and are under surveillance in the South.

Many white Northerners must have been irritated by coming off no better than Southerners in Baldwin's comparison. For six years they had had the moral luxury of watching the South struggle against the school integration ordered by *Brown v. Board of Education*. Racism seemed to speak with a Southern drawl. A decade later the progress of school integration would expose the extent of Northern racism, but Baldwin and his neighbors already knew it from bitter experience.

—D.H.—

Style Lesson 19: Varying Sentences in a Passage of Contrasts

In paragraph 19, Baldwin's contrast of the Northern response to Negroes with the Southern response runs the danger of sounding mechanical and choppy, but the variety of his sentences saves him. Here are the first two sentences of the paragraph unaltered and the information for the next five in table form:

None of this is true for the Northerner. Negroes represent nothing to him personally, except, perhaps, the dangers of carnality.

North	**South**
Negroes are never seen.	Negroes are seen all the time.
Whites never think about Negroes.	Whites never really think about anything but Negroes.
Negroes are ignored.	Negroes are under surveillance.
Negroes suffer hideously.	Negroes suffer hideously.
Whites are not able to look on the the Negro simply as a man.	Whites are not able to look on the Negro simply as a man.

Fit the tabular information into sentences built on the pattern below.

He [phrase]. Southerners [phrase]. Northerners [phrase], whereas Southerners [phrase]. [Clause] in the North and [phrase] in the South, and [phrase] in both places. Neither the Southerner nor the Northerner [phrase].

TONI CADE BAMBARA

The Hammer Man

Bambara's story brings together so many themes that it might fit into any of the first four units of *The Dolphin Reader.* The narrator is on the brink of adolescence, having her "last fling with boy things" in a way that echoes several readings from *Childhood* and *Femininity and Masculinity,* and she is involved in racial friction that connects the story with *Insiders and Outsiders.* What makes it so suited for the *Communities* unit is that it gives a convincing and humorous portrait of a neighborhood officially labeled as "deviant" (see paragraph 11) but actually working with all the drama and friction and affection one would expect in any close-knit community.

When the outside world enters this community in the form of white policemen, the narrator comes to a number of realizations at once. One is that in the face of a threat from strangers, everyone inside the community becomes brother and sister, even the "crazy" guy you've been at war with for weeks.

QUESTIONS

1. How would you describe the tone of this story?

"I was glad to hear that Manny had fallen off the roof," the story begins, and this open line establishes a tone that hovers between the shocking and the humorous. The events of the story certainly have the potential for tragedy or melodrama or didacticism. When, for example, Miss Rose and Manny's mother fight with bottles snatched from garbage cans and broken over fire hydrants, Bambara *might* have presented the scene in a way that emphasized the poverty of the environment and the anger of people caught in hopeless socio-economic circumstances, but she chose instead to bring out the humor. Despite their heavy armaments, the women roll harmlessly in the streets with their "pink drawers and fat legs" exposed to the neighbors who gather to comment that it's "much too cold for this kind of nonsense" (paragraph 6). We don't feel that the women want to hurt each other seriously; we don't feel that they are helpless products of their environments. We feel that they have their blood up and that they are a sight to behold.

The humorous tone may trouble some students, especially after they read about Manny's being unjustly arrested by the policemen and forced into a lunatic asylum. It might strike them as sheer callousness that the narrator distracts us during the arrest with fantasies about her own murder (". . . it just wasn't no kind of thing to happen to a small child like me with my confirmation picture in the paper next to my weeping parents and schoolmates") and that at the story's end she jumps lightly from a mention of Manny's commitment to an asylum to a mention of "this very boss fashion show at the center." It may appear to them that the narrator has missed the point, missed the epiphany in her own story. Perhaps she has, but Bambara has not missed the point and neither will the alert reader, who finds the injustice more jarring because it is presented so casually, as just another thing that happens in a girl's life. And my own suspicion is that *nothing* is missed on a person as quick on the uptake as the narrator: Bambara really means us to see what the narrator sees—that there is horrible injustice and that life goes on, including the boss fashion show.

2. What do the fights between Miss Rose and Manny's mother and the narrator's father and Manny's various male relatives tell us about the community the narrator lives in?

They tell us several things. Some students may be inclined to say that they reveal a pretty low state of civilization in the neighborhood: In the leafier suburbs of America adults don't usually go at their neighbors with broken bottles or smash each other's heads into mailboxes. Other students may point out that the violence is more showy than dangerous: if there were a great likelihood of serious injury or death, the onlookers would not be laconically commenting that the weather is too cold for fighting in the street. All students should agree that this is a community where tensions are played out (shouted out, fought out) rather than hidden.

It is a community where family loyalties are strong. When the narrator's father feels that his daughter is in danger, he "has a few words" not only with Manny, but with Manny's older brother Bernard. And when he bruises Bernard's head, Bernard's uncle has a few words with him.

It is also a neighborhood where loyalties extend outside the family. Miss Rose is presumably unrelated to the narrator, but she is the girl's godmother, and she takes the role seriously enough to fight for her and to buy her first corsage. She has other godchildren in the neighborhood (paragraph 10), and one suspects that the onlookers at the fight are not there entirely for their own amusement. If Miss Rose's life had been threatened, some of the people who knew her well would have come to her rescue, and one suspects that Manny's mother was under the same sort of protection.

3. What does the story seem to say about the relations between black communities and white communities in 1966? How much has the situation changed since then?

The two fights among neighbors, loud but harmless, stand in sharp contrast to the struggle between Manny and the big policeman. There the action is relatively subdued, but the harm is much greater because Manny is struggling with outsiders who have no knowledge of him as a quirky but manageable individual with a mother, brother, and uncle. Perhaps they lack the capacity to imagine him as being anything so complex: he is a "black boy" in a public place after dark. When they take him out of the neighborhood, he loses all the protection and tolerance a neighborhood can offer. He is at the mercy of the larger society the policemen represent.

As the narrator says ". . . crazy or no crazy, Manny was my brother at that moment and the cop was the enemy" (paragraph 22). In a racially segregated society, resentment of "the enemy" who enters the community and has its will with one of the neighbors becomes a recurrent theme. I am writing this comment in the year of the Rodney King beating, the acquittal of the Los Angeles policemen who beat him, and the riots that followed the acquittal. After the acquittal, any number of black children must have echoed the narrator's disillusioned comment,

> And I'm standing there thinking that none of my teachers, from kindergarten right on up, none of them knew what they were talking about. I'll be damned if I ever knew one of them rosy-cheeked cops that smiled and helped you get to school without neither you or your little raggedy dog getting hit by a truck that had a smile on its face, too. Not that I ever believed it. I knew Dick and Jane was full of crap from the get-go, especially the cop.

This tough talk is typical of the narrator's resilience and intelligence, but a little too tough for comfort. The cynicism about the cheerful official view of America as one unified community may be justified. When we hear it from the mouth of somebody so young, we realize that when a natural and perhaps laudable identification with the "home folks" become entangled with race, the results can be an early onset of bitterness and suspicion.

—D.H.—

EDNA O'BRIEN

Sister Imelda

In "Sister Imelda" we experience life in an Irish convent school during the 1950s. The narrator, a student in her last year at the school, describes a small, intimate community where students complain about the food, grumble about the rules, and speculate about the lives of the nuns. The story focuses on the narrator's passionate attachment to one of her teachers, Sister Imelda, and we see how their friendship is pruned to fit the expectations of a religious community that prohibits friendships between teachers and students.

O'Brien gives us a look at a closed community, where the rules are explicit and elaborate, where everyone knows everyone else's business, and where the tensions that occur in every community are heightened to a degree few of us have experienced.

QUESTIONS

1. How is the convent like other communities?

To answer this question your students will need to formulate their own definitions of "community." You might help them get started by asking everyone to make a list of at least five features that are characteristic of all communities. Then you can have them read their lists aloud and write their suggestions on the board. Of course our lists will vary, but they will generally include the following:

- The people in a community are bound by a common purpose or goal.
- Membership in a community is usually more or less voluntary.
- Communities have rules; some of those rules may be written, but members of the community know the rules even when they are unwritten.
- Most communities have a hierarchical structure, even though that structure may be established by a democratic process.
- People in a community expect to remain together for an extended period of time.
- Members of a community feel some responsibility for the welfare of other members.
- A community has obligations to its members.

After defining "community," your students will probably conclude that the convent has more in common with the communities they belong to than they might have guessed. In a number of ways the convent is surprisingly similar to a fraternity, a Girl Scout troop, a public high school, a Chamber of Commerce, a neighborhood association, or an A.A. group.

But even if the differences between the convent and other communities are differences of degree rather than kind, your students may conclude that those differences are significant. All communities have rules, but rules that forbid bathing (paragraph 73) or writing home more than once a week (paragraph 74) strike most of us as draconian. As H.D.F. Kitto remarks when he compares the atmosphere of the Greek *polis* to that of the huge modern state, "Difference of scale, when it is great enough, amounts to difference of kind."

2. How does the convent community shape Sister Imelda, the narrator, and Baba?

All of us are shaped by our membership in various communities. The greater our respect for a community, the greater its power over us. As Plato shows us in "Crito," it was Socrates' love for his community of Athens that compelled him to drink the cup of hemlock. In a similar fashion, Sister Imelda's love for her religion motivates her to accept the hardships of life in a convent. Her devotion to her community enables it to transform her appearance and behavior. She wears a long black habit and a stiff white wimple that covers her hair, eyebrows, and ears (paragraph 31). And, perhaps because she realizes that her lips are provocative, she develops "the habit of turning them inward" (paragraph 3). Sister Imelda also attempts, somewhat unsuccessfully, to restrain her passionate nature. In spite of her affection for the narrator, Sister Imelda tells her that they "must not become attached" (paragraph 50), and she asks the narrator to "avoid seeing her alone" (paragraph 79).

The narrator, whose commitment to the convent is at best tentative, is shaped but not transformed by the expectations of that community. Like the other girls, she wears a drab uniform, long black stockings that dye her legs black, and no makeup. Her thoughts and behavior, however, zigzag back and forth between conformity and rebellion. Sometimes she is drawn to religious life and seriously considers becoming a nun. At other times she resents the restrictions of convent life, particularly the prohibition against friendships between nuns and students. Her ambivalence is best demonstrated by her remembrance of returning to the convent after having her hair permed.

> Yes, the world outside was somehow declared in this perm, and for a second I remembered the scalding pain as the trickles of ammonia dribbled down my forehead and then the joy as the hairdresser said she would make me look like Movita, a Mexican star. Now suddenly that world and those aspirations seemed trite . . . (paragraph 41).

The narrator ultimately leaves the convent community, but only after it has become a permanent part of her emotional make-up.

Baba, who considers the convent a prison and remarks that "saner people were locked in the lunatic asylum" (paragraph 9), is—so far as we can tell—unchanged by her incarceration. She is an unruly prisoner. When she hungers for the Swiss roll she sees in a bakery window, she tries to cut through the glass with her nail file (paragraph 72). When she doesn't feel like participating in a mandatory walk, she sits on a wall and waits until the other girls return (paragraph 73). And even though she wears the required uniform, she boldly rolls down her socks to examine her legs for the varicose veins she expects as a result of "this bloody daily walk" (paragraph 73). Baba is an inhabitant of the community but never a member of it.

3. Does the narrator make the right decision when she decides not to return to the convent?

Most readers will be so put off by the restrictions of convent life that they will probably breathe a sigh of relief when the narrator decides to attend college in Dublin rather than return to the convent. Surely anything is better than convent life. But when we see the narrator two years later, we may reconsider. She and Baba are riding a bus to Howth to meet some businessmen who play golf there. The narrator and Baba have traded the rules of the convent for new rules. Their skins are "smothered beneath layers" of makeup that they never wash off; they never swim or sunbathe or do "anything good for" them. As the narrator explains,

> Life was geared to work and to meeting men, and yet one knew that mating could only lead to one's being a mother and hawking obstreperous children out to the seaside on Sunday. "They know not what they do" could surely be said of us.

In contrast to the convent, the world outside is depressing, superficial, and sprawling. The narrator has not consciously chosen her new life: she has accidentally become a part of a world where there is no sense of community, and where following the rules will at best lead to a goal she doesn't want to achieve.

—M.R.D.—

GRETEL EHRLICH

Wyoming: The Solace of Open Spaces

From the desperate city, Gretel Ehrlich moved to Wyoming, believing that life on a sheep ranch would produce the "numbness" she thought she wanted. The opposite occurred. Life in that unpopulated territory woke her up, and she stayed on: "The vitality of the people I was working with flushed out what had become a hallucinatory rawness inside me. I threw away my clothes and bought new ones; I cut my hair. The arid county was a clean slate. Its absolute indifference steadied me."

In this essay Ehrlich offers us an unusual definition of the term "community." Most of the other writers in this unit assume that a community is a number of people living in a fairly small geographic area, such as a convent, a city neighborhood, a suburban town, or a Greek city-state. Ehrlich challenges that notion. Wyoming's human population of 470,000, which, according to Ehrlich, is "visibly outnumbered by the animal," is spread over 98,000 square miles. (Manhattan has twenty-two square miles.) Except for six cities, the largest of which has a population of 50,000, the towns range from ten to 2000 residents and are as far as sixty miles apart. A rancher or a sheepherder may go for days or weeks without seeing another human. And yet Ehrlich claims that the Wyomingites are not merely isolated individuals; they are members of a community, a community united by common values, language, rituals, history, and a formal code of behavior.

Ehrlich's considerable talents as a poet are especially evident in her vivid descriptions of the land and the lifestyle she loves. For example, she describes the band of 2000 sheep she trails for five days across a fifty-mile stretch of Wyoming badlands: "Bunched together now and excited into a run by the storm, they drift across dry land, tumbling into draws like water and surging out again onto the rugged, choppy plateaus that are the building blocks of the state."

QUESTIONS

1. Which descriptive passages give you the clearest impression of Wyoming?

Of all the writers in this unit, Ehrlich is the most concerned with the physical environment of her community. Naturally so, because she feels that the landscape changed her personality. In contrast, when Plato (through Socrates) extols the virtues of Athens in "Crito," he tells us nothing about the physical features of that city-state.

Like the other tourists Ehrlich chides, before reading this essay, I had "driven through Wyoming, as if there were nothing to stop for" (paragraph 6). After reading Ehrlich, I went back to Wyoming to see what she had made visible to me: the "rugged, choppy plateaus that are the building blocks of this state" (paragraph 1), the canyons that "curve down like galaxies to meet the oncoming rush of flat land" (paragraph 4), a state that "seems to be the doing of a mad architect—tumbled and twisted, ribboned with faded deathbed colors, thrust up and pulled down as if the place had been startled out of a deep sleep and into a pure light" (paragraph 7). Her powerful descriptions do justice to a terrain that has promoted "individualism," "optimism," and—sometimes—insanity (paragraphs 27 and 37).

Ehrlich particularly stresses meteorological conditions. She describes the weather during each season: "Winter lasts six months here. . . . The landscape hardens into a dungeon of space" (paragraph 3). "Spring weather is capricious and mean. It snows, then blisters with heat. There have been tornadoes" (paragraph 20). Summers bring temperatures in the nineties or higher, mosquitoes, "battalions of bugs," poisonous vegetation, and sixteen-hour workdays (paragraph 36). She makes repeated references to the wind (paragraphs 1, 18, and 22), and she ends the essay by describing the star-filled sky on a night so clear and dry she can count eighteen satellites in one hour. The profusion of meteorological details reminds us that the weather, which is often no more than a source of mild irritation to suburban and city dwellers, is a matter of vital importance to the Westerner.

2. According to Ehrlich, which qualities of Wyomingites can be attributed to the effect of their surroundings?

For Ehrlich the single most important characteristic of Wyoming is its spaciousness. She makes repeated references to this quality: "open country, with its hundred-mile views," "towns, scattered across the expanse with as much as sixty miles between them," "the desolate look," "the big room of space," "the emptiness of the West," the "roominess of the state" (paragraphs 5, 9, 10, 22, 26, and 35). She titles her essay "Wyoming: The Solace of Open Spaces," and she concludes with a discussion of the healing power of space.

Given her fascination with open space, Ehrlich predictably claims that the roominess of the state has influenced nearly every aspect of its inhabitants' personalities. In fact, if she wanted to present this essay at the appropriate scholarly conference, she could retitle it: "The Solace of Empty Spaces: The Impact of Geographic Separation on the Personalities and Social Relationships of Inhabitants of the West."

Ehrlich tells us that the physical separation encourages people to "stay in touch, often driving two or three hours to another ranch for dinner" (paragraph 10), and that it has made friendliness a tradition in the West (paragraph 12). She further notes that the solitude has made Wyomingites quiet and has engendered a laconic style of speech in which "a few phrases imply a complex of meanings" (paragraph 16). She suggests that the open spaces have developed a people whose values are crystal clear, who faithfully observe "the Western Code" of behavior, and who are politically "conservative, but with a populist twist" (paragraphs 30–35). She admits that the same emptiness that some saw as a "geography of possibility" was "nightmarish" for others (paragraphs 25–26). Consequently, the land that makes some people individualistic and optimistic causes others to become hermits, go mad, commit suicide, or engage in lifelong family feuds (paragraph 37).

I'm not so sure that her thesis is logically convincing. Is it merely the immensity of the landscape that has made the people of Wyoming what they are? It seems to me that the climate, even more than the emptiness, may have shaped the character of Wyomingites. And are the people as uniformly affected by their surroundings as she implies? I suspect that there is at least as much variation among the Wyomingites as there is among the inhabitants of suburbia. Perhaps Ehrlich's "romance with this windswept state" coupled with her aesthetic appreciation of the vastness makes her more susceptible to the psychological impact than many of her neighbors. Maybe John, the sheepman called "Highpockets," is correct when he says, "Open spaces haven't affected me at all" (paragraph 5).

Your students should also note that many of the qualities Ehrlich seems to consider native to Wyoming are indigenous to other quite different societies. She tells us that people in the West are "tenderhearted about quirky behavior" (paragraph 32), but perhaps what she is observing is not a uniquely Western trait, merely the tendency of all people to feel protective rather than hostile toward the eccentrics we know well. Ask your students to think about whether any of the other characteristics Ehrlich ascribes to Wyomingites are just as likely to be found elsewhere.

3. On what principle is the essay structured?

I would not use this essay as an example of clear, straightforward organization. Unlike Boorstin in "Technology and Democracy" (*Progress and its Price*), Ehrlich does not begin by telling us where she is planning to take us and how we are going to get there. That doesn't mean that the essay is disorganized, only that the structure is organic rather than mechanical and that it is therefore somewhat more difficult to describe. Actually there are two organizational principles that structure the essay. One is cause and effect. In section 1 (paragraphs 1–7), Ehrlich overwhelms us with her description of the landscape. In section 2 she begins by explaining how the country affected her. "I had not planned to stay, but I couldn't make myself leave." And she uses the remainder of the essay to describe and analyze the impact of the wide open spaces on the other inhabitants of the area.

At the same time the essay is organized to suggest a seasonal progression. In the opening sentence Ehrlich tells us, "It's May . . . ." After reflecting briefly on the winter that has just ended (paragraph 3), she moves us forward to spring in paragraph 20. We learn about summer in paragraph 36, and we complete the cycle with autumn in paragraph 39.

4. Are the ranchers, sheepherders, and cowhands who live in Wyoming isolated individuals or members of a community?

You might want to begin this discussion by asking your students to list the essential characteristics of a community. Of course, your students' answers will vary according to their definitions of community, but at least they will be obliged to formulate a definition. According to the ancient Greeks, Wyomingites would not be members of a community. The ancient Greeks defined a community as a relatively small group of people who live in proximity and focus their attention on the affairs of the community. Certainly, Aristotle, who said that a man who chooses to live apart from the polis is either a god or a wild animal, would not have believed that such isolated existences could comprise a meaningful society.

The community Ehrlich describes is based on something other than geographic closeness. She observes that there is a "coziness to living in this state," that "ranchers . . . know each other statewide," that "people stay in touch, often driving two or three hours to another ranch for dinner," and that the people are united by a shared system of values, by a laconic style of language that is almost a private code, by "private histories [that] are largely public knowledge," and by their appreciation of Wyoming's vast open spaces. Although the ancient Greeks and some contemporary urban and suburban residents would say that the solitary Wyomingite is deprived of all the benefits community life should offer—theaters, shopping centers, police protection, friends who live nearby, and the opportunity to actively participate in local government, Ehrlich would counter that the residents of Wyoming are not deprived of the only benefit that is essential—the sense of connection with other people. When a man rushing to the doctor with half his foot cut off thinks to shut a neighbor's gate (paragraph 33), he must be living in a community.

—M.R.D.—

Style Lesson 20: Metaphors Supported by Word Choices

Paragraph 20 of "Wyoming" contains four stunning metaphors, each supported by surrounding language. To appreciate these metaphors fully, fill in the blanks in the passage below, paying special attention to the capitalized words:

Spring weather is capricious and mean. It snows, then blisters with heat. There have been tornadoes. They lay their ELEPHANT TRUNKS out in the sage until they find houses, then _____ everything up and leave. I've noticed that melting snowbanks _____ and rot, VIPEROUS, then drip into calm pools where ducklings hatch and livestock, being trailed to summer range, drink. With the ice cover gone, rivers CHURN a ______ BROWN, taking culverts and small bridges with them. Water in such an arid place (the average annual rainfall where I live is less than eight inches) is like ______. It festoons drab land with green VEINS; a line of cottonwoods following a stream; a strip of alfalfa; and on ditchbanks, wild asparagus growing.

ANZIA YEZIERSKA

America and I

Other pieces in this unit describe communities such as families or neighborhoods, but "America and I" examines one of the largest and most heterogeneous communities imaginable—the United States. In this thinly disguised autobiographical story, Yezierska, a Jewish Russian immigrant, describes her struggle to become a part of her adopted community. Although the story was written in 1915 and deals with incidents that occurred near the turn of the century, it poses a difficult question that America, the nation of immigrants, has yet to answer: What, if anything, do those of us whose ancestors came here generations ago owe to those of us who are newly arrived?

QUESTIONS

1. If this piece were included in all high school American history texts, how might it change our understanding of the typical immigrant experience?

In many ways this piece reinforces the flag-waving view presented by old-fashioned history books. Here we have an immigrant who is grateful to be in America, who is willing to do menial labor, who struggles to learn the language, and who takes advantage of every opportunity to better herself. Even our glimpse of the dark side—the exploitation of immigrant workers by unscrupulous employers—is consistent with the traditional view that immigrants soon become "Americanized" and move up from sweat shops to better jobs.

However, the story also challenges our stereotype of the immigrant as a person who wants nothing more than the opportunity to work in "a light, airy factory, only eight hours a day" (paragraph 57). This narrator is not content to spend her life sewing shirtwaists. Conventional wisdom has it that first generation immigrants should resign themselves to mining coal, laundering clothes, or picking tomatoes, comforted by the knowledge that their sacrifice will enable their children or grandchildren to attend college and rise above their working-class origins. Most native-born Americans casually accept the possibility that immigrants may spend their lives doing work that is neither financially rewarding nor intellectually challenging. For example, in "What's So Bad About Being Poor?" Charles Murray notes that when hundreds of thousands of immigrants came to America at the end of World War II and again after the Vietnam War, lawyers and professors had to take menial jobs. He then matter-of-factly observes, "Sometimes they worked their way up and out, but many had to remain janitors and factory workers, because they came here too late in life to retool their foreign-trained skills."

Readers who consider such situations unfortunate but inevitable may be surprised to learn that some immigrants are not willing to sacrifice themselves for future generations, and that some believe their new country owes them more than mere subsistence.

2. What is it that the narrator wants from America? Are her expectations realistic? Why or why not?

This question should lead you to the larger issues of what an immigrant or any person can justifiably expect from his or her community and vice versa. The narrator tells us that she was not satisfied with an opportunity to work for a living; she wanted to work for love (paragraph 47). And she suggests to the vocational guidance counselor that America should provide free boarding-schools for immigrants so they will have a chance to discover and develop their special talents. She reasons that a country that does not allow its people to contribute the best that is within them loses "all that richness of the soul" (paragraph 109).

Although her logic is sound, it's not likely that Congress will allocate funds for such boarding schools. As a nation we have not yet found a way to guarantee every person work of any kind, certainly not work that is intellectually challenging or emotionally satisfying. In fact, more and more people hold jobs that occupy the "hands," but not the "head" and the "feelings" (paragraph 63). Although this essay was written seventy-five years ago, Yezierska describes a problem that continues to make headlines.

3. What is the author's tone in the final paragraph?

It's difficult to know what to make of Yezierska's closing paragraph. During the course of the essay, her attitude toward America undergoes major changes. At first she is naively optimistic, confident that she will have the opportunity to "be a creator, a giver, a human being" (paragraph 6). Later, after her work experiences and her conversation with the vocational guidance counselor, she becomes disillusioned and bitter, and she sees her future as a "long desert of wasting days of drudgery" (paragraph 100). Later still, her study of the pilgrims renews her faith by revealing America as "a world still in the making" (paragraph 107), a country that can be changed and improved by the contributions of "the last comer" (paragraph 107). Near the end, she voices her conflicting feelings—joy brought by her own success as a writer and sadness occasioned by her realization that others "[waste] their days in drudgery they hate" (paragraph 110).

It is this ambivalence that makes the closing sentence a mystery. If that sentence had followed paragraph 109, which is just brimming with hope, it would seem to be a prophecy confidently describing what her adopted country *will* be. But following paragraph 110, with its bleak description of the fate of most immigrants, the closing sentence becomes a plea, beseeching the reader to make America what it *should* be.

4. How does the narrator attempt to become a part of America? How are her efforts similar to or different from your own efforts to become a member of a new community?

This question should lead to a discussion of how people become members of a new community. When the narrator arrives in America, she has "no speech, no common language, no way to win a smile of understanding" (paragraph 8) from the Americans who surround her. She knows that even her clothes identify her as a foreigner: "The outside of me still branded me for a steerage immigrant" (paragraph 18). She remedies this situation by getting a job, earning wages, and buying American clothes. But even after her clothes make her look American, she does not yet feel American (paragraph 58). Next she learns English (paragraph 65), joins the Women's Association (paragraph 72), and goes for vocational counseling (paragraph 78), but still she feels isolated: "Between my soul and the American soul were worlds of difference that no words could bridge over" (paragraph 101). Eventually she studies American history to understand how the pilgrim experience shaped the "American soul" and she decides to become a writer so she can explain the "Russian soul" to her compatriots: "I began to build a bridge of understanding between the American-born and myself" (paragraph 108).

All of your students will know what it's like to join a new community. Some may have lived in different countries, and even those who are attending college in the town where they were born have experienced entry into a new academic community. In all likelihood, most will recall their first efforts to fit in by adopting the standards for dress, hair style, and speech. And most will agree that looking like a member of the group isn't enough. Unlike the narrator, however, your students probably didn't read textbooks to learn about their new community, and they probably didn't become writers to explain themselves. Yet they somehow found a way to develop the mutual understanding that is essential to members of a community.

—M.R.D.—

MAYA ANGELOU

My Sojourn in the Lands of My Ancestors

Being a traveler in a foreign country gives a person a fresh perspective on what it means to belong to a community. Angelou's essay has special insights and a special poignancy because she is a traveler in a double sense. If she ignores her ancestral history, she is an American visiting Ghana and trying to overcome the isolation caused by differences in language and culture. If she considers her ancestry, her historical "journey" has been to America, and she is now returning, after a long stay (or captivity), to her African home. Under these circumstances, being accepted into a community as Angelou is accepted into the Ghanaian village of Dunkwa may have an emotional significance far greater than that of a Ghanaian traveler who finds herself accepted into the life of an American town.

The essay ends with Angelou reminding us that she was not a Bambara after all, and that she was accepted into the community only by assuming a false identity: she passed for a Bambara just as many African-Americans have passed for white. Yet her essay does not end in despair. In the rootless society America is becoming, "home" is often a makeshift, jury-rigged thing. Belonging briefly in a community of family, friends, or neighbors—as Angelou did in Dunkwa—may be the best that we can hope for. But that we *can* belong makes all the difference in the world.

It is worth noting that Angelou may not have fooled the villagers completely. Our friend Maxwell Boafo, a well-educated Ghanaian who translated Fanti phrases for us, tells us that *Bambara* is not only the name of a Nigerian tribe, but a word commonly used by Ghanaians to refer to any stranger (apparently because strangers are so often Bambara). Thus "Bambara Auntie" might be translated as "Aunt Stranger"—a paradox the people of Dunkwa seem to relish.

QUESTIONS

1. To what communities does Angelou seem to belong, and how thorough is this belonging?

Discussion of this question might produce a list on the chalkboard and will certainly produce some discussion of the complexity and ambiguity of our sense of community. Here are some items that may appear on the list:

- The tiny community of Angelou's immediate family—herself and her son. This community is not as snug as she might have wished, apparently. The son is "increasingly distant."
- The "circle of black American friends" she made in Ghana. Apparently, this is not a complete enough community to satisfy any of its members: they all long for the "place the heart could call home."
- The African-American community generally. Her membership in this community is announced in the opening paragraphs by her recitation of words from two spirituals sung by black American slaves. Your students need to notice two things about her belonging to this community: 1) that it is an act of imagination and 2) that it links the living with the dead. By seeing herself as part of the African-American community, she becomes connected with the slaves imprisoned in Cape Coast Castle long ago. These slaves may or may not have been her lineal ancestors (notice "unknown" in paragraph 8), but they are spiritually her "grandfathers" and "grandmothers." In a sense, Angelou's feeling of inclusion in this community must be very strong, since a visit to the castle reduces her to tears.
- The African-American community of Stamps, Arkansas, which Angelou treats as a simple subset of #3, but which provides her with a very concrete, personal picture of how a true community will rally to the sup-

port of one of its members (paragraphs 50–54). This is a community Angelou has left physically, but clearly still carries in her mind.

- The community of Africans-by-race everywhere. This Pan-African identity, like #3, is an imaginative and historical one, since genes alone can't create a community. Some black Americans who are uneasy with the label African-American might say that identification with Africa is a sentimental, romantic fantasy—nostalgia for a past the individual never experienced. Nonetheless, it has emotional power for many people; every appeal to every "old country" does, and in the case of African-Americans, the link to Africa is strengthened by our national fixation on skin color.
- The community of Dunkwa, about which we will say more after the next questions. Here the attachment is fleeting, and fleetingly very important.

One advantage of getting students to list the various communities to which Angelou belongs is that it may help them consider their various communities, tight and loose, imaginative and physical, and how these communities have affected them.

I, for example, would say that I am more a midwesterner than an academic, though both communities have their pull. I would be a midwesterner if I lived in San Francisco, and this identification would show (I think) in what one of my friends calls a "resistance to innovation" but what I prefer to think of as "imperviousness to fashion." But, because I grew up in Oklahoma and have my deepest family roots there, I might say that I am more Oklahoman than midwestern. Among other things, this makes me a shirttail member of a community that, for two or three generations back, lived in daily contact with Indians from the reservations around Anadarko. Somehow I suspect that the Oklahoma legacy keeps whispering to me that the advance of history is not entirely benign.

2. What are the signs that Angelou has found acceptance in Dunkwa?

The aim here is to get students to think about the little rituals by which one's acceptance into a community are marked. When the "old man" (Kobina) says "Foriwa, we have a guest. Bring beer," Angelou has been accepted into a status where outright suspicion, at least, is dropped. When he tells her to hand over her car keys so that someone can bring her bag, she is at a stage of trust that is rarely achieved so quickly in America: "I was either at home with friends or I would die wishing that to be so." When Patience Duodu takes her to the bathhouse and the women joke with her about the shape of her breasts and about her having only one child, and when the children of the household call her "Bambara Auntie," she seems to have become at least "a friend of the family." You may want your students to consider how rare it is in America for someone to be accepted so fully so quickly. Students might write interesting essays about occasions when they have found themselves accepted by a family or community with unaccustomed swiftness and about what gestures or words marked their acceptance.

3. Why is Angelou's acceptance in Dunkwa so important to her?

In the introduction, Angelou explains that while in Ghana, she "became a hunter for that elusive and much longed-for place the heart could call home." Your students should see that she has some personal reasons for this search. She is in a strange land, her marriage has broken up, her son is increasingly distant from her. She thinks of herself as linked to her African neighbors by common ancestry, but her attempts to make friends with them are "often rebuffed." Her loneliness permeates the opening paragraphs of the essay. She is driving alone in her car, watching people sing and shout together from the crowded trucks. She is alone thinking about Cape Coast Castle and attempting to understand the experiences of her ancestors. In paragraphs 8–13, she is a woman sitting alone in a car parked on the shoulder of the road, crying so hard that she can't see. The stage has been set for any experience that will break her isolation.

But the experience at Dunkwa is a particularly rich one because it not only connects Angelou directly with the people of a particular village, it connects her indirectly with other communities for which she is longing. Acceptance in this village is symbolically acceptance by all of Africa and so a healing of the old separation caused by slavery. The shared custom of bringing food to help a neighbor with an unexpected guest reconnects Angelou with the community of black Americans, and particularly her home community of Stamps, Arkansas: "I felt the distance narrow between my past and present" (paragraph 49). And the experience of being infolded by a family, surrounded by adults who call her "sister" and children who call her "Auntie" compensates for the troubles in her own family.

—D.H.—

Style Lesson 21:
Word Choice

Identify which word in each bracketed pair in the following passage (paragraph 12 of "My Sojourn in the Land of My Ancestors") is preferable. Be prepared to justify your choices.

I allowed the [people/shapes] to come to my [imagination/mind]; children passed, tied together by ropes and chains, tears abashed, [stumbling/walking] in [complete/a dull] exhaustion, then women, hair [disheveled/uncombed], bodies [gritted/covered] with sand, and [sagging/accordioning] in defeat. Men, muscles without memory, minds [enervated/dimmed], [marching/plodding], leaving bloodied footprints in the dirt. The quiet was awful. None of them cried, or yelled, or [bellowed/wailed]. No moans came from them. They lived in a [hushed/mute] territory, [without/dead to] feeling and protest. These were the [legions/many], sold by [their own people/sisters], stolen by brothers, bought by strangers, enslaved by the greedy, and betrayed by history.

Among the considerations that surely affected Angelou's choices was the desire to present a vision of troubled ghosts in hellish torment rather than a flat documentary view of enslaved people.

N. SCOTT MOMADAY

The Way to Rainy Mountain

There is a tendency among composition teachers (based, perhaps, on a misreading of James Britton) to see the personal experience essay as inherently simpler than more objective, analytical writing. "The Way to Rainy Mountain" should disabuse us of all such notions. The essay deals simultaneously with three levels of experience: the immediate impression of a landscape, the individual experience of a man whose grandmother has died, and the collective experience of a people who have been stripped of their identity. The great images of the story bring all three planes of experience together, as in paragraph 14, where Momaday, sitting on the stone steps of his grandmother's house on a moonlit night, sees a cricket: "My line of vision was such that the creature filled the moon like a fossil. It had gone there, I thought, to live and die, for there of all places, was its small definition made whole and eternal. A warm wind rose up and purled like the longing within me."

The passage is moving even in isolation, but when we are prepared for it by the rest of the essay it gains force. The solitary cricket outlined in the moon is almost a summary of Momaday's description of the dry, open land; it is also a mirror of Momaday's feeling of solitude in his grandmother's empty house and his grief, not just for her passing but for the passing of the Kiowa way of life he knew through her.

QUESTIONS

1. What is the function of the images of solitude that recur throughout the essay?

In the opening paragraph Momaday sets the tone for the essay with these images: "A single knoll rises out of the plain. . . . All things in the plain are isolate; there is no confusion of objects in the eye, but *one* hill or *one* tree or *one* man." In paragraph 10 he describes his memories of his grandmother. In each she is a solitary figure: "standing at the wood stove," "sitting at the south window," "going out upon a cane," and "praying." In paragraph 14 he returns to his grandmother's empty house, alone on the prairie, and sees the single cricket that fills the moon. And in the final scene, he visits his grandmother's grave and then looks back once at the mountain.

The images are appropriate for all three levels of experience that the essay deals with: (1) as a description of a majestic but barren landscape that dwarfs the humans who dwell there, (2) as an account of Momaday's personal feelings of loneliness and his sense of loss when he returns to his grandmother's house after her death, and (3) as a reminder of his grandmother's symbolic role as the last of the Kiowas. The images tie the essay together.

There are only two scenes that describe a group of people. In paragraphs 12 and 13 Momaday recalls the happy days of his childhood when his grandmother's house was filled with the sounds of "a lot of coming and going, feasting and talk." In those days, when there were enough of the old Kiowas to "come to remind and be reminded of who they were," there were "a lot of good things to eat, a lot of laughter and surprise." The other group scene is of the last time the Kiowas came together as "a living Sun Dance culture" but were dispersed by a company of soldiers (paragraph 9). In the final scene the Kiowas are reduced to "ancestral names" on "dark stones" in the cemetery.

2. What makes the essay more than just the story of an individual whose grandmother has died?

On one level the essay is the moving story of Momaday's attempt to come to terms with his sense of personal loss, a loss that would be the same even if Aho had been his sister or cousin or friend rather than his grandmother. To deal with his private sorrow, he makes a journey to his grandmother's grave and to her now-empty home, and he remembers the experiences he once shared with her. But the essay is dramatically stronger because, on another level, it is an account of the end of an era. Aho was more than a relative; she was a conduit to the past. She knew the legends of the Kiowas (paragraph 8), she could see "perfectly in [her] mind's eye" land viewed by the Kiowas as they migrated from the high country in western Montana almost three centuries earlier: "The immense landscape of the continental interior lay like memory in her blood" (paragraph 5). As a child she had taken part in the annual Sun Dances, and she had witnessed the deicide that occurred on the last such occasion. When she died, Momaday lost a grandmother, and he also lost his one contact with his cultural heritage. Momaday's visit to Aho's grave is a tribute to an individual he loved; his 1,500-mile pilgrimage across the country traversed by the migrating Kiowas is a tribute to the noble people his grandmother represented.

In some senses Momaday's experience of being cut off from his past is not as unique as it first seems. Although no other group in America has been dispossessed in the way the Native Americans were, their buffalo slaughtered, their land stolen, their religious ceremonies prohibited, all American immigrant groups have, to some extent, been destroyed by assimilation. As Alvin Toffler pointed out in *Future Shock*, the only constant in the modern world is change. No twentieth-century inhabitants of the Western world grow up in the world our grandparents knew or in the world our own grandchildren will know. As each generation passes, their descendants lose their link to their heritage.

3. What is Momaday's attitude toward the Kiowas?

Momaday respects the Kiowas, but he doesn't idealize them. He proudly states that "they were among the finest horsemen the world has ever known," and he describes them as "a lordly and dangerous society of fighters and thieves, hunters and priests of the sun" (paragraphs 3 and 4). He recognizes the weaknesses that made it impossible for them to survive as the kind of people that they were: "But warfare for the Kiowas was preeminently a matter of disposition rather than of survival, and they never understood the grim, unrelenting advance of the U.S. Cavalry" (paragraph 3). Although Momaday understands that their inability to organize for all-out warfare led to their downfall, he seems to like them the better for it.

Momaday most admires the Kiowas' relationship to nature. He tells us that his grandmother "had a reverence for the sun, a holy regard that now is all but gone out of mankind" (paragraph 9). He explains that, according to Kiowa legend, the stars of the Big Dipper are their "kinsmen in the night sky" (paragraph 8). And when he describes Devil's Tower in the Black Hills, Momaday states that "because they could not do otherwise, [the Kiowas] made a legend at the base of the rock." The Kiowas' view of nature is far removed from the attitude Brophy presents in "The Menace of Nature" *(Nature and Civilization).* It is difficult to imagine that a proud Kiowan warrior would have invented a wooden leg or deigned to use it. Momaday is not advocating a return to the old ways, but he is sorry that we have so completely lost all the good attributes of an admirable group of people.

—M.R.D.—

Style Lesson 22: A Sentence With Parallel Subparts

Combine the following sentences into one, using one colon and three semicolons (as Momaday does in paragraph 10 of "The Way to Rainy Mountain"). The exercise should help sharpen your skills at parallel sentence construction. You will, of course, have to change wording slightly to combine the sentences.

Now I can have her only in memory. I see my grandmother in the several postures. These were peculiar to her. I see her standing at the wood stove on a winter morning. I see her turning meat in a great iron skillet. I see her sitting at the south window. She is bent above her beadwork. I see her sitting there afterwards. Her vision had failed. She looked down for a very long time into the fold of her hands. I see her going out upon a cane. She went very slowly as she did when the weight of age came upon her. I see her praying.

H. D. F. KITTO

The Polis

Because textbooks tend to be homogenized products, many college students have never been exposed to prose that is both academic and spirited and may think that it is a beast seldom seen, like the Loch Ness monster. Kitto's chapter will give them at least a glimpse of the beast. It does its scholarly business thoroughly, defining the polis in a way that must be intellectually interesting even to classicists but is also clear to laypeople. In the process, it uses primary sources very well: Homer, Aristotle, Plato, Sophocles, Aristophanes, Aeschylus, Thucydides. It is, in short, the term paper grown up, and I would want my students to see it as one model for their own academic writing.

I'm not sure that every teacher will agree that Kitto is a safe model. The chapter is full of memorable sentences, quips, and—what may be surprising to your students—emotion. Kitto really *feels* that the polis gave its citizens a more vivid and comprehensive life than our modern city or state can. Without reducing his scholarship to bathos or soap-box antics, he manages to make us feel what we miss by not living in fifth-century Athens. Since not only students but professors sometimes expect academic prose to be duller and more homogenized, Kitto may be a more dangerous model than the average contributor to a scholarly journal. But safety isn't everything.

Kitto's eagerness not only to describe the Greek polis, but to praise it, means that he is writing a prescription for a good community. His essay can, therefore, provide a standard that can be held beside the various communities described in this unit, including the convent in "Sister Imelda" and the neighborhood in "The Hammer Man."

QUESTIONS

1. How is this essay organized? Can it be neatly outlined? What are the major elements?

Not the most fascinating question, but one that may be important if you ask your students to do any sort of comparable assignment (a definition paper, for example).

I think that there is a neat and even predictable outline beneath the chapter's surface. We can imagine, in fact, what Kitto's original scratch outline may have looked like.

Definition of Polis

1. introduction
2. origin and development
3. size
4. geographical meaning
5. communitarian meaning
6. cultural meaning
7. religious meaning
8. conclusion

Something like this is the almost automatic outline of a trained academic mind. With the exception of #3, it is a fairly accurate representation of the shape the finished essay takes. But in an outline of the finished essay, #3 would appear twice, once interrupting another section:

Section	*Paragraphs*
1. introduction	1
2. origin and development	2–3
3. SIZE	4–6
2. origin and development	7–16
4. geographical meaning	17–18
5. communitarian meaning	19–21
3. SIZE	23–24
6. cultural meaning	25–27
7. religious meaning	29–33
8. conclusion	34–36

Is the unruly intrusion of #3 evidence that Kitto is out of control? Of course not, but I think it is a good example of the relation between the plannable and the non-plannable elements in composition. Aware that the element of size was the crucial one for a modern audience accustomed to "states so big that they have to go by their initials," he introduced it (intuitively, surely) in the places best suited to emphasis, letting any rigid outline bend to his rhetorical needs.

2. Is the purpose of this essay to inform or to persuade?

Or, to put the same question another way, is Kitto giving us an objective definition of the polis or an argument that the polis is preferable to the modern state? Your students should see that Kitto is doing both. If they don't, you might point them to paragraphs 23 and 24, which are fairly representative. When your students read through them, they should see that a good deal of information is given: clear exposition of the smaller scale of Greek life, plus the concrete examples of liturgical taxation and the execution of incompetent commanders. All these things are informative in the most obvious sense: they could be grist for the mill of multiple-choice exams. But who can read the paragraphs without noticing the implicit indictment of modern institutions? In modern life "'work for the community,: though an admirable sentiment, "is to most of us vague and flabby." In modern life the wealthy taxpayer says of his taxes, "There! *That*'s gone down the drain!" In modern life the incompetent commander who sends young men to their deaths faces only "diffused and harmless popular indignation." Kitto wants more than modern life offers, and he wants us to want more.

3. What less attractive aspects of Greek life does Kitto gloss over?

Kitto certainly never denies the existence of slavery in Greece, but he reports it without great emphasis. He seems similarly untroubled by the position of women, whom Aristotle, for instance, tends to group with slave and oxen. We may be disturbed that only one resident in ten is a citizen; Kitto is not.

But perhaps in the context of this chapter, he needn't be. Is his assertion that the intimacy of the polis is preferable to the anonymity of the modern state really affected by the existence of these inequalities? Perhaps not. With technology replacing human labor, the modern polis could presumably free the slaves and extend citizenship to women.

4. What keeps modern cities from being *poleis*?

I suppose that the short answer could be a simple government lesson: cities today are not independent political units, but parts of nations. But why is this so? A good question, I think, for a longish paper—particularly if you urge your students to use details of modern life as effectively as Kitto uses details of Greek life. Among the many answers that follow rather naturally from the reading are

- We don't live in the sort of power vacuum the Greeks enjoyed and so must band together in larger political units to resist the aggression of other large political units. But this argument has grown weaker of late.
- Fewer and fewer of us will live our entire lives in the cities of our births; we don't have time to develop loyalty to the polis.
- We are caught up in economic webs too large to encourage the independence of small cities and in technological webs that break down geographic separation.
- Our public lives are largely economic; for non-economic things we look to the private life. (That is, by the way, very nearly Thoreau's definition of a proper relation between the individual and society.) The Greek was very different: "In the winning of his livelihood he was essentially an individualist; in the filling of his life he was essentially communist."

—D.H.—

Style Lesson 23:
A Memorable Analogy

In paragraph 6 of "The Polis," Kitto introduces a memorable analogy that shows his preference for the small Greek city-state rather than modern states "so big that they have to be referred to by their initials." With the help of a classmate, fill in the blanks, then discuss the effectiveness of the analogy: is it precise? does it clarify Kitto's attitude? does it change the reader's attitude?

The modern writer is sometimes heard to speak with splendid scorn of "those petty Greek states, with their interminable quarrels." quite so; Plataea, Sicyon, Aegina and the rest are petty, compared with modern states. The _____ itself is petty, compared with _____—but then, the atmosphere of _____ is mainly _____, and that makes a difference. We do not like breathing _____—and the Greeks would not much have liked breathing the atmosphere of the vast modern State. They knew of one such, the Persian Empire—and thought it very suitable, for _____.

PLATO

Crito

In "Crito" Plato explains why Socrates chose to die rather than disregard the laws of his community, Athens. Socrates, who wrote nothing himself, spent his life in the marketplace and the *gymnasia* talking to the citizens, persuading "old and young alike, not to take thought for [their] persons or [their] properties, but first and chiefly to care about the greatest improvement of the soul." His criticism of Athenian democracy led to his arrest and trial in 399 on the specious charge of "impiety," specifically "corruption of the young" and "neglect of the gods whom the city worships and the practice of religious novelties." After Socrates was tried, found guilty, and sentenced to die, his friend Crito came to him in prison to attempt to convince him to escape. It is their conversation that is recreated in "Crito."

Plato, who was 29 when Socrates died, had known the older philosopher from boyhood. Because Plato wrote in the dialogue form, frequently using Socrates as the central speaker, there is a great deal of scholarly disagreement as to whether certain ideas presented by Socrates in the dialogues should be attributed to Socrates, Plato, or both. My own assumption is that in this dialogue, Plato is talking for himself through Socrates' mouth.

This essay offers an interesting contrast to "Letter from Birmingham Jail" (*Insiders and Outsiders*), in which Martin Luther King, Jr. advocates disobeying unjust laws. Plato, on the other hand, comes close to saying that there is no such thing as an unjust law, that the good of the nation is always more important than the good of the individual, and that it is the duty of the citizen to die rather than disobey.

QUESTIONS

1. Why does Socrates choose not to escape?

According to Plato, Socrates drinks the hemlock because he believes in unflinching obedience to his country's laws. Plato has Socrates tell Crito that their "country is more to be valued and higher and holier far more than mother or father or any ancestor" (paragraph 88) and that "a person must do what his city and his country order him; or he must change their view of what is just" (paragraph 88). For Plato, political stability is far more significant than the welfare of any one person.

That viewpoint is clearly expressed in Plato's later work "The Republic." In that dialogue Plato describes the form of government he thinks most capable of providing justice: a rigidly stratified totalitarian society. The lowest class, the general population, is to be composed of people interested primarily in gratifying their appetites (consumers?). These workers are to receive little or no education and are to spend their lives producing. The middle or soldier class is to be drawn from people of spirit. Because their duty is to protect the state, they are to be taught gymnastics and music to make them both strong and gentle. The ruling class, the philosopher-kings, are to be people dominated by their intellects. Naturally, they are to be trained in philosophy. According to Plato, if society were ruled by benevolent, wise, selfless guardians, there would be no unjust laws. Although I don't like the utopia Plato describes, I can understand why a man who saw Athenian democracy fall apart, and who watched a democracy condemn Socrates, his friend and his teacher, would not be a liberal democrat.

It is important that your students see that the state's superiority to the individual citizen is the central tenet of "Crito"—in effect its thesis. But whose thesis is it? To answer this question, your students need to read critically, to divorce the author Plato from the subject Socrates. Remind them that the dialogue is not a literal transcription of conversation; it is Plato's presentation of his own political position.

I think Plato's political views led him to put into Socrates' mouth words that are inconsistent with Socrates' own actions. Personally, I can't believe that Socrates would have said that a citizen is "a child and slave" of the laws and should thus obey all laws unquestioningly. At least twice in his life Socrates refused to obey unjust commands. In 405, after the Battle of Arginusae, the Assembly tried and condemned six generals as a group rather than separately as the law required. As a member of the Council of 500, Socrates vociferously opposed that unconstitutional condemnation of the generals. In 404 the oligarchy of the Thirty Tyrants ordered Socrates and four other men to bring in Leon the Salaminian so that he could be put to death. The other four obeyed, but Socrates went home. His disobedience probably would have cost him his life if the counterrevolution had not occurred the next year. In the "Apology" Socrates explains those acts: "I made up my mind that I would run the risk, having law and justice with me, rather than take part in . . . injustice because I feared imprisonment and death."

But Socrates did drink the hemlock. If he wasn't acting out of absolute loyalty to the state, why did he turn down an opportunity to escape? Socrates may have been motivated by practical considerations. As he told the court, he preferred death to exile. To help your students understand why he felt so strongly, you may want to refer them to "The Polis," in which H.D.F. Kitto explains that for the ancient Greeks the polis was "more than a state, a nation, or a people: [it was] a way of life. . . ." Consequently, moving from Athens to another city such as Thebes would have meant giving up everything Socrates valued—the city he had proudly called home for seventy years; his Athenian citizenship (an honor some Athenians valued so highly that they had it inscribed on their tombstones); his friends; and the government, laws, culture, and religion of his country. In addition, Socrates may have assumed that if he left Athens, he would be compelled to wander endlessly from one city to another because he would continue to teach the young and be driven out by their fathers. Unlike Gretel Ehrlich's Wyomingites, Socrates could not have lived in isolation. For him the daily discourse about virtue, the dialogue with others who sought wisdom, and the give and take that tests ideas, were as essential as breathing.

Yet another consideration was Socrates' concern that the friends who aided his escape would have been driven into exile and deprived of their citizenship and property. As a man who refused to harm even his enemies ("Then we ought not to retaliate or render evil to any one, whatever evil you may have suffered from him" —paragraph 81), Socrates could not sacrifice his friends to save himself. Finally, and probably most important, Socrates feared that his flight would be seen as a repudiation of all that he had taught, as an admission that "the many" could force him to commit a dishonorable act.

Plato tells us that Socrates died rather than disobey the law. If that is true, Martin Luther King, Jr., was wrong to consider Socrates a champion of civil disobedience. However, what we know of Socrates' life indicates that he was a man who, regardless of the consequences, followed his conscience. When he told the court that he would rather die than "cease from the practice of teaching of philosophy," he, like King centuries later, expressed his willingness to accept the penalty for breaking an unjust law. I agree with King's assessment: "To a degree academic freedom is a reality today because Socrates practiced civil disobedience" ("Letter from Birmingham Jail").

2. Does Plato's decision to write this essay in dialogue form make it more or less effective?

Rather than structure this essay as a conventional argument, Plato presents it as a dialogue between Socrates and his good friend Crito. The advantage of the dialogue format is that it gives Plato the opportunity to present two opposing views in a dramatic form. He adds suspense by creating the illusion that the final outcome is undecided. We don't know until the closing paragraphs whether Socrates will drink the hemlock. Even if we know that Socrates never loses an argument, our curiosity may compel us to read the entire essay to find out how he refutes Crito's very persuasive opening arguments. (You will disgrace your friends, make orphans of your children, and appear to be "choosing the easier part, not the better and manlier"—paragraph 32.)

Nevertheless, I've never been fond of Plato's dialogue form. I wish I could read Greek, because those who do read it claim that the stylistic differences between the speakers help to distinguish them and develop their characters. Apparently, we lose all that in the translation, and the conversations frequently sound stiff, stilted, and awkward. At the beginning of "Crito" Crito gets a few good lines: "Now, can there be a worse disgrace than this—that I should be thought to value money more than the life of a friend?" (paragraph 26). "No man should bring children into the world who is unwilling to persevere to the end in their nurture and education" (paragraph 32). The content of the sentences, if not the language, gives us clues as to Crito's personality, but after the first three pages, Crito is allowed only one-sentence responses such as "Certainly," "Certainly not," "Clearly so," "True," and his superfluous concluding remark, "I have nothing to say, Socrates." I find those lines either annoying or comic (depending on my mood, I suppose). I admire the skill required to advance an argument through questions and answers, but I don't enjoy the form.

3. Do you accept all the premises underlying Socrates' argument?

The purpose of this question is to make your students see how Plato's argument works. I am obviously not a philosopher. When I read Descartes, I agree with him, and when I read Hume, or Kant, or Nietzsche, or Sartre, I agree with them. The problem, of course, is that once we accept certain premises, we arrive at foregone conclusions. Probably a few of your students will find that, like Crito, although they are unable to find flaws in Socrates' logic, they are dissatisfied with the outcome of the dialogue. If you encourage them to examine some of the premises, they should better understand why that occurred. Here are a few that you may wish to point out:

- "[N]ot life, but a good life, is to be chiefly valued" (paragraph 61). At first this statement seems to be a truism; however, it is actually a highly controversial statement that is at the center of the controversy about euthanasia.
- "[N]either injury nor retaliation nor warding off evil by evil is ever right" (paragraph 81). A sentiment that is easy to agree with but not so easy to live by. Except for Gandhi, few people even try.
- A citizen is the "child and slave" of the law and is "not on equal terms" with them (paragraph 89). The signers of the Declaration of Independence would have disagreed vehemently.
- Because the "duty of educating one's children" is "only the doctrine of the multitude" (paragraph 65), it is not worthy of consideration. Plato is simply sidestepping a difficult question here. It is hardly logical to suppose that the multitude is always wrong.

—M.R.D.—

CHARLES MURRAY

What's So Bad About Being Poor?

John Kenneth Galbraith ("How to Get the Poor Off Our Conscience") would perhaps remind us that Murray's argument belongs to the long tradition of blaming poor individuals rather than the economic system and its movers for the existence of poverty. But Murray's argument contains something that is quite fresh and that comes directly from his Peace Corps experience: he is able to compare the poverty of America's underclass with the poverty of a culture virtually without money. This comparison allows him to escape the funhouse world of economic statistics that can be interpreted every which way (a world he knows well) to some more fundamental questions about the quality of life.

Some students may think that this is a leap out of the frying pan and into the fire: economic statistics, after all, are something "real," and Murray's thought experiment about what it would be like for him to live in Thailand or the South Bronx is pure speculation. We'll deal with this issue in question one.

Whatever we may make of Murray's intellectual methods, he has produced a provocative essay challenging the conventional wisdom equating poverty and misery. His argument anticipates some themes students will encounter in the Progress unit, particularly in essays by Henry David Thoreau, Jomo Kenyatta, and Alice Bloom. For one of the champions of today's conservatism to find himself in such company shows that economics can create strange bedfellows.

QUESTIONS

1. What is the function of the thought experiments Murray uses in his essay?

There appear to me to be three experiments: life in the Thai village, life in the South Bronx, and the choosing of surrogate parents. Your students may count as many as five, since the last two are given with variations.

Of the surrogate parent experiment, Murray says it is "set up not to be realistic, but to evoke something about how you think" (paragraph 22). It is, in short, a values-clarification exercise. So, really, are the other two. Murray makes it clear in paragraph 9 that his rendition of life in a Thai village does not portray the situation in an average community in Southeast Asia. He has picked a nearly idyllic case because he wants to push a line of thought to the extreme and get us to see if we can imagine *any* situation where we could live contentedly in poverty. For most people, his experiment surely works: we will concede that a case does exist where we would find a life lived in poverty tolerable, even enjoyable. The South Bronx case pushes us to another clarification of values: we can imagine a situation where we would choose poverty over relative affluence. As Murray says in paragraph 26, the experiments convince us that it is *possible* that a policy that imposes poverty on people is not bad policy.

Are these discoveries about our values significant? It is hard to say. Intellectually, they are hardly overwhelming, since we have learned nothing about the world. On the other hand, Murray has accomplished the very difficult task of holding a prejudice at bay. He is surely right in assuming that conditioning has led us to react to poverty as if it were the definitive misfortune. By making us think through his cases, he slows this judgment down and keeps poverty in perspective (precisely the task he sets for himself in the first paragraph).

2. What conditions, according to Murray, can make even an economically poor community a good community to live in?

In discussing his various scenarios Murray keeps returning to the question of child-rearing: a good community is for him a community where it is possible to raise children equipped "to pursue happiness" (paragraph 28). Being so equipped requires that they have an education —at minimum, elementary schooling, religious training, and parents who own a modest library (paragraph 10). It requires that they have what every parent will eventually call "nice" friends, a "positive peer culture" (paragraph 11). And it requires, as Murray says repeatedly, the presence and influence of adults who are hard-working, who value education, and who teach children that "integrity and responsibility are primary values" (paragraph 23).

I doubt many readers will disagree that a good environment for child-rearing is essential to a good community; I'm sure some will find Murray's definition relentlessly middle-class and a bit bland. Apparently intense joy or deep friendship or religious fervor are less important to him than they might be to some others.

Beyond a proper climate for children, the adequate community needs to offer each member

- enjoyable (not necessarily ideal) work and an opportunity for advancement (paragraph 9)
- opportunities to gather with friends for "jokes and conversation" (paragraphs 12, 18)
- the opportunity to move about freely without the danger of attack.

This seems a modest enough list, but I am revising this comment in the summer of the Los Angeles riots, which reminded America that in some of its communities these conditions have not been met.

3. What distinctions does Murray make between concepts most of us confuse?

If you think your students will have trouble handling this question, you might give them the most obvious example, Murray's distinction between poverty and subsistence (see paragraphs 2, 3, and 27). Most of us do confuse the terms, forgetting that someone in the United States may be living far below the poverty level and far above the subsistence level. The distinction clarifies our thinking and makes his argument possible.

He makes a similar distinction in paragraph 9 between career choice and career satisfaction. Most of us, having absorbed a message that permeates a consumer society, automatically associate choice and satisfaction. That we might be happy with a career we wouldn't choose seems an almost shocking idea, though we at once see that it is perfectly possible. In paragraph 15 he makes the politically important distinction between happiness and the opportunity to pursue happiness, and in paragraph 19 the equally important distinction between personal and environmental poverty.

If your students will pause to consider the implications of these distinctions, they will realize how important it is to define and so control the terms used in an argument. If poverty and subsistence are not equated, then the government is not necessarily remiss if it keeps people in poverty. If career choice is not necessary to career satisfaction, then the government is not obliged to educate people to the limits of their ability and ambition. If the opportunity to pursue happiness is a good thing in itself, then the government is under less pressure to ensure that the pursuit has a good chance of ending in success. If environmental poverty is raised as a concern equal to or greater than personal poverty, then the government may have a greater obligation to improve the social fiber than to raise the income of the poor.

4. What counterarguments can be made to Murray's argument?

Your students may find several. Two occur to me. First, Murray's assumption that those who make public policy are largely people who don't know poverty first- or even second-hand (paragraphs 1 and 2) makes sense only until we begin to think about it. Then we realize that the most significant policy makers in America today are not products of America's postwar affluence. Senior government posts, elected or appointed, tend to be held by people well into middle age. In 1988 we replaced a president born in 1911 with one born in 1924. Both men lived through the Great Depression and the privations of World War II. And the leader whose policies Murray consistently attacks, Lyndon Johnson, had more personal knowledge of poverty than either Reagan or Bush: he grew up relatively poor in a region where he was exposed to people who were poorer still. We haven't yet experienced a generation of leaders that finds poverty an utter mystery, though sometime after the turn of the century we may.

The second objection I would raise has to do with the conditions of the Thailand and Bronx thought experiments. In the Thailand case, Murray begins by imagining himself selling the jeep, buying enough land to support himself and perhaps a family, and farming successfully enough from the start that he is in no danger of starvation. That is, he gives as his example of a poor man a perfectly healthy, optimistic fellow who not only owns his house free and clear but also owns his own business without encumbrances and has been mysteriously educated in how to run it. On *this* basis he allows us to imagine that poverty may not be such an awful thing. Of course, truly poor people are more likely than their rich counterparts to have health problems, defeatist attitudes, and other encumbrances that stem from their poverty rather than from a defect in their characters. There is sleight-of-hand at work here.

Similarly, in the Bronx experiment, Murray insists that we maintain our own identity, presumably the identity of healthy members of the middle class. Then, presto, he implies that because we would prefer the Thai village to the Bronx, personal poverty is not so bad as the invidious influence of the degenerates who live in American slums. But let's try another thought experiment. Let's take a forty-year-old Bronx resident living in just such an apartment as Murray describes, one with a moderate health problem—a spastic colon, say. Give her a clear choice between life in the village and life in her neighborhood, and which would she choose? It isn't entirely clear that she would choose the village. Can we discount the possibility that reality is not defined by the consciousness of readers of *The National Review*? Perhaps for some people living in poverty a closer approach to the subsistence level has no attraction, however charming the villagers might be.

—D.H.—

Style Lesson 24:
Distinguishing a Term from Related Terms

In the first paragraph of "What's So Bad About Being Poor?" Murray distinguishes between poverty and some conditions that are not synonymous to it, but are frequently taken to be. This technique of defining by distinguishing the term defined from terms commonly confused with it is a good one to master. Practice it by constructing sentences modeled on those below, but using different words for those capitalized. They should aim to clarify their key word as Murray clarifies his.

POVERTY is not equivalent to DESTITUTION. Being POOR does not necessarily mean being MALNOURISHED or ILL-CLOTHED. It does not automatically mean JOYLESSNESS or DESPAIR. To be poor is not necessarily to be without DIGNITY; it is not necessarily to be UNHAPPY.

One possible response: "Tardiness is not equivalent to irresponsibility. Being late does not necessarily mean being lazy or uncooperative. It does not automatically mean apathy or resistance. To be late is not necessarily to be without motivation; it is not necessarily to be rude."

INSIDERS AND OUTSIDERS

OVERVIEW OF UNIT

Like *Femininity and Masculinity*, this section has the advantage of raising issues that have their roots in personal experience but that bear fruit in history and public policy. Every student in your classroom has had some longing to join what C. S. Lewis calls the "Inner Ring," or having joined it, has struggled to maintain a position snugly inside by holding others out. Some have experienced the grosser forms of discrimination based on race, religion, or gender. The essays by Mary McCarthy, Brent Staples, Roger Wilkins, Perri Klass, and Adrienne Rich could serve students as models for their own memoirs of inclusions and exclusions.

Beyond the personal experience essay, I've found the topics raised here useful bases for research and argumentation. The best luck I've had with the straight research paper was sending students to newspapers and magazines from twenty-five or fifty years ago and asking them to show how the position of minorities or women then was different from what it is today. Some students made good use not only of news and feature articles but of advertisements and stories.

C.S. LEWIS

The Inner Ring

If I could assign only one essay in this reader, it would be "The Inner Ring." It's that important. The essay is actually an address to the students at King's College, the University of London, and you may want to compare it to the addresses by Virginia Woolf ("Professions for Women" in *Femininity and Masculinity*) and Adrienne Rich ("Claiming An Education" in *Understanding*). Because the essay is in essence a serious moral argument, it requires careful reading. It might be helpful to approach the essay by looking at its structure to identify the major points of the argument. A good many speakers follow the three-part "tell 'em what you're going to say, say it, and tell 'em what you said" method of organization. Lewis does something entirely different.

In Part 1 (paragraphs 1–5) Lewis describes the phenomenon of the Inner Ring, the unofficial hierarchy that exists in the Russian Army and in every school, court, hospital, business, or other human institution. This stunningly clear opening is a complete essay in itself, but Lewis doesn't stop there.

In Part 2 (paragraphs 6 and 7) he goes a step further by arguing, convincingly I think, that the desire to be inside whichever Inner Ring we most admire motivates all of us during some period of our lives.

In Part 3 (paragraphs 8–10) he pauses to explain that the existence of Inner Rings is unavoidable and is not necessarily evil. What is dangerous is our desire to enter them, our anguish at being excluded, and the kind of pleasure we feel when we are included.

In Part 4 (paragraph 11) Lewis returns to the theme of Part 2 and states not only that the desire to be an insider influences everyone at some time, but that the desire is "one of the great permanent mainsprings of human action" and that, unless we fight the temptation, it will be one of the chief motives of our lives.

In Part 5 (paragraphs 12–17) he argues that there are two reasons to resist the temptation. First (paragraph 13) because it can lead a person to become a scoundrel. Second (paragraph 15) because the thirst to enter the Inner Ring is unquenchable. No Ring is as glamorous from the inside as it seemed from the outside; as soon as we succeed in entering one, the mirage of a better dances before us. It's a little like the Groucho Marx line: I wouldn't want to belong to any club that would accept me as a member.

In the conclusion (paragraphs 18 and 19) Lewis offers hope by describing two circles that can give genuine happiness. One is the professional circle composed of sound craftsmen who take pride in doing excellent work and who respect others who do the same. The other is a social circle composed of people we like. According to Lewis these circles are incidentally rather than intentionally exclusive.

QUESTIONS

1. How does Lewis's address differ from typical commencement speeches?

Most students will find it difficult to remember the content of any of the graduation speeches they have ever heard. They will probably characterize them as long and boring. (Lewis's essay takes approximately twenty minutes to read aloud.) They may recall that most such speeches are exhortations to succeed.

The Lewis piece differs in a number of ways. First, it is considerably weightier than we might expect. It is, as he warns his audience, exactly what they should have anticipated from a middle-aged moralist. Second, Lewis does not encourage his listeners to become successful, at least not in the sense that the term is ordinarily defined. In fact, that is precisely what he is warning them against. Third, Lewis is definitely not boring.

The techniques he uses to stave off boredom are worth noting. As I mentioned earlier, he does not use the traditional three-part form of organization. Instead, his message unfolds and is gradually revealed. After he persuades us to accept one part of his argument, he introduces the next. The suspense builds. "Where is this man leading me?"

The essay is also interesting simply because the ideas Lewis presents are so novel. Who else would suggest that, Freud to the contrary, the lure of the caucus may be more powerful than the sexual impulse?

Finally, his use of specifics makes him a fascinating writer. I would probably write that the desire to penetrate the Inner Ring may or may not lead to worldly success. Lewis, on the other hand, writes that it "may end in a crash, a scandal, and penal servitude: it may end in millions, a peerage and giving the prizes at your old school" (paragraph 13).

2. How does Lewis prevent this terribly serious essay from becoming absolutely bleak?

Primarily with his tone. Although he eschews the obligatory public speaker jokes, he lightens the essay with delightful understatements: "The painless death of a pious relative at an advanced age is not an evil. But an earnest desire for her death on the part of her heirs is not reckoned a proper feeling, and the law frowns on even the gentlest attempt to expedite her departure" (paragraph 8).

Lewis avoids being preachy and offensive by including himself among those of us who are lured by the Inner Ring. In paragraph 10, for example, he uses the pronoun "we" not "they" while describing the pleasure of penetrating the Inner Ring. Lewis also wins our hearts when he wonders why these students would have a taste for middle-aged moralizing and when he worries that, in the minds of many, his association with the devil has reached the level of identification. Often he compliments his audience. For example, he assumes that he doesn't need to explain who Tolstoy is or to define the term "scoundrel." He is treating his listeners as equals rather than preaching down to them from the mountaintop.

3. Think about an Inner Ring you have had experience with and describe it.

You should get a wide variety of answers here, and some of your students may discover that this is a topic they would like to write about. The obvious topics include high school cliques; the informal hierarchies inside dormitories, fraternities, and sororities; and the pecking order that exists within the college. Other answers will vary according to your students' backgrounds but may include recognition of similar systems in religious organizations, in the work place, in communities, in neighborhoods, in families, in the legal system, and in politics.

Having seen things from Lewis's angle, students may discover new insights about prior experiences. Surely they, like Lewis's listeners, will be compelled to answer the question Lewis poses: "In the whole of your life as you now remember it, has the desire to be on the right side of the invisible line ever prompted you to any act or word on which, in the cold small hours of a wakeful night, you can look back with satisfaction?" (paragraph 9).

4. Compare Lewis's view of "insiders" to the views of other essayists included in this unit.

Most of the writers in this unit force us to consider the damage done to outsiders by insiders. In "Letter from Birmingham Jail," for example, Martin Luther King reminds us of the suffering inflicted on black Americans by whites. King seems to believe that once we understand the artificiality of the barriers currently separating insiders and outsiders, insiders will realize that it is ludicrous to exclude others because of their race.

Lewis is less optimistic about our chances for destroying inner rings:

> But your genuine Inner Ring exists for exclusion. There'd be no fun if there were no outsiders. The invisible line would have no meaning unless most people were on the wrong side of it. Exclusion is no accident: it is the essence (paragraph 17).

In Lewis's opinion, insiders don't care that the invisible line is artificial, only that they are on the right side of that line. He does not propose that we expand the inner ring; instead he urges potential members to refuse their invitation to join. Like Adrienne Rich in "Split at the Root: An Essay on Jewish Identity," Lewis focuses on the devastating effect membership in the Inner Ring (or the pursuit of that membership) has on the insiders. As he tells his audience, "The quest for the Inner Ring will break your hearts unless you break it" (paragraph 18).

—M.R.D.—

Style Lesson 25: A Periodic Sentence

In paragraph 13 of "The Inner Ring" Lewis uses a long periodic sentence to describe the insidious approach of the hint that leads a person to become a scoundrel. Imitate his sentence, writing on a subject of your choice.

Over a drink or a cup of coffee,
disguised as a triviality
        and
sandwiched between two jokes,
from the lips of a man, or woman,
        whom you have recently been getting to know rather better
        and
        whom you hope to know better still—
just at the moment when you are most anxious not to appear
        crude,
        or
        naif,
        or
        a prig—
                THE HINT WILL COME.

GEORGE ORWELL

Shooting an Elephant

Like Momaday's "The Way to Rainy Mountain" (*Communities*), Orwell's autobiographical essay "Shooting an Elephant" is a brilliant example of the way history lends dimension to personal experience and personal experience to history. Orwell proves that a writer who sees himself in the context of history can turn the personal experience essay into something other than mere reminiscence. In the essay he relates an incident that occurred while he was serving as assistant district superintendent in the Indian Imperial Police in Burma (1922–1927). Orwell uses the incident to illustrate "the real nature of imperialism—the real motives for which despotic governments act" (paragraph 3).

This essay dramatizes the uneasy relationship between the oppressed and their oppressors, a theme in much of Orwell's writing. Orwell first encountered oppression as a student at preparatory school, and he subsequently recounted his school day sufferings in an autobiographical essay, "Such, Such Were the Joys." Later, his service in the police force in Burma showed him oppression from the opposite point of view, and he liked it no better. He resigned from the imperial police and changed his lifestyle and his political orientation, first calling himself an anarchist and later a socialist. Of his many writings on oppression, the two most famous are *Animal Farm*, a political fable based on the Russian Revolution and its betrayal, and *1984*, his anti-utopian novel, which paints a frightening picture of a society ruled by a totalitarian government that perpetuates itself by a systematic rewriting of history.

"Shooting an Elephant" is an impressive essay for many reasons, one of which is Orwell's extraordinary honesty. He reveals a number of unflattering things about himself. Your students will undoubtedly note many statements that, taken out of context, would make Orwell look like the embodiment of British imperialism. For example, he admits, "And afterwards I was very glad that the coolie had been killed; it put me legally in the right and it gave me a sufficient pretext for shooting the elephant." Obviously, Orwell cannot allege that imperialism corrupts all those it touches and yet claim that he himself was unaffected by it. Orwell sees the ugliness of imperialism, but like Prospero in the closing scene of *The Tempest*, Orwell looks at Caliban and says, "This thing of darkness I acknowledge mine."

The essay is also notable for its vivid descriptions. The scene in which the mortally wounded elephant continues to suffer for what seems like days is one readers never forget, no matter how we try. And, although ultimately we do not judge this piece exclusively as narration, "Shooting an Elephant" is an example of storytelling at its best.

QUESTIONS

1. Which emotions does Orwell experience during this incident?

One mark of Orwell's honesty as a writer is his admission that his relationship with the Burmese evoked an incredible range of emotions, some of them seemingly contradictory. He is perplexed and upset by the hatred directed at him (paragraph 1). He believes that imperialism is an evil, and he hates his job as a policeman, yet he feels honor-bound to serve his country faithfully. He feels sorry for the Burmese, and he feels guilty because they are oppressed by the British, but a part of him thinks "that the greatest joy in the world would be to drive a bayonet into a Buddhist priest's guts."

Your students will understand Orwell better if you can get them to recall situations in which their inclinations and their obligations were irreconcilable. Probably all of us who have taught have been in the unenviable position of having to enforce a policy we did not agree with. In those situations I have felt angry with the administration who made the ridiculous policy and with the students who persisted in pointing out how ridiculous it was. Even though I sympathized with my students, I was upset with them, both because they blamed me for the policy and because their questions forced me either to defend something I did not believe in or to admit my powerlessness.

Surely all of your students will have had similar experiences. Camp counselors, employees in fast food places, secretaries, lifeguards, babysitters, and almost all other employees are occasionally required to enforce rules they didn't make.

Another example of the complexity of Orwell's emotional makeup is shown by his reaction to the death of the coolie and to the death of the elephant. Although Orwell describes the dead man's body in graphic detail, he says nothing about feeling sorrow because a man was dead. In fact, he coldly states that he was glad the coolie was killed because the death vindicated his decision to shoot the elephant. In contrast, he demonstrates straightforward humane horror at the agony he puts the elephant through. That difference in response may be attributed partially to the fact that he directly caused the elephant's death, but not the coolie's. It is also significant that the British are notoriously fond of animals and have led the movements to prevent cruelty to animals. Orwell reminds us that human beings are quite capable of empathizing with the pain of animals while ignoring the suffering of fellow humans.

2. Who or what ruled Burma at the time of this incident?

Ostensibly, the British were the rulers of Burma. After winning three Anglo-Burmese Wars fought between 1824 and 1885, the British annexed the whole kingdom of Burma, and in 1886 made it a province of India. That political decision added insult to injury because the Burmese differed from the Indians in race, language, culture, and religion, and the Burmese bitterly resented India for having fought on the side of Britain during the

Anglo-Burmese Wars. Nevertheless, the British government did not separate Burma from India until 1937, and Burma did not become a sovereign independent republic until 1948. When Orwell served in Burma, Britain dominated its colony economically, politically, and militarily.

But in this essay Orwell tells us that when he realized he would have to shoot the elephant because the Burmese onlookers expected it of him, he finally understood that, in a colonial system, the white man is nothing more than "an absurd puppet pushed to and fro by the will of those yellow faces" (paragraph 7). It is not, however, entirely accurate to say that the Burmese ruled the country. If that had been the case, they would have expelled the British.

If neither the British nor the Burmese rule, who or what is in charge? Orwell seems to be suggesting that the system itself, the colonial psychology, takes command. The white man does what he thinks the natives expect him to do, and the natives expect him to do the kind of thing they think white men do. The ruler's behavior is shaped by his perception of his subjects' expectations, and their expectations are shaped by their perception of the ruler's behavior. Imperialism becomes a gigantic shell game.

3. Is Orwell an insider or an outsider in Burma?

This question should demonstrate how difficult it can be to define these terms. Orwell is an outsider in that his clothing, language, and race mark him as a foreigner. But if we define insiders as the group in power, the British seem to be the insiders. They certainly have all the trappings of the "Inner Ring" described by C.S. Lewis. However, if the British are merely the titular rulers of Burma (as the answer to Question 3 suggests), they are not insiders in any sense of the world. And even if the British are the insiders, Orwell does not choose to identify himself with his countrymen. As he explains,

> [A]t that time I had already made up my mind that imperialism was an evil thing and the sooner I chucked up my job and got out of it the better. Theoretically—and secretly, of course—I was all for the Burmese and against their oppressors, the British (paragraph 2).

As an Englishman who is alienated from other Englishmen and who is hated by the Burmese, Orwell is the quintessential outsider.

4. If you judge this piece as a narrative, what are its strengths?

Orwell carefully structures the entire essay to build suspense. The title hints at the event that is to occur, but the death of the elephant is not a certainty until the penultimate paragraph. In the first two paragraphs Orwell gives us the necessary background information; he sets the stage for the drama that is to unfold. And indeed, this particular tragedy has the classical five-part structure—introduction, rising action, climax, falling action, and catastrophe.

The rising action is set in motion in paragraph 3 when the sub-inspector telephones Orwell to report that an elephant is "ravaging the bazaar" and that Orwell should "do something about it." At that point neither Orwell nor the reader knows what he can do, especially with only an old .44 Winchester, but like him we are curious enough to go along to see what is happening.

From that point on, Orwell advances and retreats. Like the crowd, the reader continues to wonder what he will do next. In paragraph 3 we learn about the destruction the elephant has caused, and we know Orwell will have to act. But in paragraph 4 it seems that no one knows where the elephant has gone. We are ready to go home. Then the body of the coolie is discovered, and Orwell sends for an elephant rifle. We assume he plans to shoot the elephant, but he surprises us by saying, "I had no intention of shooting the elephant. . ." (paragraph 5), and he spends an entire paragraph explaining why he knew with "perfect certainty" that he ought not shoot the elephant.

Paragraph 7 is the turning point. Orwell looks at the crowd and realizes that he has to shoot the elephant because he cannot disappoint the 2,000 people who have gathered to watch him. But the falling action prolongs the suspense. Orwell hesitates. In paragraphs 8 and 9 he weighs his alternatives. Finally he decides that although he is not afraid of death, he is afraid of being laughed at. He has to shoot the elephant.

Even the catastrophe is suspenseful. Once Orwell shoots, the question changes to whether he will succeed in killing the poor animal. In spite of Orwell's efforts to end the elephant's suffering, the animal and the reader agonize until paragraph 13.

5. To what extent is this essay specifically about that peculiar phenomenon, the British upper-middle-class male?

In the larger sense the essay is about the evils of imperialism, but Orwell is also making observations about a specific class of people at a specific time and place. Orwell was himself a product of the British public school system, and he certainly understood the pressure to be manly, to do the right thing, to maintain a stiff upper lip, and to demonstrate the ability to handle any situation calmly—in short, to be the kind of man Morris describes in "To Everest" (*Femininity and Maculinity*).

Orwell states repeatedly that, throughout the incident, his primary concern was to avoid being laughed at (paragraphs 7 and 9). Everyone has experienced the fear of being laughed at, but ordinarily we are concerned that it will occur when we make a mistake, when we inadvertently do something foolish. Orwell, on the other hand, fears that he will be laughed at if he does what he knows is right. He therefore chooses to do the wrong thing—to shoot the elephant—rather than risk looking a fool. Whether such a mentality caused imperialism or vice versa is immaterial. What is important is Orwell's recognition of the relationship between the two.

—M.R.D.—

Style Lesson 26:
A Description with Visceral Impact

To emphasize Orwell's ability to describe what he sees in a way that involves the reader's visceral emotions, work in groups (or as one group) to fill in the missing words in the following passage, discussing the reasons for your choices as you go. Then check your wording against the original wording from paragraph 4 of "Shooting an Elephant."

This was the rainy season and the ground was soft, and his face had _____ a _____ a foot deep and a couple of yards long. He was lying on his _____ with arms _____ and _____ sharply twisted to one side. His face was covered with _____, the eyes wide open, the teeth _____ and _____ with an expression of unendurable _____. (Never tell me, by the way, that the dead look _____. Most of the _____ I have seen look _______.) The friction of the great beast's foot had _____ the skin from his back as neatly as one _____ a _____.

MARTIN LUTHER KING, JR.

Letter from Birmingham Jail

The American civil rights struggle of the late 1950s and early 1960s was one of the most dramatic attempts in history by a group defined by law and custom as outsiders to win full participation in a society. The brightest star in the civil rights movement's constellation was Martin Luther King, Jr. Your students will undoubtedly know something about King, but you might want to give them some background information before assigning this essay. King's civil rights activities began in 1955 when he was the pastor of a Baptist church in Montgomery, Alabama. In that year Mrs. Rosa Parks, a forty-two-year-old black woman, made history by refusing to give up her seat on a bus to a white passenger. She was subsequently arrested for violating the city's segregation law, and black activists organized the Montgomery Improvement Association to boycott the city's transit system. King was chosen a leader of the group that, after a year, succeeded in desegregating the city's buses. Following that success, King formed the Southern Christian Leadership Conference, which championed the use of nonviolent resistance to effect desegregation. King quickly became a leader of international fame.

The events that led to "Letter from Birmingham Jail" began in the spring of 1963 with King's campaign to end segregation at Birmingham's lunch counters and in the city's hiring practices. Police responded by turning fire-hoses and dogs on the demonstrators and by jailing King and hundreds of his supporters, including schoolchildren. Specifically, his letter was addressed to eight local clergymen who had issued a statement entreating blacks to oppose the demonstrations.

A few of your students may have seen television selections of King's most famous speeches, including his "I have a dream" speech. If so, they will know what an eloquent and powerful speaker he was. Fortunately, King's style does not depend solely on delivery. "Letter from Birmingham Jail" is an impassioned plea for justice, even if achieving that goal requires the violation of unjust laws. As King explains, "I submit that an individual who breaks a law that conscience tells him is unjust, and who willingly accepts the penalty of imprisonment in order to arouse the conscience of the community over its injustice, is in reality expressing the highest respect for law." That position should trigger strong responses, both positive and negative, from your students.

QUESTIONS

1. Do you agree with King's statement that "one has a moral responsibility to disobey unjust laws" (paragraph 15)?

King defines an unjust law as one that is "out of harmony with the moral law," one that "degrades human personality," one that "a majority inflicts on a minority group that is not binding on itself," one "inflicted upon a minority that . . . had no part in enacting [it]," or, in some instances, one that is "just on its face but unjust in its application" (paragraphs 13–17). If we accept that definition, few would argue that such a law should be obeyed. But a problem arises when we attempt to apply the guidelines to a specific law. To illustrate how difficult it is to agree on which laws "are out of harmony with the moral law," ask your students to assume, for example, that the United States passed a Constitutional amendment prohibiting all abortions. Then ask them to use King's definition of an unjust law to determine whether the anti-abortion law should be violated. They will quickly realize that King does not formulate an objective test. In fact, some would say that his statement is in essence an assertion that we should obey the laws we like and ignore all others.

You might remind your students that King was an admirer of Gandhi and of Thoreau. In "Civil Disobedience" Thoreau asserts that when an unjust law exists, we should transgress it at once rather than obey it while we attempt to persuade the majority to alter it. Thoreau, however, makes a distinction between trivial and significant laws: "If the injustice is part of the necessary friction of the machine of government, let it go . . . but if it is of such a nature that it requires you to be the agent of injustice to another, then, I say, break the law." Thoreau undoubtedly realized that his reputation as an eccentric (that fellow who lives alone in the cabin he built on Walden Pond) might cause his critics to interpret his refusal to pay a poll tax as little more than evidence that he was a crank. He was therefore eager to explain that refusing to pay taxes used to finance the war against Mexico constitutes disobedience of a significant law. King does not distinguish between trivial and significant laws, probably because the laws he urged his followers to disobey were so obviously significant.

2. How is King's training and experience as a preacher reflected in his writing style?

King was a fourth-generation Southern Baptist preacher. Like all good preachers, King is particularly adept at appealing to his audience by making abstract concepts concrete. We may be able to oppose the abstract notion of civil disobedience, but it is impossible to disapprove of the people King compares to the civil rights activists—the Hungarian freedom fighters and the Germans who aided Jews in Hitler's Germany (paragraph 22). In this essay King also displays his ability to create unforgettable images:

> Like a boil that can never be cured so long as it is covered up but must be opened with all its ugliness to the natural medicines of air and light, injustice must be exposed. . . (paragraph 24).

> They have carved a tunnel of hope through the dark mountain of disappointment (paragraph 43).

But it is the sound of his sentences that sets his writing apart. The essay is written in language that is meant to be heard. Apparently his legacy from his preacher father, grandfather, and great-grandfather included a remarkable ear for rolling cadences that stir the heart. I think the most amazing sentence in this amazing essay is the one in paragraph 14 that begins "But when you have seen. . ." This periodic sentence, which answers those who encourage blacks to wait for change, is 322 words long. It begins with a list of the abuses American blacks have suffered, and it concludes with this understatement: "then you will understand why we find it difficult to wait." The 311-word catalogue is organized into ten subordinate clauses. Some of those clauses are long and some short, but all open with the word "when." The repetition of "when" ties the clauses together, creates the sonorous quality of the sentence, and contributes to the dramatic impact of the switch to "then" in the short independent clause that concludes the sentence. The length of the sentence underscores the length of time blacks had already waited—futilely, it seemed—for justice. You might want to read this one aloud to your class to demonstrate its power.

Another rhetorical device King uses effectively is the balanced sentence or sentences: "Shallow understanding from people of good will is more frustrating than absolute misunderstanding from people of ill will" (paragraph 23). "If I have said anything in this letter that overstates the truth and indicates an unreasonable impatience, I beg you to forgive me. If I have said anything in this letter that understates the truth and indicates my having a patience that allows me to settle for anything less than brotherhood, I beg God to forgive me" (paragraph 49). In his ability to present facts and ideas in clear, convincing, and attractive language, King is a rhetorician in the finest sense of the word.

3. Who is King's audience and how does his awareness of his audience affect what he has to say?

King's specific audience was eight white clergymen, Jewish, Catholic, and Protestant, who had issued a statement urging blacks not to support the demonstrations against segregation in Birmingham. Considerations of audience influence King's tone, the structure of his letter, and his choice of supporting examples.

His tone is consistently conciliatory. He begins by referring to the clergymen as "men of genuine good will" (paragraph 1), he tells them he is sure that each of them would want to go beyond "the superficial kind of social analysis that deals merely with effects and does not grapple with underlying causes" (paragraph 5), he emphasizes their points of agreement ("You are quite right in calling for negotiation," paragraph 10), he addresses them as "my Christian and Jewish brothers" (paragraph 23), he praises each of them for taking significant stands on the issue of segregation (paragraph 33), he states that he does not believe they would have commended the police force for keeping order if they had observed "their ugly and inhumane treatment of Negroes . . . in the city jail" (paragraph 45), and he concludes with the hope that he will soon be able to meet each of them "not as an integrationist or as a civil rights leader but as a fellow clergyman and a Christian brother" (paragraph 50).

Although King wants to win the understanding and support of these religious leaders, he cannot, in good conscience, avoid scathing criticisms of white moderates and of the white church and its leadership. Since these clergymen are white moderate church leaders, he must have wondered how to write the truth without creating even more hostility. The simplicity of his solution is brilliant. When he refers to the clergymen he is addressing, he uses the pronoun "you"; when he criticizes moderates and church leaders, he uses the pronoun "they." Thus he subtly encourages his audience to identify with the group of reasonable sincere people who will understand his position and not with those who "have remained silent behind the anesthetizing security of stained-glass windows" (paragraph 35).

King's audience also influences the structure of the essay in that it is organized to refute the criticisms these clergymen voiced in their statement opposing the demonstrations. He begins by rebutting the accusation that he and the other civil rights leaders are outsiders, and then goes on to explain why demonstrations are essential, why blacks are unwilling to patiently wait for change, and why it is sometimes necessary to violate unjust laws. It is only after defending himself against their criticisms that he counters with his own attack against the white moderates.

Mindful that he is addressing Jews, Catholics, and Protestants, King carefully chooses examples that will appeal to all three groups. He uses the words of the protestant theologians Reinhold Neibuhr and Paul Tillich (paragraphs 12 and 16), the Catholic saints Augustine and Aquinas (paragraphs 15 and 16), and Jewish philosopher Martin Buber (paragraph 16) to support his argument that unjust laws should be opposed. He praises a Greek philosopher and both Old and New Testament figures for their courageous acts of civil disobedience (Socrates; Shadrach, Meshach, and Abednego; and the early Christian martyrs, paragraph 21). And in paragraph 31, he lists as extremists Jesus, the Old Testament prophet Amos, the New Testament figure Paul, Martin Luther, the Puritan minister John Bunyan, Abraham Lincoln, and Thomas Jefferson: just the sort of company these heterogeneous religious leaders would like to keep.

—M.R.D.—

Style Lesson 27: Use of Repetition and Parallelism

Martin Luther King's style, based on a tradition of pulpit eloquence, makes heavy use of parallel patterning and repetition. To get a sense of how much redundancy is built into such a style, fill in the blanks in the following passage and explain how you decided what to insert.

A just law is a man-made code that squares with the moral law or the law of God.
A(n) ____ ____ is a code that is out of harmony with the ____ ____.
To put it in the terms of St. Thomas Aquinas:
An unjust law is a human law that is not rooted in ____ law and ____ ____.
Any ____ that uplifts human personality is ____.
Any ____ that ____ ____ ____ is ____.
All segregation statutes are ____
because ____ distorts the ____
and
____ the personality.
It gives the segregator a false sense of superiority
and
____ ____ ____ ____ ____ ____ ____.

Every writer needs to learn to distinguish occasions when such patterning is desirable (in speeches, for example) and occasions when the redundancy is a detriment (the academic paper, for example). King's excellent style is not a style for every occasion.

MARY McCARTHY

Artists in Uniform

I've probably read Mary McCarthy's account of her meeting with a smug anti-Semite ten times in the last ten years, always delighted at how perfectly it captures both the nature of casual bigotry and the helplessness of the liberal who, attempting to put a dent in the bigot's self-satisfaction, finds herself caught in prejudices of her own. The memoir was written more than forty years ago, but age hasn't dimmed it. Students may find it quaint that the action takes place on a passenger train and that the communist is treated as the ultimate outsider, but the characters and their attitudes are timeless.

Students may assume, as the editors of *Harper's* apparently did, that McCarthy's story is fictional. In her fine essay "Settling the Colonel's Hash" (*Harper's*, February 1954) McCarthy insisted that it was strictly autobiographical and that its chief interest for her was that it actually happened very much as she tells it.

QUESTIONS

1. What type of man is the Colonel? If you met the same type of man today, how would you recognize him?

This question is intended to force students to separate the accidental from the essential in the presentation of the Colonel. Reasonable people may disagree, of course, about which is which. I take it that these features are essentially accidental:

- The Colonel is Irish.
- His dominant prejudice is anti-Semitism (rather than, for example, dislike of blacks or Orientals).
- He is in the military. Though McCarthy suggests that military training may have something to do with the Colonel's undemocratic character (paragraph 18), we could surely find the same sort of smug superiority among businesspeople or academics.

I'm less sure about whether two other features are accidental or essential:

- The Colonel is male. In general, like most of us today, I'm reluctant to associate a character flaw with one sex rather than the other, but I suspect that the Colonel's particular combination of arrogance and prejudice continues to be more common in men than in women. This may be changing, of course.

- He is in his young adulthood, young enough to feel his oats and old enough to enjoy authority. Arrogance may come somewhat easier when we perceive ourselves as being at the height of our powers.

These features are, I think, essential:

- The colonel has personal magnetism. He is a dangerous bigot because people like the fanatic accountant and the sedate engineer have an instinctive admiration for him and will fasten themselves to his opinions.
- He is confident of his own superiority to practically everyone. Students should notice that it is not only Jews he assumes to be his inferiors. Because McCarthy is a woman, he treats her as his "perquisite," and he accepts a drink from the engineer as if he were a god accepting a mortal's libation (paragraph 2). He seems contemptuous of academics and artists, and he apparently has some disparaging things to say about the President of the United States (paragraph 8). Having set his own religion aside, he dismisses all religion as "a lot of bushwa" (paragraph 22). Here is a man who views the whole world as if he were sitting on the mountaintop.
- He is a man who thinks, though not very deeply. McCarthy's characterization of him in paragraph 17 tells the story. The height of the colonel's intellectual activity is the development and application of impossibly broad categories. McCarthy points out how naive he is in handling these categories in paragraph 10: the Colonel seems to believe that the statement "Most Communists are Jews" allows one to conclude that "Most Jews are Communists," a very crude mistake in logic. Still, we have to give the Colonel credit for some intellectual curiosity. When he decides that McCarthy is an Irish woman who is "for the Jews," he is eager to figure out how this can be so—it upsets his categories and forces him to concentrate (paragraph 12).
- He is a bigot, of course, but not a virulent one. He would probably not be capable of any of the "hate crimes" states and municipalities have been trying to legislate against, and he probably does understand himself to be on friendly terms with some people from the group he is prejudiced against.

It is possible that we would recognize a contemporary manifestation of the Colonel's type in, let's say, a 30-year-old female executive we meet on an airplane—one who uses a story about welfare mothers in the newspaper as a springboard for an unsolicited talk about the way "minorities" in this country want special privileges and as little work as possible. She expects immediate agreement. If you resist, she may put on a show of moderation. Not *all* blacks are this way, she concedes. Her own black friends are very hard-working. But even they will admit . . . and so forth. The keys are the use of racial stereotyping, the unshakable confidence in that her opinion is right, and the wink-and-nod assumption that, down deep, we all know it.

2. How does McCarthy present herself in this essay?

Mercilessly. Students who read attentively should realize that McCarthy presents herself as

- A coward who hides her identity. She tells us in paragraph 3 that she "preened" herself on being "an artist in disguise" and that her vanity was injured when she realized that she looked like what she was, a "Bohemian." In the case of Bohemianism, she argues that the disguise has some socially useful function, but the same cannot be said for her hiding of her Jewish ancestry (see especially paragraphs 7 and 9).
- An egotist. In paragraph 4, especially, and throughout the essay generally, she shows herself fencing with the Colonel for dominance. She wants to prove herself his superior in intelligence and knowledge of the world. In paragraph 7 she says that it hurts her *amour-propre* to think that the men in the club car could think of her as a Communist or a fellow-traveler. More subtle egotism shows in her "concept of transcendence" (paragraph 7): she wants to show the world that she, unlike the Colonel, operates according to principle rather than prejudice, and so represents humankind at its best.
- A snob; we might almost say a bigot. She realizes that the Colonel comes from "a somewhat lower social stratum" of Irish-Americans than she does, and she tries to rub his nose in the fact, suggesting that Irish anti-Semitism might be the result of "the potato diet" (paragraph 13) and pointing out that she used "to call the old clothes man a sheeny" (paragraph 19). Even her championing of the Jews has an aroma of snobbishness about it. See paragraph 12, where she realizes that "the defense of the Jews could be a subtle and safe form of anti-Semitism, an exercise in patronage: as a rational Gentile, one could feel superior to both the Jews and the anti-Semites."
- A hypocrite. McCarthy sinks low in our opinion when in paragraph 21 she solemnly tells the Colonel that he'll "have a long spell in Purgatory" if he continues to hate the Jews in "deliberate violation of Christ's commandment," then admits in paragraph 22 that she is not at all religious.

But, of course, it is McCarthy the character whose faults are thus exposed. McCarthy the author wins high marks for being so honest about her failings. (And must be aware of this, of course, which could suggest another layer of pride.)

McCarthy's willingness to show that she is not exempt from the Colonel's faults is what makes this essay particularly attractive to me, particularly thought-provoking. Like Jane Austen's *Pride and Prejudice,* it reminds us that a keen sensitivity to arrogance and prejudice in others doesn't prevent our being proud and intolerant ourselves.

3. McCarthy's style is often praised for its energy, but sometimes criticized as being difficult. Find a sentence that strikes you as both energetic and somewhat difficult, and explain what is going on in it.

Asking this question may give you some insight into the reading skills and habits of your students, even while it gets them to think about what it means to have a style. Here is the sentence I would analyze:

> I saw that still I was a doubtful quantity to them, a movement in the bushes, a noise, a flicker, that I was figuring in their crenelated thought as "she."

There is no literary allusion that might confuse a student in this case (there are in some of McCarthy's other sentences) but the style is highly metaphorical, requiring the reader to

- Imagine the men standing nervously in the woods, alarmed by movements and sounds they can't pin down;
- Imagine the men's thought—one thought for three men, notice—as a castle with crenelations at the top, an amusing suggestion of both their defensive posture and their dull anachronism.
- Catch the implications of *she* in quotation marks. McCarthy represents to these men the unfathomable mystery of Woman, manifesting itself now in the avatar of a Bohemian intellectual. The men might well say what Churchill said of Russia: this is to them a "mystery inside an enigma."

This is the sort of sentence McCarthy was master of, quick and funny, packing into thirty words what others might spread over a paragraph.

—D.H.—

Style Lesson 28: A Descriptive Sentence with Five Participles

In the first paragraph of "Artists in Uniform," McCarthy describes the accountant brilliantly. The fourth sentence of the paragraph focuses on the man's nervous movements, using participles to knit a series of actions together. To fully appreciate the architecture of this sentence, try to recreate it from the choppy sentences below.

This morning he had come in late. He had had a hangdog look. He had looked like he had a hangover. He had sat on a settee. He had sat forward. He had been tense. He had smoked cigarettes. He had followed the conversation. His nose had twitched little twitches. His body had quivered. A dog will follow a human conversation. Its mistrustful eyeballs will veer from one speaker to another. It will raise its head eagerly at its master's voice.

Note: The dog in the eleventh sentence is a simile.

BRENT STAPLES

Just Walk On By

Staples' brief essay picks up a thread from the *Femininity and Masculinity* unit: the "power to intimidate" can be, as he says, part of "the male romance." Here, however, it is not romantic at all. As a gentle black man, "a softy who is scarcely able to take a knife to a raw chicken," Staples is dismayed that he intimidates people—especially female pedestrians—by his mere presence. This accidental intimidation, alarming to his victims, is dangerous to *him*, since he may be mistaken for a mugger and shot.

The essay is a good model for two tasks we often require of students: it uses a series of examples to illustrate a point; and, in referring to essays by Norman Podhoretz and Edward Hoagland, it connects reading and personal experience. The way it discusses a highly charged topic without icy detachment on the one hand or throbbing emotion on the other sets students a good example of moderation in tone.

QUESTIONS

1. When you read Staples's first sentence only, what assumptions are you inclined to draw about the writer? When are these assumptions overturned?

"My first victim was a woman—white, well-dressed, probably in her early twenties." The sentence suggests a good deal by an implied opposition: victims are presumably unlike their attackers. It reveals that the author is probably black, probably male (in case we missed the byline), and perhaps not particularly well-off. By the use of *victim* it suggests that the writer is a mugger, if not a rapist. In short, this sounds like the beginning of a criminal's confession. Staples maintains his disguise as a mugger through most of the first paragraph. Only in the last sentence does he drop this pose. When the woman disappears safely into a side street, we realize that she cannot be a victim in quite the way we had assumed, and that Staples cannot therefore be an ordinary mugger.

This is a brilliant start for an essay on the subject of the general public's tendency to mistake all young black men for criminals. We make the mistake the woman has made. Our pulses race a bit.

2. Read Staples's closing sentence. What is implied by the comparison to the cow bell in bear country?

My first response to this comparison (and I think it is typical) was to think of the bell as a device that warns harmless people of the presence of a dangerous customer—like the bell that the fabled mice want to hang on the fabled cat. The purpose of the bell in bear country is not, however, to warn people that grizzlies are present, but to warn grizzlies that people are present. The rangers fear that a bear surprised by some bandy-legged photographer may turn on him and bite his head off. The comparison implies that Staples is *not* dangerous to the people around him, but that they are dangerous to him—because of their fear.

3. How would you describe the tone of Staples's essay?

Talking about tone is never easy for students. You might want to make it easier by asking this question in a multiple choice format: Would you describe the tone as

A. Humorous
B. Angry
C. Sorrowful

In discussion, students should be able to make a case for any of these. Some students will probably complain that you should have included "All of the above" as an option, and they will be right. There is outright humor when Staples describes himself as being unable "to take a knife to a raw chicken." There is grim humor when he describes the reactions of motorists to his crossing the street ("the *thunk, thunk, thunk, thunk* of the driver—black, white, male, or female—hammering down the door locks") and when he describes the hysteria of the jewelry-store proprietor who fetches the Doberman pinscher. There is anger in Staples's references to the Podhoretz and Hoagland essays, anger that shows in the diction—you might have your students discuss the effect of "famed (or infamous)," "extols," and "bad guy" in paragraph 5 and "annoyed" in paragraph 12. And there is sorrow not only for his own "kind of alienation that comes of being ever the suspect," but also for the plight of pedestrians, particularly women ("the danger they perceive is not a hallucination") and for the "poor and powerless young men" who are most likely to become muggers (see paragraph 9). I suppose that if I were forced to choose "one of the above," I would choose *sorrowful*, since the essay as a whole strikes me as a sigh for the state of our society.

4. Who in our society besides young black males has the power to "alter public space" in positive or negative ways?

I ask this question partly to force students to think about what Staples means by altering public space. The phrase is somewhat ambiguous in the context of this essay. Given the mention of what "seemed to be a discreet, uninflammatory distance" between Staples and the pedestrian in the first paragraph, the phrase could refer to the black man's ability to alter people's sense of what anthropologists and ethologists call "encounter distance"—the distance at which adrenaline starts to pump and the "flight-or-fight response" kicks in. But I don't think this is what Staples means. I think he is talking about his ability to alter the *atmosphere* of public space, to make a scene that is pleasant and relaxed into one that is charged with danger, real or apparent.

If we consider atmosphere to be the issue, your students should be able to compile a list of people who can easily change the atmosphere of a street corner or a shop: a celebrity, a clown, a policeman, a pregnant woman, a father with a child on his shoulders, a strikingly beautiful woman, someone with a camcorder in hand, a nun, etc. You might have your students compare Staples's situation with the situation of other people they list. Few other people alter public space as negatively and as involuntarily as he shows us a black man does.

But I think you should push this conversation a bit further in order to get at a point Staples makes well, but doesn't state with special emphasis—that all people, including black men, have some choice about the way they affect the public space around them. Contrast the "quick hunch posture" Hoagland uses to ward off panhandlers (paragraph 5) with Staples's whistling Vivaldi in the final paragraph. One is designed to insure distance, suggest toughness, the other to lower the level of threat. A street full of people in "hunch posture" has become a mean street.

—D.H.—

Style Lesson 29: Diction in a Street Scene

In the following passage, Staples describes the way that frightened women walk along a city street. Choose which word or words in each set of brackets belongs to the original, then explain your choices and compare them to Staples's choices in paragraph 6 of "Just Walk On By."

I often witness that "hunch posture" from women after dark on the [warrenlike/overcrowded] streets of Brooklyn where I live. They seem to [stare straight ahead/set their faces on neutral] and, with their purse straps across their chests [bandolier style/like a banner], they [forge ahead/walk on] as though [very much afraid/bracing themselves against being tackled]. I understand, of course, that the danger they perceive is not [unfounded/a hallucination].

ROGER WILKINS

Confessions of a Blue-Chip Black

Roger Wilkins, the nephew of NAACP president Roy Wilkins, adds to this discussion of outsiders by describing the isolation of a person who is caught between two cultures and rejected by both. As the stepson of a successful black doctor, Wilkins spent his school years during the 1940s living in an all-white neighborhood in Grand Rapids and attending an all-white school. After overcoming the hostility he encountered initially, he made friends with the white students and in his senior year was elected president of the Creston High School student council. But he was never an insider:

> With my friends in the north, race was never mentioned. Ever. I carried my race around with me like an open basket of rotten eggs. I knew I could drop one at any moment and it would explode with a stench over everything. . . . I knew that my white friends, being well brought up, were just too polite to mention this disability that I had. And I was grateful to them, but terrified, just the same, that maybe someday one of them would have the bad taste to notice what I was (paragraph 32).

At the same time Wilkins became painfully aware of an ever-widening chasm between himself and other blacks his age. He tells us that black culture evolved away from him, that he didn't know how to talk or banter or move his body, and that he was tense, stiff, and awkward when he was with his black contemporaries. Given his unusual vantage point, it is not surprising that Wilkins demonstrates a special understanding of the outsider's problems.

QUESTIONS

1. In what ways is Wilkins living what he calls a reactive life?

In paragraph 30 Wilkins writes, "I had already learned one of the great tenets of Negro survival in America: to live the reactive life." Apparently, the reactive life is based on three cardinal rules: (1) Never initiate social contact with white people. (2) Ignore cruel behavior on the part of whites. (3) Accept decent behavior from whites gratefully. In keeping with these rules, Wilkins rides away on his bike when one of the high school boys at football practice calls him a little "coon," and he ignores the spitters at school (paragraphs 25 and 27). In all-white, middle-class Creston High School, Wilkins remains isolated until the "frecklefaced kid with a crewcut" asks to borrow a pencil from him (paragraph 26). When the other boys play pickup games in the end zones of the football field, Wilkins "stands around the edge of the group watching" until one boy has to go home, the teams are unbalanced, and Wilkins is invited to play (paragraph 29). In the same way he waits for Don De Young to suggest that they walk to school together. "I hadn't suggested it for fear of a rebuff for overstepping the limits of my race" (paragraph 30). Wilkins forgets the rules only once: he invites Marge to a hayride. "Her jaw dropped and her eyes got huge. Then she uttered a small shriek and turned, hugging her books to her bosom the way girls do, and fled. I writhed in mortification in my bed that night and for many nights after" (paragraph 59).

You may need to remind your students that Wilkins's response to whites accounts for only part of his reactive life. Because young Wilkins lives in a white neighborhood, attends a white school, and has white friends, he begins to feel "almost completely alienated from his own people as well" (paragraph 49). As a result, the wariness he develops while dealing with whites also governs his relationships with blacks. Thus he avoids inviting his friend Lloyd to visit him until Lloyd says that he would like to come up and play some Saturday. Finally, when Wilkins knows that he can't put it off any longer, he responds, "Sure. Why not?" A similar incident occurs at church. Wilkins realizes that "customs, attitudes, and the other common social currencies of everyday black life had evolved" away from him. He is too uncomfortable to strike up a conversation with Nickerson, the boy his mother especially wanted him to be friends with. And when Wilkins hears Nickerson jokingly refer to him as a "technicolor paddy," his face flames, but he tries to ignore the comment (paragraph 48).

2. What other groups in our society have developed a reactive life?

Your students will probably begin with the obvious answers—women, Hispanics, Native Americans, French Canadians, Jews, and members of other minority groups. But you should insist that they come up with more original examples. Your students will have to determine what it is that causes the reactive life. I would suggest that the reactive life is caused by the outsider's fear that the group in power, the group that matters, considers him or her inferior and will consequently reject any overtures from the outsider. The outsider decides it is better to be ignored than rejected.

Ask your students to think about which other people on your campus might believe they would be rejected because of other people's perceptions of them. By the time your students list all the characteristics that sometimes cause people to think of themselves as outsiders (being old, or young, or overweight, or disabled, for example), they should realize that all of us occasionally feel that we are outsiders. Perhaps this exercise will encourage them to write about their own experiences with the reactive life.

3. When does Wilkins's fear of being an outsider lead him to do things he is ashamed of?

One effect of the insider/outsider phenomenon is obvious: the outsider feels miserable. But there are other, more insidious, consequences. For example, Wilkins shows us that the fear of isolation can drive the outsider to knowingly commit dishonorable acts that are ultimately self-destructive. In contrast to Gide's optimistic view that the suffering of Philoctetes enables him to transcend the petty concerns of ordinary mortals, Wilkins presents his observation that the dread of alienation can muffle a person's conscience.

Wilkins relates two incidents that illustrate this point. In history class, when the students stand to tell where their families originated, Wilkins lies and says his ancestors came from England and Egypt (paragraph 40). He also lies when he tells his white friends that Lloyd is his cousin. He explains his motivation to us: "I could have a Negro cousin. It wasn't voluntary. It wouldn't be as if I had gone out and made a Negro friend deliberately. A person couldn't help who his cousins were" (paragraph 47). In both cases Wilkins explains that he was ashamed to admit his race and, in retrospect, he is even more ashamed to admit that he denied both his ancestors and his friends.

In some ways Wilkins is writing specifically about his experience of being black in white America. At the same time he is telling us about the universal experience described by C. S. Lewis in "The Inner Ring." Lewis defines the Inner Ring as the apex of an unofficial hierarchy, the informal group of people "in the know" who actually wield power. Lewis claims that the desire to be inside the Inner Ring and the terror of being outside is one of the dominant elements in our lives and that "of all the passions, the passion for the Inner Ring is most skillful in making a man who is not yet a very bad man do very bad things" (paragraph 14). Adrienne Rich comes to a similar conclusion in "Split at the Root: An Essay on Jewish Identity," when she points out that the price of assimilation is to engage in persecution of other outsiders.

Discussing the essay in these more general terms may suggest several writing possibilities. After all, most of us remember at least one incident in our lives that we are now ashamed of. If your students are not intrigued by the prospect of writing confessions, you might remind them that, in spite of its title, Wilkins's essay is more than a confession. It is Wilkins's attempt to analyze the situation he faced and to understand, if not forgive, the young boy he once was. Your students might be interested in attempting similar journeys toward self-understanding.

4. Which of the stories Wilkins tells gives you the best understanding of his position as an outsider?

The purpose of this question is to highlight Wilkins's knack for telling illustrative stories. He doesn't simply tell us that the white people in his neighborhood didn't know how to react to him when he rode by on his bike; he shows us: "The people I passed would look back at me with intense and sometimes puzzled looks on their faces as I pedaled by. Nobody waved or even smiled. They just stopped what they were doing to stand and look" (paragraph 15). Again and again he tells a story that makes his point precisely:

- He bicycles to a black neighborhood and is terrified by the black boys he sees there (paragraphs 16 and 17).

- He stops to watch a high school football workout, and one of the football players refers to him as a "little coon" (paragraphs 18–19).
- He strikes up a friendship with Jerry, who is "poor in a way [he] had never seen anyone be poor." One day Jerry tells him, "I can't play with you anymore because you're not good enough for us" (paragraphs 21–24).
- He invents a scheme to explain to Lloyd why they must tell his white friends that they are cousins" (paragraphs 45–47).
- He attends church and overhears one of the boys call him a "technicolor paddy" (paragraph 48).
- He asks Marge for a date (paragraph 58).

You might ask your students to select their favorite story and write a one-sentence generalization that communicates the same idea (as I did in the first paragraph of this answer). Then compare the emotional impact of the story and the generalization.

—M.R.D.—

PERRI KLASS

Learning the Language

In "Learning the Language" Klass, who is a doctor, describes how the specialized language used by doctors separates the insiders (doctors) from the outsiders (the rest of us). She translates baffling terms such as "basic LOL in NAD" ("Little Old Lady in No Apparent Distress"), and she explains the grammatical conventions and patterns of speech. We learn, for example, that under the rules of doctorese the patient, not the patient's condition, is always the subject of the verb. Thus the correct sentence is not "The patient's blood pressure fell," but "The patient dropped his blood pressure." In addition to providing us with a fascinating glimpse into the mysterious world of medical jargon, Klass forces us to consider the consequences of exclusionary language.

This essay will remind your students of their own encounters with specialized language—both as insiders who knew the language and as outsiders who did not—and it should provide them with a greater understanding of those experiences.

QUESTIONS

1. What are the advantages and disadvantages of the special language of doctors?

Klass suggests that "doctor talk" has at least two advantages. Some phrases such as NG for nasogastric provide abbreviations that save time and probably prevent embarrassing spelling errors. In addition, the special language of doctors "contributes to a sense of closeness and professional spirit among people who are under a great deal of stress" (paragraph 8).

The primary disadvantage of medical jargon is that it enables doctors to "maintain some distance from their patients" (paragraph 18). Of course, some degree of emotional distance is essential for a doctor's mental health, but when jargon increases that distance from centimeters to light-years, doctors are no longer able to recognize their patients as fellow humans. The condescending and paternalistic label LOL in NAD (little old lady in no apparent distress) stereotypes Mrs. Tolstoy by placing her in the general category of old women who irritate their doctors by continuing to experience aches and pains even after their doctors have declared them healthy (paragraph 1). And the use of terms such as "terminal players" (paragraph 6) or "CTD" ("Circling The Drain," paragraph 11) allows doctors to forget that they are referring to *people* who are dying. The convention I find even more disturbing is that of making the patient the subject of the verb. When doctors say, "Mrs. Bacon failed chemotherapy" rather than "Chemotherapy failed to cure Mrs. Bacon's cancer" (paragraph 5), they are identifying Mrs. Bacon as their adversary rather than their patient, and they are blaming her for her failure to get well. It would be simplistic to conclude that jargon is the sole cause of the contemporary doctor-patient schism, but the attitudes fostered by such callous language can only exacerbate an already serious problem.

2. Describe the special language of a group you belong to and discuss the functions of that language.

You may want your students to write their answers to this question because, in essence, we are asking them to write an essay similar to Klass's. Some of your students may protest that they don't belong to any group that speaks a special language, but I'll bet they do. Some of them may be able to talk sports, or cars, or heavy metal—using jargon unintelligible to the outsider. Some have probably worked as waitresses, or sales clerks, or legislative aides and learned work-related languages. Others probably belong to churches, clubs, sororities, or fraternities—all distinguished by their own languages. If all else fails, ask them to consider the special language of their neighborhood, of their peer group, or of college students.

All of them will probably decide, as Klass does, that jargon has at least two functions. One function is to facilitate communication among group members; the other is to exclude those who do not belong to the group. It's the second that causes so much trouble. If your students have read Lewis's "The Inner Ring," they should recall his warning that the desire to be an insider is "one of the great permanent mainsprings of human action" and that it seldom prompts us "to any act or word on which, in the cold small hours of a wakeful night, [we] can look back with satisfaction." I suspect that most of us enjoy jargon because it allows us to demonstrate that we are among the elect. Is that why the phrases "higher order reasoning," "heuristics," "discourse communities," and "hermaneutics" come up so often during conversations at CCCC?

3. Describe an incident that caused you to feel excluded because you didn't know the special language.

Question 2 is based on the assumption that everyone is sometimes an insider. This question assumes that everyone is sometimes an outsider. Students who have been patients in hospitals may want to respond directly to Klass's essay by explaining what it is like to be puzzled and perhaps frightened by medical terminology. Others may have felt like aliens when they watched a trial, asked a mechanic what was wrong with the car, watched a soccer game, or went through rush week.

4. Do the benefits of specialized languages outweigh their detriments?

This is a difficult but crucial question. After your students have considered both the joys of inclusion and the misery of exclusion, they should be able to examine jargon more critically and decide when it is worth keeping and when we should toss it. This is a question near to my heart because I teach legal research and writing to first-year law students, and I valiantly attempt to persuade them not to write like lawyers. Law students have to make a conscious effort to write in plain English because they spend most of their waking hours reading appellate court decisions written in legalese. After a very short time, passive voice and phrases such as "said party of the first part hereinafter referred to as seller" begin to sound right.

I suggest that students who want to communicate rather than obfuscate follow two rules: (1) When you write for someone who is not a lawyer, if you simply must use a legal term, define it. Better yet, try to explain the concept without using the term. That rule generally keeps us from mystifying and excluding our clients. (2) When you write for other lawyers, distinguish between legalese and terms of art; cut out the legalese and keep the terms of art. Legalese includes "whereas," "said" (when used as an adjective), "aforementioned" and any other term that can be replaced with a simpler and less formidable word. In contrast, a term of art is a word or phrase that allows us to explain with only a few words a concept that would otherwise require a lengthy definition. "Consideration," "hearsay," and "exclusionary rule," for example, are hard workers that carry tons of information.

Perhaps similar rules for other specialized languages would allow us to retain the significant benefits while eliminating their pernicious effects.

—M.R.D.—

Style Lesson 30: Sports Metaphors in the Hospital

Try to supply the missing words from the following passage from paragraphs 6 and 7 of Klass's "Learning the Language." How do you feel about the use of the extended metaphor? Does it enliven the subject or trivialize it?

_____ metaphor is pervasive. A _____ is a night without any new admissions. A ______ is always a patient—a nitrate ______ is a patient on nitrates, a unit ______ is a patient in the intensive care unit, and so on, until you reach the terminal _______.

It is interesting to consider what it means to be ______, or doing well, in this perennial ______ game. When the intern hangs up the phone and announces, "I _____ a _____," that is not cause for _________. The team is not ______ points; rather, it is getting hit, being _______ with new patients. The object of the ______ from the point of view of the doctors, considering the ______ for whom they are already responsible, is to get as few new _____ as possible.

ADRIENNE RICH

Split at the Root: An Essay on Jewish Identity

In 1961 when Rich was thirty-one, she wrote a poem in which she described herself as "Split at the root, neither Gentile nor Jew,/ Yankee nor Rebel" (paragraph 5). In this essay (written in 1982), Rich continues to explore the many facets of her identity that make her both an outsider and an insider.

> The middle-class white girl taught to trade obedience for privilege. The Jewish lesbian raised to be a heterosexual gentile. The woman who first heard oppression named and analyzed in the Black Civil Rights struggle. The woman with three sons, the feminist who hates male violence (paragraph 56).

Rich gives us a different view of the insiders-outsiders question. Through her analysis of her own background, personality, and beliefs, Rich reminds us that every person is a complex being who differs significantly from the members of any given group. Thus, even when we seem to be insiders, we are in some ways outsiders as well.

QUESTIONS

1. By what signs does Rich learn that Christian is the norm and that everyone else is outside the norm? Are those signs still present?

Rich states, "The social world in which I grew up was christian virtually without needing to say so—christian imagery, music, language, symbols, assumptions everywhere" (paragraph 14). She later catalogues some of the signs that marked her world as Christian: Episcopal hymns, prayers, and Bible readings at her school (paragraph 18), the use of the word *Christian* "as a synonym for virtuous, just, peace-loving, generous, etc., etc." (paragraph 20), and even the celebration of a "secular, liberal Christmas" with her Jewish husband and children (paragraph 46). As Rich notes, "you could raise your children to be as vaguely or distinctly Jewish as you would, but Christian myth and calendar organized the year" (paragraph 46).

Rich was born in 1929, and some of the specifics have changed. For example, since Rich's childhood, the Supreme Court has prohibited prayer in public schools (although that issue is still a political hot potato). However, there is little doubt that Christianity is still the norm. Public schools may call the December school vacation "winter holiday," but that break always includes Christmas day. American authors who quote from the Koran or the Upanishad generally provide their readers with footnotes to identify those religious texts, but the same authors assume that their readers will know what the Bible is. Americans are also expected to recognize allusions to Biblical figures and to realize that a reference such as 1 Cor. 13:13 indicates a specific chapter and verse from the Bible. Your students, especially those who are not Christian, will have no trouble listing other indicia of Christianity's cultural dominance.

2. In how many ways does Rich see herself as an outsider? In what ways do you consider yourself an outsider?

The first part of this question will be easier to discuss in class because it requires nothing more than careful reading and analysis. Although the subtitle of the essay, "An Essay on Jewish Identity," suggests that Rich is an outsider because her father is Jewish, the answer to this question, like Rich herself, is far more complicated. Rich's recognition of her status as an outsider begins with her realization that she is outside Jewish culture and tradition. Because her mother is a gentile, according to Jewish law, Rich is not considered a Jew (paragraph 10). Because her father rejects Judaism, Rich grows up knowing nothing about Jewish religion, holidays, or foods (paragraph 24). And because she did not personally experience the Holocaust, she feels unworthy to claim kinship with the courageous people who suffered and died because they were Jews. Her sense of alienation from other Jews leads her to embrace her Jewish husband's family, people who represent "that new and mysterious Jewish world" (paragraph 41).

At the same time, Rich feels that she is outside the white southern gentile society of her childhood. Two of her grandparents are Jewish, which would have been enough for Nazis to label her *Mischling, first-degree* —non-exempt from the Final Solution" (paragraph 13). Consequently, she grows up feeling that she is "*seen* as Jewish" by the gentiles around her, and her father urges Rich, her sister, and her mother to "speak quietly in public, to dress without ostentation, to repress all vividness and spontaneity" (paragraph 32) so no one will think of them as Jewish.

Other facets of Rich's identity also label her an outsider. As a white southern woman who grew up in a world where racism was a given, she is in some ways outside the black struggle for Civil Rights, even though she is an activist committed to that cause. As a feminist, she is outside the separate strands of patriarchy represented by her father (paragraph 42) and by Judaism (paragraph 53). And as a lesbian, she is outside the "inveterate romantic heterosexual fantasy" (paragraph 11) of our society.

The second part of this question, which requires students to reveal something about themselves, may be more difficult for your class to talk about. This question might work better as a writing topic, or you might get the discussion started by describing some of the ways you saw yourself as an outsider when you were a college student.

3. Why does Rich condemn her father's decision to assimilate into the dominant gentile culture?

Among other things, this essay is a character study of Arnold Rich, the father Adrienne Rich must "expose" "in order to claim" (paragraph 1). By my count, Rich refers directly to her father in 18 of this essay's 55 paragraphs. She describes him as a modern Renaissance man—a professor of pathology at Johns Hopkins and also an amateur musician who collected books, traveled widely, knew several languages, "read poetry," and "adored encyclopedic knowledge" (paragraph 34). Rich recognizes her father's genius, and she gratefully acknowledges his contributions to her achievements.

> He taught me . . . to believe in hard work, to mistrust easy inspiration, to write and rewrite; to feel that I *was* a person of the book, even though a woman; to take ideas seriously (paragraph 35).

Nevertheless, Rich clearly faults her father for ignoring his Jewishness and thus denying her a part of her identity. She recalls that when she was a child her parents sent her to the Episcopal church and that, after church, her father read to her from Thomas Paine's *The Age of Reason* so that she would have a choice. Rich then remarks, "He . . . did not give me the choice to be a Jew" (paragraph 19).

But Rich's quarrel with her father involves more than her own private loss of heritage. As she later realizes, she and her father represent "two strains of Jewish social identity: the Jew as radical visionary and activist who understands oppression firsthand, and the Jew as part of America's devouring plan in which the persecuted, called to assimilation, learn that the price is to engage in persecution" (paragraph 48). Adrienne Rich gives us a number of examples of her father's willingness to engage (at least symbolically) in such persecution:

- Ironically, Adrienne is playing Portia in her school's production of *The Merchant of Venice.* Her father coaches her to convey "more scorn and contempt" when she says the word "Jew" (paragraph 16).
- Arnold Rich tells his daughter, "You know that I have never denied that I am a Jew. But it's not important to me. . . . I am a person, not simply a Jew" (paragraph 30).
- Adrienne Rich's parents teach her that to identify with "the 'wrong kind' of Jew" is "to court downward mobility" (paragraph 33).
- Arnold Rich refuses to attend his daughter's wedding when she marries "a Jew of the 'wrong kind' from an Orthodox eastern European background" (paragraph 39).

Adrienne Rich does not condemn her father because he rejects Judaism but because—in her view—he rejects it for the wrong reason. In her opinion, his claim that Judaism is unimportant to him because he is a scientist who has no need for organized religion is at best a half truth (paragraph 30), and she is convinced that his real motive for distancing himself from his background is less noble—that he sells his birthright for a professorship. Although Adrienne Rich also separates herself from Judaism (because it is a patriarchy that represses women), she distinguishes her motives from her father's when she says to herself, "If Jews had to wear yellow stars again,

I, too, would wear the yellow star . . ." (paragraph 53). Unlike her father, she refuses to be assimilated if doing so means that she will be implicated in the persecution of others.

Your students may not agree with Rich's assumption that everyone who opts for assimilation tacitly consents to the persecution of those who do not choose to be assimilated, but it's certainly a question worth discussing, especially in a nation that proudly calls itself a "melting pot."

—M.R.D.—

Style Lesson 31: A Sentence with an Important Appositive

Imitate the following sentence phrase by phrase, producing a sentence about your own experience as an outsider (e.g., as the only male, female, Asian, nerd, etc., in a group). The exercise should produce thoughts about weightier matters than style.

With enough excellence,
you could presumably make it stop mattering
    that you were Jewish;
you could become the *only* Jew in the gentile world,
    a Jew so "civilized,"
        so far from "common,"
        so attractively combining southern gentility
            with European cultural values
        that no one would ever confuse you
        with the raw, "pushy" Jews of New York,
            the "loud, hysterical" refugees from eastern Europe,
            the "overdressed" Jews of the urban South.

NADINE GORDIMER

Which New Era Would That Be?

Nadine Gordimer, a white South African woman, is a well-known novelist and short story writer. Many of her stories are set in her native country, and she often explores the effects of apartheid. Apparently for that reason, three of her novels were banned in South Africa. Gordimer refused to appeal the banning because she didn't want to recognize the authority of the board of censors. In response to the observation that the government considers her disloyal, she stated: "I consider myself an intensely loyal South African. I care deeply for my country. If I didn't, I wouldn't still be there."

In "Which New Era Would That Be?" Gordimer demonstrates how extraordinarily complicated race relations can be. The story centers around a social encounter between a liberal white woman, Jennifer, and a group of black men. Jennifer goes with her escort Alister, a white correspondent for a newspaper in England, to visit his black friend Jake. In fact, Jake is, according to the South African system, "coloured"—that is, a mixture of white and black ancestry. In spite of, or perhaps because of, Jennifer's attempts to understand the problems of being black in South Africa, she manages to offend and alienate Jake.

QUESTIONS

1. What does this story tell us about the possibility of improving relations between members of the oppressed and oppressing classes?

Nadine Gordimer has often been praised for her ability to understand South African blacks, and yet this short story offers a rather pessimistic view of the possibility for true understanding between the races. Jennifer Tetzel is enough like Nadine Gordimer (a progressive white woman who is opposed to the apartheid policy) to suggest that her attempt to understand Jake and communicate with him is a mirror of Gordimer's attempts to do the same. If Gordimer believes that communication is impossible, perhaps it is.

But, of course, Jennifer is not Gordimer, and Gordimer as author shows us that no matter how well-meaning Jennifer is, she makes at least three serious mistakes. One is that she relates to Jake and the other men, not as individuals, but as representatives of an oppressed group. Second, she insists that she can understand exactly how blacks in South Africa feel. And finally, because she confuses form and substance, she naively assumes that changing form is the same as changing substance. For example, when Jake attempts to introduce her as "Miss ——?" Jennifer fills in with her first name ("Jennifer. Jennifer Tetzel"), leaving the men so uncomfortable that not one of them addresses her by name (paragraphs 15 and 16). Her confusion is also apparent in her decision to live in Cape Flats, a "desolate coloured slum," because she feels guilty that anyone else should have to live there (paragraphs 34–36). Again she changes the form without realizing that the substance is unchanged. She is still free to escape to her flat in Cape Town on Sundays; the colored inhabitants do not have that option.

A somewhat different view of black and white relationships is presented by the friendship between Alister and Jake. Unlike Jennifer, Alister is comfortable with the form if not the substance of the racial barrier. Although Alister and Jake are good friends, Alister does not object when Jake addresses him as Mr. Halford. Alister obviously enjoys Jake as a likeable companion, not as a black man he should feel sorry for. Probably the most significant difference between Jennifer and Alister is that Jennifer chooses to suffer with the oppressed class (by living in Cape Flats, for example) and Alister opts to have fun with a few friends who happen to be a different color. Perhaps Gordimer is telling us that even if complete understanding between classes is impossible, communication between members of those classes can occur.

2. How does the opening clarify the relations between classes in South Africa?

Gordimer packs a great deal of information into the opening paragraphs of the story. Gordimer uses plot, dialogue, setting, and description to explain the class structure of the country and to suggest each character's place within that system. When the story opens, Jake is frying bacon while talking to a group of men in the back room of a printing shop. It is a perfectly innocuous scene. Then Jake hears a knock at the door and the mood veers abruptly. Jake silences the men, and they respond by cautiously finishing the brandy in their glasses and hiding the glasses. We are immediately put on notice that South Africa is a police state, and no black man can assume that a knock on the door is friendly.

Next we have the scene at the door. Alister identifies himself: "Me——Alister," and calls Jake by his first name. Jake, however, calls him Mr. Halford, suggesting the gulf between their classes. Jennifer steps forward, introduces herself by her first and last name, and shakes hands with Jake. But Jake refuses the forced familiarity and does not address her by name (paragraphs 3–5). In a matter of moments Gordimer has informed us that each is aware of the traditional relationships between the classes and that each responds to the traditional expectations differently.

A brief look at the setting, a building entered through an archway lettered NEW ERA BUILDING, allows Gordimer to show us that although both Jennifer and Alister are progressives, it occurs to neither that the "new era" might refer to the status of blacks in South Africa. The setting further informs us that blacks live in the rundown end of town. And the fact that the building smells of "waiting" and "acceptance" illustrates the complex attitude of black South Africans such as Jake (paragraph 6).

Next Gordimer gives us a sharply detailed physical description of Jake's and Alister's clothing, and she tells us that Jennifer was immediately recognizable to Jake as a type of white woman he knew well. In less than two pages Gordimer has given us all we need to understand the tensions that soon develop.

3. What is it about Jennifer that so irritates Jake?

Obviously, part of Jake's problem with Jennifer stems from the fact that she is white. After all, it is because she is white that she cannot believe Maxie's story about the lunch (paragraphs 91 and 92). But that can't be the major cause of his dislike for her. Alister is white, and Jake considers Alister a friend.

Actually, Jake is annoyed because Jennifer doesn't look or act the way Jake thinks women should. He tells us he likes his women "sort of round" (paragraph 53), which Jennifer's "bony brow" and "slender fingers" indicate that she is not. And his picture of the ideal European woman is one who is "big, soft . . . with curly yellow hair," "one of those women with nothing resistant about them . . ." (paragraph 59). Gordimer's description of Jennifer in paragraph 8 as a "determined woman" with "black hair" is a decided contrast. Jake's preference is for a woman who apparently would not object if he referred to her as "a little parcel" from Zululand. Jake wonders what his friend could see in women like Jennifer—"bristling, sharp, all-seeing, knowing women, who talked like men, who wanted to show all the time that, apart from sex, they were exactly the same as men" (paragraph 59). One reason Jake is so insulted by "white women who persisted in regarding themselves as your equal" (paragraph 7) is that he is quite certain that all women—white or black—are his inferiors.

Jennifer further irritates Jake by treating him as a member of a class rather than as a person who wants to be liked or disliked for his own merits or flaws. In the same way that Jennifer lives in Cape Flats, not because she likes her neighbors but because living there assuages her guilt, she is interested in Jake merely because he is black and she is a liberal. Jake, a "man interested in women, money, brandy, and boxing" (paragraph 8), is precisely the kind of person Jennifer would feel free to dislike if he were white. Jake understands that. And he resents being liked for the color of his skin as much as he resents being kept out of a bar because of it.

Ironically, although Jake dislikes Jennifer because she responds to his class membership rather than to his individual personality, he is guilty of the same sin. Here is Gordimer's description of Jake's thoughts when he meets Jennifer, "He had never met her before but he knew the type well" (paragraph 7). Throughout the story, Jake thinks of Jennifer as a representative of liberated European women, not as a unique person.

4. How does Gordimer use point of view to control our reaction to the characters?

Generally, readers empathize with the characters they know best. Although this story is written in third person and the author is nearly omniscient, Gordimer chooses to present most of the events from Jake's perspective. Jake's assessment of Jennifer is decidedly unflattering. Consequently, the reader gets a rather negative view of her. Gordimer never tells us what Jennifer is thinking or why she says or does certain things. For example, after Jennifer tells Maxie that she does not believe his story about the lunch, Gordimer writes what seems to be an objective description of Jennifer's motives, but a closer examination reveals that paragraph 92 is either Jake's view of the scene or, given the language of the passage, Jake's view as stated and endorsed by Gordimer.

Gordimer also permits us occasional glimpses into the minds of other characters. In paragraph 20 she shows us Temba, laughing heartily "at the idea of himself as a cricket-playing white public-school boy." And later she explains that Temba is embarrassed by an innocent remark he made to Jennifer: "He had not meant to sound so familiar" (paragraph 28). In another scene, after Jennifer explains her need to expiate the guilt she feels because of the racial situation, Gordimer tells us that Maxie shrugs, "as if at the mention of some expensive illness he had never been able to afford and whose symptoms he could not imagine" (paragraph 37). In each instance, what is revealed by the character's thoughts makes him more likeable.

In short, Gordimer—who knows perfectly well that most of her readers will be white liberals—uses point of view to make a white liberal the subject of criticism, ridicule, and scorn. Gordimer clearly believes that good relations between blacks and whites in South Africa depend on a certain humility in whites and an admission that they cannot fully understand the inner lives of blacks. By attacking Jennifer, Gordimer forces her white readers to recognize their limitations. Gordimer would probably agree with the following observation made by Martin Luther King, Jr., in "Letter from Birmingham Jail": "Shallow understanding from people of good will is more frustrating than absolute misunderstanding from people of ill will".

—M.R.D.—

LILIANA HEKER

The Stolen Party

Most of the selections in this unit focus on the feelings of isolation experienced by outsiders who recognize their position. In contrast, "The Stolen Party" shows us the humiliation of a child who, convinced that she is an insider, suddenly discovers that she is not. Nine-year-old Rosaura, the daughter of a maid, is invited to the birthday party of a classmate, Luciana Ines, whose mother employs Rosaura's mother. In spite of her mother's misgivings, Rosaura attends the party and has a delightful time. She is particularly pleased because she is the only child who is allowed to help serve the refreshments. When the children depart, Señora Ines gives each child a small gift—yo-yos for the boys and bracelets for the girls. But there is no gift for Rosaura. Instead, Señora Ines hands her money and says, "You really and truly earned this. . . . Thank you for all your help, my pet" (paragraph 69).

This story is more than an attempt to untangle the skein of rules governing social relationships between wealthy Argentines and their domestic servants. Reading "The Stolen Party" should cause your students to consider the complex symbol system of our own society, and may inspire some to write about how they learned to interpret the cryptic clues that tell us when we're in and when we're out.

QUESTIONS

1. Why does Señora Ines offer Rosaura money rather than a gift?

Because the point of view doesn't allow us to see inside Señora Ines's mind, we can only speculate about her motivation. In fact, some of your students might want to rewrite the story from Señora Ines's perspective.

If we want to be charitable, we can say that Señora Ines knows that Rosaura's family is poor, and she assumes that the child needs the money more than she needs a bauble. There is certainly no evidence that Señora Ines intends to hurt Rosaura. In fact, Señora Ines compliments Rosaura on her appearance (paragraph 17), hushes a party guest who persists in asking Rosaura questions about her mother's employment (paragraph 35), and tells Rosaura's mother that her daughter is "marvelous" (paragraph 66). But Señora Ines's politeness is motivated not by egalitarianism but by noblesse oblige. To demonstrate this point we have only to ask ourselves whether Señora Ines would have treated a child of her own social class in the same way.

Certainly she could not favor any other girl by complimenting her because doing so would cause everyone else to dislike the one singled out. But, of course, no one can resent the maid's daughter, who doesn't even have a new dress for the party (paragraph 15). Neither would Señora Ines end questions about the occupation of any other child's parent. Thus her "protection" of Rosaura merely confirms the girl's suspicion that she should be embarrassed to admit that her mother is a maid. Finally, Señora Ines would not tell a woman from her own social class that her daughter is marvelous. Such praise (unless it follows a specific accomplishment) suggests the superiority of the person who pronounces her judgments. It also suggests that the child's achievement is somehow surprising. Apparently, Señora Ines never imagines that the messages that might insult her social equals could also offend her maid, a woman she addresses by her first name, "Herminia" (paragraph 66).

Each of Señora Ines's kindnesses falls into the category of behavior that amounts to being nice to people in a way that tells them they are inferior to us. As Heker shows us in the final lines of the story, Señora Ines must offer Rosaura money rather than a gift if she is to fortify the fragile class barrier that separates them:

> Señora Ines, motionless, stood there with her hand outstretched. As if she didn't dare draw it back. As if the slightest change might shatter an infinitely delicate balance.

2. If Rosaura's mother could have watched the party through a hidden camera, at what point would she have realized that her daughter was not a guest at the party?

Rosaura is shocked by Señora Ines's offer of money because the girl has not yet learned to tell the difference between courtesy and friendship. Rosaura's mother would not have made that mistake. Her wariness of the upper classes is evidenced by her initial reluctance to let Rosaura attend the party (paragraph 2) and by her uneasiness when Señora Ines asks them to wait by the door for a minute (paragraph 57). Herminia would have understood the significance of each of the "kindnesses" discussed in Question 2, and she certainly would have known that no guest would be allowed to go into the kitchen or to help serve the refreshments. Your students may disagree about which incident should have been the tip-off for Rosaura, but all will agree that the girl is oblivious to social nuances that are clear to the adults of the story.

3. What is the significance of the monkey in the story?

Students always hate having their teachers "read things into a story," but the monkey is too obvious a symbol to ignore, partly because it is mentioned so often (paragraphs 1, 10–12, 18–19, 40–52, and 54). On one level the monkey is a reminder of the huge chasm separating the wealthy Señora Ines, who can afford to hire a magician and his monkey for her child's entertainment, and Rosaura's mother, who can't imagine such extravagance and accuses her daughter of believing "nonsense."

To Rosaura, the monkey symbolizes everything that is good and noble about the rich:

> As soon as she arrived she went straight to the kitchen to see if the monkey was there. It was: what a relief! She wouldn't have liked to admit that her mother had been right (paragraph 1).

Rosaura's relief suggests more than the typical youthful reluctance to hear a parent say "I told you so." If Rosaura knows that her mother is wrong about the monkey, she can also believe that her mother is wrong when she insists that Luciana is not Rosaura's friend.

But, as it turns out, Rosaura's mother is not wrong. Rosaura's status at the party is much like the monkey's. Both "employees" are treated kindly, but are expected to perform as requested. Calling the monkey "partner" (paragraph 40) doesn't make it the magician's equal any more than inviting Rosaura to the party raises her to the social level of the other guests, a fact made painfully clear in the final scene when Señora Ines addresses Rosaura as "my pet" (paragraph 69).

4. What does the story's title mean?

The titles students affix to their own writings indicate that most students give little thought to their selections. It might be worth pointing out that titles can serve a variety of functions. Some titles, such as "Adam Smith's Division of Labor," merely describe the subject matter of the writing. Others, such as Adrienne Rich's "Claiming An Education," emphasize a crucial point the writer doesn't want us to miss. Still others, such as Mary McCarthy's "Artists in Uniform," cause us to interpret the writing differently than we would have if it had been labeled "Number 27." To illustrate this point you might ask your students to look through the table of contents for the *Dolphin Reader* to find their own examples of each type. They might also want to propose a classification system other than the one I described.

Your students will probably agree that Heker's deliberately ambiguous title is one that forces us to rethink our original reading of the story. The title may be meant to show us that Señora Ines, with her final gesture of offering money, steals from Rosaura the party that, until that moment, rightfully belonged to the girl. Stealing usually involves taking something without paying for it, but, ironically, in this instance the theft occurs when Señora Ines tries to pay for Rosaura's services. On the other hand, the title may suggest that Rosaura, not Señora Ines, is the thief. From Señora Ines's perspective, the party belongs to Luciana and her peers. Yet Rosaura nearly succeeds in "stealing the show" when she wins the sack race, escapes capture during tag, and discovers that all the boys want her on their team for charades. If Rosaura leaves the party believing herself the equal of the other children, she steals not only the party, but also Señora Ines's opportunity to play generous benefactor and Señora Ines's previously unchallenged faith in the security of her own status.

—M.R.D.—

NATURE
AND
CIVILIZATION

OVERVIEW OF UNIT

How are we like and unlike the animals around us? To what extent does our happiness and welfare depend on "doing what comes naturally" and to what extent on rising above the natural? *Nature and Civilization*, besides providing some excellent models of descriptive writing, raises questions like these.

How we answer these questions will affect the way we view the shift away from nature that comes with material and economic progress, whether we see femininity and masculinity as extensions of the natural order of things or as inventions, whether we see our tendency to divide the world into insiders and outsiders as an extension of the hierarchical principles of animal societies, whether we see the human as essentially a creature of the community. The splash of civilization into nature (or vice versa) is the center of many ripples of thought, so this unit can be easily connected with the others in *The Dolphin Reader*.

Central ideas in the unit are most fully articulated by Loren Eiseley (who sees even nostalgia, the most "human" of emotions, embedded in our animal heritage), Brigid Brophy (who would sooner set her feet in a bucket of concrete than be embedded in nature), and Edward Hoagland (who regards with regret our increasing denial of our animal nature). The other essays and Doris Lessing's short story involve encounters between humans and the natural world, including some encounters (Thomas, White, Greene) that occur in nooks of the cityscape. These essays—filled with good examples of development by anecdote and description—can provide models for students who want to write about their own encounters with the natural world.

AGATHA CHRISTIE

Butterfly

In this tiny vignette about her own childhood, Agatha Christie vividly describes a traumatic horseback ride with her father, her older sister, and a guide. The guide, as a kindness to little Agatha, captures a butterfly and attaches it to her hat by sticking a pin through the live insect, which continues to flutter. The little girl is horrified, but can't bring herself to hurt the guide's feelings by explaining why she is upset. Instead, she ruins everyone's ride by crying all afternoon.

"The Butterfly" is a great model for student writing. In this very short story, Christie focuses on a single incident and describes an encounter with the natural world and her response to that encounter. After examining Christie's technique, your students should be ready to attempt similar narratives about their own experiences.

QUESTIONS

1. Why is Agatha so miserable after the guide pins the butterfly to her hat?

Students may be tempted to answer that the little girl is unhappy because she sympathizes with the suffering butterfly. Of course that's correct, but if that was the only problem, Agatha would tell the guide to unpin the butterfly (or to kill it quickly), and both she and the insect could escape their misery. Unfortunately for the girl, her sympathy for the butterfly is counterbalanced by her sympathy for the guide. She knows that he is motivated by kindness, and she cannot bring herself to hurt him by telling him that she considers his act cruel. Her suffering is intensified by the knowledge that she is ruining the trip for everyone else, and by her inability to express her feelings. Even after the butterfly stops flapping, she continues to cry because no one understands her moral dilemma. The child cannot be released from her pain until someone else intuits and articulates for her the conflicting emotions she cannot voice. That is exactly what her mother does in the final scene.

2. Is the moral revulsion the little girl feels because of the butterfly's suffering justified?

The purpose of this question is to encourage your students to consider whether we have an ethical obligation to treat animals humanely and—if their answer is yes—to attempt to define the nature of that obligation. As the controversy regarding the recent transplant of a baboon liver to a human demonstrates, our society is deeply divided by this question. At one extreme, we have animal rights activists who argue that animals should have the right to live their lives free from human exploitation, and that humans should not use animals for food, for experimentation, or for entertainment. At the opposite end of the spectrum are those who contend that, because we are superior to all other animals, we can do what we like with them, even if what we like is cockfighting. Most of us find ourselves somewhere in between, often in the awkward position of holding logically inconsistent views. Personally, I was horrified that the guide would allow that butterfly to suffer, but I wouldn't hesitate to swat a fly, and I'm not sure that I would be equally concerned about the sufferings of a mosquito or a cockroach.

To illustrate the moral morass we find ourselves in, you might ask your students to decide whether each of the following is right or wrong:

Euthanasia of unwanted pets
Fishing
Hunting
Eating meat
Wearing furs
Wearing leather
Using laboratory animals to test cosmetics
Using laboratory animals to test drugs or medical procedures
Bullfighting

Killing primates to use their organs to save human lives
Keeping animals as pets
Keeping animals in zoos

This exercise will provoke a lively debate and should encourage each student to analyze the basis of his or her own beliefs.

3. How does Christie structure the plot of this story to keep us interested?

It may be useful to point out to your students that even though "The Butterfly" looks like raw memory, it is instead a carefully structured story. To help your students recognize this story as a story, you might ask them to list some of the things Christie does not tell us about that memorable horseback ride. (For example, she does not describe either the horses or the scenery.) Like any good storyteller, Christie omits everything that is not directly related to her encounter with the butterfly, and the events that she does include are arranged for maximum dramatic effect. The story opens with a short exposition. Then the conflict arises when the guide pins the butterfly to the girl's hat, and the little girl finds herself trapped by conflicting ethical demands. We want to know whether the girl will be able to escape from that trap, but the author keeps us in suspense—first raising our hopes by suggesting possible escape routes, then dashing them when those routes turn out to be dead ends: Will she answer her father's or sister's questions about the cause of her unhappiness? No. Will they be able to guess why she is crying? No. Will she feel better after the butterfly stops flapping? No, again. Finally, after we have nearly given up hope, her mother rescues Agatha by recognizing the cause of her tears. By arranging the events so that they build steadily toward this climax, Christie transforms memories into literature.

—M.R.D.—

ANNIE DILLARD

The Fixed

In "The Fixed," a chapter from *Pilgrim at Tinker Creek*, the book that won her a Pulitzer Prize, Annie Dillard displays her incredible talent for observing nature and then describing it so vividly that the rest of us see as we have never seen before. On one level the book is a record of her observations of the natural world surrounding her home at Tinker Creek in Virginia. But to stop there is rather like saying that George Orwell's "Shooting an Elephant" is about an elephant hunt. In fact, she tells us that her purpose was to keep "what Thoreau called 'a meteorological journal of the mind,' telling some tales and describing some of the sights of this rather tamed valley, and exploring, in fear and trembling, some of the unmapped dim reaches and unholy fastnesses to which those tales and sights so dizzyingly lead."

In "The Fixed" Dillard graphically describes an incident that illustrates the tragic results of human interference with nature. She tells us that when she was ten, a classmate brought a Polyphemus moth cocoon to school in January. As the children held the cocoon in their hands, the creature inside warmed and decided to emerge. The well-meaning teacher dropped the cocoon inside a Mason jar where the moth, which often has a wingspan of six inches, finally struggled out of his cocoon. The clarity of Dillard's vision, her unrelenting honesty, and the power of her language are all evident in her picture of the event:

> He couldn't spread his wings. There was no room. The chemical that coated his wings like varnish, stiffening them permanently, dried, and hardened his wings as they were. He was a monster in a Mason jar. Those huge wings stuck on his back in a torture of random pleats and folds, wrinkled as a dirty tissue, rigid as leather. They made a single nightmare clump still wracked with useless, frantic convulsions.

QUESTIONS

1. What does the essay tell us about the relationships between people and nature?

Note that the question uses the plural—relationships— because Dillard shows us that there are different possibilities. The role she wants us to avoid is that of humans as bunglers who unwittingly and unnecessarily interfere with nature. She relates several examples of such occurrences. In paragraph 4 she describes the praying mantises who hatch in a Mason jar at school and, because "the teacher never summoned the nerve or the sense to release them," devour each other. She tells us about the praying mantis egg case that she discovered, checked on throughout the winter, and visited daily in the spring hoping to see the mantises hatch. One day the egg case was gone: "Somehow my neighbor had contrived to run a tractor-mower over that steep clay hill on which there grew nothing to mow but a few stubby thorns" (paragraph 11). And, of course, there is the horror story of the Polyphemus moth (paragraphs 15–20). At first glance, Dillard's belief that humanity can destroy nature seems to differ from Lewis Thomas's position that nature is tough enough to prevail in spite of us. But Thomas is optimistic about nature as a whole, about the survival of life in some form. Dillard's focus is on particular individuals who are undeniably fragile.

Dillard offers us a second choice. Because people are able to learn, we do not have to be bunglers. We can be moral agents who make responsible and ethical decisions. In Dillard's opinion, the knowledgeable and sensitive relationships between humans and animals that are described in the essays by Lorenz and Eiseley should be the norm rather than the exception. The crucial first step is learning to see. As she wrote in another essay, "I am no scientist. I explore the neighborhood. An infant who has just learned to hold his head up has a frank and forthright way of gazing about him in bewilderment. He hasn't the faintest clue where he is, and he aims to learn. . . . Some unwonted, taught pride diverts us from our original intent, which is to explore the neighborhood, view the landscape, to discover at least *where* it is that we have been so startlingly set down, if we can't learn why."

2. What is Dillard's purpose in writing the essay?

In all of Dillard's essays one of her purposes is to "cleanse the doors of perception." She wants to convince us that we must learn to see the lives around us if we are to avoid maiming or destroying them. She begins by demonstrating that most of us don't see very well. She tells us that once she learned to see praying mantis egg cases, she saw them everywhere. Obviously, few of us have had that experience. She then allows us to see, through her eyes, what few of us would have noted or appreciated with our own. And what we see is fascinating. Her account of the praying mantis laying eggs was, as she says of the experience, like a nature movie. With her nose an inch from the insect she describes the abdomen that "puffed like a concertina" and "throbbed like a bellows," the "bubble creature [that] seemed to have two eyes, a frantic little brain, and two busy, soft hands" (paragraph 8). In all honesty, before I read this essay, if I had been invited to my backyard to watch a praying mantis lay eggs, I might have declined. But now I'd be there with "my knees in thorns and my cheeks in clay."

In the passage about the Polyphemus moth, Dillard combines physical vision with moral vision. She is convinced that if we see and understand the consequences of our meddling, we will choose to do what is right. After all, she herself fears to touch the praying mantis egg cases because she remembers the Polyphemus moth (paragraph 13). Perhaps she is overly generous in her assessment of humans, but I prefer to think that she is correct. Certainly she does what she can to show us how tragic the results can be. The grotesque image of the moth "crawling down the driveway, crawling down the driveway hunched, crawling down the driveway on six furred feet, forever" is, for me, as unforgettable as Yeats's rough beast slouching toward Bethlehem.

3. Why does Dillard include three astonishingly grotesque scenes in an essay intended to persuade us to value the natural world?

The answer would be easier if she had included only the description of the Polyphemus moth and the newly hatched praying mantises. Both of those scenes offer evidence of humanity's unintended cruelty. But the scene in which the female mantis placidly eats the male while they are mating (paragraphs 9 and 10) reminds us that equally shocking events occur even when people are not involved.

Dillard is an honest observer of nature, and a number of the events that actually occur are, by human standards, cruel. Dillard insists that we see nature as it is, not through a soft-focus lens, but with all its hard, sharp edges. The natural world is "a world covered in chitin, where implacable realities hold sway" (paragraph 14).

Another of her essays, "Heaven and Earth in Jest" explains why it is necessary to observe every aspect of nature. She wrote, "We wake, if we ever wake at all, to mystery, rumors of death, beauty, violence. . . ." For Dillard, one of the principal reasons for studying nature is to attempt to learn our place in it. "Our life is a faint tracing on the surface of mystery, like the idle, curved tunnels of leaf miners on the face of a leaf. We must somehow take a wider view, look at the whole landscape, really see it, and describe what's going on here. Then we can at least wail the right question into the swaddling band of darkness, or, if it comes to that, choir the proper praise." To take the wider view she advocates, we must be willing to look at the terrible as well as at the beautiful.

4. What bits of description do you find particularly effective and why?

This is obviously a question with no single right answer, but your students should notice that Dillard's descriptions are often pure poetry: "Night is rising in the valley; the creek has been extinguished for an hour, and now only the naked tips of trees fire tapers into the sky like trails of sparks" (paragraph 13). They will also notice an abundance of similes. (I counted 18, but I am sure there are more.) Dillard uses the similes to translate exotic sights into images more easily visualized by her readers. I particularly liked her picture of newly hatched mantises trailing "from the egg case to the base of the Mason jar in a living bridge that looked like Arabic calligraphy, some baffling text from the Koran inscribed down the air by a fine hand" (paragraph 4).

My favorite metaphor is the waterfall described in paragraph 14. Dillard transforms the common simile "Time is like a river" into a breathtaking image. The future rushes toward the lip of the great waterfall, passes momentarily through the present, and tumbles into the past. But for humans, some moments of time are etched indelibly in our consciousness and thus remain in the present: "The Polyphemus moth never made it to the past; it crawls in that crowded, pellucid pool at the lip of the great waterfall."

—M.R.D.—

Style Lesson 32: Precise Verbs and Verbals

In paragraph 8 of "The Fixed," Dillard describes a mantis laying eggs. The description uses a series of verbs and verb forms to show the abdomen's apparently separate life and intelligence. To appreciate how much can be suggested by verb forms, try to recall the words Dillard used instead of the generalized synonyms in capital letters.

. . . I settled my nose an inch from that pulsing abdomen. It MOVED like a concertina, it MOVED like a bellows; it WENT, WORKING, over the BRIGHT, IRREGULAR surface of the egg case FEELING and TOUCHING, PUSHING and CORRECTING. It seemed to act so independently that I forgot the BREATHING brown stick at the other end. The bubble creature seemed to have two eyes, a frantic little brain, and two busy, soft hands. It looked like a hideous, harried mother PREPARING* a fat daughter for a beauty pageant, ADJUSTING* her, FUSSING over her, TOUCHING and REPAIRING and CLEANING and TOUCHING.

*In place of *preparing* and *adjusting*, Dillard uses participles formed of two words, like *giving up* (for surrendering) or *looking over* (for examining).

E. B. WHITE

Twins

"Twins" is by far the better of the two E. B. White "comments" included in *The Dolphin Reader*. The other is on the moon landing discussed at length in the Introduction, pp. 10–18 (where I mention in passing *The New Yorker*'s custom of using the editorial *we*). Good White comments are so seamlessly good that they make admiration easy and analysis hard. In this respect they are like haiku, brilliant tips of enormous icebergs.

I think one way to help your students read White well is to be sure that they have some sense of the iceberg beneath—in this case the tension between civilization and nature, which they will be more sensitive to if they have read other selections from this section. Another is to make sure they understand the effort and artistry that goes into "writing short." Faulkner, who did understand, said that he was forced to switch from sonnets to novels because he couldn't get the *it* said in fourteen lines. White himself once apologized for a long letter, saying he didn't have time to write a short one. In this respect, I think it will help to have them read the discussion of the White comment in the Introduction. The best way, though, to help them see the merit of White's work is to make them cowriters. To that end, I am inserting the following style lesson and assuming that your class will complete it before going on to the discussion questions.

Style Lesson 33:
Recreating the Style of E. B. White

After taking a few minutes to look over the original, use the following pared-down version of "Twins" as a draft to improve in class, either by remembering White's good strokes, or by providing some of your own.

One morning last week we went to the Bronx Zoo to see the moose calf. We had better luck than we expected. The cow moose and her calf were standing near the wall of the deer park below the monkey house, and in order to get a better view we went down to the lower end of the park. The path there is not much travelled. As we approached the corner we noticed a red deer getting up on her feet. Beside her, standing unsteadily, was a spotted fawn. They stood there under a beech. On the ground was another fawn. The second fawn was still wet. The scene happened right in New York City, and we felt better for seeing it.

The doe was only two feet from the wire, and we sat down to see how young fawns behave in the middle of the city. The doe, noticing us, stamped with her forefoot. Then she ate the placenta. The monkeys in the monkey house were screaming and could be heard all over the park. As we watched, the sun came out, and the red and white color of the fawns became brighter. Occasionally, someone would wander by, but of all who passed, none noticed what had occurred. "Looka the kangaroos!" a child cried. And he and his mother looked at the deer and then walked on.

In a few moments the second fawn got up and stood sniffing the deer park. The doe began to dry him with her tongue. Meanwhile, the first fawn walked unsteadily toward the shallow brook and started across. He urinated in mid-stream. Then, while his mother watched, he crossed and lay down under a leaf near the fence, in perfect concealment. Without actually going out of sight, he had disappeared completely. We watched awhile, but he never budged. Before we left we reached through the wire and scratched him between the ears without frightening him.

After they have spent some time thinking about what isn't there in this perfectly competent version, they may be better able to turn to the original and appreciate its virtues.

A great many questions about White's techniques should come up spontaneously in class discussion. Here are some you may want to raise to get things going.

QUESTIONS

1. It is perfectly obvious that two fawns born at the same time are twins. Why does White bother to say so?

Early on, our dummy version omits "and we realized that the doe had just finished twinning." No information is lost by the omission, but much else is. Much of it is a matter of ear, which some of your students will recognize and others will not. Most should see how effective the word *twinning* is here. The very idea of twins carries a hint of the miraculous about it, and this verbal use of a word we usually see as a noun catches us pleasantly by surprise—a verbal echo, if you don't mind my pushing this point a bit, of White's own pleasant surprise.

Once introduced, the word *twin* serves a useful alternative to *fawn*—one that breaks up the monotony of repetition and blurs somewhat the distinction between animal offspring and human.

2. Our version has "standing unsteadily." White has "on legs that were just learning their business." What is better about his wording?

This is partly a question of tone, and therefore part of a larger pattern. White frequently uses very conversational phrases: "better luck than we had bargained for," "working out all right," "a couple of feet from the wire." These have two closely related effects: they make the comment seem rather whimsical, "tossed off" rather than "ground out," and they allow ample contrast for the very precise diction of other passages. Note that he ends the sentence we are now looking at with a dazzling simile: "a spotted fawn, as small and perfect as a trinket seen through a reducing glass." When White wants fine writing, he can produce a line of poetry, but he realizes that a comment will work better if the diction is sometimes looser, giving the reader a little elbow room.

But even in the apparently loose and conversational phrase there is often a surprising precision. "Just learning their business" may be a sort of cliché, but the application to a fawn's legs is fresh and wonderfully apt, suggesting that they are all learning their business independently, going this way and that.

3. What intrusions from civilization has White admitted to his scene, and with what effect?

Let's think about these piecemeal, then collectively. It is a "warm, miserable morning," the kind that makes being indoors almost insupportable.

White is breaking in a new pair of shoes. The beech trunk is carved with hearts and initials. There are few other sightseers, particularly the mother and child who stare "sullenly." And at the moment when White and his readers are most caught up in the charm of the scene, a twelve o'clock whistle sounds "somewhere a long way off." We are always reminded that the scene is not in the countryside, where it would be less remarkable.

Surrounded by an urban, slightly oppressive, workaday world, the chance encounter with the deer is a gift, "a scene of rare, sylvan splendor, in one of our five favorite boroughs." It lifts White's heart, and White lifts ours.

—D.H.—

LEWIS THOMAS

Ponds

Perhaps this essay should have been titled "The Invasion of the Killer Goldfish." In it Lewis Thomas pokes fun at Manhattanites, people so civilized, so far removed from contact with nature, that they are dismayed and frightened by any animal—even a goldfish—that dares to survive outside the wildlife preserve, zoo, or fishbowl to which we have consigned it.

Thomas's vocation is medicine, his specialty pathology, and his avocation the observation of nature. In 1971 he began contributing "Notes of a Biology Watcher" to the *New England Journal of Medicine.* In 1974 several of those essays were published in *The Lives of A Cell: Notes of a Biology Watcher,* which received a National Book Award. In 1979 he published *The Medusa and the Snail: More Notes of a Biology Watcher.* The theme of both books is that symbiosis, a close relationship between organisms for their mutual benefit, is the normal state of existence. In "Ponds," which is a selection from *The Medusa and the Snail,* Thomas expresses his amusement with humans who attempt to separate themselves from nature. As he once explained, "The whole dear notion of one's own self—marvelous old free-willed, free-enterprising, autonomous, independent, isolated island of Self—is a myth."

Although "Ponds" deals with a serious issue—the proper relationship between humans and the rest of nature—Thomas's approach is humorous. He treats the existence of unauthorized goldfish in a style worthy of an epic event. His tone is demonstrated by this beautifully crafted periodic sentence in which he describes the exciting possibility of mutant goldfish:

> And with a certain amount of splashing and grayish-greenish spray, at all the edges of the pond, up all the banks of ancient New York landfill mud, crawling on their new little feet, out onto the sidewalks, up and down and across the street, into doorways and up the fire escapes, some of them with little suckers on their little feet, up the sides of buildings and into open windows, looking for something, will come the goldfish (paragraph 10).

QUESTIONS

1. What does the Manhattanites' attitude toward the goldfish reveal about their attitude toward nature and civilization?

The Manhattanites clearly believe that the purpose of civilization is to conquer nature, to force it to exist on our terms. As Thomas states, "New Yorkers cannot put up with live fish out in the open" (paragraph 3). When nature refuses to stay in its assigned spaces, the Manhattanites demand that all the powers of technology be marshaled to subdue it: Call the ASPCA. "Dynamite, if necessary. But get rid of them" (paragraph 8). Drain the pond by pumping and have the ASPCA come back with nets to catch them (paragraph 7). Purchase cats from out of town. Or "send up teams of professionals from Washington with a new kind of antifish spray. . ." (paragraph 11).

2. How does Thomas's attitude toward nature and civilization differ from that of the Manhattanites?

Thomas is amused by the Manhattanites' basic misunderstanding of the relation between nature and civilization. The Manhattanites naively believe that people control the world and can command nature to do our bidding. Thomas disagrees. He expresses his view in the following statement from "The Lives of a Cell":

> We are told that the trouble with Modern Man is that he has been trying to detach himself from nature. He sits on the topmost tiers of polymer, glass, and steel, dangling his pulsing legs, surveying at a distance the writhing life of the planet. In this scenario, Man comes on as a stupendous lethal force, and the earth is pictured as something delicate, like rising bubbles at the surface of a country pond, or flights of fragile birds. But it is an illusion to think that there is anything fragile about the life of the earth; surely this is the toughest membrane imaginable in the universe, opaque to probability, impermeable to death. We are the delicate part, transient and vulnerable as cilia.

Thomas is reassured rather than frightened by his belief that life on earth will continue even if humans do not. The New Yorkers, on the other hand, prefer to believe in human superiority. That is precisely why they find the goldfish so threatening. As Thomas suggests in paragraph 9, they are frightened by the realization that nature is hardier than civilization. "We do not like to think that life is possible under some conditions." In this instance the goldfish are thriving in an environment humans have poisoned for themselves. The mud around the pond "is not proper country mud but reconstituted Manhattan landfill, ancient garbage, fossilized coffee grounds and grapefruit rind, the defecation of a city" (paragraph 9). And the water of the fish pond is an "upwelling of the East River" so filthy that "if anyone fell in, it was an emergency for the Infectious-Disease Service, and the first measures, after resuscitation, were massive doses of whatever antibiotics the hospital pharmacy could provide." The survival of the goldfish is an unwelcome reminder that it is humanity rather than nature that is vulnerable.

But the alarm of the Manhattanites is not triggered solely by the reminder of our own vulnerability. After all, Thomas reacts differently to the same reminder. Why? Maybe it's because people often fear and consequently hate the unfamiliar. To Thomas nature is a long-time friend. He likes to think that it will survive his personal death. But the Manhattanites are so distanced from nature that they have no love for it, only fear. When I read this essay, I remembered a friend who grew up in New Jersey but went to college in Missouri. He could hardly believe that towns in Missouri were frequently fifteen miles apart, and although he was a big, strong man, he was genuinely afraid to drive from one town to another at night. "What," he asked, "if I have a flat tire out in the middle of nowhere?" We explained that he could walk to the nearest house to get help. He was not persuaded. "But what if I'm attacked by a wild animal, like a raccoon?" (Of course, people who grow up in rural areas often have equally exaggerated fears about the dangers they might encounter in cities.) In this humorous essay, Thomas suggests that such fears could be allayed by closer contact with nature.

3. How does the image of water in the first four paragraphs express Thomas's attitude toward nature?

In the introductory paragraphs Thomas suggests the tenuousness of humanity's claim to earth, even in that citadel of civilization, the concrete, steel, and glass island of Manhattan. In Thomas's view, Manhattan is a Netherlands protected by horizontal dikes under the city. Make a hole in the dike, and the water rushes in. Rather than being alarmed by that knowledge, Thomas is pleased by it. In his opinion, the first stage of Bellevue Hospital, an enormous square lake, was "the most spectacular and satisfying" (paragraph 1). And he is delighted by the prospect of an inland sea in place of the Empire State Building, or of underground canals, "a Venice underground, without pigeons," instead of subways. Long before Thomas begins to relate the goldfish tale, he has informed us of nature's power to take back her own, and of his satisfaction with that state of affairs.

—M.R.D.—

Style Lesson 34: A Periodic Sentence from Kernels

In paragraph 10 of "Ponds" Thomas writes a long, comic periodic sentence about the possibility of mutant goldfish taking over New York City. To get a sense of Thomas's style, try to recreate this sentence from the choppy sentences below. To get the full effect, you will need to put the main clause (principal action) at the end.

The goldfish will come with a certain amount of splashing and grayish-green spray. They will begin at all the edges of the pond. They will come up all the banks of ancient New York landfill mud. They will be crawling on their new little feet. They will crawl out onto the sidewalks. They will crawl up and down and across the street. They will crawl into doorways and up the fire escapes. Some of them will crawl with little suckers on their little feet. They will go up the sides of buildings and into open windows. They will be looking for something.

MELISSA GREENE

No Rms, Jungle Vu

Although "No Rms, Jungle Vu" might seem to be an essay about the animals who live in zoos, Greene devotes five or fewer paragraphs to the behavior of those animals; the rest of her essay explores the thoughts, dreams, and needs of the human animals who build and visit zoos.

In this thoroughly researched essay, Greene recounts the history of zoo design, explains the multiple purposes of the modern zoo (which range from promoting captive breeding programs to providing restrooms for zoo-goers), and describes the techniques used by contemporary landscape immersion architects to design exhibits so realistic they "will make the hair stand up on the back of your neck" (paragraph 1).

"No Rms, Jungle Vu" is both entertaining and disturbing. Everyone likes to find out how magicians do their tricks, and part of the fun of this essay comes from learning how zoo designers create the illusion of natural environments. We discover that in constructing Seattle's Woodland Park gorilla exhibit, architect Jon Charles Coe designed artificial "shaggy, weed-covered" hills, boulders warmed by heating coils, and a viewing area carefully calculated to limit the viewer's peripheral vision. We learn that the Bronx Zoo's Jungle World relies on an "old jeweler's trick" to make zoo visitors believe there is no barrier between them and the python over their walkway. We learn that Coe elevated the terrain of the Woodland Park lion exhibit and concealed its moats "to instill fear and respect in the zoo-goer." And our discoveries leave us with the disquieting realization that the only "wilderness" many of us will ever see is a high-tech illusion.

Greene forces us to ask ourselves tough questions: What do we learn about the animal in us when we see that gorillas kept in sterile, unnatural environments become neurotic? How can we justify setting aside a mountain-gorilla preserve in Rwanda to save 240 gorillas if that same land would sustain 2,000 human families who have no other place to live? If we don't save our wilderness areas and the animals living there, what do we as humans lose?

QUESTIONS

1. What does this essay teach us about the animals who design, direct, and visit zoos?

You might ask your students to list any ten things this essay taught them about the human animal. Beginning with paragraph 55, for example, Greene presents interesting tidbits of information about zoo-goers: the most common visitor constellation is a parent with one or more children in tow (paragraph 58), our most frequent questions are "Where is the bathroom?" and "Where is the snackbar?" (paragraph 59), and we can tolerate only fifty feet between animals (paragraph 61).

In addition, Greene forces us to contemplate our complex motives for building, maintaining, and visiting zoos, motives that range from competing with Disney World (paragraph 45), to preserving endangered species (paragraph 55), to slicing through our "sophisticated veneer" and recalling our own origins in the wild (paragraph 1).

2. How have changes in the purpose of zoos influenced zoo design?

This form-follows-function question is meant to make your students realize that it is not merely coincidental that the landscape revolution in zoo design occurred at the particular time it did. Greene identifies three distinct stages in zoo history. During the first stage, which began as early as pharaonic Egypt, the purpose of a wild animal exhibit was to amaze viewers with their first sight of some exotic species. (One of my uncles, who is 70, told me that he was 18 when he first saw an elephant and that he was absolutely astonished by it.) At that time a successful zoo needed little more than cages (often on wheels) and a steady supply of new animals to replace those that sickened and died (paragraph 47).

During the second stage, which began soon after Linnaeus's publication of *Systema Naturae* in 1735, the purpose of zoos became taxonomic. Zoos attempted to educate the public about the classification of animals by building reptile houses, primate houses, and carnivore houses (paragraph 42). On the inside, all animal exhibits were more or less the same: bars separated visitors and inmates, tile lined the walls, each concrete floor sloped to a central drain. The exteriors of such houses were as diverse as the architects hired to design them (paragraph 21).

In recent years, with the disappearance of the wilderness, many zoo directors have begun to think of zoos as arks that may prevent the extinction of wild animals by implementing successful captive breeding programs and by educating the public to save the wilderness. Both strategies have influenced zoo design. Encouraging animals to breed in captivity may require housing gorillas in large family groups, allowing golden lion tamarins to live in monogamous pairs (paragraph 41), or giving cheetahs spacious habitats where they can escape from viewers. Educating the public to believe that wild animals are worth saving required a revolution in zoo design. As Terry Maple points out, a visit to a traditional elephant house leaves visitors with the "unspoken impression" that "elephants are filthy, tread in their own feces, attract flies, require hosing down, eat mush, and no wonder they are housed in cinder-block garages" (paragraph 66). On the other hand, the sight of an uncaged gorilla arranging her sleeping nest or of a lion racing toward us through tall yellow grasses gives us "a taste of what is out there, what is being lost" (paragraph 55).

3. How has technology affected modern zoos?

Your students should notice that technological advances have benefited zoos in a number of ways. Technology enables zoo architects to design realistic "natural" habitats that include "entire forests of epoxy and fiber-glass trees, reinforced concrete boulders, waterfalls, and artificial vines, with mist provided by cloud machines" (paragraph 43). *In vitro* fertilization, embryo transplantation, surrogate motherhood, and computerized databases that match potential mates (paragraph 54) boost the birth rate among endangered species. Advances in veterinary medicine make it possible to inoculate animals against diseases that once killed them (paragraph 40), and thus eliminate both the rationale for keeping a zoo animal in a tile-lined, antiseptic cage with a drain in the floor (paragraph 40) and the need to replace dead animals with alarming regularity.

A few of your students should also note technology's downside. Had technology not been so phenomenally successful in preventing and treating human diseases, thus allowing the human population to increase by 150 every minute, we probably would not be destroying the rain forests at the rate of 50 acres per minute and annihilating a species of animal each day (paragraph 50). And then perhaps zoos would not be so necessary.

4. What does the use of the ark metaphor by zoo professionals suggest about their view of the relationship between humans and other animals? (paragraph 48)

In "Education by Poetry", Robert Frost warns that all metaphors break down at some point and that we have to learn how far we can safely ride them. This is a great metaphor to test-ride.

The metaphor suggests that we, like Noah, have a moral obligation to save the other animals, that annihilation of most wild species is both inevitable and imminent unless we recognize and accept this obligation, and that our motive for building the ark is not entirely altruistic. But our situation differs from Noah's in significant ways: our building instructions are not as detailed as Noah's and were not revealed to us by such an authoritative source, we don't know how much time we have to construct our ark, and we have no guarantee either that our ark will float or that our stay on it will be temporary.

You may need to point out that Greene doesn't tell us whether the tenor of this metaphor is "zoo" or "earth." If zoos are the modern ark, perhaps we still have time to preserve representative species in captivity, but if the entire planet is our ark, we may not be able to saw and hammer fast enough.

—M.R.D.—

Style Lesson 35: Multi-Level Sentence Structure in a Paragraph

Paragraph 64 of "No Rms, Jungle Vu" comprises two back-to-back examples of well-structured longer sentences, one suspended, one cumulative. Imitate them with sentences on a subject of your choice.

The zoo-goer who emerges from the research literature—
    benighted and happy-go-lucky,
        chomping his hot dog,
        holding his nose in the elephant house and
        scratching under his arm in the monkey house
            to make his children laugh
—is a walking anachronism.

He is the creation of an outmoded institution—
    the conventional zoo—
in which the primate house, carnivore house,
and reptile house,
            all lined with tile
        glow with an unreal greenish light
            as if the halls were subterranean,
and in which giraffes, zebras, and llamas
        stand politely,

        and as if on tiptoe,
            on the neatly mown lawns of the moated exhibits.

ISAK DINESEN

A Gazelle

Like many passages from *Out of Africa,* this one impresses me as a remarkable picture of harmony between the writer and the setting in which she lives, including both its natural features and its people. Our focus here will be on nature, but some of your students may be distracted by the social setting: Dinesen (Blixen) owned a coffee farm in Kenya; her employees were black, and she follows the colonists' custom of calling them "boys." If students see her as a Simon Legree, I would point out to them that her workers were not her slaves and that, by all accounts, she was a respectful, generous employer. European colonialism certainly had its share of ugliness, but the Blixen farm seems to have been one of its more benign manifestations.

The "plot" here is simplicity itself: Dinesen adopts a fawn who lives briefly at her house and who, when she returns to the wild, makes frequent return visits to the farm. What makes the reading a pleasure is Dinesen's combination of description and enchantment; she obviously felt the gazelle's presence in her life as a nearly miraculous blessing and she conveys her sense of wonder to the reader. She was, of course, a master writer of *Gothic Tales* (fairy stories for adults), and when she writes about Africa, she manages simultaneously to describe its realities and to transform it into the land that lies east of the sun and west of the moon.

QUESTIONS

1. In a sense, what Dinesen has written here is simply an account of keeping an unusual pet. What details about the gazelle and its behavior around the house would you not have imagined before you read Dinesen's account?

This may seem a pedestrian question. I think it's important, though, to see that Dinesen is doing the bread-and-butter work of a writer by giving us a steady stream of new and engaging information. Here are some of the details that were news to me:

- A very young fawn is no bigger than a cat (paragraph 7).
- A gazelle's eyes are purple (paragraph 7).
- A fawn's hooves slip out from under her on a polished floor until she learns to manage it; they then make a sound like "little angry finger taps" (paragraph 8).
- A fawn doesn't fear dogs (paragraphs 16, 37).
- A fawn will attack a horse (paragraph 18).
- A fawn throws temper tantrums in the form of a zig-zag dance (paragraph 19).

- A gazelle brought up around the house carries into adulthood a tolerance for the presence of humans (paragraphs 35, *ff.*). It loses, however, its willingness to be touched (paragraph 38).

Other details could, of course, be listed. Some student writers benefit from frequent reminders that professionals interest readers partly by giving them scraps of information they would not otherwise have known.

2. What is Dinesen's attitude toward Lulu, and how does she convey it in her writing?

Attitude? This is the sort of vague word that elicits vague answers. If your students are inclined to say something like "she likes her," try to pin them down. Likes her as a carpenter likes a hammer? No. Likes her as a child likes a parent? No. Eventually I think your students will say that Dinesen respects Lulu more than the average dog owner respects his or her pet, and that she even holds her in a certain amount of awe.

This attitude shows in her refusal to capture Lulu's fawn: ". . . I thought it would make a boorish return to Lulu's elegant confidence" (paragraph 39). It shows most strongly in paragraph 40, where Lulu is presented as an emissary from "the wild world." She has seen things few humans will ever see: "Lulu knew the place of the Giant Forest-Hog's lair and had seen the Rhino copulate," Dinesen writes, using capitalization to indicate mystery and grandeur. At the end of the paragraph, Dinesen compares Lulu's visits from the forest to the farm to a Chinese Empress's visit from the Forbidden City to her home village.

The comparison to the Empress of China is the culmination of a pattern of similes that raise Lulu to a high level of dignity. From the beginning she is talked about in human terms. She is at first like the man beaten and left by the roadside in the tale of the Good Samaritan (paragraph 5), then she is like a Chinese lady with tiny, bound feet (paragraph 7). She is "headstrong as a child," but possessed of great dignity (paragraph 8). She allows herself to be scratched behind the ears "like a young wife who pertly permits her husband a caress" (paragraph 16). She is a "young princess in exile" now "come into her rights" (paragraph 32). She is like "the married daughter of the house on a visit" (paragraph 35). In paragraph 32 she rises above humanity and is compared to a Greek goddess.

Language and attitude are closely tied. We can't tell to what extent Dinesen uses these similes to express her attitude toward Lulu and to what extent the similes *created* her attitude. The habit of mind that compares deer to empresses elevates nature, just as the habit that compares them to machines degrades it.

3. Dinesen is an excellent writer of fairy stories. Where do you see evidence of her ability to write about a real place or real event in a way that makes it seem to belong to a fabulous land? What techniques create the sense of enchantment?

The passage I would choose is Dinesen's description of a morning on the farm, found in paragraphs 29 and 30. For ease of reference, I'll reproduce it here:

> The great vault over our heads was gradually filled with clarity like a glass of wine. Suddenly, gently, the summits of the hill caught the first sunlight and blushed. And slowly, as the earth leaned toward the sun, the grassy slopes at the foot of the mountain turned a delicate gold, and the Masai woods lower down. And now the tops of the tall trees in the forest, on our side of the river, blushed like copper. This was the hour for the flight of the big, purple wood-pigeons which roosted by the other side of the river and came over to feed on the Cape-chestnuts in my forest. They were here only for a short season in the year. The birds came surprisingly fast, like a cavalry attack of the air. For this reason the morning pigeon-shooting on the farm was popular with my friends in Nairobi; to be out by the house in time, just as the sun rose, they used to come out so early that they rounded my drive with the lamps of their cars still lighted.
>
> Standing like this in the limpid shadow, looking up towards the golden heights and the clear sky, you would get the feeling that you were in reality walking along the bottom of the Sea, with the currents running by you, and were gazing up towards the surface of the Ocean.

A fraction of the lift toward the fabulous here is created by a technique I'm afraid students are over-inclined to already, the use of adjectives with more emotional than descriptive force. It wanted no ghost come from the dead to tell us that the vault of heaven is "great," and I'm not sure what color "delicate" gold is. But there aren't many such adjectives in the passage. What is present in unusual abundance is comparison. The vault of heaven (a metaphor in itself) filling with light is compared with a wine glass filling with wine. The blushing of the hills is both a straight description and a faint personification, as is the earth's leaning toward the sun. The tops of the trees blush "like copper." The coming of the birds is like "a cavalry attack of the air." And finally, ambitiously, standing on the shadowy earth and looking up at the bright sky is like standing on the bottom of the sea, looking toward the surface. This is a passage where things shrink (sky to wine glass) and swell (birds to horses) and change elements (leaves to copper). We see a flat earth from an impossible angle as if it were a plate tilting toward the sun. Even if we are reading too quickly to consciously process all these metaphors, their cumulative effect is to unsettle our view of the world as a familiar, predictable place.

What keeps this barrage of comparisons from being mere overwriting is that Dinesen anchors her figurative language firmly to reality: the passage creates a clear picture of what we assume Dinesen actually saw when she looked west toward the hills at sunrise. The digression about the hunting of the wood pigeons is one of the passage's anchors. It says, in effect, "This isn't never-never land; other people have been there, real people with real guns, come to shoot birds. I can give you details." Dinesen may lead us part way into *faërie*, where we don't have an everyday sea or ocean, but *the Sea, the Ocean*. But she also explains that the pigeon season is short because they only come to the farm to feed on the Cape-chestnuts.

—D.H.—

Style Lesson 36: Combining or Not Combining Sentences

To study the best balance between simplicity and complexity of style, examine these short sentences, drawn from paragraph 33 of "A Gazelle," and combine them into one, two, three, or four sentences, according to your best judgment.

Kamante touched my arm with one finger. He then pointed it towards the woods. I followed the direction. I saw a male bushbuck. The bushbuck was under a tall Cape-chestnut-tree. It made a small tawny silhouette at the outskirt of the forest. It had a fine pair of horns. It was immovable like a tree-stem.

HARRY CREWS

Pages from the Life of a Georgia Innocent

Crews's earthy skepticism about nature makes an interesting match with the more cerebral skepticism of Brigid Brophy and provides students who have never lived farther than two miles from the nearest McDonald's with a referent for Brophy's assertion that cities are devices for reducing stress. The essay is also a good companion for Sue Hubbell's "Beekeeper" *(Progress and its Price).* Some of the hardships Crews had to endure resemble those that Hubbell seems to enjoy.

The essay is direct and very simply organized, one of the easiest in *The Dolphin Reader*, good for a day when you feel the class could use the relief of some humor. Like the essays by White and Brophy in this section, it relies heavily on the author's voice, his ability to establish himself as a definite personality. If I were interested in generating class discussion of voice, I would assign it with one of these.

QUESTIONS

1. What is Crews's declared purpose in writing this essay? Is it his real purpose?

By beginning with the anecdote about watching the Disney film, Crews implies that irritation with the Disney/Waltons/Little House tradition of presenting country life has provoked this essay: "It seemed immoral and dangerous to show so many smiles without an occasional glimpse of the skull underneath." If you read enough Crews, you realize that this statement is probably true and false. He is never a sentimental writer, and no doubt can be irritated by the Hallmark version of practically anything. He is also fairly careful here to match the alleged provocation of the essay with the anecdotes he will give as counterexamples. The Disney characters have an idealized relation to animals who are more pets than livestock, so Crews gives a couple of stories about the gritty reality of dealing with chickens. The Disney characters seem to get free and painless medical help from an always accessible physician, so Crews tells a story about the reality of homemade health care for the rurally isolated poor.

Frankly, though, all this strikes me as an after-the-fact contrivance. Crews is always a storyteller, and my own guess is that this essay started with the story of Felix's bad tooth, or perhaps grandma's hawk-baiting, and grew outward from there. The thesis probably came late, and the supposed provocation—the Disney movie—perhaps later still. If this, or something like this, is true, then Crews's real purpose is to tell a couple of good stories rather than to advance an anti-Disney thesis.

And it is probably worth reminding your students that this is an old and noble motive, and that their composition process, too, may start from nuggets of good story and only gradually and perhaps even incompletely find their justification in a thesis.

2. By what technique does Crews develop his own character and tone in this essay?

Or, if you want to ask the somewhat more precise form of this question, how does he establish his *persona*? For this is a persona, a mask. It may be a mask that conforms fairly exactly to Crews's own face, but it is deliberately shaped, largely by diction.

It is often difficult to get students to see that relation between the words on the page and the writer's tone and persona. You might try to help them make this connection by looking closely at the two opening sentences of Crews's essay and then having them rewrite them for different effects. Here is the original:

> Not very long ago I went with my twelve-year-old *boy* to a Disney movie, one of those *things* that show a farm family, *poor but God knows honest, out there on the land building character through hunger and hard work.* The hunger and hard work seemed to be *a hell of a lot of fun.*

The words I've italicized are the ones that seem to get the effect we are interested in here. Crews is a plain fellow, his sentences tell us: he says "boy" rather than "son" and is comfortable with the all-purpose word "thing" rather than, say, "film." He isn't the sort of person who would call a movie a film at any rate, any more than he would call a farm family a rural family. His plain speaking contrasts with another voice he adopts when he parodies the movie's clichés: "poor but God knows honest, out there on the land building character through hunger and hard work." This is far too hyperbolic to be sincerely meant, and prepares us for the blunt irony of "a hell of a lot of fun."

You might have your students try writing the sentences as a suburban businessman who accepts Disney at face value would have done them:

> About a week ago, I took my twelve-year-old son to a film by Walt Disney, a picture that represents the life of a rural family, quite poor, but honest, struggling to make a living from the land. Their hunger and hard work brought them real pleasure.

Or a skeptical college professor—grossly parodied, of course:

> Not terribly long ago, I escorted my prepubescent son to a Disney film, one of those tendentious tales where the poor family is *ipso facto* honest, and malnutrition and perspiration are the foundations of character. Malnutrition and perspiration, in fact, seemed positively exhilarating.

Of course, the stories Crews tells also give an impression of his character. Neither the businessman nor the college professor would be likely to end both story and essay with the line "Hurt now, you sumbitch."

3. In the rural areas you know, how well does either Crews's version of country life or Disney's correspond to reality?

This is probably not a great question if you are teaching at City College of New York and have a class with little direct knowledge of country life. If you have a class more sophisticated about contemporary farming, you might get good discussion or essays on its technical and financial complexity. I know that when the personal computer boom started here in Columbia, Missouri, there were two instant markets, university people and farm people. And I know that when I go visit my in-laws in Iowa, I am flooded with numbers—land prices, fertilizer prices, markets, futures markets, depreciation schedules, break-even points—and with talk I can never quite understand about the virtues of various antibiotics for livestock or the BTUs produced by various heaters. And, of course, few farmers today are reduced to medical self-treatment. The ones I know get into late-model cars (rather than battered pickup trucks) and drive to a clinic in town, noting along the way which neighbors have satellite dishes.

—D.H.—

Style Lesson 37: Creating a Persona Through Style

To study the way that Crews's voice implies the personality (or persona) of the writer, rewrite the following passage as it might have been written by (1) a suburban businessperson who takes Disney at face value and (2) a skeptical college professor.

Not very long ago I went with my twelve-year-old boy to a Disney movie, one of those things that show a farm family, poor but God knows honest, out there on the land building character through hunger and hard work. The hunger and hard work seemed to be a hell of a lot of fun.

DORIS LESSING

A Sunrise on the Veld

"A Sunrise on the Veld" is a gripping tale told by a master storyteller. It is the story of a fifteen-year-old boy who goes hunting on the veld, hears a scream of pain, and finds a buck who is being eaten alive by ants. Lessing's description of that horror is unforgettable:

> There, between two trees, against a background of gaunt black rocks, was a figure from a dream, a strange beast that was horned and drunken-legged, but like something he had never even imagined. It seemed to be ragged. It looked like a small buck that had black ragged tufts of fur standing up irregularly all over it, with patches of raw flesh beneath . . . but the patches of rawness were disappearing under moving black and came again elsewhere; and all the time the creature screamed, in small gasping screams, and leaped drunkenly from side to side, as if it were blind (paragraph 22).

The sight sickens and angers the boy. It also forces him to recognize his own mortality and to reconsider his moral responsibilities to the amoral world of nature.

QUESTIONS

1. Is the exhilaration the boy feels caused by being part of nature or by overcoming nature?

The boy's exuberance is caused both by his connection to nature and by his separation from it. He is a healthy young animal in tip-top physical condition and bursting with energy. In fact, he is remarkably similar to young James Morris as Jan Morris describes him in the essay "To Everest" (*Femininity and Masculinity*):

> His body is running not in gusts and squalls, but at a steady high speed. He actually tingles with strength and energy, as though sparks might fly from his skin in the dark. Nothing sags in him. His body has no spare weight upon it, only muscles made supple by exercise.

In one scene the boy is completely overcome by the vitality of his body:

> He leapt into the air, shouting and yelling wild, unrecognisable noises. Then he began to run, not carefully, as he had before, but madly, like a wild thing. He was clean crazy, yelling mad with the joy of living and a superfluity of youth (paragraph 16).

In that instant the boy seems to be driven by the same natural forces that cause his dogs to race across the veld.

But—except for that one incident—most of the boy's happiness comes not from giving in to his body's natural urges but in controlling them. In the opening paragraphs we learn that he has trained himself to wake at "half-past four to the minute, every morning" (paragraph 2), that "he had once stayed awake three nights running, to prove he could, and then worked all day, refusing even to admit he was tired" (paragraph 3), and that by "using the steady lope he had learned by watching the natives," he can run for miles without tiring (paragraph 13). When Lessing tells us that "the exultation and pride of body mounted in him till he was shutting his teeth hard against a violent desire to shout his triumph" (paragraph 13), she is describing a triumph of the body and also a triumph over the body.

2. What does the protagonist learn when he sees the buck eaten alive by ants?

The boy's discovery of the buck screaming in pain triggers two different epiphanies. The first brings him to the angry realization that he too is mortal: "The knowledge of fatality, of what has to be, had gripped him and for the first time in his life; and he was left unable to make any movement of brain or body, except to say: 'Yes, yes. That is what living is'" (paragraph 29). Even though the boy is accustomed to seeing the deaths of other animals close up, like most young people, he is convinced of his own invulnerability. That conviction is evident when he runs wildly through the veld, and he thinks "briefly, not believing that such a thing could happen to him, that he could break his ankle at any moment, in this thick tangled grass" (paragraph 16). But when he watches the agonized dying of a buck, he understands his connection to the cycle of life and death that surrounds him: "That morning, perhaps an hour ago, this small creature had been stepping proud and free through the brush, feeling the chill on his hide even as he himself had done, exhilarated by it" (paragraph 36). The boy's identification with the vibrant young animal who died so cruelly forces him to reluctantly acknowledge his own mortality: "'Go away!' he said to the ants, very coldly. 'I am not for you—not just yet, at any rate'" (paragraph 34).

The second epiphany is even more disturbing. At first the boy attributes the buck's death to nature, to the savage necessity that governs the relationship between the eaters and the eaten who inhabit "the vast unalterable, cruel veld" (paragraph 29). He forces himself to remember that "the ants must eat too!" (paragraph 30). But his curiosity about how the ants could have trapped such a swift animal leads him to discover its broken leg, and to realize that it was human intervention—not nature—that led inexorably to the buck's torment. He initially blames the Africans who had probably thrown stones at the buck while trying to kill it for meat (paragraph 39). But then he remembers the times he had taken a shot at an animal, not knowing whether he had hit it or not, and had chosen not to track it for miles to put it out of its misery (paragraph 40). He is overwhelmed and dismayed by the responsibility he cannot deny. For the first time the boy glimpses the moral complexities of his position in the natural world. Unlike the ants, he can feel the sufferings of their victim: "[H]e found that tears were streaming down his face, and his clothes were soaked with the sweat of that other creature's pain" (paragraph 30). And unlike the ants, he can and must choose whether to inflict such pain on other victims.

3. How does Lessing manage to keep our interest throughout this story?

This is not a story filled with dramatic events. The boy isn't attacked by a lion or chased by a rhinoceros. And yet Lessing keeps us in suspense from beginning to end. First she piques our curiosity by raising a question. Then we race forward to find the answer, but just as we discover it, she poses yet another question. To demonstrate this technique, you might refer your students to specific paragraphs and ask "After reading that passage, what do you want to find out?"

Here are a few possibilities:

Paragraph 1: Why does the boy fall asleep saying "Half-past four!"?
Paragraphs 2–4: Why does he get up at 4:30 a.m.?
Paragraphs 5–6: Why is he careful not to wake his parents?
Paragraph 7: Why is he taking a gun?
Paragraph 8: Why does he have to be four miles away before dawn?
Paragraphs 9–14: Where is he going and why is he going there?
Paragraphs 15–17: What is he going to do now that it's too late to shoot guinea fowl?
Paragraphs 18–21: What is making the sound of pain that he hears?
Paragraph 22: What is the "dream figure" he sees?
Paragraph 23: Why is the grass "whispering and alive"?
Paragraph 23–35: How will the boy respond to the horror he has observed?
Paragraph 38: How did the ants manage to trap a "swift surefooted" buck?
Paragraph 39: How was the buck's leg broken?
Paragraph 41: How will the boy deal with his realization that he might have caused some other creature to suffer the buck's fate?

If you want to be sure your students appreciate Lessing's skill as a storyteller, you might ask them what would be lost if the story opened with "The boy woke at 4:30 a.m. to hunt for guinea fowl" or if paragraph 22 began with "He saw a buck covered with ants."

—M.R.D.—

LOREN EISELEY

The Brown Wasps

Loren Eiseley, who was a professional anthropologist and a student of the history of science, is as well known for his books written for the layperson as for his contributions to scientific journals. In "The Brown Wasps" Eiseley focuses on his lifelong theme, the way in which nature flows into civilization and vice versa. In this essay he tells us that one day as he cut across a field adjoining a suburban shopping center, he saw a "giant slug feeding from a runnel of pink ice cream in an abandoned Dixie cup." As he watched the slug, the significance of the event became clear. "Then, as I stood there at the edge of the concrete, contemplating the slug, I began to realize it was like standing on a shore where a different type of life creeps up and fumbles tentatively among the rocks and sea wrack. It knows its place and will only creep so far until something changes. Little by little as I stood there I began to see more of this shore that surrounds the place of man."

Eiseley's intense interest in the ever-changing, jagged edge where nature and civilization meet is shared by Annie Dillard ("The Fixed"). In her rural home at Tinker Creek in Virginia she, too, lives on that shifting shoreline. But Eiseley's emotional response to the point at which humans and other animals separate is somewhat different from Dillard's. Dillard feels so at home with nature, so connected to it, that she hardly recognizes that we are in fact separate from it. At the indistinct border where nature and civilization meld, Eiseley experiences both the pain of our separation from nature and the joy of our connection to it. When he learns that a new store will be erected in a field close to his home, he mourns "the bodies of little white-footed mice [who] would be crunched under the inexorable wheels of the bulldozers." And when he considers that "in a few years [man's] plaster and bricks would be disappearing once more into the insatiable maw of the clover," he feels "an obscure sense of satisfaction."

Even people who do not share Eiseley's attitude toward nature admire his writing. Edward Hoagland ("Dogs, and the Tug of Life," *DR*, pp. 437–445), another fine nature writer but one who has quite a different outlook, wrote of Eiseley, "He is one of those transcendent imaginative thinkers who are not limited to one branch of science, nor to science itself. . . . He's a writer so good he can stop you dead in your tracks for a day or a week."

QUESTIONS

1. Is the essay unified by a thesis?

When your students examine the structure of the essay, they should notice that it is divided into four distinct parts. Part 1, which deals with the brown wasps, ends with paragraph 7. Part 2 (paragraphs 8–16) is the story of the field mouse. Part 3 (paragraphs 17–22) describes the pigeons who frequented the El. And in the final section Eiseley tells us about his journey to sit under the shade of a nonexistent cottonwood. It could be argued that the essay is disjointed. Certainly it is true that Eiseley declines to state his thesis in the opening paragraph. In fact, if the essay ended after paragraph 7, it would be quite complete and the thesis would be different from what it finally is. After Part 1 the thesis would be that humans, like wasps, need a place at the heart of society. Part 2 seems to shift the focus, but actually Eiseley is expanding the thesis by illustrating that the place we need may exist only in memory. He demonstrates that observation first with the mouse, then with the pigeons, and finally with himself.

The condition shared by all three, and perhaps by all living things, is exile, the sense of being cut off from our place, from our fellows. The mouse is "in exile from its home" because his field was usurped by a Wanamaker suburban store (paragraph 11) and the pigeons because the El was replaced by a subway. For them the enemy is impermanence, the fact that the world is in a perpetual state of flux. "Life disappears or modifies its appearances so fast that everything takes on an aspect of illusion—a momentary fizzing and boiling with smoke rings, like pouring dissident chemicals into a retort" (paragraph 11).

Eiseley, too, has been exiled because everyone "who was supposed to wait and grow old under [the] shade" of the cottonwood he and his father had planted had instead died or moved away (paragraph 23). But Eiseley and all humans face an additional enemy, unknown to animals. Eiseley must confront not only the fact of impermanence, but his awareness of it. It is our knowledge that all things pass, our understanding of mortality, that distinguishes humans, that makes us exiles even if we live out our lives in the houses we were born in. It is the theme of exile that unifies the essay.

2. How do the metaphors help to hold the essay together?

First, each extended metaphor unifies a major section of the essay. The metaphor comparing old men in a railroad station to brown wasps who return to the deserted wasp nest to die controls the first section. The second metaphor, in which Eiseley imagines civilization as an island surrounded by the ocean of the natural world, explains why the boundaries between the two are so impermanent and sets the stage for the field mouse who is displaced by a concrete parking lot but consequently invades the realm of civilization by moving into Eiseley's apartment. In Part 3 the image of the El as a food-bearing river that comes to a sudden halt (paragraph 17) vividly explains why the pigeons are so disoriented by its closing.

In addition, the use of metaphor reinforces the major point of the essay. Because we fear disconnectedness, we value relationships, even if they exist only in our heads. The old wasps respond to "the hum of the spring hive [which] still resounded faintly in their sodden tissues" (paragraph 1). The mouse attempts to "build a remembered field" in a flower pot in Eiseley's living room (paragraph 9). "He had an image in his head, a world of seed pods and quiet, of green sheltering leaves in the dim light among the weed stems. It was the only world he knew, and it was gone" (paragraph 13). When the wreckers show up to dismantle the El, some of the pigeons who had departed flock back, convinced "that the river was about to flow once more." Eiseley writes, "It was plain . . . that they retained a memory for an insubstantial structure now compounded of air and time" (paragraph 22). Humans are motivated by similar memories, but we differ in that we are capable of consciously constructing concepts that hold things together. In that sense, a metaphor is more than an interesting illustration; it is an attempt to impose order, to unify our seemingly disjointed experiences. The birds don't know that the El is a food-bearing river, but Eiseley understands that the tree growing in his memory symbolizes his father and the love he feels for him. That is why the image of the tree can connect Eiseley to his father long after both the father and the tree are dead.

In this essay metaphor is not merely a tool to illustrate a point. In a real sense metaphor is the point. To see one thing in terms of another, to see the past in terms of the present, is the response both animals and humans make to life's disconnectedness.

3. To what extent is the role of memory the same in humans and animals?

Eiseley is convinced that animals other than humans have memories that influence their behavior. In paragraph 8 he describes the significance of memories for humans: "We cling to a time and place because without them man is lost, not only man but life." In the following paragraph he explains that animals have similar needs: "This feeling runs deep in life; it brings stray cats running over endless miles, and birds homing from the ends of the earth. It is as though all living creatures, and particularly the more intelligent, can survive only by fixing or transforming a bit of time into space or by securing a bit of space with its objects immortalized and made permanent in time."

But Eiseley also understands the difference between human and animal memory. For the lower animals, memory is built into the nervous system. They respond automatically to certain situations in predictable ways meant to assure the species' survival. Destroy a mouse's burrow, and it will remember how to build another. But the memories that motivate humans are personal and unique. When Eiseley sees that the tree is gone, he reflects on its meaning for him:

> It was obvious I was attached by a thread to a thing that had never been there, or certainly not for long. Something that had to be held in the air, or sustained in the mind, because it was a part of my orientation in the universe and I could not survive without it. There was more than an animal's attachment to a place. There was something else, the attachment of the spirit to a grouping of events in time; it was part of our morality (paragraph 31).

—M.R.D.—

Style Lesson 38: A Sentence that Imitates a Journey

In paragraph 16, Eiseley writes a sentence whose windings and delays seem to imitate the windings and delays of the field mouse's journey into his apartment. To get a sense of how Eiseley creates the movement of this sentence, imitate it, writing a sentence about another journey.

It was a small dream,
        like our dreams,
    carried a long and weary journey
        along pipes and through spider webs,
        past holes
            over which loomed the shadows of waiting cats,
        and finally, desperately, into this room
            where he had played
                in the shuttered daylight
                for an hour
                among the green ferns on the floor.

BRIGID BROPHY

The Menace of Nature

Brigid Brophy has a tough, original mind, full of surprises. An interviewer, knowing her interest in history, once asked what military action she most admired. She told him it was Horace's desertion at the battle of Philippi in 42 B.C. She is quick-witted and sharp-tongued, adept at aphorism and unworried about giving offense.

Students who read this essay will see how a much-admired stylist keeps her audience interested by confronting it directly, without much psychological distance, and challenging its comfortable assumptions. The comfortable assumption here is that nature is somehow morally and aesthetically superior to civilization, to which Brophy responds by blowing a very articulate raspberry.

QUESTIONS

1. How does Brophy's attitude toward the landscape reflect her beliefs about nature and civilization?

In a sense the answer to this question is terribly obvious, and some of your students will be inclined to go no further than to say that since she doesn't like nature and she does like civilization, it isn't surprising that she doesn't like landscape. I think they need to go a step further, though, and understand the world view that underlies this tautology. What does Brophy think civilization is all about? The direct answer, surprisingly, is in a parenthetical in paragraph 9: "The city is one of the great indispensable devices of civilisation (itself only a device for centralizing beauty and transmitting it as a heritage)." What is her view of nature? Here she doesn't give us so trenchant a definition, but notice the end of the same paragraph, where she points out that the city, like currency, "is a medium of exchange and thereby of choice—whereas the country is a place where one is under the thumb of chance. . ."

Brophy's view of the balance of nature and civilization is very much like E. M. Forster's. Nature, from Brophy's perspective, is the iron rule of mindlessness. Like death, which is one of its parts, it is inevitable. Our great triumphs come from an ability to hold it temporarily at bay while we busy ourselves with important and unnatural things. It isn't surprising that a person with such opinions would not love a walk in the wilderness.

2. What attitude does Brophy have toward her reader?

If *engaging* were not used as a synonym for merely *charming*, I would be tempted to call Brophy's prose engaging. She begins, of course, by laying a trap in the first paragraph and springing it in the second. It is a practical joke—far more sophisticated than the whoopee cushion on the guest's chair, of course, but of a similar genre. She is not quite on her best behavior; she intends to enjoy herself, and expects her reader to do the same. She doesn't maintain her authorial distance. Notice how colloquial she can be, beginning her first two paragraphs with "So?" and "Well," and using frequent contractions. The same sort of colloquialness shows in her use of italics to indicate the stress (playfully exaggerated) of her voice in some of her sentences:

> I'm not such a pig as to want the country built on or littered up with bottles and plastic bags merely because it doesn't appeal to *me*. (paragraph 3)
>
> ["To *moi*," Miss Piggy would say, with precisely the same inflection.]
>
> I'm not, however, out to dissuade *you* from spending your holiday as a sort of legalized bandit in the landscape (paragraph 4).
>
> They'll scarcely let you have a *baby* these days if you can't satisfy them beforehand you're adept at relaxing (paragraph 4).

If you want to remind your students how different the tone of other writers can be, you might compare Brophy's first four paragraphs with the first three or four paragraphs of Martin Luther King, Jr.'s "Letter from Birmingham Jail." King's prose, written in the midst of a political and moral crisis, and directed to a broad public that included some people deeply opposed to his views, does give the impression of the speaking voice, but it is a grave voice, far more formal and courteous. Brophy, writing for *The New Statesman*, assumes a reader who is willing both to think and smile.

3. What passages in this essay seem particularly ingenious or witty?

Some of Brophy's effects, humorous and otherwise, come from concatenations of images. In paragraphs 3 and 4, for example, she first portrays herself driving through the countryside in a fast car, then shows herself in a picture gallery, "pausing to look at 'Landscape with Ruins' or 'Bandits in a Landscape' but walking straight past the pure landscapes at a speed which is obviously trying to simulate the effect of being driven past in a car." Then she tells the reader that he or she can feel perfectly free to spend a holiday as "a sort of legalized bandit in the landscape." There is just an edge of insult in the final line.

More often, though, her ingenuity shows in the wording of single sentences: *bons mots*, in the manner of Shaw, whom she admires:

> We are a species that doesn't occur wild (paragraph 11).
>
> We are *homo artifex, homo faber, homo Fabergé* (paragraph 11).
>
> The whole Wordsworthian fallacy consists in gravely underestimating the toughness of plants (paragraph 12).
>
> By simply exchanging their own for a foreign city, they are released from the routine of earning their daily bread and washing up after it, but don't suffer the disorientation, the *uncorseted discomfort*, which overtakes an urbanite cast up on a beach with no timetable to live by except the tides (paragraph 4, my emphasis).

Even when I think she is dead wrong, I have to admire her ear and her lexical playfulness.

> If you don't like what you've put up on the meadow, you can take it away again and the meadow will re-*seed* itself in a year or two; but human *semen* is lucky if it *engenders* an architectural *genius* a century (paragraph 12, my emphasis).

This is not the sentence of someone who has spent much time with a jackhammer or backhoe, trying to break up a few acres of frivolous concrete, or of someone who has tried to reclaim an area made sterile by strip mining. But it *is* a terribly good sentence.

—D.H.—

Style Lesson 39: Compression

Brophy's wit not only makes for clever writing, but economical prose as well. Six times in the following sentence we have replaced Brophy's word or phrase with several words that express the same meaning. Try to recall the original or match its brevity.

By simply exchanging their own for a foreign city, they are released from the routine of WORKING IN ORDER TO MAKE MONEY TO BUY THE NECESSITIES OF EVERYDAY LIFE[1] and DOING ALL THE ROUTINE HOUSEKEEPING CHORES[2], but don't suffer the disorientation, the UNEASINESS THAT COMES FROM GETTING OUT IN NATURE AND LETTING IT ALL HANG OUT[3], which overtakes a PERSON ACCUSTOMED TO CITY LIFE WHO IS[4] cast up on a beach with no SCHEDULING PRINCIPLE[5] to live by except the RHYTHMS THAT ARE BUILT INTO NATURE[6]. (par 4)

[1]*Brophy uses 4 words;* [2]*4 words;* [3]*2 words;* [4]*1 word;* [5]*1 word;* [6]*1 word.*

EDWARD HOAGLAND

Dogs, and the Tug of Life

In a very short essay with the enormous title "Thoughts on Returning to the City after Five Months on a Mountain Where the Wolves Howl," Edward Hoagland makes a perfectly characteristic observation: "I like gourmets, even winetasters. In the city they correspond to the old-timers who knew all the berries and herbs, made money collecting the roots of the ginseng plant, and knew the taste of each hill by the springs." Equally at home in the city or country, Hoagland never seems quite urbanized, quite tame, so that even when he writes about Manhattan we feel we are being led through the city by an Indian scout whose senses are keener than our own.

Though it contains a great deal of information about dogs, this turns out to be an essay about the atrophy of urban (or suburban) man's animal nature. Its alarm is similar to that expressed by Jerry Mander in "Advertising: The Standard-Gauge Railway" (*Media*).

QUESTIONS

1. Are Hoagland's observations about canine behavior scientific?

If we mean "scientific" in anything like the strict positivist's sense, the short answer is no. If you can get your class to look closely at paragraph 11, for example, they should be able to see how unscientific Hoagland is. Here the dog *aspires* for a hierarchical position, *dislikes* running out of urine, *prefers* a scent post that has already been marked, feels a *delight* and *duty* in staking out territory and a *disappointment* when he cannot. And so Hoagland goes on, to the paragraph's end. All the way through the language is anthropomorphic, and so is the intent. Hoagland attributes human feelings to dogs in a way that would alarm investigators far less conservative than B. F. Skinner.

2. Is this essay primarily about dogs or about humans?

In a sense, the best answer to this question is that the essay is not primarily about one or the other, but about the relationship between the two. To good readers this will be obvious almost from the essay's beginning: Hoagland calls his shot in paragraph 6 by telling us that a dog's life "is a kind of cutout of our own." What is remarkable about the essay is the way that it manages to talk about dogs and humans simultaneously, making them metaphors for each other. In class discussion, I would point out, for example, how often Hoagland's description of dog behavior points to the human parallel explicitly:

> The nose is the dog's main instrument of discovery, *corresponding to our eyes*, and so it is that he is seldom offended by organic smells, such as putrefaction, and sniffs intently for the details of illness, gum bleeding, and diet in his master and his fellows, and for the story told by scats, not closing off the avenue for any reason—*just as we rarely shut our eyes against new information, even the tragic or unpleasant kind* (paragraph 12, emphasis mine).

Or by choice of words:

> In addition to an epistolary anal gland . . . the anus itself, or stool when sniffed, conveys how well the animal has been eating—in effect, its *income bracket* . . . (paragraph 10, emphasis mine).

Or by innuendo:

> The contortions of fawning and obeisance which render group adjustment possible among such otherwise forceful fighters—sometimes humping the inferior members into the shape of hyenas—are what squeezes them past our tantrums, too (paragraph 9).

If he used only a few instances of this sort, we might attribute them to illustrative convenience—comparing the thing we know little about (canine behavior) to the thing we better understand (human behavior). But the comparison is so constantly maintained, particularly in paragraphs 6–14, that we soon begin to see what is happening. Hoagland is not just using a rhetorical figure in comparing humans and dogs; he is asserting that they really *are* alike. He is saying that we, too, live in a hierarchy, fawn on superiors, intimidate inferiors, note signs of income bracket, form close relationships with our mates because of the prolonged togetherness of sexual activity, mark our territory with whatever signs we can. We are closely related animals with closely related—in a sense identical—instincts. It is only our civilized, stylized expression of these instincts that disguises the basic identity.

3. What is the point of this essay?

Or, if you prefer, "What is the thesis?" though I find that when I ask for a thesis, students begin to rummage through the essay as if they were looking for a lost pen in a desk drawer. Somewhere they have learned that there is always a thesis statement contained in a single sentence. Hoagland defines his direction far more indirectly, though we can point to a few near-theses that he drops along the way:

> On stubby, amputated-looking feet he leads his life, which if we glance at it attentively is a kind of cutout of our own, all the more so for being riskier and shorter (paragraph 6).

> The point of it is to open oneself to the possibility of becoming partly a dog. . . . One wants to rediscover the commonality of ani-

> mal and man—to see an animal eat and sleep that hasn't forgotten how to enjoy doing such things . . . (paragraph 7).

> And as we drift away from any cognizance of them [animals], we sacrifice some of the intricacy and grandeur of life. Having already lost so much, we are hardly aware of what remains, but to a primitive snatched forward from an earlier existence it might seem as if we had surrendered a richness comparable to all the tapestries of childhood (paragraph 16).

> Though animal programs on television are popular, what with the wave of nostalgia and "ecology" in the country, we can generally say about the animal kingdom, "The King is dead, long live the King" (paragraph 20).

> But the basic switch has already been accomplished—from the ancient juxtaposition of people, animals, and dreams blending the two, to people and monsters that grow solely out of people by way of dreams (paragraph 20).

> The first reason that people kept a dog was to acquire an ally on the hunt, a friend at night. Then it was to maintain an avenue to animality, as our own nearness began to recede. But as we lose our awareness of all animals, dogs are becoming a bridge to nowhere (paragraph 21).

The point that emerges from these partial theses and from innumerable small touches in the essay is that, just as we have drawn the dog inexorably and somewhat unhappily out of the natural world his instincts suit him for, we have been drawn somewhat unhappily out of the natural world. The dog is the fixed point of reference that lets us measure our movement from nature. He is like the canary that coal miners used to carry into the shafts as a precaution against poisoned air. His fate foreshadows our own.

—D.H.—

Style Lesson 40: Choosing Words for Their Associations

In the following passage from the last paragraph of "Dogs, and the Tug of Life," Hoagland pointedly inserts words that are commonly associated with human life into his discussion of the lives of dogs. Try to fill in the blanks; the sound of Hoagland's prose, as well as the content, may help you recall the missing words. Be prepared to discuss the effect of Hoagland's choices and the alternatives you create.

Though they admire us, are thrilled by us, _____ us, we regard them as a hobby or a status symbol, like a _____ _____, and substitute leash laws for leadership—expect them not simply to learn _____ but to grow _____, because their beastly paws seem stranger to us every year. If they try to _____ us with their handy-jack mouths, we read it as a bite; and like _____ _____, they are disposed of when the family relocates, changes its "bag," or in the scurry of divorce. The first reason people kept a dog was to acquire an _____ on the hunt, a _____ at night. Then it was to maintain an _____ to animality, as our own nearness began to recede. But as we lose our awareness of all animals, dogs are becoming a _____ to nowhere. We can only pity their fate.

PROGRESS
AND
ITS PRICE

OVERVIEW OF UNIT

The Progress section has one foot in nature and one foot in the marketplace, and is intended to remind students that all of us are forced into this awkward straddle. Cumulatively, the essays tend to present us as a four-million-year-old species shaped by evolution for an outdoor life of hunting and gathering, but living in an economic system that keeps most of us indoors and ties us to clock time.

Two of our writers view this change in our circumstances without regret—the majority view in American society, surely. Adam Smith believes that the benefits of industrial production outweigh the losses, and Aldous Huxley takes the long view of technology and pronounces it good. The other eight writers file opinions which are, to a greater or lesser degree, dissents from this view. This apparent imbalance is really an attempt to achieve balance; most students I meet are so unthinkingly committed to the idea that technology has made our lives better that I felt it important to call more witnesses on the other side.

In all probability, your classroom will contain a number of "technological fundamentalists," as Berry calls those who have internalized as dogma the notion that things are getting better all the time. Part of the fun and challenge of teaching this unit is to get such students to think about things in a more complex way. The Boorstin article may be particularly important for such students because it is written by a person who is obviously quite sophisticated about technological processes and can therefore raise credible concerns about them.

Your students needn't take sides to write good papers. Having them write a process analysis of fast-food meal production or some other form of simple manufacture may be a real eye-opener if they are naive about the complexity of our economic system. The essays by Smith, Thoreau, Kenyatta, and Hubbell provide good models for such process writing.

ADAM SMITH

Division of Labour

Knowing that *The Wealth of Nations* was published in 1776 and has a reputation for being hard to follow, you may be tempted to conclude that we have gone off the deep end by including a selection from it. But take a look at the selection itself, and you will see that it is interesting, compact, and lively. By fits and starts, Smith was a marvelous writer, with a much plainer and more direct style than, for example, Huxley or Thoreau. Somehow, he sounds more modern than most writers between 1776 and World War I.

Smith's essay can be productively assigned with Thoreau's or Jomo Kenyatta's. Smith argues very persuasively that specialized methods of manufacture are making life better for everyone; Thoreau argues and Kenyatta implies that division of labor may be whittling away at the integrity of life. Some of your students will want to assume that Smith must be a tough-minded manufacturer, Thoreau an ineffectual, artsy-craftsy student of nature and the arts, and Kenyatta a soft-headed academic romantic. In fact, Smith was Professor of Moral Philosophy at the University of Glasgow and was notoriously absent-minded. He once fell into a tanning pit while he was deep in talk with a friend, and it is said that he once put his bread and butter in his cup, poured boiling water over it, sipped it, and declared it a terrible cup of tea. Thoreau was a competent carpenter, a very good surveyor, and the inventor of some ingenious manufacturing process for lead pencils. Kenyatta was one of the most successful practical politicians of our century.

QUESTIONS

1. What contemporary examples of specialized manufacturing can be added to the eighteenth-century examples Smith uses?

Your students' tendency at first will be to go for complex, large-scale manufacturing of such high-tech items as computers or spacecraft. In all probability this discussion will lead nowhere because no one in the room will have enough knowledge of the manufacturing techniques to create an example in detail. This is in itself a lesson worth driving home: most manufacturing now takes place behind what we might call the corporate curtain. A few of your students may have had work experience that has taken them behind this curtain; most will have to settle for such glimpses of production as the idle citizen sees. I think, for instance, of the McDonald's on our campus, involved in what Smith would call the "trifling manufacture" of fast food. If I were to attempt to describe this workplace in the sort of detail Smith uses for the pin factory in paragraph 3, I would have to find out how many separate operations are performed by how many employees (I heard the manager say to an employee one day, "I'm putting you on drinks today, but don't worry—it's not too hard."), and with what sort of specialized equipment. All this I might do by observation. So might your students, and write good short papers on what they find. But then, if we were to note, as Smith does in paragraph 11 for the woolen coat, the more remote aspects of manufacture, we would include the manufacture of beef, its specialties and subspecialties: feed manufacture, veterinary medicine, marketing, futures trading, butchering, storage, refrigerated transport, and so forth endlessly. Or we could begin by looking at the cash register, with each product represented by a key: what a history its manufacture must have! Getting beyond the immediate workplace requires more research than your students can probably manage in a semester, but they should be encouraged to think about the intricate circuitry of trade that ties an industrial country together.

The university itself is a specialized factory of sorts and may bear analysis.

2. What factors about working life are not taken into account in Smith's discussion?

In this selection, Smith's eye is, as people say these days, on the bottom line, on the number of widgets and blodgets, rather than on the workers who make them, except insofar as these workers are useful tools. This tendency in the thinking of political economists irritates writers like Thoreau and Wendell Berry. It is certainly arguable that the specialization of the workplace can impoverish the life of the worker, that the person who turns chair legs on the lathe all day (particularly if the lathe is computerized) hasn't the satisfaction of the craftsman who makes the whole chair start to finish and is proud of the product. I know of a painter who mixes his own paints, gathering his raw materials from the same Oklahoma landscapes he paints. There must be satisfaction in such integrity.

Smith's inclination to see the worker as a part of the machinery of production shows most clearly in paragraph 7. Notice his impatience with the man who "saunters a little in turning his hand from one sort of employment to another." Smith's heart seems to freeze at the idea of *sauntering*, but Thoreau, who knew the benefits of apparent idleness, once wrote a defense of it, saying that the word derives from the wandering of medieval pilgrims going *à la Sainte Terre*, to the Holy Land, and that it still smacks of a pilgrimage to redeem the earth from the infidels, among whom he seems to include Smith.

3. In what sort of production is specialization likely to be detrimental rather than beneficial?

The obvious cases are in arts and crafts, but here some of your students will detect an element of mere quaintness. And indeed it is hard on strictly utilitarian grounds (perhaps not impossible) to favor the split-oak chair made by a traditional craftsman over the tubular aluminum wonder that costs a fraction as much and lasts till doomsday. But in some of the arts we feel that individual expression is absolutely essential and are saddened when specialization takes over. Motion pictures, for instance, because they are high-budget items put together by teams of specialists, are hamstrung as vehicles for the expression of individual insight. The novel that the movie is based on (let's assume for the sake of argument that it is a good one, not compromised from the start) must be modified by a screenwriter who must listen to the results of the studio's marketing research; the screenplay is turned over to a director who will see the story somewhat differently, will cast it partly according to his or her tastes and partly according to the box-office potential of the stars. The stars will have their own theories of their parts, and will not want to be mere puppets for the director. And there are the musical director, the director of cinematography, the costume director, etc. Movies tend to be beaten into blandness by this long process.

—D.H.—

HENRY DAVID THOREAU

The Fitness in a Man's Building His Own House

This selection from "Economy," the first chapter in *Walden*, reveals a Thoreau your students may not recognize. Those who know him as a transcendentalist prose-poet may read this shrewd, practical Yankee who can build a house for less money than most college students pay in annual rent and wonder if there are two Henry David Thoreaus. They will be right. At first it may seem that the two have nothing in common. The practical Thoreau praises the virtue of self-reliance and can tell us that the hinges and screws for his house cost $0.14. The other Thoreau writes,

> Sometimes, in a summer morning, having taken my accustomed bath, I sat in my sunny doorway from sunrise to noon, rapt in a revery, amidst the pines and hickories and sumacs, in undisturbed solitude and stillness while the birds sang around or flitted noiseless through the house, until by the sun falling in at my west window, or the noise of some traveller's wagon on the distant highway, I was reminded of the lapse of time. I grew in those seasons like corn in the night, and they were far better than any work of the hands would have been.

Thoreau's boast that he is more practical and better able to make a living than his neighbors is not antithetical to his claim that he is at the same time more spiritual, more transcendental. In fact it is his practicality that makes his spirituality possible. In Thoreau's opinion the "mass of men lead lives of quiet desperation" because they waste their lives laboring to earn money for unnecessary luxuries that are "positive hindrances to the elevation of mankind." In contrast, the person who recognizes how few things are necessary to life can obtain them easily and have time left "to entertain the true problems of life with freedom and a prospect of success."

If your students question Thoreau's relevance, you might want to assign Randall Jarrell's "A Sad Heart at the Supermarket" (*Media*) along with this essay. Jarrell argues that our wants have become so insatiable that we can now be persuaded to buy stand-by generators. Thoreau's insistence that we think about what is truly necessary seems especially appropriate in the Age of Consumerism.

QUESTIONS

1. Has Thoreau's statement that "the swiftest traveller is he who goes afoot" (paragraph 15) been invalidated by inventions like the jet?

It is not true that a person who walks would arrive before one who must first earn the fare to fly. Assuming that the jet traveler earns the minimum wage per hour and buys a bargain-rate round-trip ticket from New York to

Los Angeles for $258 (it is unlikely that anyone Thoreau considered a friend would fly first class), the air traveler working for minimum wage could earn his fare in fewer than 8 eight-hour days. And even if Thoreau consistently logged 30 miles per day, the journey would take about 100 days one way. But enough for higher math. Thoreau wouldn't want to visit New York or Los Angeles anyway.

Thoreau's point, that the person traveling by foot savors the time spent traveling while the other person may dread the time spent earning a fare, is still valid. His observation that the walker sees more of the country is even more strikingly true in the age of air travel. In "On A Greek Holiday" Alice Bloom asserts that most tourists today see little more than what she terms "international accommodation, and wherever it exists—whether in Madrid, London, Istanbul, Athens, Cleveland—it resembles an airport lounge." Thoreau's misgivings about the value of merely riding "somewhere, in next to no time, and for nothing" seem to be shared by an increasing number of twentieth-century travelers who are opting to travel at less than the maximum rate. Millions of us choose, at least occasionally, to bike, canoe, jog, swim, backpack, or otherwise propel ourselves across some portion of the globe.

2. When have you experienced comparable pleasures in returning to a simpler mode of existence?

Few of us build our own houses, but most of your students will recall accomplishments that gave them a similar sense of pride. In an age of specialization, we need to feel that we are capable of creating something all by ourselves. We achieve that sensation in an unending variety of ways. Whether we grow tomatoes, rebuild 1969 Camaros, write novels, bake whole-wheat bread, or learn to play the mountain dulcimer, we share the pleasure of seeing a process through from start to finish, of feeling that we actually have some control over one aspect of our lives. Personally I still like playing with clay (probably because I didn't attend kindergarten), and I have at times dug my own clay, mixed it with grog, built pots, and fired them in an outdoor pit. As a result I have produced some remarkably ugly, black, stubby pots which I prize because I made them. Such experiences make me feel both closer to and farther from Thoreau. I understand the feeling of satisfaction he describes. There is an indescribable joy in lifting a bowl and realizing that it fits the curve of my hands because my hands shaped it, but I am grateful I don't have to make every dish I need. It's backbreaking work, and sometimes all the pots crack because there is no way to keep the temperature in the pit constant.

3. Evaluate Thoreau's statement that students "should not *play* life, or *study* it merely . . . but earnestly *live* it from beginning to end" (middle of paragraph 13).

Thoreau claims that a "boy who had made his own jackknife from the ore which he had dug and smelted, reading as much as would be necessary for this" would advance more than a "boy who had attended the lectures on metallurgy at the Institute" (paragraph 13). Your students should be overwhelmed by the implications of Thoreau's argument. First they should notice that he is claiming that the student who is actively involved in the "experience of living" is not only learning more but is in a sense morally superior. Of the typical student who lives in housing constructed by others Thoreau says, "The student who secures his coveted leisure and retirement by systematically shirking any labor necessary to man obtains but an ignoble and unprofitable leisure. . . ." I doubt that everyone will agree that people who work with their hands rather than their heads are inherently nobler.

Second, someone should raise the objection that it would be impossible to do as Thoreau advocates and get through college in one lifetime. The explosion of knowledge that occurred during the past century has rendered obsolete the notion of the Renaissance man or woman who is accomplished in all things. We are so technologically interdependent that each specialist must rely on the expertise of others. The person who designs computers for the telephone system doesn't have time to learn about the tensile strength of the wire strung between telephone poles or of the chemical composition of the plastic used in designer telephones.

Finally, your students should note that although Thoreau advocates that students be educated through practical experience rather than traditional academic methods, he relies on a traditional academic method to educate his readers. What could be more traditional than a structured essay replete with classical allusions (the gods of Troy, for example, in paragraph 4) and metaphors (the core of truth within architectural ornaments likened to the almond at the center of sugarplums, in paragraph 8)? Thoreau may believe that we would have benefited more by building our own houses than by reading his essay, but he also believes that the essay is itself a tool that can be used to teach.

4. By building his own house, has Thoreau in fact solved the problems most people face in everyday life?

It is important to explain to your students that Thoreau was not urging his readers to build their own cabins around Walden Pond. Thoreau himself lived in his cabin at Walden for only two years (1845–1847) and, to some extent, he lived there through necessity rather than by choice. At that point in his life, Thoreau tells us that he was occupied with the question of "how to get my living honestly, with freedom left for my proper pursuits." Although Thoreau had been educated at Harvard, he had not succeeded in a profession. He was dismissed from his position as a teacher at Concord school because he refused to administer discipline. He had failed to support himself by writing, and in 1844, to pay off debts he had acquired, he went to work in his father's pencil factory. (That probably explains his opposition, in paragraph 7, to the division of labor which is so enthusiastically praised by Adam Smith.) After a year Thoreau decided that life was too precious to waste it making a living. To gain time for living, he chose to cut his expenses by eliminating all but the necessities. As he tells us, "My purpose in going to Walden Pond was not to live cheaply nor to live dearly there, but to transact some private business with the fewest obstacles. . . ." For Thoreau, that private business was life.

I cannot read Thoreau without feeling the lure of the siren's call to return to a simpler existence. I am most tempted on the days that my possessions seem to own me, when the clothes need to be ironed, the floors swept, the furniture dusted, the dishes washed, the grass mowed, the kitty litter changed, and the car filled with gas. "Surely," I think, "I would be better off without all this stuff." But then I recall the week we spent in a primitive fishing camp in Canada when one daughter was three years old and the other six weeks old. I have never been in a prettier place, nor have I ever had less time to appreciate the beauty of my surroundings. Children are dependents in ways never contemplated by the IRS. I spent hours just carrying water (for baths, for dishes, for cooking) from the lake and heating it on the wood stove. I enjoy Thoreau's account of cooking outdoors: "When it stormed before my bread was baked, I fixed a few boards over the fire, and sat under them to watch my loaf, and passed some pleasant hours in that way." But I wonder what his hours would have been like if he had been entertaining two hungry children while the bread baked. For those of us who have children to support and care for, life in a cabin on Walden Pond might be less than blissful. I think the title of this essay is perfect: "The Fitness in *A Man's* Building *His Own* House."

If we read the essay as a call to unplug our machines and return to a primitive life, it obviously has little significance to an urban, technological society. But if we read it to remind ourselves that making more money so that we can own more things is not the purpose of life, then the essay is probably even more important today than when it was written.

—M.R.D.—

Style Lesson 41: A 125-Word Sentence

In paragraph 13 of "The Fitness in a Man's Building His Own House," Thoreau constructs the long, beautifully constructed sentence broken into phrases below. Thoreau's style may be too involved for some modern tastes, but practice imitating it phrase by phrase will help you hone your skills with syntax, particularly with parallel constructions.

If I wished a boy to know something
    about the arts and sciences,
        for instance,
I would not pursue the common course,
    which is merely to send him
        into the neighborhood of some professor,
            where anything is professed and practised
                but the art of life;
    —to survey the world through a telescope or a microscope,
        and never with his natural eye;
    to study chemistry,
        and not learn how his bread is made,
    or mechanics,
        and not learn how it is earned;
    to discover new satellites to Neptune,
        and not detect the motes in his eyes,
            or to what vagabond he is a satellite himself;
    or to be devoured by the monsters that swarm all around him,
        while contemplating the monsters in a drop of vinegar.

DANIEL J. BOORSTIN

Technology and Democracy

This essay could be seen as an elaboration of an idea that Thoreau floats in a single sentence in *Walden*: "To make a railroad round the world available to all mankind is equivalent to grading the surface of the planet." The elaboration is carefully arranged, copiously illustrated, and clearly stated—really a model of the practical virtues one hopes to inculcate in a freshman composition class. It is a cogent argument about the dangers of a too-successful technology, offered by a historian whose reputation has been made by books that praise technology highly. Students who think hard about the four consequences of technological advances Boorstin discusses should look at the daily life around them through somewhat altered eyes.

The view of the advanced society Boorstin presents is similar to the one Alice Bloom presents in "On a Greek Holiday" and the one Randall Jarrell presents in "A Sad Heart at the Supermarket." His view that technology attenuates experience gains some support from Jomo Kenyatta's "Gikuyu Industries."

Because the essay is long and crowded with detail, I am providing an outline that should be useful when you prepare yourself for class discussion. Paying less attention to the section breaks in the text than to the apparent intent of the essay, I see it in six parts.

1. The introduction, paragraphs 1–4, stipulates a definition of democracy and notes the enormous success of technology in achieving democratic goals. It then poses the central question: what are the consequences of this success?

2. *Consequence 1*—the attenuation of experience—occupies almost half of the essay (paragraphs 5–26). Here is the heart of Boorstin's argument that in our pursuit of safety and convenience, we may be turning life into an experience as bland as tapioca. We can subdivide this section into seven parts:

a. definition of attenuation, paragraph 5

b. attenuation of seasons, paragraphs 6–9, including the important examples of refrigerated transport (7) and central heat (9)

c. homogenization of space, paragraphs 10–12, including the example of plate glass

d. attenuation of occasions and events, paragraphs 13–16, including the important examples of photography (13), television (15), and the pseudo-event that television creates (16)

e. neutralization of risks via insurance (17)

f. attenuation of property, paragraphs 18–25, including shares of stock (19), credit buying (20), franchising (21, 22), and packaging (23–25)

g. summary, paragraph 26

3. *Consequence 2*—the decline of congregation—is Boorstin's argument that the circumstances of modern life may leave the individual deprived of the natural camaraderie that comes with more primitive technologies. This section divides into four parts:

a. definition of decline of congregation, paragraph 27

b. effect of centralized plumbing, paragraphs 28 and 29

c. effect of television and newspapers, paragraph 30

d. summary, paragraph 31

4. *Consequence 3*—the rising sense of momentum—is the modern citizen's not entirely unjustified view that technology has its own momentum and will advance despite the efforts or interests of mere human individuals. The section divides into five parts:

a. definition of rising sense of momentum, paragraphs 32 and 33

b. the alarming example of the momentum of atomic research, paragraphs 33–36

c. the example of space exploration, paragraph 37

d. the example of foreign aid, paragraph 38

e. summary, paragraph 39

5. *An aside, in which the author frees himself for a moment from his data to announce his thesis, that "getting there is all the fun."* He poses the question, "Is it possible that while *democratizing* enriches experience, *democracy* dilutes experience?" But he poses it in such a way that he pushes us to answer yes. This section divides as follows:

a. posing and definition of thesis, paragraphs 40–41

b. example of photography as impoverishing experience, paragraphs 42 and 43

c. example of phonograph, paragraphs 44 and 45

d. example of declining community, paragraph 46

e. summary, paragraph 47

6. *A conclusion* in which the author urges us to remember that if we are content to rest on our oars, we may find life a comfortable coffin, but that we can choose to keep rowing to "reach to the open horizon." This conclusion includes the following:

a. *Consequence 4*—the belief in solutions—which Boorstin sees as "one of our most dangerous popular fallacies." He argues that while technological problems are solvable and do reach an end, democracy is *not* a problem but a process. We should not attempt to solve the problem of democracy or look forward to its being fully achieved (paragraphs 48–54).

b. a reminder that to appreciate the process, we need both a sense of our past and a poetic and imaginative view of the future, one that will encourage us to sail toward the open horizon, rather than to a narrow pragmatic goal (paragraphs 55–59).

QUESTIONS

1. How convincing is Boorstin's argument that technology and democracy dilute experience?

Boorstin's thesis here is so original that few of your students will have been over the same mental ground before. Some will be inclined to resist his ideas simply because they are alien; some will be inclined to embrace them for the same reason. The trick in class discussion will be to get them to examine the actual merits of his argument. One merit it clearly has is abundant and pertinent evidence, particularly in the section which argues that technology attenuates experience. When classroom discussion comes around to this issue of evidence, I have my students close their books and see if they can collectively reassemble the evidence of attenuation that Boorstin has assembled, in each case naming the technological or economic advance and the attenuation it creates. They usually remember the importance of refrigerated transport, central heat, plate glass, photography, television, franchising, and packaging, at least. This discussion will likely drift into question 2.

I think Boorstin's case that one effect of technology is to convert experiences that were unique or unusual to commonplace is superbly documented and almost incontrovertible. I'm not sure this gets us all the way to saying that technology dilutes our experiences. Let's take, for instance, televised baseball. In an earlier state of technology, when professional baseball was played only by day and only in a few cities, John Smith, who played a little in his youth, might be lucky to see a game in a decade. I suppose viewing of this game might have been poignant, as Boorstin suggests, but would it have been rich? Would Smith have recognized the players, known what kind of season they were having, known their batting averages against left- and right-handed hitters, known who had just come up from the minors two weeks before? Surely not. Today's television-watching John Smith would know these things, and might have an experience of the game that is admittedly less poignant but nonetheless richer. Sometimes repetition makes us more sensitive to experience rather than less. And even if we grant that repetition attenuates each experience, technology provides the opportunity of so many experiences that the enormous increase in quantity and variety may to some degree make up for the lack of poignancy. A person who can sample in a month the cuisine of a dozen countries, including fruits in and out of season, may not be losing so terribly much by not waiting all winter for that first satisfying bite of June strawberry.

These objections notwithstanding, I find Boorstin pretty convincing.

2. Explain the concept of attenuation of experience, and name one device other than those Boorstin mentions that contributes to this attenuation.

Discussion of the first question may lead inevitably to this one. I will not bore you with a restatement of Boorstin's concept of attenuation. It is, however, unusual enough to merit class discussion. Students can feel that they really understand it when they can contribute a fresh example of it. Three possibilities are

- new mass-mailing techniques, which make it possible for millions of people to get an apparently personal letter from a senator or member of congress or a company president. The effect is, of course, to diminish the effectiveness of such letters.
- tract housing, which has made it possible for millions of Americans to escape the confinement of city apartments and buy a suburban home, but has also made suburbia a synonym for mediocrity.
- mass-produced clothing, which has, as Aldous Huxley says, placed elegance within the reach of practically everyone and so has made elegance less elegant.

3. Is technological advance in fact causing a decline in congregation?

There is so much congregation on a college campus that students should view Boorstin's assertion with some skepticism. In the years beyond college, they may indeed wish that they could meet people accidentally at the well rather than deliberately at the singles bar or via a computerized dating service or by joining a hobby club. But I think that on this particular issue, Boorstin is being a little myopic. When America was largely a nation of isolated farmsteads, there must have been fewer opportunities for congregation. Or, at least, the range of those with whom one could congregate must have been exceedingly narrow.

4. How does Boorstin propose to remedy the ills he describes in the essay?

Here we deal with the last 11 paragraphs of the essay, which may provoke very different reactions in different readers. There is something uplifting and right about Boorstin's conclusion that the best solution is to keep struggling to advance democracy through technology, knowing that the satisfaction is always in the struggle. On the other hand, doesn't it practically amount to this: having stripped our life of much of its poignancy and left ourselves with less and less to look forward to, we must now keep moving, like sharks, or else we will die with stale water in our gills.

—D.H.—

Style Lesson 42:
Combining Sentences to Produce Coherence

People who make computerized style checkers often mistake shortness of sentences for "readability." But sometimes a longer sentence presents material more effectively than several short ones because it allows the writer to straighten out the relationships among concepts. The following sentences are drawn from one long sentence in paragraph 5 of "Technology and Democracy." To practice using repetition and parallel structure, combine the sentences into one, then compare to Boorstin's original.

One of the consequences of our success in technology has been the removal of distinctions. It is also a consequence of our wealth. And it is a consequence of our energy and our imagination, as well. This removal of distinctions is not just between people. It is also between everything and everything else. It removes the distinction between places and between points in time.

ALDOUS HUXLEY

Hyperion to a Satyr

This paean to progress may come as a surprise to readers who know Huxley's most famous work, *Brave New World.* That satirical anti-utopian novel, which was written in 1932 in the midst of the Great Depression, reflected Huxley's fear that technology would be used to enslave humanity. The novel is set in the seventh century A.F. (After Ford) in a world where applied science has eliminated pain and poverty and illness and aging, but the people, who are conditioned from the time of conception to fit into their assigned spot in the social hierarchy and to be delighted with their place, are merely slaves who love their servitude. They are deprived of the freedom to love, to think, to create—of all that we consider vital to the experience of being human.

Apparently Huxley had a change of heart between 1932 and the mid-1950s (when this essay was written). As he explained in the foreword he wrote to the 1946 edition of *Brave New World,* the most serious defect in the story is that the Savage is offered only two choices—"an insane life in Utopia, or the life of a primitive in an Indian village. . . ." Huxley explained, "If I were to rewrite the book, I would offer the savage a third alternative," and he then described a community in which "[s]cience and technology would be used as though, like the Sabbath, they had been made for man, not (as at present and still more so in the Brave New World) as though man were to be adapted and enslaved to them." In "Hyperion to a Satyr" Huxley praises an embodiment of that ideal, the Hyperion Activated Sludge Plant, a marvel of technology that triumphantly solved the "problem of keeping a great city [Los Angeles] clean without polluting a river or fouling the beaches, and without robbing the soil of its fertility. . . ."

In "Hyperion to a Satyr" your students will see Huxley at his best and at his worst. The essay is a tour de force in which he displays his incredible store of knowledge (with information about everything from sphincter control among primates to the role of symbols in thinking), his wry sense of humor ("In his youth, before he went into power politics as Innocent III, Lotario de' Conti . . ."), his unorthodox opinions (that improved sanitation allowed the "transformation of the English caste system into an equalitarian society"), and his ability to create unforgettable images ("At our feet, and as far as the eye could reach in all directions, the sand was covered with small whitish objects, like dead caterpillars. Recognition dawned. The dead caterpillars were made of rubber and had once been contraceptives . . . "). At times, however, Huxley's obvious display of his superior knowledge—the passages in Latin and Italian, the allusions to obscure medieval writers—can be a bit irritating. Whatever your students' response to Huxley as a writer, the essay should serve as a springboard for interesting student writings about the effects of technology.

QUESTIONS

1. How effective is Huxley in using the structure of the essay and supporting details to convince us that technology can decrease class distinctions?

Although the essay is clearly focused in that it has a single unifying thesis (that cleanliness is a prerequisite for democracy), Huxley explores an incredible range of topics only tangentially related to his argument. He considers Caesar, Gandhi, Tolstoy, and Auden; the origin of soap; the contamination of the Thames; the social significance of cotton garments; the medieval view that filth was divinely ordained; and the mechanics of sewage disposal in the twentieth century. It would be impossible to control such a mass of information without a clear plan of organization. Close examination shows that the essay can be divided into six sections.

In the introduction (paragraphs 1–4), Huxley captures our attention with his graphic description of the Los Angeles sewage disposal problem.

In part 2 (paragraphs 5–15) he describes "the all-pervading squalor" that has characterized most of humanity's existence, and he argues that such conditions led the upper classes to loathe the poor, to believe that "they should be treated as badly as they smell" (paragraph 8).

In part 3 (paragraphs 16–20) he argues that "techniques for keeping clean at a cost so low that practically everybody can afford the luxury of not being disgusting" can contribute to brotherly love within, if not between, nations (paragraph 16), and he continues with a historical overview of the development of sewage systems.

In part 4 (paragraphs 21–23) he returns to the Hyperion Activated Sludge Plant and describes that marvel of technology.

In part 5 (paragraphs 24–29) he notes that "untouchability depends on other things besides the bad sanitation of slums" and explains how innovations that allow us to be healthier and to wear clean clothing have also narrowed "the gulf of disgust" that once separated the classes.

In the conclusion (paragraphs 30–32) he warns against the danger of creating "new symbols no less compulsive in their anti-democratic tendencies than the old."

Within that framework, Huxley bombards us with supporting details for his every observation. In paragraph 25, for example, Huxley supports his generalization that "when sickness rages unchecked . . . the occasions for being disgusting are innumerable." From *Troilus and Cressida* he quotes Thersites' nauseating list of fifteen of "the commoner ailments of Shakespeare's time." He discusses the prevalence of malaria, typhus, bubonic plague, dysentery, and cancer. He reminds us that Chaucer's Cook had a gangrenous sore and the Summoner suffered a skin disease. And he concludes with stomach-turning accounts of Christians who embraced lepers, kissed sores, and swallowed pus. By the time I finished the paragraph, I was willing to concede the point rather than be forced to think about it any longer. You could examine any other passage in the essay and find equally impressive support.

2. How would you characterize Huxley's attitude toward his audience?

I'm never sure what Huxley thinks of his readers. At times I am tempted to yield to the flattering thought that he really believes that I can read Italian and Latin, that I will remember where Brother Salimbene dropped his relic of St. Dominic (paragraph 18), and that I will recognize the lines he quotes from Wordsworth (paragraph 1). After all, his grandfather was T. H. Huxley, a scientist of worldwide fame, and his brothers were the noted biologist Sir Julian Huxley and the Nobel laureate Andrew Fielding Huxley. He might have concluded that the world is populated with brilliant people. And I must admit that I feel a certain degree of pleasure when I do recognize his allusions.

But at other times I am annoyed by his too obvious flaunting of his knowledge. In his introduction to *Brave New World & Brave New World Revisited*, Martin Green made the following remarks about Huxley's statement that the "last conservative statesman was the fifth Marquess of Lansdowne": "He of course knows that not one in a hundred of his readers will remember this name, thus unconnected with party or ministry or decade; that they will all be halted in their following of his argument, and will all feel an incipient twinge of inadequacy; and by calling the statesman not Lord Lansdowne, but the Marquess, and the fifth Marquess, he spreads his peacock tail of insolent joy in his own superiority." I think it is fair to say that in this essay Huxley sometimes uses his knowledge to intimidate us rather than to enlighten us.

3. To what extent can technological developments improve the condition of humanity?

Huxley clearly believes that there are a number of human problems for which there are no technical solutions. Huxley admits that he sees no technological developments capable of bringing about the religious ideals of monotheism and human brotherhood (paragraph 15). And even when technology appears to have solved a problem, Huxley fears that our ability to deceive ourselves, to pick the wrong symbol, may resurrect the problem in a slightly different guise. He warns us, for example, that a person who is tagged with an offensive political label may be as much an outcast as one who has an offensive odor (paragraph 31). At the same time, he believes that, within limits, technology can effect real improvement in the human condition, and can even bring about some changes that are ordinarily considered religious or political goals. For example, when technology enabled us to be cleaner, it contributed to brotherly love and democracy as well as to physical comfort. Huxley seems to agree with the historian Lecky who claimed that "sanitary reformers had done more for general happiness and the alleviation of human misery than all the more spectacular figures . . . put together" (paragraph 20). In spite of technology's limitations, Huxley is quite happy to accept "such real but limited goods as Hyperion . . ." (paragraph 33).

Other writers in this unit such as Thoreau and Bloom are less sanguine about technology's ability to benefit us. In "The Fitness in a Man's Building His Own House," for example, Thoreau writes, "Our inventions are wont to be pretty toys, which distract our attention from serious things. They are but improved means to an unimproved end, an end which it was already but too easy to arrive at; as railroads lead to Boston or New York."

By the time your students have read a few of the essays in this unit, they should be thinking about both the limitations and the potential of technology. They may not be ready to take on the underlying question—What is good?—but there are a number of more concrete writing possibilities that should encourage them to consider both the positive and the negative aspects of progress. We are often accused of being a black box society, in that we rely on machines we do not understand and could neither build nor repair. Perhaps some of your students would like to try a modern version of *A Connecticut Yankee in King Arthur's Court*. They can imagine being transported to any previous period of time, then speculate about the number of modern gadgets they could reconstruct given the resources available to them. Or they might explain which aspects of technology they would miss and which they would gladly give up.

Another possibility would be to have them write about a technological advance they consider comparable in importance to sanitation. Some candidates are the clock, the printing press, the birth control pill, and the automobile. Or they could consider the possible effects of something we have not yet invented, such as the Star Wars defense plan or nuclear fusion.

One final suggestion. Your students might enjoy comparing their lives to those of their parents in regard to any one technological change. If nothing else, they should be fascinated to learn what people did with their time before the advent of television.

—M.R.D.—

Style Lesson 43: Coherence in a Short Paragraph

The following sentences form a short, well knit paragraph (paragraph 24) in "Hyperion to a Satyr." Their order has been scrambled. Reconstruct the paragraph by putting the sentences in order, then discuss the transitions and references that made the job easy.

1. Where sickness rages unchecked and where people cannot afford to buy new clothes or keep their old ones clean, the occasions for being disgusting are innumerable.
2. And we live not exclusively in health, but very often in sickness.
3. We live not merely in our houses, but even more continuously in our garments.
4. But untouchability depends on other things besides the bad sanitation of slums.

JOMO KENYATTA

Gikuyu Industries

Kenyatta's chapter, the selection from Thoreau, and the selection from Adam Smith form an interesting triad. All deal with practical details of simple manufacturing or house building, but one gives a distinctly literary view, one an economic, and one an anthropological. This grouping offers you a good opportunity to assign essays in which students contrast disciplinary approaches to the same general question. As the anthropologist in the group, Kenyatta has more interest than the other two in the way that the industries he studies fit into the general culture, including family life, religion, social obligations, and art. But his interest in these things is not merely avocational. As a deeply political man born into a colonial society, Kenyatta regretted the erosion of Gikuyu folkways and was in a good position to see that the European folkways that were beginning to replace them were not uniformly preferable. Apparently *Facing Mount Kenya* has sometimes been criticized for romanticizing the Gikuyu rather than merely reporting on them. Knowing about this accusation puts the reader in an interesting situation. Should he or she read the book as a scientific study perhaps tainted by Kenyatta's convictions, or as an essay written out of personal and political conviction but bolstered by scientific observation? Since the book was first written as a thesis under Stanislaw Malinowski's direction, we may assume that it is primarily a study, but the personal essay is a very visible thread running through it.

QUESTIONS

1. What social functions do Gikuyu ironwork and hut-building serve that are not served by manufacturing and house-building in our society?

Kenyatta does not explicitly make this comparison, but note the edge on his statement that Gikuyu methods may "seem primitive in the eyes of the machine-man of the Western world" but that they "fulfilled the needs of the community" (paragraph 6). I think Kenyatta means to imply more than material needs.

In Western society, industry occupies a separate compartment of life. People of my generation grew up essentially in the dark about what Daddy was going off to do each morning, and many children today grow up with two parents who vanish every day behind the industrial curtain—though the "industry" may not have to do with traditional manufacturing. Fairly few people in Western society today do work that is knit into their religion and family lives. We leave "all that" behind when we go to the factory or the office.

The Gikuyu do not leave it behind. In fact, the connectedness of Gikuyu life is one of the themes of *Facing Mount Kenya*. Notice, for example, the repeated references to the ceremonies that connect the living to the dead, the "ancestral spirits." Both before starting the smelting furnace (paragraph

8) and when removing the "blooms" (paragraph 9), the smith makes a small beer libation, not to *propitiate* the ancestor spirits, but to *invoke* or *greet* them: it is a very comradely gesture. The woman's hut is traditionally the abode not only of the living family but of the ancestral spirits (paragraph 14), and when the foundation is laid for a hut, there is also a libation to these spirits. We don't imagine American steelworkers or carpenters beginning a day by communing with the spirits of departed relatives.

Gikuyu work also connects the worker with the generations of the living. Kenyatta notes that when the smith gathers iron ore, his whole family participates in the process (paragraph 6). When men and women do their respective work on a hut and sing songs praising their labor, the children nearby are receiving a lesson in how to behave (paragraph 21); and when the completed hut is dedicated, both the elder (paragraph 22) and children (paragraph 24) play a special role. In hut-building, these connections extend beyond the family and include all good neighbors of both genders (paragraphs 16–20; see especially 18). The smith's work is more closely confined to the family, but it establishes for him a special status in the community because it confers on him the power to curse (paragraph 12). In contemporary industrial society, the tradition of unpaid work on behalf of neighbors has atrophied, though your students can probably think of some examples of its continuation. (It is, of course, arguable that in contemporary society our workplaces become our villages, and that we build around them rich social relations.) Your students probably won't be able to find an example of a trade that gives its practitioners the sort of clout that smiths seemed to enjoy among the Gikuyu. Even the physician's work has lost some of its mystique.

The Gikuyu worker is connected to nonhuman aspects of the cosmos as well. The society lives on more familiar terms with nature than our own does: few of us could comfortably share a hut with animals we are fattening for slaughter. But for the Gikuyu, "brute" natural and the supernatural are close cousins and are connected with traditional industries, as we can see from the story of how the Mogai taught the Gikuyu the technique of smelting in order to spare animals the pain of being slaughtered by wooden implements (paragraphs 1–4). The spirits of the departed play a role not only in the various ceremonies but in the practical matter of where a hut can be located (paragraph 19). And the close of the hut-building ceremony is a prayer to the Great Elder who dwells on Mount Kenya.

When we look at Kenyatta's explanation of Gikuyu traditions, it is hard not to conclude that the old ways were richer than the Westernized ways that will gradually replace them. Again, this presents us with a dilemma, since the richness may be in the eye of the beholder. Some of your students may want to examine the way we live and work today; perhaps they will find connections to ancestors, neighbors, nature, and the supernatural that are not immediately apparent. Or perhaps they will find the absence of such connection desirable as a source of individual freedom.

2. What evidence do you find that Kenyatta's observations are not objective?

Specific evidence of Kenyatta's sympathies can be found in the disparaging comment about the "machine-man of the Western world," whose condescension toward Gikuyu industry obviously provokes his anger in paragraph 6. It also shows in paragraph 15, where he cannot resist a comment on the benighted British practice of exacting a hut tax damaging to the Gikuyu way of life. These particulars, however, are probably less important in setting the chapter's tone than is an almost omnipresent numinousness. This quality shows itself in Kenyatta's frequent use of such words as *sacred*, *ritual*, and *communing* (with the ancestral spirits). Your students might mark several instances in which such words are used and consider their effect. It seems to me that they present the Gikuyu as a people who do virtually nothing out of mere habit or dead tradition. Many an American family I know says grace before a meal with a perfunctoriness that does not call up the words *sacred* or *communing* or even *prayer*. Interjecting these words might make the spiritual life of the family appear considerably richer than it is. I can't know, of course, whether Kenyatta has unconsciously enhanced the life of the Gikuyu in reporting it, but I understand why some anthropologists would suspect him of doing so.

3. What evidence do you find in the essay that Gikuyu technology is better or worse than Western technology in providing for the material well-being of the people?

As someone who benefited in his youth from Western medical technology, Kenyatta certainly can't be blind to the advantages Western ways can have. The essay, though, makes a pretty good case for what we now might call the "appropriateness" of Gikuyu techniques. Clearly their techniques for smelting are slow and must produce an impure metal: a high-quality steel blade would probably be as much of an improvement over the traditional iron knife as the iron knife was over the legendary wooden one, and Kenyatta shows that few metal implements are available. On the other hand, few seem to be needed, and the Gikuyu recycling of used implements is admirable. Certainly the whole system seems capable of producing as many metal implements as are essential without danger of polluting the environment or exhausting scarce resources: there is much to be said for it. As for Gikuyu hut-building, to have developed a system that allows a group of people to build in one day a dwelling that will last for ten or more years is no mean accomplishment. Even if we allow that the Gikuyu family needs two huts, the procedure compares favorably to what we do in the West. How many days per decade does the average American work to pay off his or her mortgage? Probably more than two times the number of huts in a typical Gikuyu village. Of course your students may be eager to point out that the hut has no plumbing and no electricity. But this returns us to the central question of the unit—just how heavily these "improvements" should weigh in the balance.

—D.H.—

Style Lesson 44:
Coherence in a Longer Paragraph

Many of Kenyatta's paragraphs are notably cohesive, filled with transitions and references that knit the sentences tightly together. Below are nine sentences that form paragraph 17. Unscramble them as best as you can; be prepared to explain your reasoning.

1. In the same manner the wife visits her women friends, requesting them to help in various ways.
2. During the feasting this group of men and women entertain themselves with traditional songs relating to teamwork.
3. Those who cannot take part in collecting building materials are asked to help in providing food and drink for the builders' feast, which is called *"iruga ria mwako."*
4. The man and his wife or wives receive their helpers joyfully and bid them to sit down and rest.
5. When a family is engaged in the work of building a hut or huts the help of neighbours and friends is necessary in order to expedite the work.
6. After all have arrived a feast is provided, consisting of a variety of food and drink.
7. On the day appointed many of these friends will turn up, bringing with them the required materials for building.
8. Before they part, a day is appointed when the actual building of a hut or huts will take place.
9. A man goes round asking his friends to help him, and at the same time telling them what kind of building materials he would like them to supply him with.

CAROL BLY

Getting Tired

In this selection from *Letters from the Country,* a collection of essays about rural life in Minnesota, writer and part-time farmhand Carol Bly takes a stand for the open tractor. First she describes the 6600 John Deere combine that is changing farming:

> The combine cab has huge windows flaring wider at the top; they lean forward over the ground, and the driver sits so high behind the glass in its rubber moldings it is like a movie-set spaceship.

Then she relates her experience of plowing for hours with an old Allis-Chalmers WC tractor, and she concludes that a farmer who spends days inside a glass-and-metal cab loses more than he or she gains. However, this is not the typical nostalgic essay about the good old days. Bly concedes that old-fashioned farming is difficult, demanding, and dirty. But she also insists that getting tired has its rewards.

QUESTIONS

1. What is Bly's position on things like the 6600 combine? Is it a logically defensible position?

Because this is a classic informal essay in which Bly rambles from one observation about farming to another, there is no clearly stated thesis. Nevertheless, Bly manages to convey her doubts about the value of what usually passes for technological progress. At the outset, she states two of her reservations about the 6600 combine: "this isn't the good old farming where man and soil are dusted together all day; this isn't farming a poor man can afford, either, and therefore it further threatens his hold on the American 'family farm' operation" (paragraph 2). Her second concern is certainly valid. The cost of such a combine is even more prohibitive today than it was when she wrote this essay in 1973. The 6600 described by Bly has since been superseded by the 9600, a mammoth machine that can cut a 24-foot swath through a field of wheat or harvest 12 rows of corn at a time. The price of John Deere's biggest and best combine? $170,000 in cash.

But in spite of that one reference to the cost of the 6600, this essay isn't about the finances of farming. Bly, like Daniel Boorstin in "Technology and Democracy," is worried about costs that can't be counted in dollars and cents. Like Boorstin, she is troubled by the flattening of experience that occurs when a farmer sits in a glassed-in, air-conditioned cab listening to a radio, "so isolated from field, sky, all the real world, that the brain is dulled" (paragraph 18). It's hard to defend an essentially visceral position with logical arguments, and Bly doesn't even try.

2. How does Bly attempt to persuade us that we experience life more intensely when we give up some of our technological advances?

Bly can't argue that it's more economical or efficient to use an old Aliss-Chalmers for plowing, but she can show us what the farmer sitting in a cab is missing. In paragraphs 10–16 she describes the thoughts and sensations that fill her day when she drives an open tractor hour after hour.

The strain of sitting "twisted part way around" (paragraph 10).

Her initial enthusiasm for political reforms that will aid American farmers (paragraph 10).

The shedding of cap, jacket, and sweater as the sun climbs higher (paragraph 10).

The "extrovert energy" of tractors everywhere (paragraph 12).

The stupor that follows noon dinner (paragraph 13).

The vitality and hope that surge through her when the shadows appear again (paragraph 14).

The joy of 3:00 lunch (paragraph 14).

The mental and physical exhaustion that follows a fourteen-hour day of physical labor (paragraphs 15 and 16).

As Bly says, "A thousand impressions enter as you work up and down the rows" (paragraph 17). I've never operated a 9600, but I'm sure its cab blocks most of those impressions as effectively as our cars do.

3. Are you inclined to trust or distrust Bly's testimony?

Some readers may question whether Bly is qualified to judge the merits of farming the hard way. After all, she is a writer, not a farmer. Working in the fields during a few autumn days hardly makes her an expert on the subject of farming. That said, there are still plenty of reasons to trust her. The first is that she is so up-front about her lack of credentials. Instead of passing herself off as a farmer, she admits that she is "someone with a half interest in literature and a half interest in farming doing a half-decent job plowing" (paragraph 14). And she recognizes that the "tiredness that feels so good to the occasional laborer and the athlete is disturbing to a man destined to it eight months of every year" (paragraph 17).

Our other reason for trusting Bly is that she refuses to sugar-coat the reality she wants us to swallow. This is not a Disney version of farming where the sun is shining, the birds are chirping, and the farmhands are whistling merrily as they work the fields. These farmhands get hot, dirty, bored, and tired. When they stop for lunch, no one brings them whole wheat bread fresh from the oven, just "sandwiches of white commercial bread with luncheon meat" and "cake-mix cake" (paragraph 7). If Bly had told us that jouncing over a field from 6:00 a.m. to 8:00 p.m. was fun, we would have written her off as a lunatic or a liar. But when she admits that plowing with the old Alice exhausts the body, we are more willing to consider her claim that such bone-wearying work can also revitalize the soul.

—M.R.D.—

SUE HUBBELL

Beekeeper

Fifteen years ago Sue Hubbell, until then a librarian at Brown University in Rhode Island, moved to a remote mountaintop farm in the Missouri Ozarks, one hundred and five acres, more or less, of thin soil and wild beauty. There Hubbell began a commercial beekeeping and honey-producing operation that she describes as "a shaky, marginal sort of affair that never quite leaves me free of money worries but which allows me to live in these hills that I love."

Hubbell has deliberately chosen a life more physically demanding and less technologically advanced than most of ours, but she is neither an enemy of technology nor an advocate of rural existence. Hubbell sells honey, not pastoral idylls. In *A Country Year: Living the Questions* she writes:

> Since [the 1930s] waves of people who find cities too complicated have come here, meaning to lead lives of simplicity. What they have discovered is that life is as simple or as complicated as the person living it, and that people who have found life in the city overwhelming will find it even more so here, where it is much harder to make a living. . . . Ozarkers lead lives as complicated as those of people anywhere else. However, they are competent and resourceful about living in these hills; they are quiet about it, too, so it looks easy and . . . simple.

Although Hubbell doesn't encourage her readers to invest in Ozark real estate, she does show us that a spartan life can be both intellectually stimulating and emotionally satisfying. This selection will encourage your students to consider the hardships and rewards of Hubbell's alternative lifestyle and, perhaps, to find their own individual answers to the central issue raised by this unit: how can we know when progress is progress?

QUESTIONS

1. What is Hubbell's attitude toward technology?

Because Hubbell chooses to live without a microwave, central heating, a VCR, or other necessities, your students might expect her to be a back-to-nature purist who hates all things technological. Not so. She likes her chain saw even though it makes a terrible racket, she characterizes her come-along as "a cheery, sensible tool for a woman" (paragraph 22), she is proud of her honey factory with its "machinery and equipment that whirs, thumps, hums and looks very special" (paragraph 30), and she is fond of her white truck. She tells us that she once dreamed about her soul and was pleased to discover that it is "a female white truck, buoyant, impatient, one that speeds along, almost too fast in an exhilarating way, skimming slightly above the road, not quite keeping to the pathway" (paragraph 47).

Hubbell is a rarity, a person who can look at our cornucopia of consumer goods and say, "I'll take this but not that or that or that." She never articulates her standards for deciding which machines to own, but I imagine her guidelines are similar to those set out by Wendell Berry in "Against PCs." You might want your students to consider whether Hubbell's machines, especially her chain saw, would pass Berry's test. Or you might ask them whether Hubbell would approve of Berry's test. I think she would heartily applaud Berry's criteria, particularly the ninth: "[A tool] should not replace or disrupt anything good that already exists, and this includes family and community relationships." Hubbell might add a tenth: A tool should make survival easier. After all, a chain saw is not a weekend toy for someone who must "cut wood or die."

2. Do the advantages of life on Hubbell's wild mountaintop outweigh the disadvantages?

Although Hubbell's answer to this question is an unequivocal yes, some of your students may find it difficult to believe that her lifestyle has advantages. It might help to begin this discussion by asking your students to list Hubbell's gains and losses while you write their answers on the board in appropriate columns. I imagine your class will have no trouble identifying Hubbell's privation. She is poor (living on an "income well below the poverty line") and cannot afford to eat in restaurants or sleep in motels when she travels on her honey-selling trips. She spends her days doing exhausting and sometimes dangerous physical labor—felling dead trees, cutting and hauling firewood, carrying sixty-pound supers from beehive to truck on stifling summer days. Hubbell does not romanticize those aspects of her life. Her account of Ky's first day in the outyards, carrying and stacking 2,500 pounds of supers in one-hundred-degree heat while under attack by swarms of angry bees, was enough to convince me that a jar of honey is cheap at any price.

For Hubbell, however, those burdens are easily outweighed by two intangible rewards—harmony with the natural world and control over her own life.

Hubbell's sense of being at one with her environment is illustrated in her lyrical description of the swarm of bees encircling her.

> They came flying in, swirling as they descended, spiraling around me and the post oak until I was enveloped by the swarm, the air moving gently from the beat of their wings. I am not sure how long I stood there. I lost all sense of time and felt only elation, a kind of human emotional counterpart of the springlike, optimistic, burgeoning, state that the bees were in. . . . My skin was tingling as the bees brushed past and I felt almost a part of the swarm (paragraph 8).

It is the same sense of connectedness that causes Hubbell to feel "odd, tense and anticipatory" on those springtime days when the "air feels electric" and a colony of bees decides to split in two and swarm. She doesn't attempt a scientific explanation of her response: "I notice that beekeepers don't talk about it much, probably because it is the sort of thing we don't feel comfortable about trying to put into words, something the other side of rationality" (paragraph 2).

Hubbell's relationship with her environment is more than a fortuitous emotional bonding. She consciously avoids disrupting the harmony she discovers. She decides not to kill the queen of the swarm she hives (when replacing her with a vigorous new queen would be the commercially sensible act), she takes only the surplus honey the bees do not need for winter, and she cuts only dead trees for firewood, "leaving the ones still alive to flourish." At one point she explains the satisfaction: "[T]here is also something heady about becoming a part of the forest process" (paragraph 26).

The second advantage, Hubbell's command of her life, is illustrated by her self-reliance and by her freedom from the buying-is-living credo. Hubbell takes pride in her ability to make a living from her land, to provide her own firewood for winter, to keep her chain saw in good condition, and to winch the widow maker to the ground. In addition to all those accomplishments, Hubbell has somehow learned to control her possessions rather than allow them to control her. When she visits the city and sees the look of strain on the faces of the women she meets, she remembers that she once "lived on the edge of lives like" these and happily escapes back to the Ozarks, thankful not to be one of the "women out buying things to drape on themselves, and things to put in their houses, and things to take care of the things hanging on themselves and the things in their houses" (paragraph 55).

One of my favorite images is that of Hubbell sitting beside Ky and "taking a few companionable stings" on her knuckles to prevent arthritic pains (paragraph 38). How perfect for a woman who chooses which pains she will or will not endure.

3. Would the other writers in this unit approve or disapprove of Hubbell's lifestyle?

For "other writers in this unit" you can substitute Bloom, Huxley, or any other writer you have assigned. Whoever you choose, this question will encourage your students to see the unit as a conversation among writers concerned with many of the same issues. In "On a Greek Holiday," for example, Alice Bloom regrets that those of us who live in technologically advanced cultures seldom experience the satisfaction that comes from providing our own food and shelter. Bloom should admire Hubbell's ability to cut her own firewood and her practical (not theoretical) understanding of the consequences should she fail to do so.

4. How successful is Hubbell in describing processes such as felling a tree, taking honey from a hive, or desensitizing someone to bee stings?

You might begin by asking your students to list the steps in any one of the processes Hubbell describes and decide whether they could follow her instructions well enough to perform that task themselves. After reading Hubbell, I think I could probably desensitize someone (other than me) to bee stings, but I don't really understand how to use a come-along, probably because Hubbell's account of her tree-felling experience is a lesson in patience, not an instruction manual.

Your students should notice that, like Thoreau, Kenyatta, and Smith, Hubbell is a good technical writer who writes clear descriptions of physical processes. What is more, her accounts of these processes are not merely accurate: they are captivating. Before reading Hubbell, I would not have guessed that I had a latent interest in honeybees. Now I find myself wanting to check out entomology books. Fortunately for us, Hubbell's writing, like that of a flower handbook she commends, is not based on the assumption that it "is necessary to be dull to be taken seriously."

If your students aren't impressed with Hubbell's technical skills, you might ask them to imagine the papers they would have written if you had assigned the topic "How to Fell a Tree."

—M.R.D.—

ALICE BLOOM

On a Greek Holiday

Alice Bloom compares two women, one a representative of the haves of the world and the other a representative of the have-nots, and concludes that actually the have-nots have more. Bloom tells us that a Greek peasant woman has three important experiences that inhabitants of "developed" nations lack: (1) She participates in a public life, a daily gathering on the streets that "lends to every day and night the feel of mild, but lively festival." (2) She lives in a culture where, because there are no shelters for the unfit, the streets are shared by all sorts of people including the old, the feeble of mind and body, and the outcast. Consequently, she sees the fullness and variety of life in a village. (3) Because she lives in a world that is less technologically mystifying, she can observe, and understand, and control many of the details of life, such as food and shelter, which people in more technologically complex nations cannot comprehend.

Bloom concludes that such experiences result in a kind of contentment seldom felt by the more privileged classes. You may want to pair this essay with Harry Crews's "Pages from the Life of a Georgia Innocent," which presents a sharply contrasting view of the simple life of the poor. The two essays will definitely stimulate class discussion.

Whether your students agree or disagree with Bloom's thesis, they should enjoy her writing. The images and rhythms of her sentences delight both the eye and the ear. In the following passage from paragraph 4 she describes a tourist she sees on the beach:

> She can undoubtedly read and write, most blond people can, and has, wherever she comes from, a vote, a voice, a degree of some kind, a job, a career perhaps, money certainly, opinions, friends, health, talents, habits, central heating, living relatives, personalized checks, a return ticket, a summer wardrobe, the usual bits and clamor we all, tourists, have. But presence, she has not.

QUESTIONS

1. To what extent does Bloom's argument depend on tone and style rather than supporting detail?

Bloom's argument is that "in literal, daily fact, the Greek woman has more than the tourist, and the tourist, wherever she comes from and despite her list of equipment and privileges, is also, in literal daily fact, deprived" (paragraph 6). In some respects Bloom is making an argument much like that of Boorstin in "Technology and Democracy." Boorstin, however, supports his claim with numerous examples—explaining, for instance, how central heating and air conditioning have diminished the differences between the seasons. In contrast, Bloom relies less on logic than on language. Look at her characterization of the Greek woman in paragraph 3:

> She looks, at once, as if she could do everything she's ever done, anything needed, and also at once, she gives off an emanation of humor, powers, secrets, determinations, acts. She is moving straight ahead, like a moving church, a black peaked roof, a hot black hat, a dark tent, like a doom, a government, a force for good and evil, an ultimatum, a determined animal.

That passage is hardly a reasoned argument that the Greek woman has presence, but the metaphors establish her as a woman whose presence is undeniable.

Bloom's style is lush, luxuriant. The rhythms and images of her sentences have a power that is distinct from the force of a logical argument. Her most effective sentences combine a generalization illustrated by a string of details: the Greek woman "is beautiful, she could crush you, love you, mend you, deliver you of child or calf or lamb or illusion, bleed a pig, spear a fish, wring a supper's neck, till a field, coax an egg into life" (paragraph 3).

At times Bloom may seem wordy. With her parentheticals and qualifiers she moves one step forward and then takes one step to the side. The second sentence in paragraph 6 is particularly tortuous.

> With *so* little fact *at hand* about either *of these lives, fact that might* make things plain and profound *as only fact can do,* there

> is little but romance, theories, guesswork, and yet, *it seems*, this accidental conjunction of women in the sun, *considered*, says it is not a matter of *the one*, the blonde, being discontent in spite of much and *the other*, the farm woman *in black*, being smugly, *perhaps ignorantly* content with little. (76 words)

Assuming that we are interested primarily in efficiency in prose, we can reduce the number of words in that sentence by roughly one-third by eliminating or rewording the italicized segments. You might ask your students to rewrite this or another sentence to try it. The result will be something like this: "With little fact about either life to make things plain and profound, there is little but romance, theories, guesswork, and yet this accidental conjunction of women in the sun says it is not a matter of the blonde being discontent in spite of much and the farm woman being smugly content with little." (53 words) But, of course, efficiency is not the only goal of prose. The shorter version of the sentence changes both the tone and the effect. Without the qualifiers, the "it seems" and the "perhaps," Bloom's statement becomes a confident assertion of fact rather than a hesitant groping for understanding.

Eliminating other words in the sentence destroys the rhythm, the carefully orchestrated patterns of sound that appeal to our ears as well as to our minds. By writing "the other, the farm woman in black" Bloom creates a powerful visual image that is emphasized by the pause after "other." Both the rhythmic emphasis and the color image are lost in the revised phrase "the farm woman." If you ask your students to read the two, Bloom's sentence and my revision, most will prefer the sound of the original. Those who don't should be advised to avoid Thomas Wolfe.

2. Is Bloom's essay effective in persuading the reader that the Greek woman is better off than the tourist?

I imagine the answers will vary according to our perceptions of "the good life," but Bloom certainly doesn't tempt me to wish that I could trade places with the Greek woman. Regardless of how beautifully written the essay is, the logic is flawed. In paragraph 11, for example, Bloom sets up the following equation: poverty = producing one's own food = the ability to see and comprehend more details = more acute and more satisfied intelligence. Conversely, wealth = ability to buy the end product = lack of knowledge of processes = unhappy peevishness and dissatisfaction. Really now.

Of course I admire a person who is strong and self-reliant, and I wish that I could be as capable as the Greek woman is. But I also feel sorry for her because she has undoubtedly had a physically grueling life, and if she can't read or write, she has been denied the opportunity to experience much that is beautiful and exciting and intellectually challenging. Gutting a fish may be educational the first time it's done, but I don't believe the next five hundred repetitions of the process produce "a more satisfied intelligence." If the Greek woman had a choice, I think she would prefer to travel to

America, watch Americans going about their daily lives, and then write an article about her observations for *Harper's.*

3. Evaluate Bloom's statement that "the less money you have to spend . . . the more your chances of getting a whiff, now and then, of what another place is like" (paragraph 16).

Your students should enjoy writing about experiences that support or rebut this assertion. Thoreau would certainly agree with Bloom. In "The Fitness in a Man's Building His Own House" he advocates walking "for seeing the country and getting experience of that kind." Most of us would concede that Bloom is correct in stating that "the less money you spend the closer you come to partaking of very annoying, confusing, exhausting, foreign, debilitating, sometimes outrageous discomfort" (paragraph 16). But I imagine that there are a great many travelers who don't have the slightest desire to learn what a country is really like and who are quite happy at the Hilton.

—M.R.D.—

Style Lesson 45:
Use of Catalogues in a Description

Bloom's style in "On a Greek Holiday" relies heavily on sentences that catalogue details and examples. Practice this style by imitating the sentence below (from paragraph 3), describing a person you have seen. Hint: Mix literal and metaphorical description as Bloom does.

The Greek woman is short and heavy, waistless,
    and is wearing a black dress,
    a black scarf pulled low around her eyes,
    a black sweater,
    thick black stockings,
    black shoes.
She is stupendously there,
    black but for the walnut of her face,
    in the white sun, against the white space.
She looks, at once, as if she could do
    everything she's ever done, anything needed,
    and also at once, she gives off an emanation of
        humor, powers, secrets, determinations, acts.
She is moving straight ahead,
    like a moving church,
        a black peaked roof,
        a hot black hat,
        a dark tent,
    like a doom,
        a government,
        a force for good and evil,
        an ultimatum,
        a determined animal.
She probably can't read, or write;
she may never in her life have left this island;
but she is beautiful,
she could crush you,
    love you,
    mend you,
    deliver you of child or calf or lamb or illusion,
    bleed a pig,
    spear a fish,
    wring a supper's neck,
    till a field,
    coax an egg into life.

WENDELL BERRY

Against PCs

One of the reasons that I've included this essay followed by letters to the editor in this edition of *The Dolphin Reader* is that the letter to the editor is a useful form for students to practice. It requires close reading of the article, the formulation of a personal response, and a pithy style. It also allows you, if you like, to hold students to a high standard of correctness for a reason that will make real-world sense to them: editors inundated with letters are not going to trouble to make corrections or rewrite awkward sentences. Bad work goes into the wastebasket. The letters following the Berry essay give students some sense of the variety of publishable responses there can be to an essay or article. The responses to the Berry article happen to be negative, some attacking the author's logic, some extending his line of argument and making it a springboard for humor, so students may need to be reminded that many letters to the editor support the author, often by contributing anecdotes from personal experience.

My best luck in assigning letters to the editor has come when I have discussed a sample set of letters responding to one essay and then had students write letters responding to another.

But there is more to be got from the Berry essays and letters than a model for a type of assignment. If students look closely at the whole set, I think they'll find that Berry's rejoinder is clearer and more persuasive than his original essay. Having discovered a group of intelligent readers who did not share his assumptions, Berry went back to first principles, so to speak. The rejoinder gets to the heart of the issue when it talks about the ethics of consumption and the distrust of centralized (and therefore diffused or delayed) action. It is also, it seems to me, much more crisply written. His opponents have stung Berry into focus.

QUESTIONS

1. Nathaniel Borenstein suggests that the quill pen would fit Berry's criteria for technological improvement. Discuss a more recent invention that would also fit, or else discuss your inability to think of one.

If students give much thought to Berry's list, they'll soon discover that, if universally adopted, it would bring technological innovations almost to a halt. In capitalist societies, at least, not much money is spent developing products less expensive than the ones they will replace, and advanced technology, almost by definition, involves circuitry that cannot be produced or repaired near home—certainly not near Berry's home. Even the manual typewriter that Berry admires could not have passed his test at the point it was introduced, since it could hardly have been smaller and cheaper than pen and ink. And because it allowed the use of carbon paper, it disrupted the system of hand copying and eliminated a class of semiskilled workers. Virtually every invention, when new, is disruptive. As a society we are inclined to think that over the long haul the gains outweigh the losses, but we may be wrong.

In fact, as inventions go, the PC does fairly well by Berry's standards. Hardly anything is getting smaller and cheaper faster than the PC. I am sitting in an airport typing this comment on a laptop PC that costs considerably less than the barely luggable desktop computer I bought seven years ago and is about one-tenth the size. It uses, I am sure, less energy, since it is designed to run on a battery, and the battery is rechargeable—in principle, at least—via the solar collectors they now advertise for recharging car and boat batteries. It was purchased within walking distance of my home and, unless something exotic goes awry, it will be repairable at the same place. As for disrupting family and community relationships, it has made it easier for me to leave my hometown and bring my work with me on some prolonged visits with my parents.

Does the laptop make my work better? I doubt it. Berry is probably right about the advantages of turning work over to a sympathetic and alert typist. On the other hand, just as Berry says he can't afford the computer (a questionable statement, given what a few hundred dollars will now buy), I'll say I can't afford a typist.

2. Imagine that you are an editor for *Harper's.* Which of the letters to the editor would you find most publishable and why?

Class discussion of this question would be a good way to set up a subsequent letter-to-the-editor writing assignment. Particularly attractive, I think, are the Inkeles letter and the Borenstein letter. Inkeles's is a gem of irony, perhaps inspired by the often-anthologized Judy Syfer's essay "Why I Want a Wife." Whatever his inspiration, Inkeles follows through well. The capitalization of *Wife* is a nice touch, as is the definition "a low-tech energy-saving device." In fact, Inkeles's irony is carried by his diction: notice "*enslaved* by the computer," "she's *cheap, repairable* near home," "two more *nasty* machines." Inkeles does a good job of turning Berry's words and his rather humorless tone against him.

Borenstein's letter begins with a burst of sarcasm, but does most of its work by challenging the logic of Berry's position. Can one product really be "better" than another for every potential user? Should Berry dismiss so absolutely a tool that Borenstein and others use in the struggle to preserve the environment? Berry's rejoinder concentrates on Borenstein's letter because Borenstein has raised the hard issues.

3. How successful is Berry's rejoinder in answering the criticisms raised by the letter?

The rejoinder is impressive. On my own first reading of this computer controversy, my sympathies shifted at every turn. Despite rather liking PCs, I read Berry's initial essay with much head-nodding and only a little resistance. The letters won me over almost entirely, and Berry's reply shifted my allegiance again.

On the wife (or Wife) issue, what makes Berry's rejoinder work is that he reveals the irony of Inkeles's and Koosman's positions: "These gentlemen obviously think themselves feminists of the most correct and principled sort, and yet they do not hesitate to stereotype and insult, on the basis of one fact, a woman they do not know." There is real anger here: "They are audacious and irresponsible gossips." Now, I still like Inkeles's letter, and I wish that Berry could have enjoyed the humor of it. I continue to be uncomfortable with the implications of the traditional arrangement in which the wife types the husband's manuscript. But Berry has certainly backed *me* off. I'm not going to claim that his wife is "characterless" or "subservient."

On the more general issue of how we deal with the environmental damage created by advances in technology, Berry scores three points. First, he insinuates that his detractors are dupes parroting the line promulgated by industrialists. This may be *ad hominem*, but no one who has read Orwell can dismiss it out of hand. Second, Berry points out that Johnson commits the fallacy of extension, arguing against a purist position that he never took. Third, and perhaps most important, Berry points out that even the conservation groups have failed to place much emphasis on the ethics of consumption (over which individuals have much control) rather than the ethics of production (over which they have little). In the final paragraphs, he effectively characterizes his essay as a small contribution to the ethics of consumption.

Berry also turns some very telling phrases, which your students should savor. My favorite is ". . . that does not mean that his conscience is clear; it means that his conscience is not working." Here Berry stings back, not with humor, but with a darker irony.

—D.H.—

Style Lesson 46: Diction that Underscores Sarcasm

Gordon Inkeles's response to "Against PCs" is a piece of withering sarcasm, the tone of which shows in his choice of words that parody Berry's attitudes and particularly mock his comparison of his wife to a computer. Try to recall the words he used in lieu of those we have capitalized below.

Wendell Berry provides writers ATTRACTED TO the computer with a handy alternative: Wife—a SIMPLE, ECONOMICAL AIDE. DELIVER a pile of handwritten notes TO Wife and you get back a finished manuscript, edited while it was typed. What computer can do that? Wife meets all of Berry's CRITERIA* for technological innovation: she's INEXPENSIVE, CURABLE near home, and good for the family structure. Best of all, Wife is PROGRESSIVE* because she breaks a writer's "direct dependence on strip-mined coal."

**Inkeles uses two words where we have substituted the single words* criteria *and* progressive.

E. M. FORSTER

The Machine Stops

This story is, I believe, Forster's only venture into science fiction. Like other good writers in that genre, he uses the freedom to alter the external circumstances of humanity as a technique to reveal something about the human soul and the perils that surround it. The particular peril here is that technology ("the Machine"), by removing us from direct bodily experience of the world, may destroy our spirit. Or, as Forster warns at the story's end, humanity may die strangled in the increasingly sophisticated "garments" it weaves for its comfort and convenience. A science fiction story written in 1909, when many of our advanced technologies were in their infancy, is certain to strike us as quaint in some respects, but here quaintness is a virtue. It allows us to evaluate how someone standing near the beginning of our century reacted to the emergence of air travel and electronic communication.

Unlike most of the selections in *The Dolphin Reader*, "The Machine Stops" is quite long. You'll not want to assign it lightly, since students may feel some resentment if they spend 60–80 minutes reading a story that is never discussed. I think that because the story can be approached from so many angles—scientific, literary, social—it could be an excellent topic for an essay.

QUESTIONS

1. How does Forster's presentation of the technology of the future reflect the state of technology in 1909?

This question has good potential as an essay topic, in which case you might want to instruct your students to do some research on how new the technologies were when Forster wrote and what the course of the development actually was. A particularly good resource is *The McGraw-Hill Dictionary of Science and Technology*, but any good encyclopedia will do. Here I will only present what a few minutes of research produces. Much more could be learned and written in a few hours.

Students will find that long-distance telecommunications were in their infancy in 1909: It wasn't possible to make a coast-to-coast phone call in the United States until 1915, and although telegraphic messages were being sent ship-to-shore by radio in 1909, the first significant voice transmission by radio didn't come till 1915. The first demonstration of a working television didn't come until 1926, although Russian scientist Boris Rosing had managed to transmit some crude pictures about 1907. The Wright brothers' flight came in 1903; the great accomplishment for heavier-than-air aircraft in 1909 was the first flight across the English Channel. More promising in terms of passenger service were the flights of the dirigibles being developed in Germany by Ferdinand, Graf von Zeppelin.

Students who pay attention to the technology of Forster's story will see that he imagines a world where telecommunications depend on the whole world being interconnected by wires (paragraph 218)—an awkward scenario, but plausible enough in a world where no voices traveled through the air. The inability of the Machine to "transmit *nuances* of expression" (paragraph 42) probably reflects the technical difficulties faced by the early experimenters with television, for whom "resolution" was a major concern. The huge airships that "rise" from the vomitories, "sail" through the skies, and "draw up at the wharves" (paragraph 88) seem to behave like dirigibles, though the one that crashes into the city in the last paragraph has "wings of steel." These curious hybrid machines travel slowly (we learn in paragraph 27 that it takes two days to travel from Vashti's home (Sumatra) to Kuno's (England). Forster imagines faster "racing aeroplanes" that attempt (and fail) to "keep pace with the sun" (paragraph 94). Thinking about these things will help students realize the enormous technological changes people of Forster's generation lived through and that we inherited as *faits accomplis*.

2. How accurate is Forster's story as a piece of prophecy?

Forster's failings as a prophet of the details of technological progress are dealt with in question 1. It may be worth pointing out that in other respects, he foresaw pretty well: Vashti's room is equipped with an answering machine, a vision phone (or whatever we now call these), and other devices. After you have discussed the merely technical angle with your students, they should be ready to move on to what surely interests Forster more: the effect of technological progress on society and the individual. Here his accuracy or inaccuracy can be disputed. I would try to nudge students into a discussion of these predictions, at least:

- That progress in technology will result first in more travel (e.g., the construction of the system for automobile and air travel), but finally in less. In the long run, people will want experience brought to them rather than vice-versa and places will become increasingly alike.
- That people will have (and will desire) less and less "direct experience" with the world or with other people, substituting instead "ideas" experienced through "the Machine."
- That technology will be viewed with increasing reverence as individuals understand less and less about how the devices around them work.
- That we will lose the sense of human proportions that have traditionally given meaning to space, ownership, strength, and even love. (See paragraph 148, where Kuno discovers that "Man is the Measure.")

These predictions correspond to concerns expressed throughout this unit of *The Dolphin Reader*. The first, for example, is very directly addressed in Alice Bloom's "On a Greek Holiday," the second in Daniel Boorstin's "Technology and Democracy." A productive essay assignment might be to have students evaluate the validity of Forster's fears about a highly technological society by referring both to their own experience and to the comments of other writers in this unit.

3. Throughout his story, Forster suggests that the quality of life in the high-tech future will be lower than the quality of life in the low-tech past. Is it likely that he is right about this?

This question brings us back, somewhat more pointedly, to issues that students will likely discuss in answering Question 2.

In paragraph 252, after "the Machine" goes slightly awry, Forster notes that among other things the artificial fruit has become mouldy and the "poetry machine" is spitting out "defective rhymes." There is, of course, a double message here, since we can safely assume that the artificial fruit was never really as good as natural fruit and the poetry produced by the machine never had the interest of human poetry. The people in Forster's future have accustomed themselves to trade convenience for quality. Thus in paragraph 42, Vashti, looking into the round plate of her vision phone, fancies that Kuno looks sad:

> She could not be sure, for the Machine did not transmit *nuances* of expression. It only gave a general idea of people—an idea that was good enough for all practical purposes, Vashti thought. The imponderable bloom, declared by a discredited philosophy to be the actual essence of intercourse, was rightly ignored by the Machine, just as the imponderable bloom of the grape was ignored by the manufacturers of artificial fruit. Something 'good enough' had long since been accepted by our race.

Your students will, of course, note that in the particular case of transmission of visual images, Forster has been a poor prophet. Even our present television is pretty good at transmitting nuances of expression, and the coming high-resolution televisions will presumably be better.

Nonetheless, the general notion is worth contemplating. Mass production and mass marketing of goods does often produce a change in quality. Our battery-grown chickens don't taste the same as the free-ranging chickens of the past. Tomatoes bred and grown for their ability to withstand transportation aren't as flavorful as those grown in the backyard garden. To the palette accustomed to spaghetti sauce made from fresh tomatoes, canned sauce is a letdown. To the theater-goer, a play watched on the small two-dimensional screen of a television is a diminished experience. To some degree we, like the Vashti, often follow our own convenience and the convenience of the economic "Machine" and settle for what is "good enough."

In "The Machine Stops," people live in small underground cells and fear the sun and the harsh outdoor air. They live, in short, like termites, and because they get no exercise they have developed soft, white bodies that might remind us of termites. To call this a dog's life would be to glorify it.

But, of course, this life can be seen as a mere inversion and exaggeration of the life of some city dwellers who rarely leave their television- and telephone-equipped apartments except to drive or ride to an office or a store. In Forster's story, the termite colonies are built above ground, but this doesn't always improve the view. Jerry Mander argues in "Advertising: The Standard-Gauge Railroad" that modern urban life is an experience in sensory deprivation, an experience of living in air-conditioned cubicles and buying a few stimulators (like television) to provide a fraction of the sensory experience that surrounded our less advanced great-grandparents. We do find people enriching this cubicle life by participating in sports or visiting galleries, or even by camping out, but these activities all seem instances of what Vashti would call "atavism," distinctly "unmechanical."

—D.H.—

MEDIA

OVERVIEW OF UNIT

The *Media* unit is concerned not just with the forms of mass communication, but with the phenomenon of *mediation*, which puts us consumers in the position of taking more and more of our experience at second hand. Celebrity autobiographies often carry an "as told to" by-line to acknowledge that we aren't reading the words of the celebrities themselves. These days, much of reality comes to us in a similarly pre-digested form: politics as told to the anchors of the network news programs, the realities of American life in the 1990s as told to the producers of *Murphy Brown*, foreign cultures as told to the producers of *National Geographic Explorer* or *Young Indiana Jones*, nature as told to the producers of *Nature*. Since no one is attaching warning labels to televisions and other media ports, warning that too high a proportion of mediated experience may damage the viewer's sense of reality, instilling some sense of the dangers seems to be one of the missions of higher education.

The unit can be parsed into four parts:

- The essays by Randall Jarrell and Jerry Mander address the mediation question in its broadest form.
- Neil Postman and Kiku Adatto concentrate on the phenomenological problem of television news—how the presentation creates the reality it reports.
- Beth Austin, Katha Pollitt, and Donald Hall talk about the ethical impact of the media on youngsters, with Austin and Hall concentrating on movies and Pollitt on sexual stereotyping in cartoons, movies, and books.
- Gloria Steinem's essay shows how economic pressures alter the truth a publisher *can* present, and though she writes about the particular case of *Ms.* magazine, students should see that the same problems afflict producers, writers, and directors in all the mass media. Garrison Keillor's story about the rise and fall of a radio talk show deals in a humorous way with the problem of marketability.

Though the Jarrell and Mander essays may be too abstract and even ideological for the tastes of some of the students, we recommend that you assign at least one of them to give a sense of how much is at stake in the mediation of experience. If you haven't time to assign the whole unit, you might then concentrate on one of the other groups.

As a subject to write about, "the Medium" as Jarrell calls it, is inexhaustible. Every student has access to familiar television programs, movies, and books. The key to getting good essays is to establish a framework within which students can write something intellectually coherent—something the readings should help you do.

RANDALL JARRELL

A Sad Heart at the Supermarket

If you used the first edition of *The Dolphin Reader*, you may remember this essay in its longer form. In this edition, we retain the essay's first half, Jarrell's energetic diatribe against the consumer society and the popular media that support it. The omitted second half is the poet's lament about the fate of the artist in such a society. Many students seem better able to give the first part of the essay a fair reading, since it is not subject to the accusation (as the second part is) of special pleading or poor-misunderstood-me-ism. Contempt rather than complaint is the dominant emotion in this excerpt.

For some students, the essay will be an eye-opener because they will not have heard the unpopular antimaterialist position put so strongly. As Jarrell says (paragraph 9), it seems "deeply un-American" to oppose the consumer society, and some of your students will quite seriously feel that the essay is seditious, part of a conspiracy against values that have become entangled with their patriotism. It may not mollify them to point out Jarrell's allusion to an alternative American tradition associated with Emerson and Thoreau (paragraph 15), but it will give them something to think about.

Students who are more receptive to Jarrell's viewpoint or at least want to consider it further would do well to read Jerry Mander's "Advertising: The Standard Guage Railway" and Gloria Steinem's "Sex, Lies, and Advertising." As talented insiders in the world of the Medium, both Mander and Steinem confirm much that Jarrell the outsider has to say.

QUESTIONS

1. Describe the tone of the essay and show how this tone is achieved.

Jarrell's tone is not conciliatory. He doesn't search for common ground with the people of the Medium. He doesn't show a trace of sympathy for the family that owns a backup generator. This is an essay that takes no hostages. Its tone might sometimes be described as supercilious or arrogant (see the Weimaraner comment at the end of paragraph 6), but overall I'm inclined to think that combative is a better characterization. When Jarrell presents his Charge-A-Plate travesty of Michelangelo's painting of the creation (paragraph 5), he raises the emotional temperature of the essay considerably. Even for the secular reader, this smacks a bit of sacrilege: It is at least as shocking as the grafitti moustache that inevitably appears on reproductions of the Mona Lisa. Jarrell's intent, of course, is to make us see that some comparable sacrilege is being perpetrated every day by the people who control the Medium. He is deliberately inflammatory; he doesn't ask for quarter or offer it.

Consider paragraph 9, which contains something to offend almost everyone. I would assume that because he was writing in 1962, before our era of relative androgyny and widespread feminism, he intended to offend male readers with this paragraph by calling them effeminate in their compulsion to buy things. These days the paragraph may be more likely to offend women, who will bridle at the broadness of the caricature of the average woman Jarrell presents as an average American.

Or consider Jarrell's statement at the end of paragraph 7: "We may still go to Methodist or Baptist or Presbyterian churches on Sunday, but the Protestant ethic of frugal industry, of production for its own sake, is gone." If Jarrell assumes (as he must) that many of his readers are either Protestants or identify with the traditional values associated with the Protestant ethic, he is deliberately telling them that they aren't what they pretend to be.

The tone of the essay would offend so many people that you may want to have your class speculate on why Jarrell adopts it. One possibility, of course, is that he is at the end of his rope, too exasperated to be diplomatic. Another is that he imagines himself to be preaching to the converted, as he very well might have been: His reputation in the scholarly community of *Daedalus* readers was so large and his views so well known that many would be prejudiced in his favor. A third and to me more intriguing possibility is that Jarrell recognized that his message, quite independent of tone, would be a bitter pill for most Americans to swallow. Knowing that only those with a taste for bitterness could down it, he didn't attempt any sugar coating.

2. In paragraph 8, Jarrell says that both the advertisements and the articles in popular magazines urge the reader to be a consumer. Test this assumption by examining a current issue of a popular magazine.

Which magazine your students choose will obviously affect their findings. Though Jarrell has his hackles up too much to admit it, there is a difference between the *New Yorker* and *House Beautiful* in this respect. When I wrote this commentary in 1988, I took for my test case the December 1988 issue of the *Saturday Evening Post*, which had Barbara Bush on the cover, 111 numbered pages of text, and 40 pages covered completely with advertisements. The magazine also included two pages of disguised ads called the "Post Sampler." Perhaps one "text" page in four was partly filled by advertising. A fair estimate, then, would say that about one-third of the magazine was given over to direct advertisement. What troubles Jarrell more is indirect advertisement, of which the *Post* contained a good deal. The magazine included two short stories: one about a school teacher who has a heartwarming encounter with a boy caught stealing money to get his mother a bus ticket for a Christmas visit, one about a tame polar bear who escapes from the arctic to Miami Beach to live the good life (no kidding!). Nothing here seems to be urging consumption.

Of the nine feature articles, however, one was made up of recommendations for Christmas gifts, and one was an Andy Rooney piece on Christmas shopping. A third consisted of recipes for fancy breads, and a fourth of celebrity reminiscences about Christmas. Here is some evidence for Jarrell's thesis: these are articles that encourage the reader to want more money, more celebrity, or perhaps more exposure to celebrities. Arguably, they inspire the sort of discontent he refers to in paragraph 8.

The nine "departments" (regular features) in the magazine included "Post People" (gossip about the rich and famous), "Vets on Pets" (a sort of consumer training; it encourages the reader to buy the right toys for kittens), "Travel" (this month encouraging a Christmas trip to the New Orleans area), "Medical Mailbox" (this month featuring news of an innovative liver-transplant procedure and information on vitamin supplements), and "Food" (this month concentrating on holiday entrées).

About half of the articles and departments, then, were of the sort that so alarms Jarrell—"buying something, going somewhere seems a necessary completion." The stories, as I said before, seem less consumer-oriented, but it is worth considering that both schoolboy and polar bear attempt to solve an emotional crisis by travel. Certainly a good deal of what a person in fact learns from this magazine is how to be a consumer, more or less knowledgeable, but your students might not feel that this predominant orientation is in itself a bad thing. The question is whether the readers are being programmed. Jarrell clearly believes that they are (paragraph 5).

3. Jarrell asks us to consider whether buying or fantasy-buying is an important part of our emotional lives. Is it an important part of yours? What is the connection between your emotionally charged buying and what Jarrell calls the Medium?

This question is an invitation to personal experience essays in which students contemplate their susceptibility to media influences. I am myself indifferent to such consumer items as clothes (notoriously indifferent, according to my family), cars, and foods. I am, however, somewhat susceptible to electronic gadgetry, and am a sucker for certain types of advertisements. Laptop computers, I'm embarrassed to say, have had a strong emotional appeal to me, and if I were undertaking an essay in response to this question, I would want to look back at the very clever advertisements that associate the laptop with freedom and travel. No more being chained to the desk. No more wasted time on flights (though I rarely fly). I would talk about the longing these ads and occasional reviews in the computer magazines created in me, and my sometimes furtive trips to magazine racks and computer stores to moon over more and more sophisticated machines that were lighter and lighter, slimmer and slimmer. I think I understood the impulse behind anorexia more clearly then than at any other point in my existence. Eventually, I bought. It is a good machine; I am content; it is better to marry than to burn. But now I read that there are one-pound "portfolio" laptops on the market with all the capacity of my 10-pound behemoth. I'm not going to give in, but I *will* torment myself with a few trips to the magazine racks.

—D.H.—

Style Lesson 47: A Two-Sentence Definition of a Way of Life

Throughout "A Sad Heart at the Supermarket," Jarrell gives thumbnail descriptions of a way of life that dismays him. The two sentences below (from paragraph 7) form one such sketch, featuring parallel predicate verbs in the first sentence and infinitives as subjects in the second. To practice Jarrell's style while thinking about the issues he raises, imitate his sentences while writing about a way of life very difference from the consumer's.

Everything about the knowledgeable consumer[1]
    looks like
    or sounds like
    or feels like
        money
            and informed money at that.
To live is
    to consume,
to understand life is
    to know what to consume:
he has learned to understand this,
    so that his life is a series of choices
        —correct ones—
            among the products and services of the world.

[1]*Note that we have omitted part of sentence 1.*

JERRY MANDER

Advertising: The Standard-Gauge Railroad

This chapter from Jerry Mander's controversial first book is certain to create some discomfort among students, since it tells them that they are not in control of their lives, not even in control of their desires. Mander, a reformed advertising man, believes that the "commodity system" and its handmaiden advertising are fairly firmly (and culpably) in control. This sounds like a conspiracy theory, and Mander is aware that he sometimes sounds like a crank. But your students need to recognize that he is not talking about the machinations of a supposed ring of conspirators. He is talking about a century-spanning change from reliance on the self and the small community to reliance on the market system. This transformation is the "conspirator" that has created an economic system that, as Randall Jarrell puts it, needs us to need. It is true, Mander points out, that a relatively small group of rich producers benefits most from the economic system and wants to keep it healthy by keeping the rest of us consuming; but these people are better seen as the heirs of a conspiracy than as the conspirators themselves.

Mander's edgy argumentative essay can be linked with essays from *Progress and Its Price* and *Nature and Civilization*. It echoes points made by Henry David Thoreau, Daniel Boorstin, Carol Bly, Jomo Kenyatta, and Alice Bloom about ways that technology may impoverish our lives in some areas, even if it enriches them in others. Mander's picture of modern "commodity people" in paragraphs 27–42 corresponds remarkably to E. M. Forster's portrayal of the people of the future in "The Machine Stops." His concern about the way contemporary life suppresses or distorts instincts evolved over millions of years is shared by Edward Hoagland and Melissa Greene. Inside the *Media* unit, Mander's essay is particularly allied with essays by Randall Jarrell and Barbara Ehrenreich, both of whom are alarmed by the substitution of media experiences for what was once called life.

QUESTIONS

1. How, according to Mander, is the situation of the chimpanzees described in paragraphs 27–35 comparable to the situation of people living in a consumer society? Do you think that their situation is actually comparable?

Though the question points students to a particular example, the example is so central that it is essentially a comprehension question over the whole text. The chimps in question are, of course, those who were "isolated, one to a room" and allowed to communicate their desires (for food, for hugs from scientists, etc.) only by pushing a dozen buttons. Because they had access to no satisfactions other than those offered by the buttons, Mander says, they learned to concentrate all their desiring on those twelve available items. Though Mander cites no evidence that these particular chimps suffered greatly under this regimen (they were not restricted to it for a lifetime), he suspects, reasonably enough, that over an extended period they would suffer the same ill effects as other animals in captivity: stress, lethargy, early death, even suicide.

Mander concedes (paragraph 36) that the analogy to the human situation is "not precise," but insists that it isn't "farfetched" either. We, too, live in confinement most of our lives—Mander insists that most of our indoor spaces are monotonous and unstimulating compared to the outdoor world—and within our confinement we are allowed a limited range of experiences: television, movies, video games, eating frozen dinners, reading and writing, and so forth. Like the chimps, we channel desires created by millions of years of evolution into the narrow range of experiences made available to us (in this case by the market-and-media system): Our desire to run and chase, for example, is transformed into a dues-paying membership at the racquet club. Like the chimps, we may find the range of choices available to us cripplingly narrow and we may become neurotic or psychotic.

The analogy is fascinating, but is it accurate enough to be useful? Your students may point out weaknesses:

- We are brainier than the chimps, so that even when we are sitting still in a dull room, we may be living a full life in our minds.
- The chimps' confinement is involuntary, ours is voluntary. We can walk out of outdoors when we want.
- The chimps' range of choices is very narrow, ours is broad. We have many channels on that television, thousands of CD's at the music store, many movies at the mall.

These objections to the analogy certainly have merit, but they also have limitations. Yes, we are a brainy species, but several generations of brainy psychologists and psychiatrists have taught us that becoming brainy did not eliminate the demands of the body and that denying those demands is costly. Yes, we are freer than the chimps to escape from our cells, but this freedom depends on many factors, including economic and social status: the college professor may rise up from her desk for a stroll around campus; the typist will be less free. And if the typist works and lives in some parts of the city or the suburbs, there is a chance that her walk along the sidewalks will be as dull as her time at the office.

As for choice of experiences, Mander is probably right when he says that it is easy to overestimate the range of choices available in a consumer culture: "It ought to be self-evident that if I choose a Ford and you choose a Volvo, we are not expressing diversity, we are expressing unity" (paragraph 50). You might ask your students to think about how they make choices of what to do on a free evening. I think many will find that by habit, they choose from a limited range of activities the society is marketing: dinner out, a movie, a concert, television-watching. But we'll return to this in the next question.

2. In paragraph 38, Mander praises the traditional Eskimo who can distinguish fifty-six varieties of snowflakes. In paragraph 50, he criticizes the modern consumer who sees a real difference between a Ford and a Volvo. Is his logic faulty?

I think the short answer is yes, but we need to consider what seduces Mander into the contradiction. Partly it is the sort of sentimental response to nature that Brigid Brophy objects to in "The Menace of Nature": snowflakes are natural, automobiles are not; therefore, knowledge of one is somehow purer than knowledge of the other. When we remove the sentiment, we may see things differently. The informed consumer—or better yet, the trained mechanic—who can recognize and appreciate the tens of thousands of details that go into the design and building of a car surely shouldn't be dismissed as inferior to the Eskimo who knows his snowflakes.

Mander argues that because humans evolved in the natural world, they take a delight in dealing with natural forms that can never be replicated by dealing with the "grosser, more monolithic, human made commercial forms" (paragraph 37). This is not an argument to be dismissed lightly, but it may underrate the diversity of man-made forms and overrate our evolutionary attachment to particular natural forms: all those millennia of evolution in Africa can't have done much to prepare humans to love snow, and one suspects that the Eskimo is genetically as well prepared to distinguish among styles of architecture as among styles of snowflakes.

The preference of the natural for the man-made is only part of the issue, though. Mander wants to dismiss the choice between a Volvo and a Ford as trivial because it "confuses diversity of product choice with diversity of life-style or thoughts." This seems a valid point at first glance. But the members of a traditional society, however good they might be at distinguishing among snowflakes or classifying dreams or recognizing the strata occupied by insects, don't have much choice about "life-style." The inevitability of only *one* life-style (and the fixed roles within it) is part of what we mean by "traditional." Neither the Eskimo nor the consumer is choosing a life-style; both are acting within tradition; both are using their inbred capacity to observe and compare.

3. Is life in traditional cultures preferable to life in a "commodity" culture?

The sophisticated student will almost instinctively answer a question like this with a firm "it depends." And, of course, it does depend. If we are talking about the situation described in paragraph 18, where living in a traditional culture means having a beach house near a plentiful supply of fresh food and living in a commodity culture means moving to a cinder-block house, working in a factory, and eating from cans, then it's hard to deny the appeal of the traditional culture. This example stacks the deck both ways, however. There are traditional cultures where life involves not only anxiety, but well-founded fear—fear of starvation, disease, warfare. And within our commodity culture, many people enjoy lives full of variety and interest.

On balance, most of the peoples of the world, faced with an opportunity to become "commodity people" have wanted to do so. To insist as stridently as Mander sometimes does on the superiority of pre-industrial culture seems naive.

I don't think, though, that the real Mander message depends on the inherent superiority of all native cultures to all commercial ones. He isn't seriously advocating that we *become* Eskimo or Senoi. Native cultures are for him a way of pointing out alternatives to a life-style whose most tantalizing feature may be that it *theoretically* offers most of us a choice of life-styles. Our culture has succeeded well enough in solving the material problems of keeping people alive and healthy that we could—individually at least—opt out of "the cycle of work-consume, work-consume, work-consume." He suspects that we would opt out if only we could imagine a better life. Our media, however, are so entangled with the commodity culture that *they* can't show us another way. Traditional cultures, for all their limitations, may be the only schools in which the subject of a truly alternative life-style can be studied.

—D.H.—

Style Lesson 48: Exemplification

Throughout "Advertising: The Standard Gauge Railway," Mander matches generalizations with examples that make his points clear. We have omitted some of these clarifying examples from paragraph 25, inserting a blank for every word omitted. Try to re-insert examples—Mander's or your own. Don't worry about matching the number of words in an example precisely.

People who take more pleasure in talking with friends than in machines, commodities and spectacles are outrageous to the system. People joining with their neighbors to share _____ [Example 1] or _____ [Example 2] or _____ [Example 3] are less "productive" than those who live in isolation from each other, obtaining their very own of every object. Any collective act, from sharing washing machines to _____ [Example 4] to _____ _____ [Example 5], is less productive to the wider system in the end than everyone functioning separately in nuclear family units and private homes. Isolation maximizes production. Human beings who are satisfied with natural experience, from sexuality to breast feeding to cycles of mood, are not as productive as the not-so-satisfied, who seek _____ _____ [Example 6], _____ _____ _____ _____ [Example 7], _____ _____ _____ _____ _____ _____ _____ _____ [Example 8], and commodities to substitute for experience.

GLORIA STEINEM

Sex, Lies, and Advertising

In this eye-opening essay, Steinem explains how advertisers influence the content of magazines, especially women's magazines. From 1971 until 1987, Steinem was the editor of *Ms.*, the most significant feminist magazine in the United States. In that role she quickly learned what advertisers for "women's products" demand from women's magazines:

> what the ad world euphemistically describes as "supportive editorial atmosphere" or "complementary copy" (for instance, articles that praise food/fashion/beauty subjects to "support" and "complement" food/fashion/beauty ads) . . . (paragraph 5).

Because Steinem refused to surrender to those demands, very few makers of "women's products" placed ads in *Ms.* To compound the magazine's financial woes, makers of "people products" purchased by both men and women were reluctant to advertise in *Ms.* because it is a women's magazine. Consequently, in an effort to generate enough ad revenue to keep the magazine afloat, Steinem "spent more time persuading advertisers than editing or writing for *Ms.*" and "ended up with an unsentimental education in the seamy underside of publishing that few writers see (and even fewer magazines can publish)" (paragraph 17).

"Sex, Lies, and Advertising" can serve as variety of teaching purposes.

- The essay demonstrates the surprising effects of gender stereotypes, which long prevented the makers of autos and computers from advertising in women's magazines. To make that point, you might want to assign this piece along with selections from *Femininity and Masculinity* such as "X" by Lois Gould.
- The essay can sharpen your students' critical reading skills by teaching them to distinguish between editorial wheat and advertising chaff.
- The essay can serve as a starting point for research. You might have each student examine one magazine to determine what percentage is advertising and what percentage is editorial.
- The essay provides "real world" writing assignments. For example, Steinem suggests that readers who are concerned about advertising's power over the press write to editors and publishers stating that they are "willing to pay *more* for magazines with editorial independence" (paragraph 95).
- The essay is a great writing model that can be used to demonstrate how to structure and support a persuasive essay.

QUESTIONS

1. Examine one issue of any magazine that prints advertisements and decide what percentage is advertising rather than content. Come to class prepared to report your findings.

To be sure that your students review a variety of magazines, you might want to type a list of twenty-five possibilities and have your students sign their names beside their choices. You will want to include general interest magazines (such as *Newsweek*), traditional women's magazines (such as *Good Housekeeping*) and other special interest magazines that are a target for advertisers trying to sell a way of life (*Runner's World* and *Southern Living* and *P.C.* come to mind).

Your students should discover that women's magazines have the highest proportion of advertising and "complementary copy." They will also find that it can be surprisingly difficult to distinguish between ads and content. Is a product review of running shoes or computer software really an ad? Is the cover story an inducement to buy something? What is the danger of running ads that look like articles?

2. This essay can be divided into six distinct parts, some of which are indicated by Steinem's Roman numeral divisions. (Part 1 = paragraphs 1–8, Part 2 = paragraphs 9–17, Part 3 = paragraphs 18–67, Part 4 = paragraphs 68–72, Part 5 = paragraphs 73–93, Part 6 = paragraphs 94–103.) What is the purpose of each section and how effective is this organizational structure?

This essay is a classic example of problem-solution organization. In part 1 Steinem presents the problem: "advertising's media-wide influence on most of what we read" (paragraph 4). In part 2 she explains how *Ms.* initially planned to avoid that problem by running ads for "people products" and by taking ads for "women's products" only if those advertisers relinquished "the usual quid pro quo of 'complementary copy'" (paragraph 3). In part 3 she gives us example after example of companies that refused to advertise in *Ms.* because Steinem would not compromise the magazine's editorial integrity. In part 4 she explains how the financial problems caused by low ad revenues led first to the sale of *Ms.* and eventually to its existence as an ad-free, reader-supported magazine. In part 5 she explains how the tradition of controlling the content of women's magazines developed. In part 6 she suggests a solution to the problem of advertising's undue influence over women's magazines.

You might point out that this essay would be coherent even if we omitted parts 2, 3, 4, and 5. However, it would be far less persuasive. The power of this essay comes from the cumulative impact of the detailed examples Steinem uses to support her thesis. Sometimes, of course, an essay of this kind focuses on the solution rather than the problem. That's the usual approach when the problem is one that people already recognize. In this instance, however, Steinem realizes that most of her readers will know nothing about advertising's impact on the content of magazines. Unless she first convinces us that the problem exists, she cannot convince us that we should act to solve it.

3. What does Steinem hope to accomplish by telling us the details about why various companies refused to advertise in *Ms.*? Does she accomplish her goal?

I think Steinem knew that her audience (readers of *Ms.*) would believe exactly what Steinem once believed—that advertisers are reasonable people who act in their own economic self-interest. If that were true, we would have to conclude that there was some logical basis for their decisions not to place ads in *Ms.* Steinem has the difficult task of persuading us that logic had nothing to do with those decisions. But rather than tell us, she shows us. With each story she first gives us the sales pitch she presented to the advertiser. We are sold. Then, like Steinem, we are appalled when the advertiser ignores sound economic arguments and finds some utterly inane reason not to advertise in *Ms.* Without Steinem's eye-witness testimony, who would have believed that Clairol would not advertise in *Ms.* because *Ms.*, along with a number of newspapers, reported on "the congressional hearing into chemicals used in hair dyes that are absorbed through the skin and may be carcinogenic" (paragraph 23)? Who would have believed that Revlon would not advertise in *Ms.* because the Soviet women featured on one cover were not wearing makeup (paragraph 46)? Who would have believed that Estee Lauder would not advertise in *Ms.* because that company was selling "a kept-woman mentality" (paragraph 65)? With these striking examples Steinem eventually convinces us that the sales techniques that work for general interest magazines—market reports, readership surveys, circulation figures—don't work for women's magazines. Consequently, if we want to solve the problem, we will have to consider Steinem's proposals.

4. What did this article teach you about what the real life of a magazine editor is like?

This essay was a real shocker for me. Before I read it, I would never have guessed that Steinem, as the editor of a major magazine, spent her days courting advertisers and her nights worrying that *Ms.* wouldn't "be able to pay the printer or the post office" (paragraph 60). No, I would have imagined a much more glamorous and intellectually stimulating existence—brainstorming with her staff to consider which women's issues to investigate next, attending feminist conferences to keep up with current developments, testifying before Congressional committees charged with investigating health care for women and children, researching and writing articles about gender discrimination, and formulating editorial policies and decisions consistent with the goals of *Ms.* I suppose I would have visualized *Ms.* as a feminist think tank where writers and editors would be provided with the time and the resources to search for solutions to the problems facing women.

Instead, we learn that, to ensure the survival of *Ms.*, Steinem spent sixteen years as a saleswoman, studying marketing surveys, preparing reports, and meeting with advertisers of cars, cigarettes, cosmetics, and toy trains to try—usually unsuccessfully—to persuade them to place ads in *Ms.* What a waste of vision and talent.

—M.R.D.—

KIKU ADATTO

The Incredible Shrinking Sound Bite

The third edition of *The Dolphin Reader* went to press in the middle of the 1992 presidential campaign, too early for us to find articles that analyze news coverage of the Bush–Clinton contest as Adatto here analyzes coverage of the 1988 Bush–Dukakis contest. To judge from what I have seen so far, however, the trend that she writes about is continuing: television news continues to cover the campaign by broadcasting the visual images so carefully manipulated by the candidates' handlers, accompanied by the briefest sound bites.

The best reason for assigning Adatto's essay may be that it encourages students to think about the dangers such a system of coverage creates for the democratic process. As Neil Postman points out in "And Now . . . This" (an essay that is a good companion to Adatto's), images bypass the mind's ability to check the truth of assertions; they appeal to emotion, leave reason behind. If the verbal (and therefore logical) anchor for the image is a ten-second sound bite removed from its context, voters who depend on television for campaign information may be in danger of drifting out to sea, toward the Nuremberg triangle.

QUESTIONS

1. What sort of research underlies this essay? Is it possible for any of us to do similar research?

I ask this question partly on general principle: students should learn to evaluate the research *implied* in an essay that doesn't fully describe its research methods. In this case, there are pretty clear clues. "An analysis of all weekday evening network newscasts (over 280) from Labor Day to Election Day in 1968 reveals that the average 'sound bite' fell from 42.3 seconds in 1968 to only 9.8 seconds in 1988," Adatto reports in paragraph 2. As the headnote indicates, she was a fellow at Harvard's Joan Shorenstein Barone Center on Press, Politics, and Public Policy. We can assume that through the Center she had access to the necessary videotapes, and we can imagine her doing her dutiful labor as a graduate student, sitting in front of a television set with a note pad and stopwatch at the ready. The result is that

Adatto can write as an authority—who in the world could know her subject better than she does?

An undergraduate in a composition class can hardly be expected to do research so extensive and would, at any rate, have difficulty getting access to the archived videotapes necessary for this sort of historical research, but your students should realize that the widespread availability of VCRs opens up the possibility of using techniques like Adatto's on a smaller scale, and so, like Adatto, putting themselves in a position to write with authority. If there is an election in the offing, they could record evening news programs on a given channel for a week and do in miniature the same sort of analysis as Adatto does here. Or if they are interested in the images of women presented on network shows, they could record a prime-time block (8:00–9:00 P.M. Monday–Friday, for example), and develop a system for analyzing the presentation of "types." A discussion of the VCR as a tool for research may inspire students to find media subjects worth researching.

2. Why is the 300% increase in "visuals" Adatto mentions in paragraph 2 a matter of alarm for her?

This question is here simply as a comprehension check on some of the most important ideas that run through Adatto's essay. She is concerned about these images partly because they are planned and largely controlled by the candidates' media consultants (see paragraphs 3–4, 14), so that by airing them, the networks are not being journalistic watchdogs, but "electronic billboards for the candidates." She is concerned because the news programs, competing for visual appeal, will rebroadcast exciting images even when they know they are false or misleading (paragraphs 12, 16–17). At bottom, she is concerned—as we can see from her discussion of the Willie Horton ad in paragraphs 17–20—that images can work so powerfully and subtly on the minds of viewers that they will have the planned effect even if they are being shown and discussed as examples of misleading advertisements. If the illogical image shouts "red" and the words whisper "not red, but green," the typical television viewer will believe red. Show the viewer the red image again and explain why red is irrational and green desirable; the viewer will remember red, forget green. If I understand Adatto correctly, she thinks that no amount of verbalized reasoning can overcome the impact of images like those in the Willie Horton ad.

For a very different view of the relative merits of words and images, see George Orwell's "Politics and the English Language" in *Understanding*.

3. What do Lee Friedlander's photographs that include the author's shadow or image in every frame have in common with media coverage of elections?

Adatto tells us that 1960s postmodernist art like Friedlander's photography "foreshadowed the form television news would take in the 1980s" (paragraph 32). She says that television news has "come to partake of the postwar modernist sensibility" (paragraph 29). She doesn't quite say that postmodernism in art *caused* the sort of news coverage we now get, but she comes very close.

The cause-and-effect question aside, students should be able to identify what the common element in postmodern art and contemporary election coverage is, and they should find it interesting. To borrow and perhaps slightly distort the meaning of Marshall McLuhan's dictum, the medium has become the message. Increasingly, newspeople report not political events and ideas, but *media* events and ideas, including reports on media coverage of media events. In this respect they are like Friedlander's photographs that always contain an image of the photographer. The analogy may strike some of your students as far-fetched, but having just watched several hours of television coverage of the 1992 Democratic National Convention, I have to say that it seems fundamentally sound. What I saw on the floor was not political debate, but a show put on for the camera. And too often the camera wasn't even on the convention floor; it was on journalists interviewing other journalists about how the spin doctors might affect the public perception of what was happening on the convention floor. If there is political discussion going on somewhere, it is presumably too dull to be broadcast. "People of the Medium" as Jarrell calls us want to hear about the medium, not the world.

—D.H.—

Style Lesson 49:
Expanding a Sentence with Modifiers

In "The Incredible Shrinking Sound Bite," Adatto often supplies background information economically, tucking it into the grammatical crannies of a sentence. In her opening sentence, for example, she gives information we can separate into the two main clauses (capitalized) and answers to a series of questions:

EDMUND MUSKIE TRIED TO SPEAK, BUT PROTESTORS DROWNED HIM OUT.

What kind of protestors? Anti-war protestors.
How many? I don't know precisely—a group of them.
What was his role then? He was the Democratic vice presidential nominee.
What was the setting? He was standing before a campaign rally.
Where? In Pennsylvania
When? In 1968

Use the answers to these questions, combined with the capitalized sentence, to form a single sentence, then compare your sentence to Adatto's. Then propose questions about the sentence below, using the answers to expand the sentence into one that gives background which readers ten years from now might need to understand the significance of the main clauses.

ROSS PEROT WITHDREW, BUT SUPPORTERS GOT HIS NAME ON THE BALLOT.

NEIL POSTMAN

"Now . . . This"

Although Postman's *Amusing Ourselves to Death* is now nearly a decade old, it continues to be the liveliest and most influential damnation of television that I know of. Here at the University of Missouri, where a disproportionate number of undergraduates are in journalism, copies are almost continuously checked out of the library and their margins are crowded with pro- and anti-Postman graffiti. The idea that a given medium may be *incapable* of presenting the Truth is itself mind-boggling to many students, and when the suspect medium is television, some students understandably react as if they had been told they had been poisoned by their mother's milk.

It is possible to accuse Postman of being an old fogy, so wedded to old-fashioned print-based media that he just doesn't "get" television: Camille Paglia makes this charge in a debate with him that was published in *Harper's* in November 1991. If your students are inclined to take this tack, you might remind them that it is possible to be both an old fogy and right. When I was a child, I used to think that the adults who wanted me to go out and play rather than watch television until I turned into a vegetable were old fogies. They were, and they were right. They could remember the days when people did things outdoors. Postman seems to be able to remember the days when people read books.

QUESTIONS

1. By Postman's standards, what would an ideal television news program be like? Why would he want it to be this way?

This question requires that students both comprehend Postman's argument and go a bit beyond what he says. Postman's chapter is essentially negative, an attack on news programming as it exists now. He offers his alternative only by implication.

He does admit in paragraph 23 that "typography is the universe I'm 'coming from.'" We can gather from the chapter that his ideal television news program would mirror as closely as possible the qualities of a book. Certainly there would be no music on the program: Postman tells us in paragraph 10 that music is a way of comforting the viewer, even though the news ought to make us uncomfortable. The stories would be long: not only does Postman criticize the standard 45-second story of network news shows, he complains that even on the "MacNeil–Lehrer Newshour" a story is typically "only" five to ten minutes long (paragraph 16). There would be very little film footage: "Pictures have little difficulty in overwhelming words, and short-circuiting introspection" (paragraph 11). Whatever images appeared would be carefully explained, so that the viewer would understand why they "intruded" on "public consciousness." In fact, one gathers that the Neil Postman Newsevening would consist largely of what television directors call (usually with disapproval) "talking heads"—journalists and interviewees looking directly into the camera and saying what they have to say. The journalistic talking heads would probably not be particularly attractive ones, since Postman is irritated by the "talking hair-do's" who tend to be cast as television journalists.

One might be tempted to summarize by saying that Postman's television news program would resemble as closely as possible the Sunday edition of the *New York Times,* but this summary misses two key issues. First, Postman actually criticizes one aspect of television journalism for being too print-like: the newscasters' style of delivery is too unemotional to suit him; they "do not pause to grimace or shiver" (paragraph 12). So we can conclude that he would favor newscasters who used the visual qualities of television to convey personal emotions. Second, Postman is dismayed by the presence of advertisements, which trivialize the news (paragraph 13). But the *New York Times* is chock-a-block with advertisements, albeit ones that are easier to ignore than those on television.

So Postman's program would be essentially a series of lectures and interviews, illustrated (perhaps) by a modest use of still photographs and film clips and uninterrupted by commercials. Like the "MacNeil–Lehrer Newshour" it would have to run on public television and would have, as Postman realizes, a "minuscule" audience. Why all this severity? Because the commercially viable (entertaining) news program is, as Postman repeatedly tells us, essentially an anaesthetic that prevents us from recognizing the importance of the events reported. This is the big point he has to make, his thesis, and you will want to discuss it thoroughly enough to ensure that your students have understood. Paragraph 12 and 13 are particularly important on the tendency of television to draw us into an "assumption that all reports of cruelty and death are greatly exaggerated and, in any case, not to be taken seriously or responded to sanely."

2. Does Postman make claims that you find incredible or exaggerated? Where?

As a controversialist, Postman is sometimes inclined to be provocative, even at the expense of credulity. Here are some examples:

- There is no murder so brutal, no earthquake so devastating, no political blunder so costly . . . that it cannot be erased from our minds by a newscaster saying, "Now . . . this" (paragraph 2).
- Viewers, after all, are partners with the newscasters in the "Now . . . this" culture, and they expect the newscaster to play out his or her role as a character who is marginally serious but who stays well clear of authentic understanding (paragraph 12).
- The result of all this is that Americans are the best entertained and quite likely the least well-informed people in the Western world (paragraph 18).

Your students will find many other examples of Postman's tendency to be hyperbolic. Surely some events reported on the news *do* stay in our memory: witness the reaction to the police beating of Rodney King. Surely most viewers would say that they preferred a newscaster who understood the news. And one wonders what evidence Postman could produce to show that Americans are, on average, less well-informed than not only the British and Italians, but Bolivians and Cubans.

How much damage is done by Postman's tendency to hyperbole? A great deal, I think. He is arguing that television tends to misinform, but his chapter itself reminds us that print media may do the same thing.

3. Do you find evidence in this chapter that Postman, like the newscasters he criticizes, sometimes puts more emphasis on entertaining his audience than informing it?

Some of your students will undoubtedly find Postman very dry, but others will probably notice that he can use his own medium's capacity to shock or amuse. The hyperboles noted above are examples. Here are others:

- Of the television producer's method of assembling a news team: "You will try, in other words, to assemble a cast of talking hair-do's" (paragraph 5).
- Of discontinuities in newscasts: ". . . we are no longer struck dumb, as any sane person would be, by a newscaster who having just reported that a nuclear war is inevitable goes on to say that he will be right back after this word from Burger King . . ." (paragraph 13).
- Of the "type of discourse" used on the news: "In the parlance of the theater, it is known as vaudeville" (paragraph 14).
- Of the tendency for television to control us by keeping us amused: "Big Brother turns out to be Howdy Doody" (paragraph 25).

In short, Postman will sometimes interrupt the flow of "serious public discourse" to get off a good one-liner. Written communication, like television, mixes attempts to entertain and attempts to inform. This doesn't do great damage to Postman's argument, of course, unless we believe that his one-liners, like the images on a television screen, have the capacity to overwhelm the audience's reason. But who would contend that Postman's skill with a phrase renders us unable to distinguish newscasts from vaudeville performances, for instance, or unable to distinguish the average American from someone clinically insane. To toy with an idea, as Postman may make us do, is not the same as to accept it subliminally, as Postman believes television viewers do.

—D.H.—

Style Lesson 50:
A Periodic Sentence Moving From Cause to Effect

To practice writing a periodic sentence with parallel clauses, imitate the following one from paragraph 3 of Postman's "Now . . . This."

In part because television
sells its time in seconds and minutes,
in part because television
must use images rather than words,
in part because its audience
can move freely to and from the television set,
programs are structured so that
almost each eight-minute segment may stand
as a complete event in itself.

GARRISON KEILLOR

The Tip-Top Club

Most of your students will know Garrison Keillor as the creator, writer, and host of the popular radio program *A Prairie Home Companion* and its successor *The American Radio Company of the Air* or as the author of *Happy to be Here* and *Lake Woebegone Days*. If so, they will expect an amusing story about ordinary small-town midwestern people. They won't be disappointed. This story chronicles the birth, life, and death of a radio club. The Tip-Top Club consists of radio talk-show fans dedicated to the notion that a talk show should be, above all else, cheerful. "Controversy was the very thing that distinguished 'The Tip-Top Club.' It had none" (paragraph 8). For eighteen years the club members call in to give each other helpful advice such as the "idea of pouring warm soapy water into overshoes and wearing them around the house to give yourself a relaxing footbath" (paragraph 2). Then their beloved host retires, and the club members have to deal with the unthinkable—change.

Like all Keillor stories, this one is more than an anecdote. Keillor is quite willing to entertain us, but he is not willing to let us read without thinking. In "The Tip-Top Club" Keillor asks us hard questions about the relationship between the media and the public.

QUESTIONS

1. Find examples of statements made by particular people in the story that could not have been spoken by anyone else.

Keillor has an amazing ability to reproduce the way people talk. The speech patterns of his characters are no more interchangeable than the people themselves. You might ask your students to write the examples they select on the board to see if the rest of the class can name the speakers. If you choose to list your own examples, here are a few I would bet that your students can correctly identify:

- "Every foulmouth in town will be slobbering into his telephone for the chance to get on the air" (paragraph 19). [Roy Jr. the distrustful]
- "Well, I don't know. Let me know what *you* think" (paragraph 12). [Bud the self-effacing]
- "I was slapping them down like barnyard flies. We were up to our ears in crazies. Finally, my fingers got sore, and Alice pulled the plug on the switchboard and her and me sat down and had a cup of coffee and left that poor dumb SOB sit and die by himself" (paragraph 51). [Harlan the profane pragmatist]
- "I appreciate your honesty, sir. I don't necessarily agree with that statement, but I think it's important that you feel you can be honest with me" (paragraph 43). [Wayne the psychobabbler]

- "The distinguished gentleman who spoke earlier on cats was very well-informed on most points, but I feel he may have overlooked the fact that cats will not shed if brushed regularly" (paragraph 29). [Tip-Top caller speaking to Bud—unfailingly courteous]
- "You make me absolutely sick. You're the biggest mistake they've made down there" (paragraph 43). [Tip-Top caller speaking to Wayne—unwaveringly cruel]

I can't distinguish among the voices of the Tip-Top callers (I don't think Keillor wants us to), but it's easy to identify their listener.

2. Does Keillor, who was himself the host for a morning "music and call-ins" radio program, seem to favor Bud's or Wayne's style of hosting?

Some of your students will base their answer on their knowledge of Keillor's style on *A Prairie Home Companion* and *The American Radio Company of the Air*. They may, for example, point out that Keillor reads greetings from his studio audience to their friends and relatives at home. That's something we can imagine Bud doing—if Bud had a studio audience. But your students should be able to answer this question even if they've never listened to Keillor on the radio.

I think your students will decide that even though Keillor seems to like both Bud and Wayne, he doesn't enthusiastically approve of either. Both have good intentions. Bud is a kind man who "*never* asks [his callers] about their occupations, not after the first few times: the answers were always apologetic sounding . . ." (paragraph 35). But Bud is a host who allows his guests to usurp his role. The "listeners" become the hosts who choose the topics, do all the talking, and offer opinions on every noncontroversial subject from hobbies to housework. Bud becomes the listener, "the recording secretary" (paragraph 2), and if he has any opinions, he keeps them to himself. When a caller reports that Communists are trained "to insinuate their beliefs into a conversation without anyone being the wiser," Bud replies, "Appreciate your concern, sir, and believe me, we'll be on guard" (paragraph 25). After listening "to the same stuff" for eighteen years, Bud loses "whatever personality he had in the beginning." "A goddamn ghost," Harlan said, "When he comes in, I don't even see him anymore. He don't really exist, except on the air" (paragraph 38).

Wayne is Bud's antithesis. Bud is self-effacing; Wayne is self-absorbed. Bud says, "Tell me about yourself" (paragraph 29); Wayne's favorite topic is Wayne. (Ask your students to count the number of times Wayne uses the pronoun "I" in paragraph 41. I find 18.) Bud's style of speaking is "warm and reassuring" and he always tries "to look on the bright side"; Wayne expresses doubts about his own abilities, and he discusses depressing topics like his divorce (paragraph 51). Bud identifies with his audience; Wayne feels alienated from and superior to the Tip-Top Club members. He tells them, "I had a hard time relating to working-class people" (paragraph 53).

But Keillor doesn't make Wayne despicable. Keillor forces us to admire Wayne's courage and his determination to "keep on trying." He makes us sympathize when Wayne is bombarded by abuse that surprises even Harlan. And he gives Wayne some lines that few of Keillor's readers are likely to dispute: "There's a lot of anger and violence out there—and I don't say people shouldn't feel that way, but I do feel people should be willing to change. Life is change. We all change. I've changed" (paragraph 53).

Bud, of course, never insisted that his audience change. For eighteen years he allowed them to stay in their comfortable patterns of thought. He screened the callers: "no kids, no foreign accents, and nobody who seemed unusually intense or determined to get on the air" (paragraph 26). He limited the topics of discussion: no politics, no religion, no criticism of others, and no promotion of products, services, clubs, fund drives, or events (paragraph 26). I think most readers will be inclined to agree with Harlan's assessment: "What's left to talk about? Not a god-damn helluva lot."

Keillor the radio show host is probably a combination of Bud and Wayne, a man who can be interested in the hobbies of the Tip-Top Club members and in Woody Allen movies, a man who is both attracted and repelled by the notion of a homogeneous community willing to sacrifice everything for cheeriness.

3. What does this story tell us about how the media and the public should interact?

Some of your students will undoubtedly object that such a question requires a too serious approach to a lighthearted story. Maybe. I agree that the story is fun to read, and many of the lines make me laugh, but I don't think the story is all that light. In fact, very few of Keillor's stories are merely humorous. If you remind your students that Keillor wrote this story while he was a radio show host, they may be willing to concede that this is the kind of question that should have interested him.

A number of writers in this unit blame the media for offering us a bland, superficial, dumbed-down view of the world. In "The Incredible Shrinking Sound Bite," for example, Kiku Adatto criticizes television for reducing complex political issues to sound bites lasting an average of 9.8 seconds. And in "Pretty Worthless" Beth Austin faults Hollywood for churning out movies that proclaim "Spend quality time with your kids and the problems of the world will magically disappear." Media representatives defend their actions by telling us that they simply give us viewers/listeners/readers what we want and that what we want is mindless entertainment, not in-depth explanations of complicated issues like the S & L fiasco.

In "The Tip-Top Club" Keillor presents two contrasting models for media/public interactions. Bud represents what I think of as the "commercial" television approach: Let viewers "choose" what they want, but offer them such a narrow range of options that their only real choice is which sit-com to watch next. Bud's listeners can choose their topics, as long as they don't discuss politics or religion, criticize other people, or promote products, services, clubs, fund drives, or events. Wayne represents the "public" television approach: Broadcast a six-part series on the migration of the monarch butterfly and tell people that they ought to watch it because it will be educational and therefore good for them. Wayne's listeners hear about Szechuan cuisine and Woody Allen movies because Wayne has decided that this information will improve his listeners' lives—even if they don't want their lives improved.

After reading this story we know that we should have another option, and we suspect that the public and the media share the responsibility for creating that third and better choice.

—M.R.D.—

KATHA POLLITT

The Smurfette Principle

This little gem of an essay is high on my list of models for students, partly because many of its best qualities are within reach for writers of average ability. Pollitt's line of argument, far from being the product of a solitary genius, is familiar to anyone acquainted with mainstream feminism; her point is systematically buttressed by examples, and her style is graceful, direct, and uncluttered. Because the essay deals with sexual stereotyping in children's television and children's books, it might have been placed in three other units: *Childhood and Childhood's End, Femininity and Masculinity,* or *Progress and Its Price.*

QUESTIONS

1. How accurate are Pollitt's observation about the presentation of females in media directed at children?

Some of your students will have a clear enough memory of the childhood reading and viewing to give an answer about how things were *then,* but this may be an area in which (despite Pollitt's complaints) ten or twenty years makes a great difference. Some of your students may spend enough time with younger sisters and brothers to have an opinion about how things stand today.

I think it would be worthwhile to discuss with your class what practical techniques they might use to research this question. Pollitt's informal research apparently included

- a trip to the local video store, where she found that "9 out of 10 offerings" starred boys
- channel cruising for a week, presumably with some guidance from a television schedule, since she confidently announces that Nickelodeon has one puppet show and one cartoon starring a female

- reading *Newsweek*'s latest (1991) Christmas roundup of children's books and learning how few are about girls

These methods are easy to replicate; they don't require a great deal of expertise and time. In addition, students could go to a local bookstore or library and browse the children's shelves, keeping some sort of scorecard. Or they could locate a recent children's best-seller list (the *World Almanac* includes one) and examine the books that appear on it. They could read summarizing reviews of the most popular new movies for children (*Film Review Digest*). With a VCR, they could record and then skim every children's program broadcast by one television station for a day and then make notes on what they have captured. Your class will undoubtedly come up with other ideas, and the students may become eager to do the research and make it the subject of their next paper.

2. How much practical difference does it make whether creatures as essentially sexless as the Muppets are male or female?

One could argue that a creature like Big Bird is so clearly different from an adult male human that few little girls will fail to identify with him just because someone calls him "him." Obviously, the girl mentioned in paragraph 5 *is* put off by Big Bird's merely grammatical gender, but can this be a typical reaction?

I'm not sure, and I think you would do well to ask your class how conscious of the sex of the muppets and various cartoon characters they were when they were growing up and how much more strongly they identified with the ones of their own sex. I've certainly known women to report that they identified strongly with Spider Man or Charlie Brown, but this may be unusual. And it may be that the important impact on children is subconscious and delayed: at age eight girls may identify with a male superhero, but the impression that heroes are male may bear bitter fruit in future years.

It's worth noting that children in this society have reason to be cued in to the smallest hints of gender. As Lois Gould's "X" shows us, we are conditioned from the cradle to distinguish between girls' clothes and boys', girls' names and boys', girls' sports' and boys'. We shouldn't be surprised if children confronted with a puppet shapeless as a sock immediately wonder whether it is a boy or a girl.

3. Pollitt treats as common knowledge the idea that such classic children's stories as Cinderella and Sleeping Beauty are sexist. What is there in such stories that would offend a feminist?

Asking this question will probably be lobbing a fat pitch to some of your feminist batters. Other students may benefit by hearing them unload. Cinderella presents three female characters and one male. Two of the females—the stepsisters—are utter horrors: they are ugly and yet vain, eager to win the Prince's affection (and wealth) by fair means or foul, cruel to and jealous of their beautiful stepsister. Cinderella (alas!) just *takes it*, doing the washing and cooking (what else?) and mooning over the Prince (if I recall the Disney version correctly) as though the arrival of the right man was the only alternative to sleeping in the ashes. The Prince has all the cards—looks and wealth and immense popularity—and is able to get the ladies of the kingdom lathered up about putting their feet into a pair of *tiny* glass slippers. (In the Grimm version, the stepsisters actually cut off their heels in an attempt to conform to the male-dictated fashion of the hour.) When Cinderella puts her delicate feet into the slippers and becomes a princess, the stepsisters are not delighted at her good fortune: no sisterly solidarity here. In the Disney version, Cinderella maintains a syrupy sweetness from first to last, but in the Grimm version, she orders her allies, the birds, to peck the stepsisters' eyes out. What are girls who hear this story learning about what it means to be a woman? That if you are to avoid being bad, you should be submissive. That the most important thing you can do is win the affection of the right man. That you mustn't trust other women, since they are your competitors and they may be inclined to ruthlessness.

Snow White and Sleeping Beauty are subject to the same sort of criticism. Other children's classics may fare somewhat better. *The Wizard of Oz* has a spunkier protagonist, takes an ironic view of the dominant male power (the Wizard), and tells us that Glinda, the Good Witch of the East, has a great deal of authority in Munchkinland. But the Munchkins seem so easy to dominate that Glinda doesn't need to be a terribly commanding figure, and I think most children are more impressed by her beauty and kindness than her power. And then there is the Wicked Witch of the West. Now *there's* a picture of spinsterhood to conjure by. Seeing her stare into her crystal ball and growl as she prepares another torment for "pretty" Dorothy and her companions must be unnerving to other "little girls" who are entering a world where prettiness or ugliness have an apparently mysterious importance.

There are surely rebuttals to this sort of criticism of children's stories, but I think it's an important consciousness-raising experience to see the stories from a feminist perspective, if only to make explicit some of our vague worries about how the media may distort the personalities of the young.

—D.H.—

Style Lesson 51: Cohesion and Coherence in a Paragraph

The following sentences can be rearranged to form paragraph 4 of Pollitt's essay. Attempt to put them in the "right" order; be prepared to explain your reasoning. What references and transitions hold the paragraph together? Compare the order you and your class prefer to Pollitt's order. How much "freedom" of order is there?

1. The message is clear.
2. In the worst cartoons—the ones that blend seamlessly into the animated cereal commercials—the female is usually a little-sister type, a bunny in a pink dress and hair ribbons who tags along with the adventurous bears and badgers.
3. Girls exist only in relation to boys.
4. Piggy, of "Muppet Babies," is a pint-size version of Miss Piggy, the camp glamour queen of the Muppet movies.
5. Contemporary shows are either essentially all-male, like "Garfield," or are organized on what I call the Smurfette principle: a group of male buddies will be accented by a lone female, stereotypically defined.
6. April, of the wildly popular "Teen-Age Mutant Ninja Turtles," functions as a girl Friday to a quartet of male superheroes.
7. Boys are the norm, girls the variation; boys are central, girls peripheral; boys are individuals, girls types.
8. Boys define the group, its story, and its code of values.
9. Thus, Kanga, the only female in "Winnie-the-Pooh," is a mother.
10. But the Smurfette principle rules the more carefully made shows, too.

BARBARA EHRENREICH

Spudding Out

Readers who know Ehrenreich's reputation as a serious social critic may be surprised to discover that she also has a flair for comedy. In "Spudding Out" she takes on one of the great questions of our time: "What drives [couch potatoes]—or rather, leaves them sapped and spineless on their reclining chairs? What are they seeking—beyond such obvious goals as a tastefully colorized version of *The Maltese Falcon*?" Ehrenreich's answer to that question is both humorous and thought provoking: We love television because it brings us a world where "you will never see people watching television." "Spudding Out" will entertain and challenge your students, and it will demonstrate that a serious topic can be presented humorously.

QUESTIONS

1. According to Ehrenreich, what are the negative effects of watching television? Do you agree? Why or why not?

Chances are your students can recite the usual criticisms of television: that children who watch more than two hours of television each day get lower grades, eat more junk food, and tend to be overweight; that television violence desensitizes us; that television commercials prompt us to buy products we don't need; and that television contributes to our high rate of illiteracy. Ehrenreich's complaints are different. She charges that our addiction to television has turned us into less active, less sociable, and consequently less interesting people.

It's hard to dispute Ehrenreich's observation that "there are still a few things that cannot be done in the den, especially by someone zipped into a body bag. These include racquetball, voting, and meeting strange people in bars" (paragraph 3). However, your students may point out that some people work out on their exercise bikes or Nordic-Trac skiers while they watch television. And the "activities" that filled pre-television days might not be all that superior to television viewing. Would our lives really be richer if we spent more time playing cards, putting together jig-saw puzzles, or embroidering pillow cases?

Ehrenreich also blames television for the fact that we no longer know our neighbors, a concern shared by Daniel Boorstin in "Technology and Democracy." Boorstin argues that "with the coming of television, everybody acquired his private theater" and that this privatization of experience has led directly to what Boorstin calls the "decline of congregation." But perhaps it would be more accurate to say that we continue to congregate, but under different circumstances. When we were a rural nation, most men spent their days alone in their fields while women spent their days alone in their houses. No wonder they looked forward to visiting with their neighbors at night. Now most of us work outside our homes in stores, restaurants, offices, and factories filled with people. Perhaps we have had our fill of congregation by the end of the day.

As for the charge that television viewing makes us less interesting, maybe that depends on what we watch. Ehrenreich seems to assume that everyone watches sit-coms. Even if that were true, some sit-coms stretch our minds more than others, and some television programs such as the Civil War series provide us with so much information that we might even qualify as contestants on *Jeopardy!*

2. According to Ehrenreich, what are the three reasons why we have become a nation of couch potatoes? What are other reasons for watching television?

Ehrenreich lists three causes of spudding out: fear of the outside world, disgust with our own boring families, and a desire to watch people who are not watching television. Your students may be able to come up with more positive reasons for watching television. For example, Aric Press, a senior editor of *Newsweek*, claims that men watched "thirtysomething" because the show "offered models of behavior for the stymied and supplied a vocabulary for the speechless." (*Newsweek*, June 3, 1991). You might ask your students to focus on any one television series and explain what makes the lives of those characters so interesting that we continue to tune in.

3. What makes this essay funny?

Although Ehrenreich is making a serious point, she keeps us laughing by combining the incongruous and the hyperbolic. For example, she writes that her "youngest . . . relies on a remote that controls his TV, stereo, and VCR." No surprises there, but then she adds "and can also shut down the neighbor's pacemaker at fifteen yards" (paragraph 2). To demonstrate her technique, you might write the following sentences on the board but omit the underlined words, and have your students try to fill in the blanks.

> Some experts say that there are virtues in mass agoraphobia, that it strengthens the family and *reduces highway deaths* (paragraph 3).
>
> Americans used to be a great and restless people, fond of the outdoors in all of its manifestations, from *Disney World to miniature golf* (paragraph 3).
>
> The list of reasons to stay safely tucked indoors lengthens yearly. First there was crime, then AIDS, then *side-stream smoke.* To this list should be added *"fear of the infrastructure"* . . . (paragraph 4).
>
> Emerging from *Family Ties* or *My Two Dads*, we are forced to acknowledge that our own families are made up of *slow-witted emotionally crippled people who would be lucky to qualify for seats in the studio audience of Jeopardy!* (paragraph 6).

I found my mind wandered to more interesting things, like *whether to get up and make ice cubes* (paragraph 7).

—M.R.D.—

Style Lesson 52: Parallel Modifying Clauses and Phrases

You may not consider yourself a couch potato, but you may see yourself as part of a comparable group—sports addicts, Nintendo fanatics, computer buffs, or compulsive romance novel readers. Replace "spuds" in the following sentence (from paragraph 10 of "Spudding Out") with a topic of your choice, and then imitate the rest, providing content appropriate to the choice.

In fact,
deep in their hearts,
this is what the spuds crave most:
a rich, new, participatory life,
in which family members look each other in the eye,
in which people walk outside and
banter with the neighbors,
where there is adventure,
possibility,
danger,
feeling,
all in natural color,
stereophonic sound, and
three dimensions,
without commercial interruptions,
and starring
. . . us.

BETH AUSTIN

Pretty Worthless

Last year Americans purchased 1.2 billion movie tickets. In this essay, Austin asks us to consider the values promoted by the movies we watch. She approaches the topic by comparing recent box-office successes such as *Defending Your Life, When Harry Met Sally, Home Alone,* and *Pretty Woman* with classics of earlier eras: *On the Waterfront, Mr. Smith Goes to Washington,* and *To Kill A Mockingbird.* She concludes that, in movies of the Reagan–Bush era, "family values" have become our only values. Austin writes, "In trying to produce 'family' movies, today's popular filmmakers have confused niceness with morality and ended up creating a moral universe that stops at the front door."

This essay is a gold mine of writing opportunities. For example, students might want to look at World Almanac volumes for the past five years to see which movies earned the highest gross receipts. Then they could examine the top movies of each year to determine whether those films support Austin's thesis. Other students might want to find out which movies were most popular during the years that *On the Waterfront, Mr. Smith Goes to Washington,* and *To Kill A Mockingbird* were released. Then they could check out a few videos to see if the classics Austin praises are representative of their era. Or they might want to review the movies that—in Austin's view—"confuse the rule" (*Dances With Wolves, Glory, The Hunt for Red October,* and *Guilty by Suspicion*) to identify the values promoted by those films.

QUESTIONS

1. Do you agree with Austin's conclusion that movies of the Reagan–Bush era exalt family values?

This question is intended to encourage your students to examine Austin's supporting evidence. Students could approach this question in at least two ways. First, they could ask themselves whether they agree with Austin's characterization of various movies. Does *Rain Man* tell us that it's all right to institutionalize relatives who require "too much maintenance" (paragraph 19)? Does *Big* teach us that "home is all that matters" (paragraph 27)? Different interpretations of those movies would lead to different conclusions about the messages Hollywood is sending.

Second, students could ask themselves whether Austin is loading the deck by selecting movies that support her thesis and ignoring those that don't. Austin admits that *Dances With Wolves, Glory, The Hunt for Red October,* and *Guilty by Suspicion* "confuse the rule" (paragraph 7). Your students may list other important movies that Austin overlooks. And they may find that if they examine ten recent movies that were not mentioned in this essay, they will detect trends quite unlike those described by Austin.

2. In Austin's opinion, why are pro-family movies morally inferior to the classics of earlier eras? Do you agree with her? Why or why not?

Students need to realize that Austin is not opposed to family values, but she does challenge the assumption "that a parent's highest responsibility is to provide complete emotional and financial security for his child" (paragraph 7). That's an assumption most of us find seductive. Before I had children, I thought of myself as a social reformer who would gladly make personal sacrifices to improve the world, but after the birth of my first child, I discovered that the world had shrunk to the size of Shannon's crib. Instead of campaigning for adequate day care and health care for all children, I found myself searching for the perfect baby sitter and pediatrician for *my* daughter. It's particularly difficult to fight this form of selfishness when society commends us for waving a white flag. If we send our children to expensive private schools rather than work to improve public schools, we are praised for sacrificing ourselves to pay the tuition. If we decline to serve on the city council, the library board, or the human rights commission so that we can spend time with our children, we are applauded as good parents. As Austin notes, "Atticus Finch would be considered a bad parent today because he risks his family's safety for his work" (paragraph 21).

Somehow we have to balance our obligations to our own families and our responsibilities to the rest of the world. It's tempting to say that if we all take care of our own children, there won't be any social problems. Maybe not. But the reality is that not all parents can or will provide happy homes for their children. So who is responsible for those little ones? One of my friends has three children and also cares for three foster children. Her foster children, who arrived on her doorstep with the predictable range of emotional problems, require a great deal of love and attention. If we accept the "family-first" ethic, my friend is "neglecting" her own children by expecting them to share their parents and their home with "strangers." But if we accept Austin's argument that a "vital part of loving your children—of loving anyone—is living a life they will admire" (paragraph 21), my friend is a role model who will show her children "what these good families are good for" (paragraph 28). As Austin notes, moral "decisions are never simple, but they are filled with excitement and satisfaction to which Hollywood these days seems oblivious" (paragraph 30).

3. Choose any one of your heroes and explain how history might have been different if he or she had accepted the proposition that "family happiness is always the paramount issue"?

Of course this question is intended to illustrate the flaw in the family-is-all approach to life. Most of our heroes have accepted their responsibility to a community greater than their own families. Three of my personal heroes, Mahatma Gandhi, Martin Luther King, and Margaret Sanger made the difficult decision to put their obligations to the world before their personal relationships. But for their devotion to ideals beyond family happiness, India might not be an independent nation, segregation might still be legal in the United States, and American women might still be denied access to contraceptives. We all know that the people who change history make personal sacrifices that involve their families, but when we choose our political leaders, we still insist that they bear the pro-family stamp of approval.

—M.R.D.—

Style Lesson 53: Diction of Fairy Tales/Diction of Marketplace

In her discussion of Pretty Woman, *Austin uses surprising word choices to show the confusion of the world of the fairy tale with the world of business. In each bracketed space below (from paragraph 15 of "Pretty Worthless") we have suggested a word that might be expected to fill the blank. Try to recall or guess the word Austin uses instead.*

Gere may turn to more productive work, but he doesn't sacrifice one thread of his thousand dollar suits—which is fortunate, since, to deliver the [not GOODS, but . . .], he has to prove over and over again that he's Roberts's knight in [not SHINING, but . . .] armor. He changes for her and he fights for her, but in the movie's most thrilling moments, he's always [not PRAYING, but . . .] for her. He lifts her up from the [not ASHES, but . . .] to a [not PALACE, but . . .(two words)] with a sweeping view. He decks her out in jewels and whisks her away in a private jet to San Francisco for the opera. With his [not UNLIMITED, but . . .] credit card, he [not IMPRESSES, but . . .] shopkeepers for her along Rodeo Drive, scooping up every item in sight as Roberts's smiles (and eyes) grow bigger and bigger. Eventually he chases after her to carry her off—in a silver [not COACH, but . . .].

DONALD HALL

Purpose, Blame, and Fire

This memoir was written for the anthology *The Movie That Changed My Life.* In it Hall recalls *The Last Train From Madrid*, a movie he attended fifty-four years earlier when he was eight years old, a movie that caused him to burn his "collection of war cards and put away [his] toy soldiers forever." Like Beth Austin's "Pretty Worthless" this essay raises important questions about the impact of movies on their viewers.

The essay also shows how research can supplement the personal experience essay. To prepare this account of his childhood response to *The Last Train From Madrid*, Hall checks out a video of the film and also goes to the library to look up the movie reviews printed in 1937 by the *New Haven Register* and the *New York Times.*

QUESTIONS

1. What is it about *The Last Train From Madrid* that so frightens eight-year-old Donald Hall?

Unless your students read carefully, they may conclude that it is the violence of war that frightens young Donald Hall. But it isn't violence per se that horrifies him, it's the arbitrariness of that violence. When the boy watches *The Last Train From Madrid*, he is struck—for the first time—by the realization that war is nothing more than "the panic of unmotivated murder" (paragraph 25). Hall's summary of the movie's plot focuses on the meaninglessness of the characters' deaths; the word "arbitrary" becomes a haunting refrain:

> She sees her father, he is shot. . . . The killing feels wholly arbitrary (paragraph 17).
>
> Like the earlier execution by firing squad, this street killing—idyll destroyed by bullet—presents itself as wholly arbitrary (paragraph 18).
>
> Mack dies on the way—again arbitrarily (paragraph 19).

Before viewing that movie the boy had believed that war deaths involve battlefields where soldiers are willing to die *for a reason*, but the movie shows him a city where civilians (including women) die unwillingly *for no apparent reason.* The propaganda of 1937 had convinced the boy that Americans "were good, brave, loyal, outnumbered and victorious against all odds" while our enemies "were evil, cruel, cowardly, vicious, dumb, shrewd, and doomed" (paragraph 8). If one side is right and the other wrong, dying to assure the triumph of right has some purpose. But the movie shows him a universe with no moral absolutes, just an army that "lacks not only name but idea" and civilians overwhelmed by "panic, chaos, and violent death" (paragraph 15). The same war horror that moved Picasso to paint

Guernica—"the random slaughter of civilians" (paragraph 13)—sends young Hall down to the coal furnace in his cellar to burn his war cards.

The underlying question here is why we, as well as Hall, are so troubled by murder without motive. After all, dead is dead. But for some reason we are particularly horrified by what we call "senseless" violence—the lunatic with a rifle who shoots strangers at a McDonald's. Our need to believe that people act for understandable reasons is so entrenched that it is almost impossible for our law enforcement agencies to track down or convict murderers who have no apparent motive. That difficulty is dramatized in Susan Glaspell's play, "Trifles" (*Understanding*) when a man is murdered, but the prosecutor decides not to bring charges against his only suspect (the victim's wife) because he can't find a motive for the crime.

Our classification of some deaths as senseless suggests a corollary—that other deaths are meaningful. Perhaps the death of a firefighter who rescues a child from a burning building but loses her own life in the attempt is meaningful because the firefighter's death serves a purpose so significant that she voluntarily sacrifices herself for that purpose. But if that's our criterion, meaningful deaths are rare. And, as Hall suggests, if design doesn't govern our deaths, perhaps it doesn't govern our lives.

2. Why did *The Last Train From Madrid* have a more striking impact on young Hall than war cards and newsreels of the war had?

This question should make your students question why some media have more impact than others. It is certainly ironic that the war cards and newsreels, media that supposedly mirror the real world by presenting actual events, had less impact than the movie, a work of fiction that is at least twice removed from reality. The relative ineffectiveness of the war cards and newsreels wasn't because they failed to present graphic photos of real tragedies. One card pictured "a Japanese bomb hitting a crowded Chinese bus, maybe in Shanghai: Bodies being torn apart hurtled through the air, intestines stretched and tangled, headless bodies littering the ground" (paragraph 10). One newsreel showed "the bombing and strafing of refugees" (paragraph 9). In contrast, the movie featured fictitious characters and events, had fewer deaths, and showed less gore.

Perhaps it all comes down to packaging. War cards looked just like baseball cards, and they were sold in packs of bubble gum. Maybe it was hard to be alarmed by information packaged between pieces of gum "pink as a dog's tongue" (paragraph 6). Newsreels, which were usually sandwiched between shorts and previews of coming attractions, may have seemed no more significant than their companion pieces. In contrast, the feature movie (although shown on the same screen as the newsreel) always announced its importance. The lights dimmed, the curtains opened, the music swelled, and the credits began to roll. How could a viewer fail to pay attention?

Then again, Hall's epiphany may demonstrate the truth of Hamlet's observation that "the readiness is all." In "Think About It" (*Understanding*)

Frank Conroy suggests that we sometimes acquire a piece of information before we are able to understand it. But we remember it, and later—maybe years later—after our lives catch up with that information, the light bulb goes on. It could be that *The Last Train From Madrid* merely lighted the bulb that appeared over Hall's head when he read his first war card.

3. What, if anything, does Hall accomplish by waiting until paragraph 14 to describe *The Last Train From Madrid*?

This question should focus your students' attention on the structure of the essay. A student writer considering a movie that changed his or her life would probably begin with a plot summary of the movie and then consider its impact. By reversing that procedure, Hall accomplishes at least three things:

- He gives us a vivid picture of who he was in 1937 and what the United States was like in that year. His portrait of himself as a naive little boy growing up in a world clearly divided into good guys and bad guys helps us understand the movie's impact.
- He makes us curious about the movie that so affected him.
- By describing an era when a lunch cost thirty-nine cents and little boys wore woolen stockings pulled up over the bottoms of corduroy knickers, Hall makes us understand how long ago 1937 was, and how striking the movie must have been for Hall to remember it still.

4. Can you recall a movie that had a surprisingly strong impact on you when you were a child but probably wouldn't have the same effect now? What was it? How did it affect you? How do you account for that effect?

This question asks your students to do more or less what Hall did in "Purpose, Blame, and Fire." However, your students don't have to select a movie that frightened them or changed their lives, just one that had some effect on them as kids that it wouldn't have on them now. When my son Camden was three, watching *Superman* convinced him that the only thing he needed to get airborne was a red cape. I made him the cape, but had no idea that it was supposed to confer such powers until I saw him "fly" out of his tree house.

This question can also lead to a discussion of movie ratings. If, as Hall suggests, children can be deeply affected by movies that have little impact on adults, some kind of warning labels may be necessary. But if it's also true (as the movie review by Frank S. Nugent suggests) that adults don't even notice the things that trouble children, how can we know what to warn against?

—M.R.D.—

UNDERSTANDING

OVERVIEW OF UNIT

The final section of *The Dolphin Reader* contains nine essays and one play about the protean nature of truth—about its shape-shifting according to the perspective and preparation of the person who perceives it. If you are acquainted with the work of William G. Perry and other "stage theorists," you will understand the importance of this section for a composition class. Many students enter college with a fairly naive view of the world that creates an obstacle to their education. Because they believe that "a fact is a fact," they tend not to be curious (as most of their professors are) about the way that "facts" are established. Until they develop some sense of the difficulty of getting at (or inventing) the truth, much of what they read or hear in their classes strikes them as mere nonsense. Rhetoric may fare worst of all: until students understand that the world is full of questions on which reasonable and well-informed people can disagree, they have no sense that the art of persuasion and the pursuit of truth are close cousins, so they naturally assume that rhetoric is flim-flam. As students become more skeptical about the factualness of facts, they become less skeptical about the value of rhetoric, and more eager to write papers that advance a controversial thesis.

The essays by Jacob Bronowski, William G. Perry, and Adrienne Rich address enlightened skepticism most directly: Bronowski demonstrating that science does not consist of the accumulation of facts, Perry showing that the student bullster is closer to the spirit of university education than the student who diligently and unquestioningly accumulates facts, and Rich reminding students that what they learn at college is not reality, but a version of reality created largely by white male academics. Several teachers we know assign one or two of these at the beginning of the semester to set the tone for the class. They will serve as announcements that in this class, the facts will not speak for themselves; we will have to interpret them, have to persuade people to see things our way.

The other essays in the section deal one way and another with obstacles to finding the truth simple. The essays by Annie Dillard and Samuel Scudder and the play by Susan Glaspell show that even seeing something with our own eyes involves active theorizing. George Orwell's essay deals with the way that language may deceive not only the audience but the speaker or writer, Frank Conroy's with episodes in which understanding comes only with subsequent experience, Carol Bly's with the narrowness of "problem solving" as a mode of dealing with the world.

Taken as a whole, then, the selections in the unit help clear the way for student writing by showing (1) that the facts rarely speak for themselves, (2) that reasonable people will say different things about the same set of facts, and (3) that the only way to keep ourselves from being hoodwinked by unscrupulous or unreliable interpreters is to be capable of developing our own interpretations.

ADRIENNE RICH

Claiming an Education

Once upon a time, when I was an undergraduate, I borrowed notes from a friend who sat next to me in French. When I read through Ann's notes, I was puzzled by a sprinkling of T's and O's in the margins. The next day I asked her what the letters meant, and she explained, "T stands for truth and O stands for the professor's opinion. I don't want to get them mixed up." I was stunned by the revelation that truth and my professor's opinion might not be the same.

If your students' understanding of the complex nature of truth is as simplistic as mine was, "Claiming an Education" is a great semester starter. In this essay (which was originally a speech to the students at Douglass College) Rich tells students that "the truth" they are taught at college is merely one version of reality (the white male version) and that students must take responsibility for their own education. As Rich explains, students must actively "claim" education, not passively "receive" it. This essay may provoke some hostility from students impatient with feminism, but "Claiming An Education" is more than a feminist tract. Like other writers in this unit, especially Perry, Rich insists that facts do not speak for themselves, that the meaning of data changes when we change our frame of reference, and that an educated person should be able to recognize the assumptions implicit in a given statement of "fact." As Perry points out in "Examsmanship and the Liberal Arts," the claim that Columbus discovered America in 1492 is based on a European calendar and a European definition of "discover."

Students familiar with other essays by Rich may be interested to learn that Rich addressed "Claiming An Education" to the students at Douglass during the same week that she delivered her well-known "Taking Women Students Seriously" to the faculty.

QUESTIONS

1. In Rich's opinion, what is the purpose of a university education?

At the start Rich rejects the idea that a university education is merely "the processing of human beings into expected roles, through credit hours, tests, and grades . . ." (paragraph 1). Instead, she offers as the ideal an environment in which each "student sees herself engaged *with* her teachers in an active, ongoing struggle for a real education" (paragraph 10). For Rich, a university education is not an end but a beginning; a university should teach students "the most important thing, which is that clear thinking, active discussion, and excellent writing are all necessary for intellectual freedom, and that these require *hard work*" (paragraph 9). Obviously, Rich does not define education as the transfer of information from the teacher's mind to the student's. She warns students, particularly female students, that they cannot afford to think of themselves as passive recipients of education. Instead, they must view themselves as active participants in the process of claiming education. Rich asserts that a university should teach students to think for themselves, to respect their own brains, to challenge narrow versions of truth, and to "insist on a life of meaningful work" (paragraph 8). In Rich's view, in large part that meaningful work consists of reinterpreting a world formerly defined exclusively by white males. In class discussion or a writing assignment, your students might want to use Rich's criteria to evaluate their own educations.

2. Why doesn't Rich offer more support for her assertion that what students learn in college is a white male version of reality? Do you think she misjudged her audience?

Rich offers few concrete examples to support what must seem to her (but perhaps not to your students) a self-evident observation. Rich warns her audience that what they can learn at Douglass or at any other college is "what men, above all white men, in their male subjectivity, have decided is important" (paragraph 3). She claims that women's experiences and thoughts have been omitted from the curriculum and that women have been excluded from the decision-making levels of universities. As evidence that the curriculum has casually ignored half of humanity while pretending to describe all of us, she submits a list of college texts such as *The Descent of Man, The Future of Man,* and *From Man to Man.* I imagine a fair number of your students will find her "evidence" unimpressive. They may even scoff at the notion that the wording of book titles is significant. After all, we know that when the author says "man," *he* means everybody. (You may want to use this opportunity to discuss the pernicious effect of **sexist language.**)

Once your students notice that Rich makes little if any attempt to argue her case, you can ask them why Rich, a noted polemicist, takes such a low-key approach. That question will force them to consider the writer's audience and her purpose. Speaking to women students at a women's college in 1977, Rich undoubtedly assumed that she need not preach to the converted. She expected the women in her audience to know from their own personal experiences that women were under-represented in the curriculum and in the power structure of the university. She expected them to know that whether a woman majored in English literature, history, science, art, or mathematics, she studied the achievements of white males. Judging by the college students I knew in 1977, I doubt that every woman sitting in that audience had thought deeply about the possibility that the content of history classes represented a white male view of reality.

I think Rich races through what she considers preliminary matters because she makes certain assumptions about her audience (that may or may not have been correct) and because she wants to devote time to the central purpose of her talk, which is not to advocate women's studies, but to convince women to take responsibility toward themselves (paragraph 6). When Rich arrives at the primary purpose of her talk, her style changes dramatically. She shifts from third person "they" to second person "you," ceases to make general observations about our cultural past, and passionately exhorts her audience to change their personal futures. If your students find the second part of the essay more persuasive than the beginning, they may decide that Rich misjudged her audience.

3. To what extent have your own educational experiences demonstrated that schools teach only a white male view of reality?

In a National Public Radio interview Rich told the story of a female acquaintance who once confided to a male professor that she wanted to be a poet. He responded, "My dear, you don't need to write poems. You are a poem." Because very few educational institutions are as blatantly sexist today as they were twenty years ago (a success due in large part to the efforts of women like Rich), your younger students may not have had comparable experiences. In fact, they may argue that schools no longer present only one version of truth. Perhaps they are right. I noticed last year that my son's fifth-grade history book included a chapter about Sojourner Truth. But I suspect that most of our students are not attuned to more insidious forms of gender bias that range from relying on admission tests that favor males to conducting class in ways that intimidate females. Perri Klass's essay, "Learning the Language," suggests other subtle ways in which a male-dominated educational system (medical school) handicaps female students.

4. Is Rich's advice for "taking responsibility for yourself" applicable to men as well as to women?

Rich's advice is addressed to women who, because they have been taught to be passive, may find it particularly difficult to claim their place in the world of serious thought. Naturally, some of Rich's remarks are gender specific ("getting pregnant as an evasion of already existing problems," paragraph 8), but many are not. Her statement that "responsibility to yourself means refusing to let others do your thinking, talking, and naming for you" (paragraph 7) is certainly as applicable to men as to women.

Your students will probably decide that men are as likely as women to let others think for them, but that male abdication of responsibility takes other forms. Many men, like Mr. Metzger's friend in Perry's "Examsmanship and the Liberal Arts" and the men in Glaspell's "Trifles," escape this responsibility by substituting diligence for thinking. Mr. Metzger's friend wants to receive (not claim) an education by memorizing any and all facts presented by his professors. The men in "Trifles" want to find evidence of motive by searching a house but not their souls.

5. Must a "university administered overwhelmingly by men" be inferior to one administered by a mix of equally qualified men and women?

This question should set off a firestorm in your classroom. I think Rich's answer would be "yes, at least in the world as it now exists." Some of your students should take the other side. They should argue that many men are sensitive to women's concerns, that more men than women have the experience necessary to make them good administrators, and that assumptions like this lead to reverse discrimination against men. For even more controversy, ask whether a college with a dearth of women administrators or professors should establish a policy of hiring women rather than equally qualified men whenever possible.

Your students will probably focus the discussion on questions of fairness to applicants for administrative and teaching positions. You may want to shift the focus by asking, "What is fair to students?" If we agree with Perry that a liberal education should teach students frames of reference so that they can understand "how the other fellow orders knowledge," aren't we ethically obligated to hire administrators and professors who can contribute multiple perspectives? As the recent Supreme Court decisions concerning affirmative action programs demonstrate, there are no easy answers to this question.

—M.R.D.—

Style Lesson 54:
Varying Sentence Length for Emphasis

To get a sense of how Rich varies her sentence lengths to achieve emphasis, combine the choppy sentences below into as many sentences as you feel appropriate. Rich herself writes two sentences, a long first one leading to the impact of the shorter second one. (See paragraph 6 of "Claiming an Education" after you are finished.)

1. I think that any Douglass student should investigate women's studies courses.
2. I think every Douglass student should enroll in women's studies courses.
3. She has everything to gain by doing this.
4. But at the same time I want to suggest something else.
5. There is a more essential experience.
6. You owe yourselves this experience.
7. Courses in womens' studies can greatly enrich it.
8. But finally, this experience depends on you.
9. It depends on your interactions with yourself.
10. It depends on your interactions with your world.
11. It depends on all of them.
12. This is the experience of *taking responsibility for yourself.*

SAMUEL SCUDDER

Learning to See

This autobiographical narrative—written 120 years ago—has achieved fame because it is a naturally occurring parable. That is, Scudder's apparently simple intentions are to praise his teacher Louis Agassiz and reminisce about his college days, but the method of instruction he describes raises profound issues about the nature of education and the nature of knowledge. To tell students to look at a fish (or a sonnet or a society) until they see what is there is to lift the veil on the great epistemological questions that unsettle every active mind from time to time and periodically unhinge whole academic disciplines.

One can easily imagine three types of response to this reading. Some students may see it as a more-or-less interesting anecdote about an eccentric man, something in the "My Most Unforgettable Character" vein. Some—especially some education majors—may see it as a tribute to what is sometimes called "discovery learning." Some may see it as an essay that raises questions it never really deals with: in what sense is Scudder more right when he says that "the fish has symmetrical sides with paired organs" than when he says that it has "fleshy lips and lidless eyes"? What does Agassiz mean when he says that "facts are stupid things until brought into connection with some general law"? Where do these general laws come from?

The essay's theme of first seeing-without-seeing and then learning to look is shared with Annie Dillard's "Seeing," an essay very different in style and tone.

QUESTIONS

1. By what means does Scudder build drama into this essay?

Some of your students may be inclined to say that such drama as the essay has was just *there,* in the episode itself, and that Scudder can take no credit for it. In fact, the narrative is "shaped" to fit our society's concept of a dramatic story. Scudder presents Agassiz so as to make him a memorable character and he plots the rising action carefully. To show students how this plotting works, you might introduce the five-part pyramid used by dramatic theorist Gustav Freytag.

c
b d
a e

a. The *introduction* (paragraphs 1–8), besides giving us enough information to orient ourselves in time and space, reveals the key conflict: Scudder's desire on the one hand to please the eminent professor and his aversion, on the other hand, to the tasks the professor sets him, which seem fishy in more than one sense ("gazing at a fish did not commend itself to an ardent entomologist").

b. The phase of *rising action* (paragraphs 9–18) shows Scudder alternating between hope and despair. He begins in difficulty, alone with the loathsome fish for hours. His state begins to improve when he decides to sketch the fish and is able to "discover new features in the creature." He plunges back into despair when Agassiz tells him he has missed "one of the most conspicuous features," but hope rises again when, piqued, he sees "one new thing after another" about the fish and also sees "how little he saw before." Each alternation between despair and hope seems more significant than the last.

c. The *climax* (paragraphs 19–23) is Agassiz's challenge to Scudder to be "ready with a better answer in the morning" and Scudder's success in answering.

d. The phase of *falling action* (paragraphs 24–30) outlines Scudder's continuing progress with the haemulons.

e. The *dénouement* (paragraphs 31–33) judges Agassiz's teaching not so fishy after all: "what I had gained . . . has been of greater value than years of later investigation in my favorite groups."

Once students see the structure of the essay, they can appreciate the skill with which Scudder builds to the climax. At each juncture during the rising action, he gives us a sense of the tension between his frustration and his hope. He shows us what ingenuity and intelligence he has shown and *still* failed to satisfy the professor. And so at the climax the question seems genuinely in doubt, and we sympathize with the difficulties (and sleeplessness) Scudder describes in paragraph 20.

2. In what sense is Scudder more right when he observes that "the fish has symmetrical sides and paired organs" than when he observes that it has "fringed gill-arches and a movable operculum"?

Of course, it is possible to argue (and some students may) that Scudder was equally right in both cases, but that he wasn't saying what the professor wanted to hear. If a fact is a fact, then answers are either right or wrong, and there are no degrees of rightness. But as we can see from paragraph 32, Agassiz was not persuaded that all facts are equally valuable: "Facts are stupid things . . . until brought into connection with some general law." It appears that Agassiz's method of instruction was to insist, on the one hand, that students learn to observe as many factual details as possible and, on the other, that they be able to distinguish those details that have broad implications and applications from those that don't. I am not enough of a biologist to understand the full significance of "symmetrical sides and paired organs," but I do know that this sort of symmetry exists not only among fish but among, essentially, all animals from the lowly flatworm up, with the number of specialized organs increasing as the species get larger and more complex. This bilateral symmetry has implications for comparative anatomy (fins as homologues to arms and wings) and for embryology—every field that has to do with the complex organization and development of animals. To the non-biologist, the striking differences between, say, an oak tree and a grasshopper may be size and mobility. The biologist may think it more important that the oak tree has few specialized organs and that those it has (flower parts, for instance) can be produced in any number according to environmental circumstances, while the grasshopper has many specialized organs, placed according to an exact plan. The presence and placement of these organs has a great deal to do both with why grasshoppers do not keep growing to indefinite size, as trees do, and with why they are able to move around. Agassiz is training Scudder to find significance where trained biologists find it.

3. Is Agassiz's method of instruction preferable to the more traditional use of textbooks and lectures? Is it applicable in other disciplines?

"Preferable" raises all sorts of issues that may come up in class. What the professor prefers, the student may not. What the passionately committed student prefers, the casual one may not. If the aim of education is to convey information, Agassiz's method is, in the short term at least, agonizingly slow. Even if the aim is to equip students to make discoveries on their own, it could be argued that *teaching* a method of investigation is better than putting students in a situation where they will have to invent one.

On the other hand, there are powerful arguments for discovery learning, and as a teacher and former student, you know them too well for me to need to repeat them. The difference in the quality of students' attention when they are being lectured at and when they are trying to work out a problem on their own is remarkable. The business of education might better be defined as producing thinking people than as producing people who have received a certain quantity of knowledge and are prepared to receive more, etc.

Is the Agassiz method applicable to other fields? It will be interesting to see what your students have to say about this. I am inclined to think that with some adaptations, it can be widely applied. A friend of mine in the history department gives undergraduate history students a "document" (a handbill produced by the Lowell mill women, for example) and asks them to figure out its significance for themselves and write up a report. In literature classes, I am inclined to set a sonnet in front of the class with almost as little prologue as Agassiz used when he set the fish in front of Scudder.

—D.H.—

Style Lesson 55: "Not Only . . . But Also"

Linguists tell us that by the time we reach adolescence, we have acquired all the grammatical structures of our language. This doesn't mean, however, that we produce them readily either in speech or in writing. One useful construction we underuse is the coordinating conjunction not only . . . but also, *which allows the writer to organize a good deal of material into a sentence with a climax. Imitate the following example from paragraph 20 of Scudder's essay, writing on a subject of your choice:*

Not only must I think of my fish all night,
    studying
        without the object before me,
    what this unknown
        but most visible
    feature might be;
but also,
        without reviewing my discoveries,
    I must give an exact account of them the next day.

ANNIE DILLARD

Seeing

We elected to use this half-chapter from *Pilgrim at Tinker Creek* rather than "Sight into Insight," the widely anthologized essay containing some of the same material, because the *Pilgrim* version gives a clearer picture of how much the mind controls what we see. Most of us take our vision for granted, of course. Unless we are caught by surprise (by a *trompe l'oeil* painting, perhaps, or a wall-sized mirror) we forget that we are constantly interpreting our seamless visual field and mentally constructing three-dimensional space and separate objects. As people who have worked with "object recognition" in robotics know very well, this is an enormously difficult task.

As with most difficult intellectual tasks, we routinely lower the level of difficulty by resorting to categories (or clichés). When we were children learning to see, we might have inspected a piece of dining-room furniture minutely before categorizing it as a chair. Now we hardly glance. We are so good at recognizing chairs that we lose the individual specimen in the category; we don't notice the nicks on the chair legs or the way the seat has discolored with use. We routinely see only as much as is necessary. In a sense, all of *Pilgrim at Tinker Creek* is devoted to countering this routinization, but "Seeing" is Dillard's clearest explanation of her resistance.

QUESTIONS

1. In paragraph 2 Dillard cites the example of one cataract patient who thinks that "Everything looks flat with dark patches" and in paragraph 3 she cites the example of another who thinks that a dog who steps behind a chair no longer exists. What do these two examples suggest about the way people with ordinary eyesight see?

There are a number of possible answers here, most of which have to do with the fact that seeing involves the mind quite as much as the eye.

One thing these examples help us understand is why normally sighted toddlers behave as they do: throwing toys from their high chair or crib, putting things into containers and taking them out immediately, walking backward while they keep their eyes fixed on a television or a chair, stopping in the middle of a sidewalk to stoop down and touch their shadow. To someone who is paying attention strictly to what the eyes reveal, it isn't self-evident that objects only *seem* to diminish in size as they get further from us, or that they aren't erased when they leave our sight, or that light and shadows don't have substance. All of these things have to be established out through experimentation and theorizing, with enormous mental effort.

The examples also tell us how many visual phenomena we ignore because we have become accustomed to interpreting them according to our standard assumptions that (1) space is three-dimensional, (2) objects can exist without our being able to perceive them, and (3) light and shadow are essentially substanceless. These *are* assumptions, however much they have become part of what we call common sense. The conversation between the girl and her mother about the photograph is a philosopher's delight. The girl in paragraph 2 can't (without a mental skill she hasn't mastered) see the dark patches as shadows and the world the photograph represents as having depth, but neither can the mother (without an unaccustomed mental effort) see the photograph as a flat sheet with dark patches on it. Surely the girl's interpretation is at least as valid as her mother's. If the girl has not yet understood roundness, the mother has been blinded to flatness. Similarly, the patient who thinks that when objects leave his visual field, they vanish from existence may be wrong (I personally think he is), but he is not being illogical. He is trusting the evidence of his senses in a way that most of us have learned not to do. When the chair partially eclipses the dog, we don't notice that her hindquarters are missing. Instead, we unconsciously supply the hindquarters from memory. We don't trust our senses too far. If we did, we would be considered mentally unbalanced.

2. After discussing van Senden's book, Dillard discusses two contrasting ways that she sees the world. Explain these two ways in your own words.

It's probably important to get your student's eyes off their books to discuss this question. Dillard makes the distinction between two ways of seeing very clear, but she does so largely by metaphor, and students need to distance themselves from her metaphors before they can be sure of their own understanding. We could say that one type of seeing is scrupulous, the other, as she enjoys putting it, "unscrupulous" (paragraph 12). Students might call the second way "laid-back" or "mystical" or "stoned." The scrupulous method is guided by words, and words are attached to concepts. The unscrupulous leaves words and concepts behind. The scrupulous is scientific; it is the method Samuel Scudder uses in "Learning to See." The unscrupulous makes no attempt to learn or analyze; it tries to see the world as the newly sighted would see it.

What Dillard doesn't say and students need to realize is that both the scrupulous and the unscrupulous methods are quite different from our ordinary dullness of sight. Ordinarily, language and experience limit our vision without focusing it. We see a bright light in the sky and say to ourselves that it is the moon. Period. If we were scrupulous observers, we might at least notice which phase it is in and the constellation; we might notice its color in the present conditions of the atmosphere; we might name (and therefore notice) the visible craters. If we were unscrupulous, we might be dazzled by the moon, feel it as a presence; we might reach for it, as children do (see paragraph 8).

3. In paragraph 8, Dillard reports that she finds it hard to "unpeach the peaches." What does she mean by this? Why is it hard?

This might be the best single question to ask as a way of testing your students' comprehension. The apparently enigmatic phrase encapsulates the whole idea of seeing "Eden before Adam gave names" (paragraph 9). Unnamed and unshaped by experience, the peaches would not be peaches at all, but color patches among other color patches. To be able to see them this way would be, for Dillard, a glorious thing—a return to the senses (see the allusion to Thoreau in paragraph 14). But unmediated experience is next to impossible. Having learned to see the world as three-dimensional, we can't long sustain a vision of it as two-dimensional (unless we happen to be, say, impressionist painters). Having learned that these particular patches of a particularly beautiful color are peaches, we can look at one only briefly before the general idea of peachiness overtakes us and we lose interest in the particular thing in front of us.

Dillard can unpeach the peach better than most of us. Paragraph 13, where she "unpeaches" Tinker Creek with fish beneath its surface and petals on top and sees instead an unscrolling field of pale circles and linear flashes is a good example. But, of course, the moment she puts her vision into words, she has begun to re-peach the peach, reducing what she actually saw into the categories of "circles" and "flashes." Some students will misunderstand this passage and think it is merely a bit of pretty writing. It is probably better thought of as an ambitious attempt to record a brief escape from the tyranny of words. George Orwell, though his methods are different, would understand.

—D.H.—

PATRICIA HAMPL

Memory and Imagination

If I wanted to inspire my students to do serious autobiographical writing, I would begin with "Memory and Imagination." The essay is a first-rate defense of the memoir against those who see it as mere self-indulgence, and it contains passages so well written that when I set the essay aside, I find myself looking at my yellow pad with fresh appreciation for what is possible.

The essay begins with a memoir about 1,200 words long, about the length of many of the personal experience papers students write in their composition classes. For reasons she explains later in the essay, Hampl sees this piece as a rough draft, but it is a beauty. When I read it, I wanted to know how the writer felt about it, what she thought it meant, where she thought it was leading her, what she saw as the value of writing this sort of memoir. Hampl teaches a course in memoir writing and is especially articulate on these questions.

QUESTIONS

1. What good does it do for a person of no particular public importance to write a memoir?

I ask this question in this way to get one issue out of the way as quickly as possible. The memoirs of public figures, generally ghost-written or "as told to" books, serve one set of functions. They are sometimes resources for historians, sometimes sources of public gossip. They are always written with the audience in mind and sometimes, as E. B. White puts it, according to "the dulcet notion that the reader is feeble-minded." The sort of memoir Hampl writes conducts more private business, and one gathers that she would find it worth writing if it never found its way into print. It is a search for truth.

She gives us two very good reasons for undertaking such a search. One is therapeutic, neatly expressed in a single sentence that could be unpacked into several books: "Our capacity to move forward as developing beings rests on a healthy relation to the past" (paragraph 45). The memoirist is engaged in psychotherapy. Notice, for instance, that on examining her first draft, Hampl has to relive a portion of her childhood: her admiration of Mary Katherine Reilly, her longings and disappointments, of which the red piano book becomes the symbol. Writing the memoir brings the emotions back to the surface. "Stalking the relationship, seeking the congruence between stored image and hidden emotion—that's the real job of memoir" (paragraph 34).

The second reason is more political and philosophical. In class discussion, I might want to start on this one by considering Hampl's statement that "even legal documents are only valiant attempts to consign the truth, the whole truth, and nothing but the truth to paper. Even they remain versions" (paragraph 46). A philosophy professor once told me that college freshmen are generally naive realists: they believe that there is one truth about an event, unaffected by the perspective of the beholder. (See Perry's "Examsmanship and the Liberal Arts" for a discussion of this world view.) Only as their education progresses and they are exposed to contradictory frames of reference do they begin to understand the relativity of truth. Who discovered America? Columbus, of course—unless you happen to be an American Indian or a fancier of Leif Ericson or Thor Heyerdahl. There are versions of the truth, and until we begin to make our own version especially of the things nearest to us, we are naked, helpless, subject to the first version presented to us: "The version we dare to write is the only truth, the only relationship we can have with the past. Refuse to write your life and you have no life" (paragraph 47, see also paragraphs 43 and 44).

Beyond these two forthright reasons for memoir, there is another truth too subtle for me to articulate, one Hampl makes a careful reader feel in the last nine paragraphs: "the attempt to find not only a self but a world," "the endless and tragic recollection that is history," "the attractive impersonality of something more significant than ourselves." Memoir makes palpable once more a world that has dissolved, but that is at the same time more permanent than the present, removed from the turbulence of the passing moment, more real: "But the past is radiant. It has the light of lived life. A memoirist wishes to touch it."

2. Despite Hampl's very personal motives for writing the memoir of her piano lesson, it is a pleasure for a stranger to read. Why?

What makes "First Piano Lesson" a memoir rather than a journal entry is that it is written to interest and inform an audience of strangers. It says things better than we would ever need to say them to ourselves or to a friend. All your students will have their favorite bits. I enjoy the humor of congruities and incongruities, chords and discords. I smile every time I read about sister Olive looking like an olive "rolled out of a can and laid on the white plate of her broad, spotless wimple." It is a sight gag, something out of a Magritte painting, but it is also part of the childlike sweetness of the piece, every child's search for things that fit. It is precisely of a piece with the discovery that "Middle C is the belly button of the piano." The flip side, of course, is Sister Olive's sneezing in the sun: "Things were not, after all, necessarily what they seemed. Appearance deceived: here was the sun acting totally out of character. . . ." All this is amusing because it is not a literal transcription of events, but a presentation of events in a way that brings order to them. The interplay of congruities and incongruities must amuse Hampl as much as it amuses us, but she would surely not have discovered it if she were writing to herself.

3. Why does Hampl say that "A careful first draft is a failed first draft"?

A full answer to this question is a review of the entire essay, which I won't inflict on you here. Hampl's comments should help you reinforce the point that writing proceeds by stages and that in the early stages, most writers are better off being less engaged with presenting a well-packaged product than with exploring their subject. Certainly this is true of a writer like Hampl, who relies heavily on subconscious processes. Writers in more technical or objective fields like Garrett Hardin and John Kenneth Galbraith may be somewhat more careful, but Galbraith once said that what he writes on a bad day requires five revisions and that what he writes when inspired only needs four. This amount of labor from so intelligent and experienced a writer suggests that, like Hampl, he begins with the "mess of my mind trying to find out what it wants to say" (paragraph 25).

4. Where does Hampl's style draw attention to itself? Is the effect of such passages good or bad?

I hope this question will lead your class to discuss the thorny questions of overwriting and underwriting. Overwriting is, of course, the danger commonly warned against. George Orwell, for instance, insists that prose should be like a windowpane through which the reader can see the subject undistracted, yet the careful reader will stop several times in "Politics and the English Language" to admire an apt simile. E. B. White's advice to young writers is to "keep yourself in the background," but the impact of his own essays is always a result of a tone and style his admirers would recognize if they found it buried in the instructions for a tax form. The advice that prose should not draw attention to itself is surely too simple. Perhaps we should say that a good stylist never harasses the reader with superfluous shows, but occasionally writes a phrase so striking that the reader instinctively underlines it.

Most of my underlines in "Memory and Imagination" are beneath similes and metaphors. Besides the delightful Sister-Olive-as-olive metaphors in paragraph 2 and the Middle C metaphors in paragraph 4, I like the following:

- ". . . the powerful waves of the sentences laying themselves on the smooth beach of the page one after another faultlessly" (paragraph 24)
- the reader as cat and the writer as dog (paragraph 26)
- the first draft as "a mystery which drops clues to the riddle of my feelings, like a culprit who wishes to be apprehended" (paragraph 32)
- the Thompson piano book as "the small red door leading straight into the dark room of my childhood longing and disappointment" (paragraph 39)
- the memoirist as a pilgrim (final paragraph)

Each of these figures of speech would pass Orwell's tests of freshness and usefulness in making meaning clear.

Other things I marked were aphorisms, fragments, and other short, muscular expressions:

> "A careful first draft is a failed first draft" (paragraph 30).
>
> "Pain likes to be vivid" (paragraph 33).
>
> "Just can't be done" (paragraph 47).
>
> "Maybe, but I don't buy that" (paragraph 52).

This sort of expression ballasts the essay, keeps its more musical passages from drawing it into the clouds. My favorite of all Hampl lines, by the way, does not appear in *The Dolphin Reader*. "To make a metaphor is to make a fuss," she once wrote. All the monkeys since the dawn of time pounding at all the keyboards ever made couldn't have produced that sentence. It is pure Hampl.

—D.H.—

Style Lesson 56: Contrasting Metaphors

In paragraph 26, Hampl uses contrasting metaphors to clarify her vision of the reader and the writer. To practice both her metaphorical technique and her syntax, imitate the passage, either developing your own vision of the reader and writer or developing a contrast between two other things that interest you. Remember that the quality of the metaphor is what counts: both its aptness and its interest.

I sometimes think of the reader as a cat,
    endlessly fastidious,
    capable, by turns,
            of mordant indifference and
                riveted attention,
    luxurious,
    recumbent, and
    ever poised.
Whereas the writer is absolutely a dog,
    panting and moping,
    too eager
        for an affectionate scratch behind the ears,
    lunging frantically
        after any old stick thrown in the distance.

FRANK CONROY

Think About It

In this essay about the retrospective nature of understanding, the way that the meaning of an event may only come to us long after the event itself, Conroy describes three seemingly unrelated incidents. The first involves two black men who run a shoeshine shop in the subway; the second concerns jazz pianist Red Garland; the third features Justice William O. Douglas and Judge Learned Hand. Conroy uses these incidents to illustrate two different kinds of understanding: understanding that comes when a problem is solved "with a resolving kind of click" and understanding that comes when we realize that some problems will never resolve. Conroy's two categories echo what Carol Bly in "Growing Up Expressive" refers to as our "two kinds of receptivity to life"—our mental capacity to solve solvable problems and our spiritual capacity to ponder the great questions—"love, death, power, time, the universe"—that can never be reduced to solvable problems.

This essay invites student writing. Conroy describes two instances when he is presented with information he can't understand. Later, however, after his life experiences provide a context for that information, he experiences a blinding flash of illumination. Your students can follow this pattern—confusion/subsequent experience/understanding—to describe their own experiences of delayed understanding. Or they may prefer to write about "those problems that will never resolve." Conroy suggests that law is one of those problems, and your students will be able to suggest other areas of understanding that continue to evolve.

QUESTIONS

1. What are the two kinds of understanding described by Conroy?

Conroy distinguishes between two different kinds of understanding. The first, which we might label the "Aha" experience, occurs when the incomprehensible suddenly becomes clear. Conroy relates two incidents that illustrate that kind of understanding. In one he finally realizes why two black men who run a shoeshine stand in the subway always stare over their shoulders into the distance. In the second he eventually makes sense of jazz pianist Red Garland's statement that he is playing sixths. In both examples the "aha" comes in the final chapter of a mystery that begins when Conroy is presented with information that doesn't fit into what he already knows, and concludes when his life catches up with that information. "The light bulb may appear over your head . . . but it may be awhile before it actually goes on" (paragraph 5).

The second kind of understanding, which we could label the "Hmm" experience, occurs when the certain gradually becomes uncertain. To illustrate this process, Conroy recalls his "brief time as a messenger boy" for Justice William O. Douglas and Judge Learned Hand, who are indirectly exchanging thoughts about *Dennis v. United States.* When Douglas tells Conroy to ask Hand about "clear and present danger," Conroy is reluctant to do so because Douglas's argument seems "crushing—the last word really" and Conroy doesn't want to embarrass Hand by showing how wrong he is (paragraph 15). Hand, of course, is not crushed. Instead, he counters with an equally crushing argument. Conroy looks forward to delivering Hand's rebuttal, and he hopes that a few more exchanges will resolve the matter, but Douglas is gone. Conroy is disappointed, but he eventually realizes that no matter how many times he went back and forth between the two men, the matter would not be resolved. He recognizes that understanding the law is not a matter of getting an answer, but of living in the ebb and flow of conflicting, powerful, irreconcilable arguments.

2. How successful is Conroy in presenting Justice William O. Douglas and Judge Learned Hand as human beings rather than awe-inspiring great men? How do his character sketches of these two jurists add to our understanding of the nature of law?

It isn't easy to present "great men" as human beings, but Conroy succeeds in doing just that. For most people, the titles "Justice of the United States Supreme Court" and "Judge of the United States Court of Appeals" evoke pictures of solemn old men in long black robes. To dispel that image, Conroy focuses on the private personalities of these two men rather than on their public achievements.

Conroy introduces Douglas by describing him as Conroy first saw him—a "strange man sitting by himself" at a student hangout on a college campus (paragraph 8). After Douglas tells Conroy that he is on the Supreme Court, Douglas counters that startling bit of news with the request, "Call me Bill" (paragraph 9). Conroy gives us no additional information about Douglas's reputation, achievements, awards, and honors. For example, he doesn't tell us that Douglas was known as a defender of civil liberties, that he served on the Supreme Court for thirty-six and one half years (1939–1975), that he was an avid naturalist and conservationist, and that in addition to writing court opinions and articles for legal periodicals, he published approximately thirty books, including *Beyond the High Himalayas, We The Judges, Mr. Lincoln and the Negroes,* and *A Wilderness Bill of Rights.*

Conroy also introduces Hand in an unorthodox way, characterizing him as "my girlfriend's grandfather" before labeling him "chief judge of the most important court in the country save the Supreme Court itself" (paragraph 9). Conroy uses only one sentence to note that Hand had served on the bench for fifty years and had become a famous man, a weighty observation that Conroy lightens by stating that Hand had become "a living legend, to his own dismay" (paragraph 8). Again, Conroy's sketch of Hand is notable for what it omits. He doesn't tell us that Hand studied philosophy at Harvard under Professors Santayana, Royce, and William James; that, in an opinion written in 1947, Hand devised a formula for determining negligence that is still studied by first-year law students; and that Hand's judicial opinions are known for their stylistic brilliance. If your students are curious about which other facts Conroy omitted, you might refer them to *Current Biography*. Curiously, biographical sketches of both Douglas and Hand are included in the 1950 volume.

After introducing each jurist, Conroy fleshes them out. To illustrate the use of memorable specifics, you might put "Douglas" and "Hand" on the board and then write down all the particular details your students can remember without looking back at the essay. For example, they may recall that Conroy compares Douglas's eyes to "blue ice" and states, "His eyes gave nothing away about himself while at the same time creating in me the eerie impression that he was looking directly into my soul" (paragraph 9). And they will probably remember that Hand "had a large repertoire of dramatic expressions involving the use of his eyebrows" (paragraph 10), and that after Conroy conveyed Douglas's comment about clear and present danger, "Hand's eyebrows writhed on his face like two huge caterpillars" (paragraph 19).

Conroy's portraits of these two legal giants are fascinating in and of themselves. These vivid character sketches also remind us that the personalities and intellects of our jurists greatly influence the interpretation and evolution of our laws.

3. What does Conroy's encounter with Justice Douglas and Judge Hand teach him about the nature of law? Which other areas of understanding develop in similar ways?

With only the information provided in the essay, your students will realize that Conroy learns that law is not an immutable truth. But they may not understand why Douglas and Hand were both so interested in the *Dennis*, and their knowledge of our legal system may be limited to information and misinformation gained from *L.A. Law*. Consequently, you may want to provide them with some background information.

Like Conroy, most people (including first-year law students) think of "the law" as a set of clear rules. The first week of law school disabuses law students of that erroneous notion. They soon learn that "the law" involves complicated interactions among many different laws, including statutes and case law (judge-made law). Each year 15,000 statutes are enacted by Congress, our fifty legislatures, and the various local governments. Each year 55,000 cases decided by state and federal courts are published (for a total thus far of 3,000,000). And in each of those cases one or more judges takes a general principle of law (such as clear and present danger) and decides how that principle applies to the specific facts of the case before the court. To make case law as uniform and predictable as possible, judges are required to follow precedent, which means that their decisions must be consistent with earlier decisions handed down by higher courts in their jurisdiction. (In other words, a Missouri court has to follow precedent established by the Missouri Supreme Court, but it can ignore the decisions of other state courts.) Naturally, a judge's personal philosophy can influence the outcome of the case. Considering these complexities, your students should understand why Aaron Burr defined the law as "that which is boldly asserted and plausibly maintained."

The case Conroy refers to, *Dennis v. United States*, began when Eugene Dennis and ten other defendants were indicted for violating a federal statute (the Smith Act), which made it unlawful to advocate the violent overthrow of the United States government. Among other things, they were accused of conspiring to organize as the Communist Party of the United States of America. After a trial that lasted nine months and resulted in a record 16,000 pages long, the defendants were found guilty. They appealed their conviction to the Second Circuit Court of Appeals (where Judge Learned Hand was the chief judge), claiming that the Smith Act unconstitutionally violated their First Amendment rights. The Court of Appeals affirmed their conviction. The defendants then asked the United States Supreme Court to consider the case. The Supreme Court did so, but it too affirmed the convictions. The Supreme Court opinion written by Chief Justice Vinson adopted Judge Hand's definition of clear and present danger: "In each case [courts] must ask whether the gravity of the 'evil,' discounted by its improbability, justifies such invasion of speech as is necessary to avoid the danger." Justice Douglas wrote a ten-page dissent. And, as Conroy suggests, the definition of "clear and present danger" continues to evolve.

Your students should be able to list a number of other areas where there are no final truths. Philosophy, literary criticism, medical ethics, economics, and physics are good choices. All lead us to "embrace the tension of never being certain, never being absolutely sure, never being done . . ." (paragraph 22).

—M.R.D.—

CAROL BLY

Growing Up Expressive

In this essay Bly offers an unusual criticism of American public schools. No, she doesn't complain that Johnny and Heather can't read, can't locate Iraq on a world map, can't speak Japanese, and can't do fifty pushups. In fact she urges us to tell our teachers that "we don't give a damn if LeRoy and Merv never in their lives get the sentence balance of past conditional and perfect subjunctive clauses right."

Bly's concern is that our schools have been too successful in teaching children to become problem-solvers. She argues that an education focused on solving tiny, solvable problems causes students to develop a kind of tunnel vision that blinds them to the great subjects—"love, death, power, time, the universe"—because "there are no immediate answers to the questions [those subjects] ask us." Bly offers an alternative, an approach to teaching that she believes will encourage children "to grow up into lovers, lobby supporters, and Amnesty International members, instead of only township officers and annual protestors against daylight saving time."

QUESTIONS

1. In Bly's opinion, what do we lose because our schools teach our students to be problem solvers? Do you agree?

Bly describes two different human impulses: the impulse to solve the solvable and the impulse to contemplate the insolvable. She labels the first "the mental genius of our species" and the second "the spiritual genius of our species." Her concern is that because our schools encourage only the first impulse, our children will learn to ignore the second and will grow into spiritually crippled adults who can recognize an adjective but who have lost the ability to be moved by "love, death, the cruelty of power, and time's curve past the stars" (paragraph 1). Such spiritually undernourished adults will work hard to smooth out the "sticky places in county government," but they will never contemplate the morality of germ warfare (paragraph 4).

Students may resist Bly's conclusion, at least partly because they are products of the education system she condemns and they may be reluctant to label themselves spiritually stunted. Even if they agree that our spiritual/mystical impulses need nurturing, they may argue that families and religious leaders, not schools, should provide that kind of education.

2. Which professionals do you think of as obvious examples of people who are trained as problem solvers? Which professionals does Bly discuss? Why would she choose them?

You might begin this discussion by asking your students to name professionals who are trained to solve problems. It seems to me that the obvious answers are engineers, business graduates, and lawyers (but I realize lawyers would not be an obvious answer for students who believe lawyers are trained to create problems). Bly, however, mentions less obvious choices—teachers, doctors, and the clergy.

It is certainly true that teachers learn the problem-solving approach while they are in college. Methodology classes teach would-be teachers to establish specific objectives, plan activities that will enable their students to achieve those objectives, and design test questions that will determine whether students mastered those objectives. That's the process Bly criticizes in paragraph 4. Bly doesn't discuss the training methods used by medical schools, but she does note that a doctor who has the problem-solving mentality will not want to be near dying patients because they "definitely are not a solvable problem" (paragraph 2). We have to infer that doctors acquire that problem-solving mentality while they are in medical school, but that inference is supported by Dr. Perri Klass in "Learning the Language" (*Insiders and Outsiders*). Bly also claims that religious leaders are now trained in "psychological problem solving" (paragraph 23) and that churches "see life and death as a *problem*—a problem of salvation—with a solution to be worked at (paragraph 24).

It's more than a little disconcerting to think that teachers, doctors, and clergy—the professionals charged with nurturing our minds, our bodies, and our souls—may be learning to disregard everything that can't be reduced to a problem-solution format.

3. As a thought experiment, imagine a school that would meet Bly's expectations. How would it be structured? What would the curriculum include? What would the teachers be like? What would the students do from hour to hour? How would grades be determined? What obstacles would you encounter if you tried to persuade a school's board of education, administration, and faculty to try your ideas?

This question will demonstrate that Bly presents us with a vision, not a plan. She suggests questions that a teacher might ask about three specific assignments, and she recommends that we make English teachers responsible for encouraging the development of our children's mystical-spiritual potential, but she leaves the details of implementation to us. Consequently, your students' concepts of a Bly school should vary greatly. Some plans may be quite traditional—except for their English classes. Other plans may call for a complete restructuring of curriculum and scheduling. But all should mention specific ways to promote what Bly calls "imaginative inquiry" (paragraph 11).

The obstacles your students imagine will, of course, vary according to their proposals. My guess is that most school boards would first want to know whether this plan would be more expensive. I think the answer to that question would have to be "yes" because we would need at least twice as many English teachers to read and respond fully to students' writings. School boards might also worry that this approach would lead to the teaching of values, always a minefield in a heterogeneous society where there is no consensus about which values to teach. Administrators would raise concerns about accountability. Now that standardized tests reign supreme, schools are blamed when their students are not (like the children of Lake Woebegone) "all above average," and administrators are understandably reluctant to allow time for anything that isn't measured by those tests. Teachers who don't teach English classes probably wouldn't care (so long as English teachers continued to teach their students to do library research, to write clear and concise answers on essay exams, to read critically, to write term papers, etc., etc., etc.).

English teachers presented with Bly's idea would surely consider a new career:

> I would like to commend this responsibility to our English teachers: that they help our children preserve pity, happiness, and grief inside themselves. They can enhance those feelings by having young children both write and draw pictures. They can be very en-

thusiastic about the children's first drawings of death in the sky (paragraph 25).

Actually, that's precisely what most English teachers would like to do. People don't become English teachers because they enjoy marking spelling errors. But the typical high school English teacher has at least 150 students, at least five classes to teach each day, and at least a three-foot-high stack of papers to grade. Under those circumstances, how could any teacher take on the time-consuming and emotionally overwhelming task of teaching our children "the fearless contemplation of gigantic things"?

—M.R.D.—

Style Lesson 57:
An Extended Sentence-Combining Exercise

The following kernel sentences are culled from paragraph 16 of "Growing Up Expressive." Practice economy and coherence by combining them to form 4–10 sentences (Bly's original has 6.) Your arrangement may require changes in order and wording. In square brackets are hints about Bly's wording.

1. A few years ago there was a stupid movement.
2. It was a movement to discourage children from reading a book.
3. The book was Grimms' fairy tales.
4. Later psychology became more sophisticated. [*with*]
5. We learned that a kind of stepmother is a reality to all children.
6. This kind of stepmother is hostile and overweening.
7. We learned that the cutting-off of a hand is a reality to all children.
8. The hand belongs to the hero.
9. It is his right hand.
10. It is replaced with another hand. [*-ing of*]
11. The other hand is made of silver.
12. There is an inner landscape. [Bly holds this till #17.]
13. Spaceships are part of it.
14. Witches' gingerbread houses are part of it.
15. Orphanages are part of it.
16. Being the last two people to survive on earth is part of it.
17. The inner landscape is something children know about. [*—all these*]
18. Therefore we need a better set of questions.
19. We need to ask children these questions.
20. We need to ask them when we are examining their artwork.
21. Some young people are going to lay their stuff in front of adults.
22. It is wild stuff.
23. These are young people who are not repressed. [*who*]
24. They will do this until the sands of life are run.
25. They are hoping for comment of some kind.
26. They are hoping for praise if possible.
27. We had better try to be good at responding to them. [*so*]
28. We are enthusiastic when they tell us something.
29. The something is "Mama, I've got the mowing done."
30. We had better be half as enthusiastic in another situation.
31. That situation is when they lay their stuff in front of us.
32. Otherwise we are acting as if we want to raise drones.
33. These drones are suitable only for conveyor-belt shifts.

WILLIAM RODMAN

When Questions Are Answers: The Message of Anthropology, According to the People of Ambae

If one of the aims of your course is to prepare students to write in a number of academic disciplines, you could treat Rodman's essay as an example from the social sciences. It has the earmarks of a standard journal publication: citation of sources, terms of art, use of headings, list of references cited. The essay's appeal for most readers, however, has nothing (directly) to do with the way it illustrates the folkways of publishing scholars. It can be read as a narrative in the tradition of *Gulliver's Travels*, fascinating because of the strange customs of the people it introduces us to, doubly fascinating when we compare our own strange customs to theirs. Rodman's story has yet another fascination Swift's does not—the Ambaens are real.

Two things make Rodman's essay fit well in *Understanding*. Generally, the meeting of two cultures shows how context can change the meaning of an event. More specifically, the Ambaen practice of *qaltavalu* ("hidden talk") provides students with a clear and colorful example of the way that subtext, narrative, and social context interact to create meaning. You may find yourself telling your students to *qaltavalu* more skillfully when they write narrative essays or even when they choose the words in individual sentences.

Place names can be confusing to readers of this essay. Here's the gazetteer in a nutshell:

Vanatu is the name of the country formerly called New Hebrides

Ambae is the name of an island in *Vanatu*; it was formerly called *Aoba*.

Longana is the name of a small district on *Ambae*.

[Espiritu] Santo is the name of another island in *Vanatu*.

To simplify my comments, I have used *Ambae* and *Ambaen* wherever possible, thereby avoiding the names of the larger nation or the smaller district.

QUESTIONS

1. What is the meaning of *qaltavalu* in Ambaen culture, and what might it mean if applied to American culture?

Of course, an outsider on Ambaen culture will answer the first part of the question very imperfectly, as an Ambaen who has learned a bit about the United States could only imperfectly answer a question like "What is the meaning of *politics* in American culture?" And the second part of the question involves the added difficulty of finding equivalents in dissimilar cultures. Nonetheless, much can be learned by struggling with this question.

Students may be inclined to think that Rodman's simple translation "hidden talk" (paragraph 84) is a sufficient answer to both halves of the question. I would challenge this with follow-up questions. Would it be *qaltavalu* if a speaker confronted a single listener and talked to him in terms that he or she couldn't understand? No; *qaltavalu* must be understood by the listener. Would it be *qaltavalu* if the speaker lied to the listener, but failed to deceive the listener? No; *qaltavalu* assumes that the speaker wants to impart the information that a knowing listener receives. To avoid a misunderstanding that may be created by students who read the essay hastily, you may want to ask if *qaltavalu* is always intended to impart instruction. No; instruction is just one of the uses of *qaltavalu* (see paragraph 85).

Eventually students should recognize that *qaltavalu* is always directed at a listener who is capable of understanding the speaker's double meaning. It always occurs in situations where there is a reason to avoid direct expression—when a lover makes a first ambiguous overture, for example, or when a chief threatens to humiliate another chief (paragraph 85). Even when the message of the *qaltavalu* is hostile, the method itself reminds the hearer that he or she shares an implicit understanding with the speaker ("... *you* understand my meaning, even if everyone else does not"). To some extent, then a *qaltavalu* is an indication of that both speaker and listener are insiders. For this reason, as Rodman himself feels, it involves a compliment: "He was shaming me, in a sense, but he was also flattering me, trusting my local knowledge; a novice wouldn't catch the *qaltavalu*" (paragraph 100).

After thinking carefully about what is implied by *qaltavalu*, students will probably recognize that it does have analogs in Western culture. In a sense, all sarcasm is *qaltavalu*, including Bart Simpson's wisecracks, the *double-entendres* of the singles' bar and locker room. The language of diplomats is full of *qaltavalu*, most of which is lost on the general public, or else it wouldn't be true *qaltavalu*. But even the casual newspaper reader eventually realizes that when the State Department spokesperson issues a statement that the U.S. will "take most seriously" such and such an act by an unfriendly nation, she intends diplomats on the other end to understand that she is avoiding the plain language of a threat, but is hinting at what the threat would be if she uttered it. A fable or parable like Lois Gould's "X" is *qaltavalu*: she expects the reader to recognize that the story of the fabulous child is a fiction revealing truths about our society that she doesn't want to belabor by too much direct statement.

2. What is the meaning of *kastom* in Ambaen culture, and what might it mean if applied to American culture?

Of course, the meaning of *kastom* in Ambaen culture is the subject of some dispute among the Ambaens themselves. Some use the word only to refer to ritual pig-killing, but Andrew Namala's definition is more interesting: he sees it as the whole set of traditional activities—including farming, cooking, sand-drawing and pig-killing—raised to the level of art (see paragraphs 94–100). This definition forces broader application and a new distinction. Now many things either belong to *kastom* or they don't. For Andrew Namala, a traditional sand drawing, done with great artistry, clearly belongs to *kastom*, but a Sony Walkman does not. An awkward rank-taking, which some Ambaen's might see as synonymous with *kastom*, is for Andrew Namala a delusion: "I guess this is *kastom*, but it's sure a mess!" Business and money are for Andrew Namala are antithetical to *kastom*, and when pig-killing became a kind of business, it lost its customary significance.

Some of your students may want to argue that the things Andrew Namala sees as antithetical to *his kastom* are very much part of ours. "The business of America is business," the argument goes, and the teenager with a Walkman is acting in a way that is customary in our society. I'm not sure that this analysis is correct. *Kastom*, as William Rodman and Andrew Namala define it, is painstaking. It implies dedication and a willingness to forego the easiest and most obvious ways of acquiring status and other satisfactions. It implies apprenticeship. I'm not yet convinced that the teenager who sells fast food at the Mall and then spends his or her paycheck on a Walkman is observing American *kastom*. The cabinetmaker whose work is better than it needs to be for marketability, the angler who ties his or her own flies, and the musician (amateur or professional, electronic or acoustical) who wishes there were more hours a day to practice all strike me as cleaving more closely to *kastom*.

3. How would you describe Rodman's attitude toward the Ambaen people he studies?

Despite living in an age where cultural cocksureness is unstylish among well-educated people, some of your students may be unable to shake the assumption that non-Western cultures are simply backward. Indeed, I suspect that most of us tend to adopt this attitude unconsciously and to smile knowingly when we hear someone from Ambae report that his ancestors used to be able to make cyclones. I don't think your students will detect any signs of this smile in Rodman's essay. Rather than assuming the rightness of the Western "scientific" world view, he seems to submerge himself in Ambaen culture and so alter his world view in a way that makes him more able to understand the Ambaen view. From what my friends in anthropology tell me, I gather that this amounts to working within the "culture" (*kastom*?) of the discipline. Contemporary anthropologists recognize the "dialogic" and "reflexive" nature of the business, and realize that to *know* what they want to know will necessarily alter the minds that do the knowing. Continue to sneer at the idea of making a cyclone and you are forever cut off from certain levels of understanding.

Rodman's attitude goes beyond the non-judgmental stance necessary to his profession, however. His *personal* interest in and admiration for Nicodemus Wai and Andrew Namala is very evident. When he says that Nicodemus, "the 'revolutionary pussycat' was leading one of the most interesting lives of anyone I knew," (paragraph 16) he doesn't mean merely "anyone on Ambae." I wonder if Rodman would find the life of say, Ross Perot, more interesting. When he describes Andrew at his rank-taking (". . . a man radiant with energy, in complete control of his body, his every movement clean and precise"—paragraph 84) and in his storytelling (". . . Andrew was a master of the form"—paragraph 100) his admiration is obviously strong and sincere.

Given the residue of chauvinism in most Westerners' attitudes toward other cultures, Rodman has accomplished a great deal merely by opening himself up to this sort of admiration. To have written an essay that makes us feel the admiration, too, is a double coup—one that may reflect the best *kastom* of his discipline.

—D.H.—

Style Lesson 58: Order of Sentences in an Explanatory Paragraph

The following sentences, when unscrambled, form paragraph 84 of "When Questions are Answers." Put the sentences in logical order, using references and transitions as guides. You may discover an arrangement different from but as logical as Rodman's original; the goal is not to get the "right answer," but to be able to discuss the logical structuring of a paragraph.

1. It took me a while, but eventually I understood.
2. More commonly, it occurs as a rhetorical device in speeches: rival chiefs use *qaltavalu* against each other to devastating effect.
3. *Qaltavalu* says to a rival: "Look, I am speaking about you in public, and *you* understand my meaning, even if everyone else does not. Shall I make my meaning explicit, or will you change your way of acting?
4. The key to understanding Andrew's interpretation of his talk with the anthropologist (and also the key to the way in which he told me the story) is *qaltavalu*, literally "hidden talk," a form of communication based on a system of implicit meanings.
5. "Hidden talk" is the process; shame is the product.
6. The threat of public exposure is sanction (or blackmail) enough in a society in which people dread public humiliation.
7. People sometimes *qaltavalu* in everyday life; for example, a man may ask a woman for a plate of rice and not have food in mind at all.
8. Some mysteries, if you dream on them enough and have enough context, reveal themselves.
9. Or, perhaps, ". . . provide me with the support I need?"

JACOB BRONOWSKI

The Creative Mind

In the long pull, I think this is one of the most important essays in *The Dolphin Reader.* I want my liberal arts students to read it in order to avoid the naive view that science is the uncreative world of plain facts, and I want my science students to read it for precisely the same reason. I am anxious for everyone to read it because I think it is spectacularly well written—disciplined, exact, and sometimes stirring.

On the other hand, it isn't an essay with a short payoff. Many students will read an essay like "Answering the Howl" (*Femininity and Masculinity*) or "Confessions of a Blue-Chip Black" (*Insiders and Outsiders*) and get the itch to write something in the same vein. Few undergraduates are prepared to work Bronowski's vein. His is an essay to read because some of it will flake off into the sediment of our thinking and periodically be stirred up over the decades.

When you consider writing assignments, therefore, you'll not want to imitate my colleague who waves his hands vaguely in the air and tells his students to write something like *this.* With such essays, the best writing assignments may call for one-page answers to comprehension questions. Eventually, when students have some other essays from the unit and some class discussion under their belt, they might bring Bronowski into a more general essay evaluating their own education or proposing improvements in the way school is conducted.

QUESTIONS

1. Explain the significance of Bronowski's statement that "All science is the search for unity in hidden likenesses."

The statement occurs in paragraph 26, but its meaning permeates the essay. It is at least half of the essay's thesis. You will need first to make sure that your students understand what the statement means in the plainest terms. I like at this point to remind them of how central metaphor (in a rather loose sense) is to all our thinking. There is simply no way to explain the unknown except in terms of the known. When someone asks me what writing this manual is like, I tell them it is like having a long conversation with another teacher. Or, if it is a bad day, I tell them it is like a long bout of flu. There are more practical, hard-working metaphors you might point to. Every tennis coach tells his students in lesson one to hold their racquets as though they were shaking hands with them. Science, particularly when it deals with the sort of invisible things it has concentrated on in the last century, really does, as a practical matter, advance by similar metaphors. Light, physicists decided some time ago, is something like a particle and something like a wave. The difference between the scientific use of metaphor and the popular use is largely that in popular use a metaphor of limited value can be happily retained. Tennis coaches can continue to compare racquets to hands till doomsday: we are not troubled because we can't find the thumb, and when we find a detached racquet on the court, we don't faint or call the police. A scientific metaphor becomes a paradigm and is viewed critically from every angle and replaced when it begins to break down.

This sense that the metaphor must be of more than limited convenience is presumably what Bronowski means when he says that science is "the search for unity" in likenesses. It is not enough that the force that holds the moon in its orbit be *like* the force that makes the apple fall. At some level of abstraction, it must be the same.

2. Why is the story of Newton and the apple a good illustration for Bronowski to use?

Here is a question we can give several answers to. Throw the ball up and see what your class does with it. A rhetorician might answer that it is a familiar enough example to appeal even to the least scientific layperson. I think it is a particularly good example here because it runs clean contrary to the common notion that science is the product of method and hard work and precise calculation (both Bronowski and Perry seem to think that diligence is an overrated virtue). Newton is loafing, for goodness sake, when he sees the apple fall. And he confirms his theory of universal gravitation by a swift calculation that doesn't quite check out: "I found the answer pretty nearly" (paragraph 29). Since Bronowski is setting out to change our image of science and the scientist, Newton in the garden is a better illustration than Marie Curie in the lab, applying herself diligently.

3. Explain Bronowski's statement (paragraph 34) that "The poem or the discovery exists in two moments of vision: the moment of appreciation as much as that of creation . . ."

This takes us to the heart of the Experiments with Truth section. It also takes us back to paragraph 22, where Bronowski implies that an electronic brain, a computer, has no chance of making a scientific discovery. Consider the line from *Romeo and Juliet* that Bronowski uses in paragraph 31: "Death that hath suckt the honey of thy breath." In principle, a computer could translate the line into contemporary English, locate it in the play, estimate its time of composition, give us other lines that use the words *death* and *suckt* together. It could even tell us what critics have said about the line. But all this does no good unless we see the comparison of death to a bee, and at the moment we see it, we are seeing what Shakespeare saw and no computer ever can. Computers don't do metaphor, they don't have flashes of insight, their hearts don't skip beats. The result is not merely that they aren't good at reading poetry. They are incapable of dealing with scientific theory. Most of us are incapable of understanding Einstein's theory of relativity, but at least we can try—by the time-honored analogies of incredibly fast trains, bullets shot from jets, and so forth. We won't get there, but we'll come far closer than the largest computer ever made.

4. Where in the midst of this abstract argument does Bronowski introduce emotion and humor?

The first section of this essay is a record of what really was the turning point in Bronowski's life. It is also one of the best short passages in *The Dolphin Reader*. Slow your students down and make sure they savor it. One bit of magic that always works on me is the song title, "Is You Is Or Is You Ain't Ma Baby?" When Bronowski introduces it at the end of paragraph 1, it seems a sad ironic comment: the silliness of the song is out of place in the grim surroundings. When he uses it again at the end of the section it acquires new meaning, and I get that little rush of adrenaline that tells me I am in the hands of a great writer.

Look now at the first sentence of paragraph 4, with its double-distilled humor: "The man whom I imagine to be asking this question, wrily with a sense of shame, is not a scientist; he is a civilized man." Only someone whose scientific credentials are in order could make that joke. I am also fond of Orpheus as lion tamer (paragraph 18) and the scientist and historian as two filing cabinets rasping at each other. Bronowski never forgets that we are human beings, capable of sharing his emotion and his wit as well as his argument.

—D.H.—

Style Lesson 59: Balance of Elements in Adjacent Sentences

Consider the following sentences from paragraph 34 of "The Creative Mind." Discuss (using whatever grammatical terms you are comfortable with) Bronowski's balancing of words, phrases, and clauses. Then imitate the sentences, writing, if possible, about a moment of insight or discovery.

When a simile
        takes us aback and
        persuades us together,
when we find a juxtaposition in a picture both
        odd and
        intriguing,
when a theory is at once
        fresh and
        convincing,
we do not merely nod over someone else's work.
We re-enact the creative act, and
we ourselves make the discovery again.

WILLIAM G. PERRY

Examsmanship and the Liberal Arts

Perry's essay is addressed to the Harvard faculty, and is playful in ways that not all your students will be able to appreciate. Consider, for instance, the end of paragraph 9:

> Metzger greeted him and extended appropriate condolences. He inquired, too, what course his friend was being tested in. "Oh, Soc. Sci. something-or-other." "What's it all about?" asked Metzger, and this, as Homer remarked of Patroclus, was the beginning of evil for him.

For a well-educated faculty member, the juxtaposition of student life (condolences on tests, the something-or-other indifference to courses) and the *Iliad* is certain to provoke a smile. Students who don't know who Patroclus is will feel left out. Still, even those who only appreciate half of Perry's humor will find something to be amused by.

At any rate, we haven't included the essay for its humor, but for the clarity with which it makes a potentially abstruse point. Even students who are baffled by the reference to Patroclus will find themselves caught up in the story of the Abominable Mr. Metzger, and will soon be embroiled in an argument about the nature of knowledge.

QUESTIONS

1. Explain Perry's statement that "Too early a moral judgment is precisely what stands between many able students and a liberal education."

The quotation is from paragraph 5, but a full answer requires a thorough understanding of the whole essay. The "moral judgment" Perry fears is the condemnation of bull and the glorification of hard work, no matter how dreary and unproductive. On a question like this, I'd encourage students not to rely heavily on the text, but to explain Perry's point in their own language and using their own examples.

The emphasis on hard work is now popularly associated with "the Protestant ethic." Keep your nose to the grindstone, the Ethic says, which we translate into university language by saying "take good notes, review them once a week, make up flashcards before the test, manage your time wisely." The payoff for this diligence is supposed to be an A on the test, earned by solid effort. In fact, Perry wants us to consider the virtues of keeping our noses far enough off the grindstone to be able to look around us. "Too early" a commitment to diligent work may result in aimless and fruitless drudgery. When I was in law school, I found that perhaps a fourth of the first-year students attempted to excel by main force. Not only did they read every assignment, they read every reference the professor mentioned in class. You could find them waiting at the library door at 7:00 a.m. and leaving at 11:00 p.m. When exam results came back, they tended to be in the bottom half of the class because, as the professors said, they had facts at their disposal but hadn't made a good argument on the exam. No wonder. Who among them had *time* to learn to practice and savor argument? They would have been better off leaving the library at 8:00 and going down to the Old Heidelberg restaurant and bar, where their beer-swilling classmates were arguing so loudly that other patrons were complaining. The best law students were, like Metzger, able to pull together an argument from a few scraps of table talk and an occasional walk through the bookstore.

Many students condemn this sort of bullsterism because they are naive realists: they believe that the facts speak for themselves and that "the standard against which the rightness or wrongness of a fact may be judged exists *someplace.*" Since they believe that there is *one truth* and that it lies somewhere outside their heads, they assume that any attempt to finesse a hard question by taking an indirect approach to it is essentially a lie. Better to leave the space blank. If they could suspend their moral judgment for a time and learn to finesse hard questions, they would eventually come to see that some such finessing is precisely the method of learning in every discipline:

> A liberal education is founded in an awareness of frame of reference even in the most immediate and empirical examination of data. Its acquirement involves relinquishing hope of absolutes. . . . It leads, not away from, but *through* the arts of gamesmanship to a new trust (paragraph 40).

2. Perry repeatedly uses the example of Christopher Columbus's "discovery" of America in 1492 as an example of a fact an able bullster can easily bring into question. Can you think of other such "facts"? How could your facts be brought into question?

It is a fact, they say, that Shakespeare wrote *Antony and Cleopatra.* And yet he based most of his incidents and his characterization on Plutarch's "Life of Antony," and some of his language is lifted almost directly from Thomas North's translation of Plutarch. His dramatic technique derives partly from such predecessors as Marlowe, and there is some evidence that the players in his company contributed occasional lines.

It is a fact, they say, that the two great revolutions of the late eighteenth century were in America and France. And yet some historians claim that the American Revolution was no revolution at all, that the landed gentry that held real power in the colonies before the revolution continued in power afterward, that the majority of the people were no more free, and that the supposed yoke of English rule was one of the lightest the American people had to bear.

It is a fact, they used to say, that all matter is made up of irreducible units called atoms. Now we can split atoms and have found innumerable subatomic particles, including quarks, which if they were not joined with other quarks would be heavier than moving vans. They used, of course, to say that a sub-unit had to be smaller than the whole, and that when you put two things together the result couldn't be smaller than either of the original things.

They used to say 2 + 2 = 4; now we say that if we are in base three 2 + 2 = 11. In Euclidean geometry, we used to say that the angles on a rectangle were 90°; but in non-Euclidean geometry, there's no reason they can't be 93°.

William Rodman's essay in this unit is a challenge to the widespread assumption that psychiatrist's can tell the sane from the insane, and Adrienne Rich's to the assumption that universities teach the truth.

3. How would you describe Perry's tone and style in this essay? What sentences would you cite as examples?

Obviously, Perry's tone is light. His relation of Metzger's story is made funnier by a style that is mock-heroic and mock-academic at the same time:

> Bull in pure form is rare; there is usually some *contamination by data*. The community has reason to be grateful to Mr. Metzger for having *created an instance of laboratory purity*, free from any *adulteration by matter* (paragraph 7).
>
> *As for the culprit*, we can reduce his guilt no further than to suppose that he was ignorant of the rule, or, *in the face of the momentous challenge before him*, forgetful (paragraph 15).

But the tone of the essay is not uniformly amused and amusing. Perry has his serious point to make, and when he makes it, his language is plain and firm:

> Students who have dared to understand man's real relation to his knowledge have shown themselves to be in a strong position to learn content rapidly and meaningfully, and to retain it (paragraph 35).

4. How accurately does the description of a typical student's progress through school (paragraph 38) describe your own progress?

At this university, most of my students have not turned the epistemological corner Perry hopes they will. They still believe, despite the astonishing paradigm changes in the natural sciences, that the truth there is unchanging, or can be. They still assume that disagreements among professors in the social sciences and the humanities are indications that somebody is talking through his or her hat, or that the entire discipline is bogus. I like to have them get this position on the table so that students who have turned the corner can challenge it.

5. What does Perry mean in paragraph 42 when he tells us that behind cow may lie "the potential for a deeper and more dangerous despair"?

Read this paragraph closely and you'll see that I am asking this question to extricate a worthwhile point from an obtuse passage. For the Harvard faculty, paragraph 42 may be perfectly clear, but for the rest of us it teeters on the brink of incomprehensibility. I take it that we can translate "an unconsidered proprietary absolutism" (a phrase that would make Orwell tear his hair out) as a state in which we are controlled by the standards that we assume we have created. The historical allusion must be partly to Nazi Germany, with its slogans about work making one free and its lemming-like march to destruction in pursuit of ends that few citizens questioned by means that few citizens challenged.

Perry's point about the dangers of cow is too important to be buried in the snowdrift of this paragraph. An addiction to cow can lead to an unquestioning obedience that invites tyranny. It can also lead to the daily desperation of millions of people who keep their nose to some grotesque grindstone for fear that if they examine their basic assumptions, their worlds may unravel. No self-respecting bullster would have swallowed the propaganda at the Nuremburg rally or the Kool-Aid at Jonestown.

—D.H.—

Style Lesson 60: "If . . . Then" and Other Qualifiers

As a product of academic culture, William Perry has developed a style that qualifies and limits direct statements. In paragraph 32 of "Examsmanship and the Liberal Arts," he states that "Bulling . . . expresses . . . what a pluralistic university holds dear," but he spends another 60 words qualifying and defining his terms. Try out the academic style by writing a parallel sentence on a subject other than bulling. A concrete subject like basketball or hamburgers might get interesting results.

If a liberal education should teach students "how to think,"
    not only in their own fields
    but in fields outside their own
    —that is, to understand
        "how the other fellow orders knowledge,"
then BULLING,
        even in its purest form,
    EXPRESSES an important part of
        WHAT A PLURALISTIC UNIVERSITY HOLDS DEAR,
    surely a more important part
        than the collecting of "facts that are facts"
            which schoolboys learn to do.

GEORGE ORWELL

Politics and the English Language

This is an indisputably great essay that can lead to a tough day in class. Part of the difficulty is that the essay is aging: the allusions to the political situation in the years after World War II will be meaningless to many of your students, and some of the political clichés Orwell condemns have passed out of the language. My way to get over these hurdles is simply to go around them. I tell my students not to worry about what Orwell has to say about *politics* and the language, but to read very carefully for what he has to say about *freedom* and the language, because this is the real and timeless issue in the essay. Certainly Orwell is concerned with political systems, but his focus here is more strongly on the mental freedom of the individual. One can succumb to "the invasion of one's mind by ready-made phrases" that "anesthetize a portion of one's brain," or one can be "constantly on guard against them" and so preserve the irreducible freedom of thinking one's own thoughts (paragraph 17).

Orwell is a great delight to those who learn to read him, but I think his mental habits put some students off. He always presents himself rough side out, pointing out the negative in order to get at the positive. I've come to respect this in him, and now it even endears him to me, but in framing the questions on this essay, I've attempted to turn the smooth side out so that students can more readily see the positive things Orwell advocates. It will be a bit easier for students to see this positive side if they have read "Shooting an Elephant" (*Insiders and Outsiders*).

QUESTIONS

1. From reading this essay, what would you say that Orwell's political ideal is, and how is this related to his picture of the ideal writer?

I hope that by saying "political *ideal*" we can lift the discussion out of any particular temporal context and avoid getting bogged down in the particulars of Orwell's reaction to Stalinism and fascism.

To answer this question well, your students will have to withdraw their attention from the "catalogue of swindles and perversions" with which Orwell begins the essay, and focus instead on paragraphs 12 through 20. If they look closely at this section, they will see an ideal of mental freedom emerging, freedom of the sort that Winston Smith gains and loses in *1984*. It is a central Orwellian theme: "Shooting an Elephant" is partly about Orwell's struggle to stay independent of imperialist mentality; Always, freedom for Orwell means first the freedom to think. And always the freedom to think is earned by hard labor against the prevailing political (or, here, linguistic) grain. Orwell begins paragraph 17 with the observation that "if thought corrupts language, language can also corrupt thought." If your students don't see how language can be either a threat to freedom or a tool for freedom, they have missed Orwell's point entirely.

On the negative side, language as threat, I would be particularly sure that students notice these statements:

- "They will construct your sentences for you—even think your thoughts for you, to a certain extent—and at need they will perform the important service of partially concealing your meaning even from yourself" (paragraph 12). *They* in fact refers to "ready-made phrases," but when we take the sentence out of context we see how much it might refer to the makers of the Newspeak dictionary in *1984*.
- "When one watches some tired hack on the platform mechanically repeating the familiar phrases . . . one often has a curious feeling that one is not watching a live human being but some kind of dummy" (paragraph 13). And, as Orwell goes on to say, such a speaker "has gone some distance towards turning himself into a machine." The machine-man, Winston Smith with his will removed, is Orwell's constant symbol of unfreedom.
- "This invasion of the mind by ready-made phrases . . . can only be prevented if one is constantly on guard against them, and every such phrase anesthetizes a portion of one's brain" (paragraph 17).
- "In prose, the worst thing one can do with words is to surrender to them" (paragraph 19). A seldom-noted gem of wisdom. Your students should especially note the political spin on the infinitive.

On the positive side, we have less to show (Orwell's habitual tendency to turn a subject rough side out), but there are these glimpses of the free person's use of language: the mention of the "fresh, vivid, home-made turn of speech" (paragraph 13), and the delineation of circumstances in which one can "choose—not simply *accept*—the phrases that will best cover the meaning" (paragraph 19). There are, of course, the indented rules in paragraph 19, but these are negatively stated. More positive, and more important, is the statement in paragraph 12: "A scrupulous writer, in every sentence that he writes, will ask himself at least four questions, thus: What am I trying to say? What words will express it? What image or idiom will make it clearer? Is this image fresh enough to have an effect?" Always, in Orwell, there is this insistence that freedom means the unrelenting exercise of judgment. To be free of the need to make judgments is to be a slave. *Scrupulous* is laden with meaning here. Orwell must primarily mean "very conscientious and exacting," but in so political a context he probably means "principled; responsible" as well.

2. Are words or images more important to Orwell?

I know this question sounds a bit simple-minded, but I think Orwell takes a surprisingly strong stand on the importance of images, and I want to make sure that your students notice it. Paragraph 19 contains the longest discussion of imagery. Here Orwell urges the writer to do something very few composition teachers would recommend:

> Probably it is better to put off using words as long as possible and get one's meaning as clear as one can through pictures or sensations. Afterwards one can choose—not simply *accept*—the phrases that will best cover the meaning.

Orwell apparently believes that we can think wordlessly and that our wordless thoughts, our images, are more reliably ours than worded thoughts are. When your students realize how important Orwell believes images are to the process of thought, they will begin to understand why he makes such an issue of stale imagery throughout the essay. You might point out that he begins his criticism of the five bad examples by saying that they share a "staleness of imagery" and that his first praise of the passage from Ecclesiastes is that "the first sentence contains six vivid images" (paragraph 11). His comment on mixed metaphor is that "the writer is not seeing a mental image of the objects he is naming: *in other words he is not really thinking* (paragraph 12—emphasis mine). Notice that in the last paragraph of the essay, Orwell puts some political distance between himself and Stuart Chase, who comes "near to claiming that all abstract words are meaningless," but there appears to be little distance between the men's attitude toward language. We think in pictures, Orwell almost says, and we write by communicating these pictures.

3. What particularly vivid images does Orwell himself use?

This is merely a signal for a hunting expedition. It might be worth asking each of your students to come to class with half a dozen examples noted. Among my favorites are these:

> It [modern writing] consists in gumming together long strips of words which have already been set in order by someone else . . . (paragraph 12).
>
> A mass of Latin words falls upon the facts like soft snow, blurring the outlines and covering up all the details (paragraph 16).
>
> Phrases like *a not unjustifiable assumption* . . . are a continuous temptation, a packet of aspirins always at one's elbow (paragraph 17).

I look back at this list of images and am astonished by how Orwellian it is, how willing to embrace hardness and pain even, but not regimentation or mindlessness.

—D.H.—

Style Lesson 61: Memorable Similes and Metaphors

The similes and metaphors Orwell uses in "Politics in the English Language" are remarkably vivid and memorable. To test how memorable, work with other students in an attempt to fill in the blanks in the following passages:

As soon as certain topics are raised, the concrete melts into the abstract and no one seems able to think of turns of speech that are not hackneyed: prose consists less and less of *words* chosen for the sake of their own meaning and more and more of *phrases* _____ together like the _____ _____ a _____ _____-_____ (paragraph 4).

[T]he writer knows more or less what he wants to say, but an accumulation of stale phrases chokes him like _____ _____ _____ a _____ (paragraph 12).

"When one watches some tired hack on the platform mechanically repeating the familiar phrases . . . one often has a curious feeling that one is not watching a live human being but some kind of _____: a feeling which suddenly becomes stronger at moments when the light catches the speaker's spectacles and turns them into _____ _____ which seem to have no _____ behind them" (paragraph 13).

A mass of Latin words falls upon the facts like _____ _____, blurring the outlines and covering up all the details (paragraph 16).

When there is a gap between one's real and one's declared aims, one turns as it were instinctively to long words and exhausted idioms, like a _____ _____ out _____ (paragraph 16).

Phrases like *a not unjustifiable assumption* . . . are a continuous temptation, a _____ of _____ always at one's elbow (paragraph 17).

SUSAN GLASPELL

Trifles

This unusual murder mystery offers yet another answer to the central question posed by this unit: How do we discover "truth"? The one-act play is set in the gloomy kitchen of a farmhouse one day after someone slipped a rope around farmer John Wright's neck and "choked the life out of him" while he and his wife lay sleeping in their bed. When the play opens, Mrs. Wright has been arrested and jailed even though she insists that she doesn't know who strangled her husband and explains that she is a sound sleeper. The sheriff, the county attorney, and a neighboring farmer come to the house to look for evidence that Mrs. Wright had a motive for murdering her husband. The men are accompanied by the sheriff's wife and the neighboring farmer's wife, who have agreed to pack up a few clothes for Mrs. Wright. While the three men search futilely for clues, the women see evidence invisible to the men and learn, almost unwillingly, who killed John Wright and why.

Glaspell's characters demonstrate two quite different ways of knowing. The men search for knowledge outside themselves, and they place their faith in objective evidence, hard facts, the kind of data Perry labels "cow" in "Examsmanship and the Liberal Arts." In contrast, the women look inward for knowledge, trust their intuition, and try to use their knowledge of their own internal lives to understand the inner life of another. You may want to ask your students to label their own approaches to learning or to consider the strengths and weaknesses of the two approaches demonstrated in the play.

QUESTIONS

1. How does the play's title point to a contrast between the male and female characters?

A "trifle" is something having little value or significance, but in this play "trifles" provoke a murder, prevent the male investigators from discovering the evidence they seek, and compel the women to conceal that evidence.

When the county attorney complains that the shelf inside a cupboard is sticky, Mrs. Peters realizes that Mrs. Wright's jars of fruit preserves have frozen. She remarks that Mrs. Wright had "worried about that when it turned so cold." The three men then make the following comments:

> SHERIFF. Well, can you beat the woman! Held for murder and worryin' about her preserves.
>
> COUNTY ATTORNEY. I guess before we're through she may have something more serious than preserves to worry about.

HALE. Well, women are used to worrying over trifles (paragraphs 27–30).

That short exchange is the key to the entire play. The men have no understanding of the labor involved in preserving fruit (especially in a primitive kitchen that has no running water). To them, preserves are merely something to spread on toast every morning. The men casually deprecate the lives of farm women by labeling their concerns "trifles." The men's arrogant assumption that women's contributions are inconsequential undermines their investigation by causing them to overlook important evidence and by offending and alienating the women who might have assisted them.

First the men fail to thoroughly investigate the kitchen.

COUNTY ATTORNEY. You're convinced that there was nothing important here—nothing that would point to any motive.

SHERIFF. Nothing here but kitchen things. (paragraphs 24 and 25)

Later, for the same reason, the county attorney declines to examine the sewing basket and fails to discover the bird hidden inside it.

SHERIFF. Do you want to see what Mrs. Peters is going to take in?

COUNTY ATTORNEY. Oh, I guess they are not very dangerous things the ladies have picked out (paragraphs 142 and 143).

In contrast, the women understand the significance of the trifles that destroyed Minnie Foster, a lively town girl who once wore pretty clothes and sang in the choir (paragraph 56). Thirty years ago Minnie married John Wright, a man Mrs. Hale characterizes by saying, "I don't think a place'd be any cheerfuller for John Wright's being in it" (paragraph 44), and moved to a farm, a "lonesome place," "down in a hollow [so] you don't see the road" (paragraph 99). The Wrights never had children, and John, who was close with his money, refused to put in a telephone or buy his wife decent clothes. Mrs. Hale says that Minnie didn't "even belong to the Ladies Aid" because "you don't enjoy things when you feel shabby" (paragraph 56). After coming to an intuitive understanding of Minnie's bleak existence, both women know what the canary's death meant to her.

MRS. HALE. If there'd been years and years of nothing, then a bird to sing to you, it would be awful—still, after the bird was still (paragraph 130).

This final trifle—the stillness following the bird's death—moves Mrs. Peters to identify with Minnie and to protect her.

2. How do Mrs. Hale's and Mrs. Peters's attitudes toward Minnie and toward the investigators differ? How do those attitudes change during the play?

From the beginning Mrs. Hale, a neighbor who has known and liked Minnie for more than thirty years, is sympathetic to Minnie and openly critical of the men. She tells Mrs. Peters, "I'd hate to have men coming into my kitchen, snooping around and criticising" (paragraph 49). She later remarks, "You know, it seems kind of *sneaking*. Locking her up in town and then coming out here and trying to get her own house to turn against her!" (paragraph 68). Mrs. Hale is steadfastly loyal. At first she believes Minnie innocent, saying "Well, I don't think she did [it]. Asking for her apron and her little shawl. Worrying about her fruit" (paragraph 62). When Mrs. Hale sees evidence to the contrary (the uneven stitches in one quilt block), she immediately rips out the sewing and restitches it (paragraph 77). And after she fits the last puzzle piece into place (the canary with its neck "all—other side *to*," (paragraph 113), she concludes that if Minnie did strangle her husband, her act was nothing more than justifiable homicide.

In contrast, Mrs. Peters, who is the sheriff's wife, initially defends the men's investigation, saying, "Of course it's no more than their duty" (paragraph 50). Later, Mrs. Peters, who "wasn't raised around" there and met Minnie only the day before at the jail, says she doesn't know whether Mrs. Wright killed her husband (paragraph 61). Although Mrs. Peters continues to dutifully recite the platitudes she has been taught ("The law is the law" and "The law has got to punish crime, Mrs. Hale," paragraphs 69 and 133), she ultimately rejects those abstract principles and trusts her heart to guide her actions. She protects Minnie by convincing the men that a cat killed the bird and by remaining silent when Mrs. Hale conceals the bird in her pocket.

3. Do the women do the right thing when they hide the evidence that would incriminate Minnie?

This question should spark some spirited debate about truth, justice, and the American way. I think most readers (male and female) will respect the women's decision to save their friend. Glaspell forces us to identify with her women characters. (We are privy to conversations between the women when the men are off-stage but never to the men's private conversations.) The women are kind, gentle, compassionate, and long-suffering. In contrast, the men are insensitive louts who are oblivious to the effects of their demeaning comments about women.

Once we move outside the world of this play, it is more difficult to condone the women's actions. How many of us are ready to assert that a man who kills a canary deserves to be strangled? How many of us would argue that it is all right for people to knowingly conceal evidence of a crime?

In *The Lessons of History*, Will and Ariel Durant explain why radicals who are willing to reject established social institutions, although often valuable, can be dangerous:

> Out of every hundred new ideas, ninety-nine or more will probably be inferior to the traditional responses they propose to replace. No one man, however brilliant or well-informed, can come in one

> lifetime to such fullness of understanding as to safely judge and dismiss the customs and institutions of society, for these are the wisdom of generations after centuries of experiment in the laboratory of history.

The Durants argue that new ideas should always be heard but then tested by the trial heat of "objection, opposition, and contumely."

It is possible to read this play as the story of two dangerous radicals who surreptitiously reject one of the most cherished of American rights—that of trial by jury—without testing their ideas in the crucible of public debate. On the other hand, if we recall that this play was written during a period in our history when jurors were nearly always male, we could conclude that Mrs. Hale and Mrs. Peters merely extended to Minnie a right then enjoyed only by men. There is no doubt about Glaspell's interpretation. In 1917 she republished this play as a short story titled "A Jury of Her Peers."

4. What is the difference between the way the men in this play attempt to grasp reality and the way the women in this play attempt to grasp reality?

Both the men and the women in this play seem content to accept too narrow a definition of truth. The men (who might be labeled dualists by William Perry) look outside themselves for knowledge. (They check the barn and the windows for external clues.) They, like Mr. Metzger's friend in Perry's "Examsmanship and the Liberal Arts," are committed to what Perry calls "cow." They assume that facts are facts and that once they accumulate enough data (evidence), the mystery will solve itself. They believe in the ethic of hard work and dutifully clump around in their big boots, first up to the cold upstairs bedroom and then out to the colder barn, looking "for some definite thing" (paragraph 139) to show a jury. Unlike Perry's "abominable Mr. Metzger," they are unable to enter someone else's frame of reference to give meaning to the data they observe.

These investigators know that the state cannot prove its case against Minnie unless it presents evidence of means, opportunity, and motive. The men's "cow" approach yields means and opportunity, both externals, but is useless in the search for motive, an internal force. Because these rather dull-witted men have never been interested in the internal lives of women, it is impossible for them to discover Minnie's motive.

Neither Perry's "cow" nor his "bull" classification seems to describe the approach to understanding taken by the women in the play. It may be more helpful to borrow a term from *Women's Ways of Knowing* (Belenky, Clinchy, Goldberger, and Tarule) and label them subjectivists, people who listen to and trust their inner voices. Mrs. Hale and Mrs. Peters believe they can find truth by looking inside themselves, and that, because women are united by shared experience, truth for one woman is truth for another.

> MRS. HALE. I might have known she needed help! I know how things can be—for women. I tell you, it's queer, Mrs. Peters. We live close together and we live far apart. We all go through the same

things—it's all just a different kind of the same thing (paragraph 136).

This approach enables the women to empathize with Minnie (whose experiences have been very like theirs), but not with the men. The women, especially Mrs. Hale, seem as unwilling as the men to attempt to imagine a frame of reference quite unlike their own. From the outset Mrs. Hale dismisses male institutions such as the law as irrelevant. When Mrs. Peters says, "The law's the law," Mrs. Hale responds, "I s'pose 'tis" and tells Mrs. Peters to unbutton her coat while they are inside (paragraph 70). Later, after they realize Minnie must have killed her husband, and Mrs. Peters insists that "the law has got to punish crime, Mrs. Hale," Mrs. Hale merely says, "I wish you'd seen Minnie Foster when she wore a white dress with ribbons and stood up there in the choir and sang" (paragraph 134). To Mrs. Hale, men's abstractions are trifles.

Mrs. Hale never attempts to use reason or logic (methods she may have rejected as male) to convert Mrs. Peters to her way of knowing; instead Mrs. Hale relates the details of Minnie's life, and Mrs. Peters begins to feel the connection between Minnie's life and her own. Mrs. Peters remembers her childhood, and her blind anger when she saw a boy kill her kitten with a hatchet (paragraph 123). And she recalls the stillness in her house after her first baby died (paragraph 131). Without attempting to reconcile the conflict between her head and her heart, Mrs. Peters listens to her heart, a dramatically effective but intellectually unsatisfying solution to a complex problem.

—M.R.D.—

APPENDIXES

A RHETORICAL TABLE OF CONTENTS

Rhetorical tables of contents always contain a number of white lies, since few essays fall neatly into a single rhetorical mode. The list below fits five examples under each of the most common modes without stretching the coat too much at the seams.

Narration

Description

Illustration

Comparison and Contrast

Division and Classification

Process Analysis

DILLARD The Fixed (Nature and Civilization)
HAMPL Memory and Imagination (Understanding)
HUBBELL Beekeeper (Progress and Its Price)
KENYATTA Gikuyu Industries (Progress and Its Price)
SMITH Division of Labour (Progress and Its Price)

Cause and Effect

LEWIS The Inner Ring (Insiders and Outsiders)
MANDER Advertising: The Standard-Gauge Railway (Media)
POSTMAN "Now . . . This" (Media)
RODMAN When Questions Are Answers (Understanding)
WINN Children Without Childhood (Childhood and Childhood's End)

Definition

BROWNMILLER Femininity (Femininity and Masculinity)
EHRENREICH Spudding Out (Media)
MURRAY What's So Bad About Being Poor? (Communities)
PERRIN The Androgynous Man (Femininity and Masculinity)
POLLITT The Smurfette Principle (Media)

Argument and Persuasion

BLY Growing Up Expressive (Understanding)
BRONOWSKI The Creative Mind (Understanding)
KING Letter from Birmingham Jail (Insiders and Outsiders)
PERRY Examsmanship and the Liberal Arts (Understanding)
PLATO Crito (Communities)

ESSAYS AND STORIES LISTED IN ORDER OF DIFFICULTY WITHIN TEXT (descending from hardest to easiest)

This is a very subjective rating. How difficult an essay is depends largely on the reader. We have tried to take into account vocabulary, syntax, range of allusion, presence of irony, and sheer fatigue when an essay is long and difficult. We have no confidence that any essay is in fact more difficult than the one listed five below it, but we do feel that essays separated by twenty ranks are at different levels of difficulty. Stories are ranked separately at the bottom. Following this listing is another giving the order of difficulty within units.

PLATO Crito
HUXLEY Hyperion to a Satyr
PERRY Examsmanship and the Liberal Arts
BRONOWSKI The Creative Mind
ORWELL Politics and the English Language
KITTO The Polis
RODMAN When Questions Are Answers
THOREAU The Fitness in a Man's Building His Own House
KING Letter from Birmingham Jail
MANDER Advertising: The Standard-Gauge Railway
JARRELL A Sad Heart at the Supermarket
POSTMAN "Now . . . This"
RICH Split at the Root
HOAGLAND Dogs, and the Tug of Life
STEINEM Sex, Lies, and Advertising
BOORSTIN Technology and Democracy
WOOLF Professions for Women
LEWIS The Inner Ring
SMITH Division of Labour
EISELEY The Brown Wasps
MOMADAY The Way to Rainy Mountain
BLY Growing Up Expressive
EHRLICH Wyoming: The Solace of Open Spaces
MCCARTHY Artists in Uniform
SANDERS Reasons of the Body
ADATTO The Incredible Shrinking Sound Bite
GREENE No Rms, Jungle Vu
HOLT Escape from Childhood
HAMPL Memory and Imagination
DIDION On Going Home
BROPHY The Menace of Nature
BLOOM On a Greek Holiday
CONROY Think About It
TWAIN The Mesmerizer

Stories

GLASPELL Trifles
HAMILTON Rehearsing "The Firebird"
MUNRO Boys and Girls
LESSING Sunrise on the Veld
KEILLOR The Tip-Top Club
HEKER The Stolen Party
CAMERON Homework
BAMBARA The Hammer Man

ESSAYS LISTED IN ORDER OF DIFFICULTY WITHIN UNITS
(descending order from hardest to easiest)

Childhood and Childhood's End

HOLT Escape from Childhood
TWAIN The Mesmerizer
MITFORD Thirteen
WINN Children Without Childhood
ANDERSON Discovery of a Father
RIVERA First Communion
DILLARD Skin
ANGELOU Momma

Femininity and Masculinity

WOOLF Professions for Women
SANDERS Reasons of the Body
MORRIS To Everest
BROWNMILLER Femininity
KINGSTON Daughter
HARRIGAN Answering the Howl
GOULD X
PERRIN The Androgynous Man
WALKER Brothers and Sisters
BARRY Lost in the Kitchen

Communities

PLATO Crito
KITTO The Polis
MOMADAY The Way to Rainy Mountain
EHRLICH Wyoming: The Solace of Open Spaces
DIDION On Going Home
RODRIGUEZ Going Home Again: The New American Scholarship Boy
ANGELOU My Sojourn in the Lands of My Ancestors
BALDWIN Fifth Avenue, Uptown
MURRAY What's So Bad About Being Poor?
YEZIERSKA America and I

Insiders and Outsiders

KING Letter from Birmingham Jail
RICH Split at the Root
LEWIS The Inner Ring
McCARTHY Artists in Uniform
ORWELL Shooting an Elephant
WILKINS Confessions of a Blue-Chip Black

KLASS Learning the Language
STAPLES Just Walk On By

Nature and Civilization

HOAGLAND Dogs, and the Tug of Life
EISELEY The Brown Wasps
GREENE No Rms, Jungle Vu
BROPHY The Menace of Nature
DINESEN A Gazelle
DILLARD The Fixed
CREWS Pages from the Life of a Georgia Innocent
WHITE Twins
THOMAS Ponds
CHRISTIE Butterfly

Progress and Its Price

HUXLEY Hyperion to a Satyr
THOREAU The Fitness in a Man's Building His Own House
BOORSTIN Technology and Democracy
SMITH Division of Labour
BLOOM On a Greek Holiday
KENYATTA Gikuyu Industries
BLY Getting Tired
BERRY Against PCs
HUBBELL Beekeeper

Media

MANDER Advertising: The Standard-Gauge Railway
JARRELL A Sad Heart at the Supermarket
POSTMAN "Now . . . This"
STEINEM Sex, Lies, and Advertising
ADATTO The Incredible Shrinking Sound Bite
AUSTIN Pretty Worthless
HALL Purpose, Blame, and Fire
POLLITT The Smurfette Principle
EHRENREICH Spudding Out

Understanding

PERRY Examsmanship and the Liberal Arts
BRONOWSKI The Creative Mind
ORWELL Politics and the English Language
RODMAN When Questions Are Answers
BLY Growing Up Expressive
HAMPL Memory and Imagination
CONROY Think About It

APPROXIMATE READING TIMES

The times here assume a reading speed of about 220 words per minute for essays of average difficulty. For essays that seem particularly difficult or particularly easy, I have added or subtracted time by no formula but instinct. Notice that I am estimating simple reading time. To prepare an essay for class discussion will presumably take longer.

5-Minute Readings

BARRY Lost in the Kitchen
CHRISTIE Butterfly
EHRENREICH Spudding Out
HARRIGAN Answering the Howl
KLASS Learning the Language
SCUDDER Learning to See
WALKER Brothers and Sisters
WHITE Twins
WINN Children Without Childhood

10-Minute Readings

ANDERSON Discovery of a Father
ANGELOU Momma
BERRY Against PCs
BLY Getting Tired
BROWNMILLER Femininity
CAMERON Homework
CONROY Think About It
CREWS Pages from the Life of a Georgia Innocent
DIDION On Going Home
DILLARD Skin
HEKER The Stolen Party
JARRELL A Sad Heart at the Supermarket
KINGSTON Daughter
PERRIN The Androgynous Man
POLLITT The Smurfette Principle
RICH Claiming an Education
STAPLES Just Walk On By
THOMAS Ponds
WOOLF Professions for Women

15-Minute Readings

ADATTO The Incredible Shrinking Soundbite
ANGELOU My Sojourn in the Lands of My Ancestors
BAMBARA The Hammer Man
BLOOM On a Greek Holiday
BLY Growing Up Expressive

BROPHY The Menace of Nature
DILLARD The Fixed
DILLARD Seeing
EISELEY The Brown Wasps
HALL Purpose, Blame, and Fire
HOLT Escape from Childhood
LESSING Sunrise on the Veld
MITFORD Thirteen
MOMADAY The Way to Rainy Mountain
MORRIS To Everest
ORWELL Shooting an Elephant

20-Minute Readings

AUSTIN Pretty Worthless
BALDWIN Fifth Avenue, Uptown
EHRLICH Wyoming: The Solace of Open Spaces
GOULD X
HOAGLAND Dogs, and the Tug of life
KENYATTA Gikuyu Industries
LEWIS The Inner Ring
MURRAY What's So Bad About Being Poor?
O'BRIEN Sister Imelda
RIVERA First Communion
SMITH Division of Labor
TWAIN The Mesmerizer
YEZIERSKA America and I

25-Minute Readings

DINESEN A Gazelle
HAMPL Memory and Imagination
HUBBELL Beekeeper
KEILLOR The Tip-Top Club
MANDER Advertising: The Standard-Gauge Railway
POSTMAN "Now . . . This"
PERRY Examsmanship and the Liberal Arts
PLATO Crito
RODRIGUEZ Going Home Again: The New American Scholarship Boy
THOREAU The Fitness in a Man's Building His Own House
WILKINS Confessions of a Blue-Chip Black

30-Minute Readings

GLASPELL Trifles
GORDIMER Which New Era Would That Be?
GREENE No Rms, Jungle Vu
KITTO The Polis
MCCARTHY Artists in Uniform

SMUNRO Boys and Girls
ORWELL Politics and the English Language
SANDERS Reasons of the Body

35-Minute Readings

BOORSTIN Technology and Democracy
BRONOWSKI The Creative Mind
HAMILTON Rehearsing "The Firebird"
RODMAN When Questions Are Answers
STEINEM Sex, Lies, and Advertising
KING Letter from Birmingham Jail

40-Minute Readings

HUXLEY Hyperion to a Satyr
RICH Split at the Root

60-Minute Reading

FORSTER The Machine Stops